A ROSARIO CASTELLANOS READER

THE TEXAS PAN AMERICAN SERIES

A ROSARIO CASTELLANOS READER

An Anthology of Her Poetry, Short Fiction, Essays, and Drama

Edited and with a Critical Introduction by Maureen Ahern

Translated by Maureen Ahern and Others

UNIVERSITY OF TEXAS PRESS, AUSTIN

Second paperback printing, 1992

Requests for permission to reproduce material from this work should be sent to Permissions,
University of Texas Press, Box 7819,. Austin, Texas 78713-7819.

∞ The paper used in this publication meets the minimum requirements of American
National Standard for Information Sciences—Permanence of Paper for Printed Library
Materials, ANSI Z39.48-1984.

LIBRARY OF CONGRESS CATALOGING-IN-PUBLICATION DATA

Castellanos, Rosario.
    A Rosario Castellanos reader.
    (The Texas Pan American series)
    Bibliography: p.
    Includes index.
    I. Ahern, Maureen,   II. Series.
PQ7297.C596A6   1988   861   88-10800
ISBN 0-292-77039-1
ISBN 0-292-77036-7 (pbk.)

*The Texas Pan American Series is published with the assistance of a revolving
publication fund established by the Pan American Sulphur Company.*

Permissions follow the index.

Contents

Acknowledgments   ix

Introduction   xiii

Reading Rosario Castellanos: Contexts, Voices, and Signs   1

  Contexts   1

  Poetry: Silences and Otherness   5

  Speakers and Addressees in the Poetry of Rosario Castellanos   10

  The Appropriation of Signs: Intertexts and Subtexts   24

  Fiction: Under a Man's Hand   31

  Essays: Writing Her Self   39

  The Eternal Feminine: Destroying the Myths   53

  Notes   57

  Works Cited   64

  Rosario Castellanos: A Basic Bibliography of Her Writing   70

  A Select Bibliography of Rosario Castellanos Criticism   71

POETRY

Translated by Maureen Ahern

  Silence Near an Ancient Stone   81

  To a Tiny Mayan Badger   82

  The Other   83

  Monologue of a Foreign Woman   84

  Routine   87

  Presence   88

  Passage   89

  Consciousness   90

  Metamorphosis of the Sorceress   92

Chess	94
Brief Chronicle	95
Malinche	96
Memorandum on Tlatelolco	98
Self-Portrait	100
Speaking of Gabriel	102
Home Economics	103
Learning about Things	105
Postscript	108
You Are Not Poetry	109
Re: Mutilations	110
Meditation on the Brink	111
Kinsey Report	112
Looking at the Mona Lisa	116
Nobodying	117
Nazareth	118

SHORT FICTION

The Eagle 121
Translated by Laura Carp Solomon

Three Knots in the Net 129
Translated by Laura Carp Solomon

Fleeting Friendships 144
Translated by Lesley Salas

The Widower Román 155
Translated by Ruth Peacock

Cooking Lesson 207
Translated by Maureen Ahern

ESSAYS

Incident at Yalentay 219
Translated by Maureen Ahern

Once Again Sor Juana 222
Translated by Maureen Ahern

An Attempt at Self-Criticism   226
Translated by Laura Carp Solomon

Discrimination in the United States and in Chiapas   229
Translated by Maureen Ahern

A Man of Destiny   232
Translated by Maureen Ahern

Woman and Her Image   236
Translated by Maureen Ahern

The Nineteenth-Century Mexican Woman   245
Translated by Maureen Ahern

Language as an Instrument of Domination   250
Translated by Maureen Ahern

If Not Poetry, Then What?   254
Translated by Maureen Ahern

Self-Sacrifice Is a Mad Virtue   259
Translated by Laura Carp Solomon

The Liberation of Love   264
Translated by Laura Carp Solomon

Herlinda Leaves   267
Translated by Maureen Ahern

THEATER

The Eternal Feminine   273
Translated by Diane E. Marting and Betty Tyree Osiek

Notes   363

Notes on the Editor and the Translators   369

Index   371

For Ursula and Crescencia
—for keeping the faith
—for the future

Acknowledgments

This anthology has been in the making since 1973 when I read Rosario Castellanos' poetry in a ten-peso pamphlet I picked up at a Mexico City newsstand. Those poems drew me to her writing and into the project of translating it into English. During the long process of research, writing, and translation that has taken place over the years, I owe debts for support and encouragement to more people than it is possible to mention here, but there are some who deserve special recognition.

This book has been formed and informed by the research that I have conducted in Mexican archives and by many private conversations with the author's friends and colleagues in Mexico City to whom I am greatly endebted for their generous assistance in many phases of this project: José Emilio Pacheco, Raúl Ortiz, Elva Macías, Aurora Ocampo, Octavio Gordillo, Emma Teresa Armendáriz, Rafael López Miarnau, and María Luisa Mendoza. Special thanks are due to Gabriel Guerra Castellanos for authorizing the translations of his mother's writing that comprise this collection and to Alicia Hammer formerly of Fondo de Cultura Económica for her able assistance in securing permissions.

Dialogues with other readers of Rosario Castellanos and discourses of the other have provided stimulating questions and comments that helped clarify my ideas about her work and its translation. For their intellectual gifts and warm friendships I am grateful to Eliana Rivero, Marta Paley de Francescato, Regina Harrison, Ingrid Muller, Mary S. Vásquez, Rolena Adorno, Helen Nader, Harriet Turner, and Jeanette Sherbondy. I particularly wish to thank Anne Leibold of the Reference Department of Hayden Library, Arizona State University, for her assistance with searches and development of bibliographical materials over the years, particularly during the summer of 1987.

These translations have passed through many versions since I read some of Castellanos' poems at a Department of Foreign Languages Symposium at Arizona State University in the spring of 1974. During this period they have benefited from the insights of a number of readers, among whom I gratefully recognize Jane Radcliffe, Nora Jácquez, Mary S. Vásquez,

David Tipton, and Clayton Eshleman. None of them are responsible for any errors or awkwardness that may be found herein, but many valuable suggestions are owed to them. Marian Smolen's skillful editorial assistance in the reading and correction of the first drafts of my translations of the essays and the first version of the critical study is especially appreciated.

I also wish to thank two other writer-translators for their support: Margaret Randall for her many readings of my translations of Castellanos' poetry throughout the United States and Canada, and her initiative with *Caliban* that marked their first publication in 1978, and David Tipton, whose enthusiasm for this Mexican author's writing in my English versions made possible their publication in a number of English magazines and later that of my collection of twenty-four poems in Rivelin/Ecuatorial's edition of *Looking at the Mona Lisa* in 1981.

Several people associated with the University of Texas Press contributed to the book's final outcome. Their editorial patience and professional skills during the final stages of the permission process and manuscript preparation have been key to its successful completion.

My deepest appreciation is due my contributing translators, Diane E. Marting, Betty Tyree Osiek, Ruth Peacock, Lesley Salas, and Laura Carp Solomon, for their unstinting patience and prompt cooperation in the process of reading and revising that produced their valuable contributions to the anthology.

I wish to acknowledge the support that I received from the Center for Women's Studies of the College of Liberal Arts and Sciences at Arizona State University in the form of a Summer Research Grant, funded by the Office of the Academic Vice-President, Dr. Jack Kinsinger, in 1985, which enabled me to complete my translations of the essays and the first draft of the critical study.

And, finally, I want to recognize the important debt I owe to my father, William Coffey Ahern, my first feminist mentor, who taught me that independent ideas and dreams are important. Although his own did not come true, they made mine possible. A second debt is due my aunt, Elizabeth M. Ahern, another feminist mentor who understood why I wanted to go to Mexico and helped me to get there.

This book is dedicated to my daughters, Ursula and Crescencia Maurer, who have been the source of intellectual gifts, insights, and encouragement during every stage of the years that it has taken to complete this book. Their strength, love, and unflagging support have sustained me through many trials. The translations and development of my own essay owe much to Ursula's thoughtful reading and insights. To Crescencia, who worked as my research and editorial assistant for the final stage of this manuscript in summer 1987, I owe many stimulating readings of the introductory essay, the organization of the bibliographies, and the completion of the manuscript. They have taught me that there are other ways to be!

M.A.

Introduction

. . . the word does not forget where it has been and can never wholly free itself from the dominion of the contexts of which it has been a part. —MIKHAIL BAKHTIN,
Problems of Dostoevsky's Poetics, 167

This is a book about connections—between words and women, between readers and texts. Rosario Castellanos explored otherness as she urged us to invent ourselves. Searching for her own voice she discovered the silences in others. She saw women in their relationships to each other, their writing, and the power of their words. This anthology is about the contexts, voices, and signs that made those connections happen and the translations that bring them from one culture into another. The goal of this book is to introduce the writing of Rosario Castellanos to the English-speaking world in terms of the ways that her major texts produce meaning.

At the core of Castellanos' work is her concern with the ideology of culture and the issues that link women and their writing to the specific realities of gender, race, and class in Mexico. "When people reread her work it will become evident that nobody in her time had as clear a consciousness of the twofold condition of being a woman and a Mexican. And no one else has made of that consciousness the subject matter and the central line of a body of literary work. Of course we didn't know how to read her," the poet José Emilio Pacheco wrote in 1974 (16). More than a decade later we are still learning how to read her.

This anthology proposes a reading of the entire range of that expression in twenty-five poems, five short stories, twelve essays, and a play that represent Castellanos' best writing over the two and one-half decades from 1948 until her death in 1974. Except for the poems, and her first novel, most of Castellanos' writing has never been available to the English-language reader. Here the major texts are brought together in a single volume that is organized to chart the connections between them. The translations are conceived as an integral part of this process: signs executed as transcultural acts that carry on Castellanos' search for "another language . . . another starting point . . . another way to be."

Moving from contexts to voices to signs, the critical study analyzes seven dimensions of Castellanos' work that create a plurality of meanings within her discourse. The first section, "Contexts," provides the frame of reference, focusing on the author's biography and the Mexican world that shaped it. "Poetry: Silences and Otherness" considers two concepts central to all her writing: the exploration of otherness and the silences imposed on female experience in Mexico. "Speakers and Addressees in the Poetry of Rosario Castellanos" analyzes the interactions between the speaking subjects and their addressees that shape the reading experiences. These voices explore a woman's world through domesticity as creativity, subverting signs, "saying the unsayable," the body as sign, language as oppressor, punning as poetry. "The Appropriation of Signs" examines how Castellanos borrows signs from other texts to create new ones of her own. The concept of *subtext* serves to illuminate Castellanos' dialogue with other social, visual, and literary texts.

"Fiction: Under a Man's Hand" inquires into the changes that took place in Castellanos' aesthetic expression and the role of the "Generation of 1950" in contemporary Mexican letters. Critical attention focuses on the perversion of signs as a tool of oppression of indigenous peoples in Chiapas and the representation of women as signs of conflict and solitude, particularly their relationships to each other, and their struggles for lives of their own. "Cooking Lesson" demonstrates the author's superb command of feminine speech act and metaphor to transform traditional sign values into radical messages through the feminization of all the elements of her aesthetic message.

"Essays: Writing Her Self" is the first comprehensive analysis of Castellanos' essays as signifying processes that inscribe cultural ideology. After discussing the impact upon her writing and thinking exercised by her reading of Simone de Beauvoir, Simone Weil, and Virginia Woolf, I consider her own reading of Mexican women. As early as 1963 in "Once Again Sor Juana," the archetypal figures of Malinche, the Virgin of Guadalupe, and Sor Juana Inés de la Cruz became metaphors to probe the inequalities that define women in Mexico. "Woman and Her Image" takes issue with the forces that have kept women outside history by using the discourse of scientific reporting as caricature. When Castellanos inquired into women's lives within history in Mexico, she used the diaries of a nineteenth-century forerunner to do so, creating a gripping colloquium of female voices that span 170 years of Mexican life, detecting the silences that speak louder than their words. "The Liberation of Love" deftly reverses male rhetoric to show how women become willing accomplices in their own degradation, while other texts use ironic humor to demolish self-sacrifice as a feminine ideal. Women as oppressors of other women, domesticity as a discursive strategy, and language as an instrument of domination are also addressed.

The final section discusses the writing and staging of Castellanos' controversial play *The Eternal Feminine*, in which her self-inscription works to defuse audience negativity. Critique of Mexican culture becomes performance that leads to invention. "It isn't even enough to discover who we are. We have to invent ourselves" (Act III).

Thus, well before the call by French feminists to write the self, decode the body, and destroy the myths inside and outside ourselves, Rosario Castellanos was practicing an *écriture féminine* in Mexico: the body as sign, puns as poems, language as oppressor, silence as meaning. Because most of the critical discussion about Castellanos' writing has been published in Spanish, the essay offers the English-language reader a comprehensive critical study that integrates biography with the semiotic analysis of her discourse. A bibliography of her writing and a bibliography of the major critical responses to Castellanos' works have been included to guide the reader to further exploration.

The criterion employed in the ordering of the texts that constitute *A Rosario Castellanos Reader* is the charting of connections that link the different dimensions of her writing, tracing the development of the sign systems she created. Poetry was the first genre in which she published, and poems were the first texts that she considered to be of literary value. Here they propel the reader into the full range of Castellanos' talent demonstrated in the short stories and essays, where many of her poetic motifs are expanded into prose equivalents. Other poems are forerunners of the powerful characters and concepts that culminate in the three-act play, *The Eternal Feminine*, in which a gallery of Mexican women shatter the stereotyped images and roles that their history and culture have assigned them.

In tune with her roots, ahead of her time, laughing at herself, Rosario Castellanos in her lucidity has become mirror and model for several generations of writers throughout Latin America. Read as a discursive whole, rather than separately, as has been the case even for the Spanish versions, her poetry, prose, and theater gain entirely new dimensions that illuminate the coherence of Castellanos' legacy: a lucid discourse on the ideology of culture and the female experience in Mexico through the exploration of woman as sign.

Translating Rosario Castellanos: The Text as Other

During the years that this anthology has been in the making, its translations have undergone many versions—the result of a process of growing sensitivity to the text as other: to the links between Castellanos' biography and her writing; to the presence of other voices within her own; to the reader who will read her writing through mine. Re-creating the new texts has been an act of mediating that otherness between myself and Castellanos, between her texts and these new ones (Díaz-Diocaretz, 25). It has enriched my understanding of Castellanos tenfold—and of translation as a process as much again.

Although many of my ideas about the translations that bring this author's writing from Mexican culture into the Anglo-American one were set out in earlier studies written in 1985 and 1986, my reading of Myriam Díaz-Diocaretz' *Translating Poetic Discourse: Questions on Feminist Strategies in Adrienne Rich* in June 1987 shed a wider and brighter light on the signifying processes that I had already identified in Castellanos' discourse. Díaz-Diocaretz' theoretical concepts lent many new insights into Castellanos' feminist strategies, as did my reading of Hélène Cixous' "The Laugh of the Medusa" and recent feminist criticism by Maggie Humm, Gayle Greene and Coppélia Kahn, and Ann Rosalind Jones. These are significant debts that I wish to recognize as this book begins. In part, then, my essay and the new versions of my translations are the result of a third critical reading, that of feminist scholarship in translation theory and literary criticism.

Because the process of translating is not a separate, but an integral, part of reading and decoding Rosario Castellanos' writing, I discuss the specific points involved in its translation as part of my analysis of the discrete texts that comprise this anthology. My underlying precept is that "the interpretative process of translating is part of the semiotics of reading . . . The translator, as interpreter and reader of various codes that form the message, handles a multileveled text with its variability, impelled by cultural and ideological suppositions and presuppositions" (Díaz-Diocaretz, 32).

However, some observations are in order about the basic concepts that have guided the translation of Castellanos' writing for this collection. First is the fundamental premise that translation is a semiotic process because it transmits a plurality of signs—linguistic, cultural, aesthetic, and ideological. A second principle has been to consider the translation of the individual texts and their problems in terms of Castellanos' discourse as a whole. Third, strategies that promote an active readership abound in her writing, and transmission of the specific elements that convey them is critical to the production of meaning throughout her work.

To become an active reader of Castellanos' writing, or even a passive one for that matter, often requires a specialized knowledge of Mexican culture and formal features of its language of which the reader may be unaware. The quintessential Mexicanness of her discourse challenges the translator. Because so much of the author's work is culture bound, cultural equivalences take precedence over lexical ones. The nature of Castellanos' linguistic creativity—its penchant for punning on linguistic, social, or literary phenomena, its oral paradigm—presents complex problems for transmission as my analysis of items like *Ninguneo* or *Poesía no eres tú* points out.

Another major challenge facing the translator of Rosario Castellanos' writing is how to transmit implicit or situational information that shapes the reading of the texts as much as does their explicit lexical content. The original Spanish poems are characterized by a great deal of cultural information that is automatically shared by the Spanish-language readers, but not usually by the reader of English. It is, in fact, a significant generator of her aesthetic message because Castellanos counts on a reader who uses implicit referents. The conversion of implicit cultural or speech act information into explicit information in various forms for the receptor language reader is not an option but an obligation if the communication elements are to survive their leaps across cultures. Thus, the notes by the translators become an integral part of many texts.

Yet a fourth cluster of challenges are found in the elements that make up Castellanos' stylistic strategies: the orality, ambiguity, intertextuality, gender explicitness, and rhetorical reversal that play so large a part in the production of her ironic humor and her cultural critique. Tone is a significant generator of those messages, because Castellanos, like Emily Dickinson whom she translated, creates a poetry of "ferocious wit" (Stevensen, 161). The intense orality of her writing has meant matching a number of very exact tones: the flat, impersonal voice of quiet desperation in "Meditation on the Brink," obedient submission in "Learning about Things," mock-serious reporting of ludicrous or degrading events by willing accomplices in the essays, radical recipes from the kitchen in "Cooking Lesson." The feminine patterns of middle-class Mexican speech that her personae assume are full of the same clichés, truisms, stilted expressions, and idioms that abound in the nightly *telenovelas*. They must *not* be smoothed out but, rather, retained because they are significant generators of the cultural and ironic humor that became Castellanos' hallmark—though at times it is impossible to render their full nuances in English. I have looked for ways to transmit the specific gender markers in the inflected Spanish system that are lost when they cross into the uninflected English forms, because their elements are the ones that feminize her discourse. In other cases, features that create ambiguity have also been preserved, not smoothed out. For example, "oneself" for the third person reflexive in "Meditation on the Brink" should not be turned into the personal "yourself" as English may grammatically elect to do. For it is this element that transmits the flatness of the voice that is relating life and death in the lives of other women. But in the case of "The Liberation of Love," where male rhetoric satirizes itself, the translation of *mujercita* must somehow convey the condescension that this form carries in the Mexican context. My translator's rule of thumb has once again been the perspective of the active reader: to attempt to offer the same degree of reading difficulty to the reader of the translation that the Spanish-language reader faces in the original.

An awareness of the polyphony of Castellanos' texts makes the translator listen for echoes of other voices that inhabit her writing, for often they are the elements that create the new text. The echo of Descartes' dictum, the words of Virginia Woolf's "Angel in the House," and the lively nineteenth-century voices from Fanny Calderón's diaries all create new messages. In other cases the translator must read through Castellanos' own readings, or in others, see through her eyes, to reach appropriate choices. In translating "Metamorphosis of the Sorceress," the peculiar flowing quality of Remedios Varo's cosmic paintings of women are simulated in Castellanos' elongated syntax and line.

An essential criterion has been that the translations selected for this volume must stand as aesthetic creations in their own right in English. In practice, this principle has led my understanding of Castellanos' writing in particular, and of translation in general, in a number of new directions. One result has been to subject my earlier translations to extensive rereading, mulling over and recasting to replace gender specificity and to render rhetoric more natural in "new" readings of the earlier versions of Castellanos' poetry that were published in magazines and anthologies and in the chapbook *Looking at the Mona Lisa*. Some, like "Malinche" and "Tlatelolco," underwent major changes, while others, like "Learning about Things," required none.

As editor I have worked toward achieving a unified translation policy, by serving as critical reader for the short fiction, essays, and play. Thus, translations executed by myself and my collaborators, Diane Marting, Betty Tyree Osiek, Ruth Peacock, Laura Solomon, and Lesley Salas, are firmly grounded in the conviction that, beyond the operations of decoding and recoding from Spanish into English, translating the writing of Rosario Castellanos in all the genres is a complex semiotic process that will generate new readings. As such, it has demanded a crucial awareness of the author's textual strategies and how the interactions between ideology and

the author, translator, and reader function to produce meaning (Díaz-
Diocaretz, 14–16). Fundamental to this process is an intimate knowledge
of Mexican culture on the part of the translators in order to detect the
subtle cultural codes that determine the linguistic ones. An invaluable as-
set has been our immersion in Mexican culture during different periods of
our lives and the assistance of Mexican writers and colleagues who knew
and worked with Castellanos.

In our own creative acts of bringing Castellanos' texts from one social
context to another, as arbiters in the production of cultural as well as linguistic meanings, as writers ourselves, our goal has been to become
Rosario Castellanos' closest readers, through whose eyes the pages that follow will be read.

MAUREEN AHERN
Tempe, Arizona

We have to create another language, we have to find another starting point . . .

—Rosario Castellanos
"Language as an Instrument of Domination"

Reading Rosario Castellanos:
Contexts, Voices, and Signs

It is in her life and her writing that we Mexican women recognize
each other. —ELENA PONIATOWSKA,
"Rosario Castellanos: ¡Vida, nada te debo!," 99

Woman must write her self: must write about women and bring
women to writing, from which they have been driven away as
violently as from their own bodies . . . Woman must put herself
into the text—as into the world and into history—by her own
movement. —HÉLÈNE CIXOUS,
"The Laugh of the Medusa," 279

Two acts of reading converge in *A Rosario Castellanos Reader.* The first is the translator's reading of the Spanish-language texts to decode their elements of meaning within the context of the whole discourse and ideology of this author. When the translator recodes those elements to produce the new text she too becomes a writer. The second reading is practiced by the reader of the new texts in English: an active process that empowers them with new meanings in the receptor culture (Díaz-Diocaretz, 21–22). The translator thus becomes "a first mediator between the sign provider and sign perceiver. The 'two individuals' become at least three—poet, translator, reader" (Díaz-Diocaretz, 11). It is the aim of this introduction to provide the contexts that shape these acts of meditation through an inquiry into the connections between Rosario Castellanos' biography and her writing, the voices in her texts that speak for and as a woman (Jacobus, 15), and the ways that Castellanos' signs produce meaning throughout all the genres.[1]

Contexts

Rosario Castellanos was born in Mexico City on May 25, 1925, the first child of Adriana Figueroa and César Castellanos, who returned to their native Chiapas when she was a year old. She grew up on a ranch on the Jataté River near the Guatemalan border and, later, in the town of Comitán, a region of centuries-old conflicts between the Chamula Indians and the landholding families, privileged for generations by class, race, and language. It is an area whose social structure and cultural life are markedly distinct from that of the Mexican highlands to the north and west and more akin to Guatemala (to which it once belonged) than to Mexico.[2]

Castellanos' early life was marked by solitude, death, and rejection. She was cared for by her Indian nanny, Rufina, and a Chamula Indian girl her same age, María Escandón, but her parents' favorite child was clearly her younger brother, Benjamín. His sudden death when she was very young sharpened her parents' rejection of her, as they withdrew into their grief. She said, "I grew up in a family that . . . was solitary and isolated, a family that had lost its interest in living." "Your father and I love you because we're obliged to," her mother told her.[3] Her essay "A Man of Destiny" describes the stifling Chiapas womanhood that she was spared by President Lázaro Cárdenas' land reform program in 1941, which stripped the provincial elite of most of their holdings. When the Castellanos family lost their properties, Rosario and her parents moved to Mexico City, where she entered the preparatory school at age sixteen. The changes in status from provincial landowners to a life of limited means in the capital city held profound repercussions for the adolescent Rosario, which are retold in her uncollected story "Three Knots in the Net." "On the one hand it destroyed any certainty of my racial, social, and economic superiority . . . and on the other it forced me to find values to achieve and make my own in order to feel worthy of living" (*Artes Hispánicas*, 67). The poems that she had begun to write in 1940 soon began to appear in student magazines.

At the National University of Mexico, the girl from Chiapas enrolled in the College of Philosophy and Letters, where she became part of the group of young Mexican and Central American writers who later became known as the "Generation of 1950." Budding dramatists and critics Emilio Carballido, Sergio Magaña, and Luisa Josefina Hernández; poets Dolores Castro, Miguel Guardia, and Jaime Sabines; Nicaraguans Ernesto Cardenal and Ernesto Mejía Sánchez; and Guatemalans Augusto Monterroso, Otto Raúl González, and Carlos Illescas—all met on Saturdays to read and discuss their work under the mentorship of Efrén Hernández, director of *América, Revista Antológica*, where many of their earliest pieces were published. Castellanos' decision to study philosophy, instead of literature, characterized the independence of mind and clearness of vision that became her hallmark. "In the College of Philosophy and Letters they give you a set of recipes for writing, but you can't write with recipes," she told Elena Poniatowska in their first interview in 1958 (7). Later Castellanos explained, "Literature interested me so much that I used to search for the essential books by myself; I tried to discover on my own how to write. On the other hand, Philosophy was a discipline so alien to my temperament that only through obligation would I be able to learn it . . . I was looking for something more profound . . . the answer to all problems and an orientation to aesthetics" (*Artes Hispánicas*, 67).[4]

The year 1948 marked a period of emotional, religious, and intellectual crisis in Castellanos' life that resulted in the freedom she needed to become her own person. The death of her parents within a month of each other and the experience of reading a long vanguard poem on death converged in the publication of her first two long poems. She was finally free, she said, from "a knot of pathological affection and relationships" to assume the responsibility for managing her own life and, above all, to "dedicate myself professionally to literature" (*Confrontaciones: Los narradores ante el público*, 89).

The thesis *On Feminine Culture* that the young scholar defended in 1950, for her master's degree in philosophy from the National University, initiated a life-long inquiry into the question of women's place in culture. A scholarship from the Hispanic Cultural Institute enabled her to study aesthetics and stylistics at the University of Madrid and to travel in Europe with her friend and fellow poet Dolores Castro.

When she returned to Mexico at the end of 1951, she became the director of cultural programs for the state of Chiapas. However, a bout of tuberculosis forced her to spend three months in a sanatorium in Mexico City and another year convalescing—a period she used to read Tolstoy, Mann, and Proust. It also enabled her to meditate on the experiences in Chiapas that would become her chapbook of poems, *El rescate del mundo* (1952). In 1953 the Mexican Writers Center awarded her a grant to conduct research on the contribution of women to Mexican culture. During 1954–55, a fellowship from the Rockefeller Foundation enabled her to develop her first novel, *The Nine Guardians* (*Balún-Canán*), which earned Castellanos national recognition in the form of the Mexican Critics' award for the best novel of 1957 and the Chiapas prize in 1958. The English translation by Irene Nicholson was published in London by Faber & Faber that same year.

Castellanos returned to Chiapas in 1956 to direct the puppet theater, El Teatro Petul, for the National Indigenist Institute in San Cristóbal de las Casas. For the next two years, the team took their troupe over mountain and jungle roads to perform in remote towns and villages throughout the state, affording Castellanos the direct contact she wanted with the rich Indian cultures of her native region. She also began to work on her second novel, *Oficio de tinieblas*, which won major critical acclaim when it was published in 1962. When she returned to Mexico City she continued to work with the National Indigenist Institute in the preparation of textbooks for Indian children.

In 1957, at the age of thirty-two, Rosario Castellanos married Ricardo Guerra, a philosophy professor at her alma mater. Her friends recall that she was apprehensive about a marriage that she soon came to perceive as a lonely failure. Two miscarriages prior to the birth of her son, Gabriel Guerra Castellanos, in 1961, caused a sense of profound loss. Eventually she obtained a divorce. The poems in *Lívida luz* (1960) and *Materia memorable* (1962) reflect those experiences of grief, solitude, and rejection.

From 1960 to 1966, Castellanos was press and information director for the National University of Mexico. In 1963 she began to write articles and columns for the weekly cultural supplements of *Novedades* and *¡Siempre!* and, later, *Excélsior*, which were partly collected in her four volumes of essays. During 1967 Castellanos held visiting professorships in Latin American literature at the Universities of Wisconsin, Indiana, and Colorado. Her stay in the United States coincided with the march commemorating the fiftieth anniversary of women's suffrage in this country and the demonstrations that dramatized the Women's Liberation Movement. These events galvanized Castellanos' thinking about women, culture, and literature, which had already been significantly changed by her extensive reading of the works of Simone Weil, Simone de Beauvoir, and Virginia Woolf.

Castellanos returned to Mexico to accept a Chair of Comparative Literature at the National University. She wrote another novel, "Rito de iniciación," which was set on that campus in the forties, about "the way an adolescent girl finds her way to the vocation of literature" (Sommers, "The Present Moment," 264), but she withdrew it from publication just before it was due to come out. It was not up to her own standards, she wrote later to her friend Raúl Ortiz.[5] In the early seventies she finished *Album de familia* (1971), a quartet of short stories about women and their alienation in urban Mexico, and the edition of her collected poems, *Poesía no eres tú* (1972).

President Luis Echeverría named her Mexican ambassador to Israel in 1971. It was not a question of becoming part of the establishment, Poniatowska has clarified: "She knew, of course, that in Mexico women are not given these chances to excell. More than advancement, Rosario saw it as a chance at life in a new country on a new basis for herself and her son" (Poniatowska, "Vida," 130). Those three years that she and Gabriel lived in Israel, where she also held a lectureship in Latin American literature at the Hebrew University in Jerusalem, were among the happiest ones she had ever known. Israeli colleagues and students responded warmly to her skillful representation of Mexican culture and art, and by all accounts she was a splendidly successful ambassador. She found time to write the play about Mexican cultural stereotypes that her friends in Mexico City had been urging her to compose for their stage production there. Her essays about Mexican women's cultural issues and women writers were published in 1971 in the volume *Mujer que sabe latín*. In July 1974, she compiled another collection called *El mar y sus pescaditos*. "In Israel, Rosario Castellanos, free and by herself, learned self-fulfillment on her own, a Rosario who didn't care if she had lost a man because she had found herself. That's why the accident that killed her was so absurd . . ." (Poniatowska, "Vida," 131).

Rosario Castellanos was electrocuted on August 7, 1974, in her residence in Tel Aviv when she turned on a lamp in her living room after stepping out of the shower. A servant found her unconscious but she died alone in the ambulance before it reached the hospital. A stunned Mexico paused to pay tribute to her at a state funeral while commemorative observances were held by the literary communities of Israel, Europe, the United States, Central America, and Chile.

Poetry: Silences and Otherness

Rosario Castellanos' trajectory as a poet set in motion concepts that are fundamental to the development of her poetic language and to our reading of her writing as sets of contiguous texts. In no other portion of Castellanos' total literary production can we trace a clearer pattern of the changing status of her discourse than in her poetry, an evolving corpus that Castellanos herself compiled in 1971 as *Poesía no eres tú*. It included all her previously published books as well as three unpublished collections written after 1969—ample testimony to her maturing talent.

A Voice of Her Own

Castellanos' first published poem appeared in a Chiapas literary magazine, *El Estudiante*, in 1940 when she was fifteen years old, and was entitled, "To Death."[6] Her first book of poetry, *Trayectoria del polvo* (1948), was written after she read José Gorostiza's poem "Death without End."[7] Death continued to punctuate her work up to the closing poem in her last book, which begins: "I walk the land of Anahuac / the land of my dead."[8] Over the years the stark concepts remained the same but her language changed significantly.

The search for that language of her own underlies all her writing.

"I came to poetry after discovering that other roads were not viable for survival. In those years survival was what most interested me. The words of poetry constituted the only way to achieve permanence in this world" (Carballo, 412). But in the next two books,[9] she struggled to find her own voice. "The rhetoric simply swept me away . . . most of the forms were not my own" (García Flores, *Cartas marcadas*, 170). The exit from this blind alley was the models that she found in her readings of the Bible and the poems of the Chilean writer, Gabriela Mistral and the Spanish poet Jorge Guillén. They helped achieve a transition to her own style in her fourth book of verse, *El rescate del mundo* (1952). "Form was transparent, crystalline. Objects, totally pure, struggled to reveal their secrets" (Carballo, 414). In *Poemas: 1953–1955*, Castellanos began to achieve the correspondence she sought between what she wanted to say and what she actually wrote. It was in *Al pie de la letra* (1959), she later wrote, that "I began to recognize my own voice and could see three cardinal points to develop: humor, solemn meditation and contact with my carnal and historical roots. And everything was bathed by that livid light of death that makes all matter memorable" ("If Not Poetry, Then What?"). This anthology opens with the poems that reflect these cardinal points: a meditation on language and cultural identity in "Silence Near an Ancient Stone," death in "The Other," and wry delight with Chiapas in "To a Tiny Mayan Badger."

Silences and Myths

The reconstruction of female experience in long poems—"Dido," "Judith," and "Salome"—dramatized women of antiquity. "Malinche" signaled a new direction toward reversing the myths assigned to women by patriarchal tradition. The poetic speaker of this monologue is Cortés' Indian interpreter and mistress, whose name Mexican folk history, as well as its language, has made the literal word for betrayal.[10] In terms of historical fact, in the sixteenth century Bernal Díaz recorded that it was really this remarkable woman who was betrayed when her own family sold her into slavery before she was delivered to Cortés as a gift. Malinche's speaking voice in Castellanos' twentieth-century text humanizes a woman traditionally cast as a historical monster in Mexico, expressing the terror and fear she felt when her mother sold her to alien traders:

> I advance toward destiny in chains
> leaving behind all that I can still hear,
> the funereal murmurs with which I am buried.

And the voice of my mother in tears—in tears!
She who decrees my death.

In this poem, Malinche is a woman, but in the essay "Once Again Sor Juana" we see how she becomes a sign, which offers yet another dimension of Malinche, depicting her as the national symbol of female sexuality and its oppression in Mexico. By reversing this myth Castellanos shed new light on the ethnic and gender stereotypes that constrain Mexican popular culture.[11]

The last poem in this anthology, "Nazareth," meditates on a female figure from yet a wider patriarchal tradition:

. . . Mary, that chosen vessel.

Like all vessels, fragile.
Like all vessels too small
for the destiny poured into it.

Both "Malinche" and "Nazareth" create voices from among the many silences that Castellanos detected in official history. These voices about whom patriarchal tradition has said so much now speak out for themselves. Thus, Rosario Castellanos reversed Mexican myths as she searched for a historical and social place for women within a cultural tradition that silenced them. It is a theme for which she will find many variations, because "silence contains all potential sounds" (Gubar, 23).[12]

If male myth has distorted the image of woman, the language that encodes it alienates her. "I've forgotten my own country / and I no longer understand the language they use there / . . . that heavy jewel-studded velvet that people where I live use to cover their rags" declares the female speaker in "Monologue of a Foreign Woman." It was one of Castellanos' favorite poems, she told Margarita García Flores: "I wasn't aware of it at the time that I wrote it. I thought I was telling the story of another woman but when I finished I realized that I was talking about myself, that it was my own story that once again I had transformed and used in that oblique form of reference that creates distance between the object and expression . . . that is perhaps aesthetic distance" ("La lucidez como forma de vida," 6). These transformations became twelve volumes of poems.

Otherness

Many critics have sought to explain Rosario Castellanos' work through an apparent obsession with death, but, when considered in the context of her total discourse, death is only one element of a much wider concept that permeates all her poetry: the exploration of the other, whether that other be woman, indigenous culture, language, silence, or writing itself. From a broader perspective it is clear that the origins of Rosario Castellanos' creativity lie in the tension between self and other that underscores all her verse and prose. Above all, it is important to realize the breadth and heterogeneity of that otherness.

An early definition found in the poem "The Other" perceives it to be "all we need to be whole": the link between death and life.

> Look around you: there is the other, always the other,
> He breathes what chokes you.
> He eats your hunger.
> He dies with the purest half of your death.

In *Lívida luz* (1960), a male lover becomes the link with another kind of death; solitude. "You meet in the dark. A kiss mingles / the taste of tears. / And your embrace encircles / memories of that orphanhood, that death" ("Routine").

It is in *Materia memorable* (1969), the collection that marked a midway point in her poetry, that the other transcends the self to become that awareness of community that enables her to define life in death, self in other, utterance in muteness. "Consciousness" begins domestically with coffee over the morning newspaper, in which a photo catapults the speaker, who is "still a woman alone," into a faraway rice paddy, face to face with the other.

> I find a man who is different from me
> in color and language but
> equal in the lightning illuminating this moment
> in which he, his adversary, and I (who can't see them)
> come together: we are one single being
> and the universe breathes in us.

No longer "just a person, a body, and a niche for a name," she leaps beyond: "I am a wide patio, a great open house, / a memory." In this other, beyond hearth and tribe, is the essence of self and life in humankind.

> In the midst of this circle of presences
> I am myself: matter
> that burns, diffuses heat and light.
> I snap out the reply, rejoicing: "All's well!"

"You Are Not Poetry" will take these meditations one step further, where otherness becomes dialogue and the passage to writing itself.

The other: mediator, judge, balance
between opposites, witness,
knot that binds up all that had broken.

The other, muteness begging a voice
from the speaker
claiming an ear
from the listener.

The other. With the other
humanity, dialogue, poetry, begin.

In Castellanos' writing, the concept of otherness transcends gender. It has become a yet wider patio that embraces sex, society, and writing—in short, creativity itself. The companion text to this poem is found in her essay "If Not Poetry, Then What?," which is a guide to her writing: "What happened is that I developed very slowly from the most closed subjectivity to the disturbing discovery that the other existed, and finally to the rupture of the pattern of the couple to integrate myself into the social sphere that is the one in which the poet defines, understands, and expresses herself."

Castellanos considered her most mature poetry to be that written after 1969, texts that comprise the final three sections of her *Poesía no eres tú*. Here, she declared to Margarita García Flores in one of her last interviews in 1974, "I use a series of incidents or experiences which are not formally considered to be poetic. I feel I have the freedom to leave the poetic canon behind and to find something outside it which is valid for me . . . the last part I like best because of its freedom . . . no worrying anymore if this word is legitimate or if it is acceptable but simply if the word is essential, exact. Furthermore, they are vital experiences at a level of awareness and a level of maturity which I hope have become part of the poems" ("La lucidez como forma de vida," 6). Beyond the female images and voices whose existence under patriarchal constraints led to suicide, silence, and self-denial, Castellanos searched for "another way" of imagining and realizing lives for women that is beyond madness, muteness, or penance.

There must be another way that's not named Sappho
or Mesalina or Mary of Egypt
or Magdalene or Clemence Isaure.

Another way to be human and free.

Another way to be. ("Meditation on the Brink")

Rosario Castellanos' poetic journey from self to otherness, the struggle to find a voice of her own among silences, and the reversal of cultural myths are part of the larger paradigm that her writing represents in the development of feminine poetry in Latin America in the twentieth century (Rivero, 406). Let us now turn to the textual strategies in her poetry, where the interaction of the female speakers and addressees combines with metaphors from domestic events, as well as intertextual elements to produce some of her most memorable compositions.

Speakers and Addressees in the Poetry of Rosario Castellanos

Gender Identification: Saying I/We/You

To a large extent the experience of reading Rosario Castellanos' poems is shaped by their speaking subjects and addressees. Thus, one way to approach the production of meaning in her poetry, which has been overlooked as a major textual clue to reading, is to examine the interactions between the speaking subjects, who are the source of the utterances in the poetic text, and the addressees or receptors of those enunciations. In particular, the interplay between "I," "We," and "You" in the communication structure requires attention. "The existence of an individual subject supposes an identity created and assumed to give expression to that portion of the world of the poem which determines the perspective from which the poet speaks, and provides the passage through which the poet's text as a totality is envisioned. In other words, it provides the viewpoint from which the poet 'penetrates the reading audience, and that of the reader [that] penetrates the consciousness of the poet (Lotman, 1977:29)'" (Díaz-Diocaretz, 85).

This speaking voice is a construct inferred by the reader from the signs in the textual world, as well as from her or his own extratextual set of presuppositions, brought to the act of reading.[13] However, it should be made clear that a man or woman author does not always write from the same gender perspective; thus, in a poem written by a woman the speaking subject is not necessarily identified as feminine but may be perceived as ambiguous or male (Díaz-Diocaretz, 86–87). By feminine identified, we refer to the gender identity that the reader allocates to the speaker or addressee through linguistic, intertextual, and extratextual clues that affect the reader's interpretation of the poem (Díaz-Diocaretz, 45–46). Nonetheless, in the case of Castellanos' poems, the central self that speaks most of her poems is forcefully defined from linguistic gender cues or by referential cues interpreted by the reader as a female speaking subject. In Spanish-language texts these are signified by explicitly marked features that accompany or form the "I," "We," or "You" of the poetic construct: principally orientation markers that are called person deitics, which include the first- and second-person pronouns and verb endings that refer to the speakers and addressees and their corresponding gender markers that express male or female, singular or plural nouns, pronouns, and adjectives. "In languages such as English that do not have an obligatory differentiation in certain gender markers, because of indeterminacy, the reader is the only one to ideate the speaker as male or female" (Díaz-Diocaretz, 45).[14]

Because the translator is a "prior reader" (Díaz-Diocaretz, 25–33) who will ideate the genders for the English version of Castellanos' poetry, I propose a correlation of the chain of different identities of the persons implied in the "I," "We," and "You" of her texts. The same holds true for her addressees, particularly those identities hidden in the transfer to the ambiguous English "You," which may potentially refer to various identities in Spanish.[15]

Language and Identity

In the Spanish source texts of Castellanos' poems, it is clear that the "*yo,*" or "I," in fact refers to a number of different speaking identities. The first one, which we meet in her earliest poems, is an I-speaker who is identified as female by the inflected Spanish gender system but whose specificity is *not* apparent in the translation when they cross into the uninflected English forms, which are not marked for gender. In "Silence Near an Ancient Stone," the speaker creates the central metaphor of the woman in the assertive first line:

Estoy aqui, sentada, con todas mis palabras
como una cesta de fruta verde, intactas.

I'm a woman sitting here with all my words intact
like a basket of green fruit.

Identity is achieved, first through the linguistic gender marker for feminine singular in the *a* of the adjective *sentada* and second, through the immediate cultural association of the simile of words and a basket of green fruit, which evokes the image of an Indian woman vending her fruit at the market—a common sight throughout Mexico. It is this feminine voice that reflects on the alienation of cultural heritage through the loss of language. The powerful contrast of past cultural glory with present emptiness is textually achieved through a series of semantic oppositions manifested in the dialectics of silence/words, intact/fragments, sight/blindness, here/behind, sea/desert, present/past.

Yet a third generator of meaning in this poem is produced when the English reader fills in a gap inferred by the title. It presupposes that he or she can associate the "ancient stone" to the *stelae* where the biographies of Mayan leaders were inscribed in glyphs, evoking the oppositions of past written and visual codes with the present absence of contemporary signs.

The feminine speaker and her words become the central metaphor, which, set off spatially, creates the rest of the poem. In a sense, this "I" also functions as a paradigm for the formation of speakers in the rest of Castellanos' literary constructs: feminine identified, reflective *personae* whose voices merge dramatized feminine experience with cultural history. Lacking explicit addressees, these strong "I" speakers belong to a dramatic, monologic mode that sets the stage for the focus of her discourse as a whole and for this anthology: women, the voices of their past and present experiences—the power of language in their lives—the silences that have shaped them.

From the first, it is clear that aesthetic meaning in this author's poetry is gender and culture based, reader as well as author based. The speaking voices trigger the production of meanings that converge in the reading process. In English translation, however, the textually explicit gender of the speaking voice is usually lost—thus a translation that replaces it in this poem with "I'm a woman sitting here with all my words intact," instead of "I'm sitting here with all my words intact," succeeds in transmitting both the gender and culture cues that create poetic meaning in this key text.

Among Castellanos' poems structured around the gender identified "I" speaker, some of the voices reflecting on feminine experiences are explicitly autobiographical. "Passage" is particularly interesting; once again English blurs the explicitly feminine markers that form this lyric voice: for example, in the line "*Niña ciega, palpaba mi rostro con mis manos*" (A blind girl, I touched my face with my hands), if *niña* were translated as child instead of girl, feminine identification, the critical difference in the poem, is lost. This same poetic speaker is one who "never learned / to blot out the name Rosario" as she climbed up, "Beyond the limits. Here, / depth or heights, a place / uninhabitable for my species." She aspires to the heights that man moves in, "a transparent atmosphere of eagles," the symbol of Mexican nationhood. Within parentheses, a sardonic reflection brings her own identity to bear:

> (I should have covered my face with a veil
> so that no one could see this color of jungle
> —splendor and catastrophe—
> that is still with me.)

This poem about women going "beyond the limits" is about naming ourselves, our own real identities, our authentic aspirations, looking up not down, ahead not behind. All are integral to the issue of identity that lies at the heart of women's writing in the Americas.

Testimonial Voices

A second pattern of speakers and addressees in Castellanos' poems involves those where the lyric speaker is an "I" marked by a first-person singular verb form, who is *not* gender identified as male or female; whose words are directed to an explicitly second-person familiar "*tú*" addressee, who is *not* gender identified either, even though it carries a masculine marker. Díaz-Diocaretz calls these persons deitics, "generic" identities for whom a reader in Spanish does not ideate a specific gender. The strong-speaking "I" of "Presence," for example, talking to a "brother, lover, child, friend," who is in fact "mankind," uses the masculine singular ending in Spanish, which is used for any general reference to person. "Memorandum on Tlatelolco" integrates a complex interplay of two generic speakers, "I" and "We," addressing a generic singular receptor, "You" (*tú*), that is unmarked for gender to create one of Castellanos' most powerful poems. It was written at the request of Elena Poniatowska as a poetic prologue for her *Massacre in Mexico*; together these two texts present the most moving testimonial to the Tlatelolco massacre in 1968, a bloody event that signaled a profound political crisis in Mexico.[16]

The poem begins with a matter-of-fact neutral third-person enunciation of terrible events that provokes a series of probing questions for which there are no answers.

> And in that brief livid light, who is it? Who is killing?
> Who are in agony, who are dying?
> Who are the ones fleeing without shoes?
> The ones who will end up in the jailpens?
> The ones who are rotting in hospitals?
> The ones who keep silent forever, out of fear?
> Who? Who are they? No one. The next day, no one.

The descriptive tone returns in the next stanza, scanning the scene of the empty plaza, blank newscasts, hollow ceremonies. Officially, nothing had happened. Suddenly the poem gathers intensity when the focus shifts to the addressee in the second-person command form that follows: "Don't search for what is not there: clues, corpses / . . . Don't comb through the files because nothing has been entered / on the books." After the refrain, the speaking voice switches to a rhetorical "I" ("*mas he aqui que toco una llaga: es mi memoria*"):

> But here I touch an open wound: my memory.
> It hurts, therefore it is true. It bleeds real blood.
> Yet if I call it mine I betray them all.

The blood of the living becomes the memory of the dead. In the final stanzas the oppositions of I/We in parallel litany deliver the poem to powerful closure as personal "I" moves to collective "We" of humankind.

> I remember, we remember.
>
> This is our way of helping dawn to break
> upon so many stained consciences,
> upon an irate text, upon an open grate,
> upon the face shielded behind the mask.
>
> I remember, we must remember
> until justice be done among us.

These neutral speaking and addressee entities, who do not carry specific gender-identified forms in Spanish, could be any one of us—we must share a collective memory in order to shoulder social responsibility. A third configuration of speaking subjects and addressees is a female-identified speaking "I" and her male-identified addressee lover or friend, who shape the male-female dialogues in "Routine," "Brief Chronicle," and "Consciousness," where at closure the female-identified "I" and the male-identified "You" (*amor mío*) become "We"—the immense leap in which self becomes other.

Women Speaking to Women: Domesticity as Poetic Discourse

By far the largest group of poems, however, particularly those selected from the collections written after 1969, manifest feminine-identified speakers and addressees who use the intimate mode of *tú* to create texts in which women speak to other women. Interwoven with these female voices are the typically "unpoetic" domestic or biographical events that serve as metaphors for an agenda of larger social issues. This is the case for "Home Economics," where the feminine identity of the speaker is inferred from the subject matter of the title and the reference to the proverb about neatness and order that corresponds closely to several cultural equivalents in English, among them "a place for everything and everything in its place." But in this case the distinctly feminine routine of the traditional good housekeeper, the orderly division of the table linen and china for daily use from the finest pieces, and the harmonious arrangement of dust-free furniture form both a contrast and a focus on the speaker's emotional life: sorrow, pain, or anxiety that are simply tossed into a drawer of catchalls that are *not* in order—that do not obey the rules handed down by her mother. Rebellion against the mother's traditional domestic order produces guilt and anxiety. "Re: Mutilations" is shaped by semantic references to domestic acts of clipping a fingernail or bobbing her hair, stripping the *tú* addressee's identity to the point of discarding even the letters of her own name.

"Rosario Castellanos makes literature out of the day-to-day events of her life," Elena Poniatowska wrote ("Vida," 67). Many of her poems and essays use metaphors or scenes from events like drinking the morning coffee, paying the bills, burning the rice, applying makeup, playing chess, gossiping, raising a child, watching soap operas, selecting a menu, taking a tranquilizer. Often these events from the domestic realms of human activity are combined with elements of the ludicrous, manifested in the guise of a singular feminine "I" and "You," that are self-deprecating or self-effacing. It is the voice of the social and domestic klutz of "Self-Portrait" telling us, "I'm rather ugly. It all depends on / the hand that applies the makeup. / . . . I'm mediocre," who in the same breath dramatizes the way women are socialized to behave in order to be acceptable: passive, self-effacing, playing roles that hold little connection with their authentic persons. Even at the task she was socialized to perform—manipulation through tears—this speaker turns out to be incompetent.

> I'd be happy if I knew how.
> I mean, if they had taught me the gestures,
> the small talk, etiquette.
>
> Instead they taught me how to cry. But crying in me
> is a broken-down mechanism;
> I don't cry at funerals,
> on sublime occasions, or when disaster strikes.

I cry when I burn the rice or when I lose
the latest tax receipt.

Several significant points need to be made about Castellanos' preference for the ordinary events of the domestic orbit—a sphere, on the one
hand, traditionally considered to be trivial and, on the other, to be safe. In
Rosario Castellanos' writing, domesticity, not unlike the female body, is
the most accessible medium of self-expression. It is a way of writing self
and writing woman from women's space.[17] Domesticity is her creative
springboard, apt for transformation to memorable matter—where it is
central to creativity—not trivial, as some critics have suggested. "The art
of producing the essential—children, food, cloth—is woman's ultimate
creativity. If it is taken as absence in the context of patriarchal culture, it is
celebrated within the female community by the matrilineal traditions of
oral storytelling" (Gubar, 24). And it is widely celebrated in the poetry
written by women in Latin America.[18]

In Castellanos' writing the prevalence of female imagery coupled with
domestic metaphor may also be seen as a way to preserve the domestic
within the realm of true creativity—a way, to paraphrase Felsteiner, of
making the familiar strange (5). Since these metaphors are often crafted
from biography, recent scholarship on women's autobiography merits
consideration here. "By androcentric standards female autobiography
seems disorderly. Estelle Jelinek prefers the term 'discontinuous' and she
and Suzanne Juhasz have pointed out that women's lives are not usually
linear, but, rather, cyclical, repetitive, disjointed and other-directed.
Progress toward a goal often proceeds erratically, usually because of exi-
gencies beyond the individual's control, such as a family crisis. As Jelinek
argues, women's autobiographies reflect this discontinuity" (Voss, 221).[19]

Castellanos used explicit female imagery and daily experience to create
poetry and essays that speak as a woman and about other women. She
practiced her vocation of writing daily, bridging the gap between the outside world of literature, Mexico, ideas, and that of her private world of
personal relationships, home, and emotion. In Castellanos' poetry, as occurs in her essays, the roles of "woman" and "writer" meet.

There are still other readings that can be garnered regarding the domestic component of her poetry. In traditional Mexican society, the feminine
is the realm of marriage, children, and the socially acceptable position of
wife—and the duties that she performs within the home. It is, therefore, a
"safe" pulpit from which to say things to women about women because
the messages can be said in codes that are traditionally "theirs." Thus, the

domestic metaphor is a subtle way of criticizing the basic institutions of this society in a socially acceptable or innocuous way. In other words, a "safe" messenger speaks in a "safe" voice to a "safe" addressee, delivering what in fact turns out to be a radical message. The self-deprecating voices ring culturally true because a "dumb little tourist lady," a "mediocre" klutz, or a docile girl are innocuous and inferior speakers, as their *tú* forms confirm. But, as I will point out, they transmit subversive messages; the enormous gap between how the message is conveyed and what it actually says generates the incisive irony for which Castellanos' parodies are famous.

Feminine Lessons: Signs That Subvert

Yet another set of speaker/addressee situations must be mentioned: where the skillful manipulation of multiple levels of discourse in a single poem highlight how women are socialized into roles of passivity and humility that become self-effacement and conformity. "Learning about Things" is such a text in which two levels of discourse operate at both poles of the communication axis; that is, there are two sets of speakers and addressees, even though technically all emanate from the performative initial I.[20]

This terrible parody does not begin with a strong female "I" but rather with a passive enunciation where the form initiating the utterance is *me*, the recipient or object of the socialization process: "*Me enseñaron las cosas equivocadamente,*" a syntactical feature that English translation deletes.

> They taught me things all wrong
> the ones who teach things:
> my parents, the teacher, the priest.
> You have to be a good girl, they told me.

After enumerating the signs of patriarchal authority that stand for family, education, and religion, the stanza shifts to their voices, albeit indirectly: "You have to be a good girl, *they told me.*" At this second level of discourse, the voices of societal authority become the speakers and the original female speaker becomes the addressee, addressed by the Spanish *tú* form used to speak to subordinates or any social inferiors. In the Hispanic world it is universally used to address children, here becoming the mode that converts this segment into a lecture. The voices of authority preach to our "good girl" the traditional formula that gains societal approval: turn the other cheek, be submissive, accept suffering, don't ask questions, and forgive whatever is done to you, "because God is testing the mettle of your soul." The poem then returns to the original female "I" speaker, who continues this devastating monologue in her own voice. When the "I" feminine-identified speaker becomes the feminine addressee of the patriarchal chorus, we the readers witness the internalization of the oppressor's discourse—the incorporation into the woman's voice of the traditional lines of control used over women by Christianity, until at last she identifies herself as a "cog" in the wheel, self-effacing to the end.

> Conformity? Perhaps. Which in a cog, like me
> is not in any way a merit,
> but rather, at best, a condition.

Once again it is the speaker/addressee construct that generates the central metaphor of a woman/child. The second-level authorities impart their lessons to the child addressee within the woman speaker, a chilling discursive allegory about the way a female person is perceived. "Custom," Castellanos wrote in an essay, "holds that a man has to be very 'macho' and a woman very self-sacrificing. The complicity between executioner and victim is so old that it is impossible to distinguish who is who" ("La participación de la mujer mexicana en la educación formal," 38). "Learning about Things" and "Postscript" trace this internalization of the ideology of subservience into the discourse of its victims, through that maxim of self-sacrifice that begins by indoctrinating children of both sexes into the very values by which women themselves have been subordinated (Gerda Lerner, 170).

Castellanos' mordant satire is heightened by the flat, matter-of-fact tone in which the feminine speaker's repression is stated as her accepted truth,[21] when she says, "Until I finally understood." The resulting irony subverts the "transparent" message of the text, emitting a second contradictory message. In this way, Castellanos' mature poems, as do her essays, go beyond mere inquiry into women's place in society to explore multiple relationships of the female subculture to the dominant ideology. Through subversive discourse, where elements like tone and speaking voices simultaneously transmit a message contradictory to that conveyed by the poetic personae, her poems are able to fulfill two central critical tasks: on the one hand, they represent the complexity and ambivalency of female roles in relation to male custom, in that they can collude as well as challenge, and, second, they expose and dismantle the structures that have marginalized women in traditional societies like Mexico.[22]

Female Sexuality: "Saying the Unsayable"

The speech act situation changes in "Kinsey Report," where the production of meaning is generated by the addressees.[23] The poem is composed of six different answers to the questions of a survey enunciated by a speaker, who, although extratextual, remains within the reader's inference from the association generated by the title, which reads in the original Spanish text as "Kinsey Report." In other words, not even a translation was needed for the source language reader, who immediately fills this gap from the general knowledge that the original Kinsey Report contained the results of a questionnaire about human sexual behavior. On this second level the addressees of the original questions now become the speakers. They are all Mexican women, as deduced from gender markers and cultural references within their speech acts, who run the gamut from a traditional middle-class housewife to a lesbian to a teenage virgin waiting for her Prince Charming. Their answers express sadness, anger, and ignorance.

In Mexico, a land where *machismo* reigns, sexuality is an area where social conduct and linguistic conventions are highly distinct between male and female—where the norm of the double standard is linguistic as well as social. Thus it comes as no surprise that women there have not had access to the full code of language either.[24] For women in Mexico, as in many other parts of Latin America, the language of sexuality is taboo. There are entire codes of lexical items that are acceptable for men and other separate codes for the same referents that women use. They may vary according to the speech act situation, whether the company is hetero or homogeneous, or its age group.[25] Castellanos was well aware of these prescriptions and the automatic social taboo brought upon their transgressors. For these reasons, this poem was a confrontation with an oppressive norm, couched in a way that could be printed and accepted; it was revolutionary in its own time. Through her parody of euphemistic female speech patterns set in a frame provided by an already existing scientific text, which reported on male sexuality (an opposition that provides yet another ironic reversal), Castellanos found a way of "saying the unsayable" (Voss, 231) about female sexuality in Mexico, which had been taboo for "decent women" to utter for centuries. In a country where female sexuality has been suspect for as far back as Aztec times, during the colonial period it was perceived as a negative force, belonging to the dark powers associated with indigenous culture, beyond the pale of Hispanic Catholic control and therefore dangerous.[26]

Because Castellanos cast the poem in a format of scientific inquiry, the responses become personal testimony to sexual experiences that failed to live up to any of these women's social expectations or emotional needs. In most of them, the discourse of the oppressor has been internalized by its female victims as they voice male criteria and the double standard. The reversal of voices achieves a double reversal of myth. Mexican women are sexual beings for whom the practice of *machismo* is rarely sexually satisfying. This parody of cultural mythology is not a new strategy but one related to the discourse of resistance to political repression in Latin America in the decades of the 1970s and 1980s.[27]

Body as Sign

The wry, flat tone of the objective female speaker in "Brief Chronicle" uses the metaphor of menstrual flow to transmit an unromanticized view of sexuality that is a far cry from the views expressed by the women in "Kinsey Report" or the maudlin stereotypes broadcast by Mexican soap operas or popular photo romances:

> Between the two of us there was
> that which exists between two people who love each other:
> blood of a torn hymen. (Can you imagine?
> A virgin at thirty! And a poetess! Knock on wood.)
> The menstrual hemorrhage in which a child says
> yes or no to life.

But this poem is really about what blood signifies as a feminine sign: blood as a way to write the record of our emotional lives, that "brief chronicle" of our experiential existence. Blood as the scribe of our emotional history, the body as memory. Blood when the hymen is ruptured certifies virginity, marking the sexual coming of age; the absence of blood when the menstrual flow stops marks pregnancy; blood flowing from a slashed wrist determines suicide or life. There are other body fluids that record the events in our lives: sweat, bile, semen, saliva, tears, "nothing, in short, that a good bath won't wash out." But how can "mere ink" compare to blood, she asks, if "ink flows from such alien springs"? Is writing also alien to womanhood? Once again Castellanos uses the most primary imagery of female creativity—"the centrality of blood as a symbol furnished by the female body" (Gubar, 17)—to link sexuality with textuality.[28] This was written at least four years before the French feminist Hélène Cixous' manifesto calling for women to write their bodies: "write your self. Your body must be heard. Only then will the immense riches of the unconscious spring forth. . . . To Write. An act which will not only 'realize' the decensored relation of woman to her sexuality, to her womanly being, giving her access to her native strength; it will give her back her goods, her pleasures, her organs, her immense bodily territories which have been kept under seal" ("The Laugh of the Medusa," 284).

"Speaking of Gabriel" looks at pregnancy and motherhood, not as a mystical, sacred state but as a time of physical discomfort and emotional adjustment to the growth of oneself, and to the child who is the other within her body. Pregnancy, the ultimate female metaphor, links literary and biological creativity, an example of how biography and domesticity become the mainsprings for some of Castellanos' richest creations.[29] This unconventional poem about pregnancy in terms of the relationship between body, self, and other is yet another example of how far ahead of her time Castellanos' writing was at that point between 1969 and 1971 when it was written. What makes this startlingly evident is the overlap of ideas, even of imagery, with sections of Cixous' "The Laugh of the Medusa," which was published in 1975:

> Oral drive, anal drive, vocal drive—all these drives are our strengths, and among them is the gestation drive—just like the desire to write: a desire to live self from within, a desire for the swollen belly, for language, for blood. We are not going to refuse, if it should strike our fancy, the unsurpassed pleasures of pregnancy which have actually been always exaggerated or conjured away—or cursed—in the classic texts. For if there's one thing that's been repressed here's just the place to find it: in the taboo of the pregnant woman. This says a lot about the power she seems invested with at the time, because it has always been suspected, that, when pregnant, the woman not only doubles her market value, but—what's more important—takes on intrinsic value as a woman in her own eyes and, undeniably, acquires body and sex.
>
> There are thousands of ways of living one's pregnancy; to have or not to have with that still invisible other a relationship of another intensity. (295)

The relationships between Castellanos' texts and those written by Cixous, Irigaray, and other French feminists, a half to full decade later, remain to be written. Nevertheless, any discussion of Castellanos' writing on feminine sexuality and the feminization of her discourse must take their textual interfacing into account.

Language as Oppression

As Castellanos' poems voice women's experiences in a patriarchal world, their relationship to language and society emerges. "Nobodying" explores this link between language and oppression, where the "We" of authoritarian utterance symbolizes the tradition of social, political, and intellectual discounting that the Mexican establishment metes out to women and indigenous peoples through language: an issue Castellanos examines in her essays "Language as an Instrument of Domination" and "Discrimination in the United States and in Chiapas."

The first generator of aesthetic meaning is the title of the text—"Ninguneo" (Nobodying), a sociolinguistic pun that is the essential trigger for the entire poem. The readers of both the source and the receptor texts must understand its function as a social sign in order to capture the full dimensions of the message. In Mexican Spanish, *el ninguneo* is the noun that describes the action of *ningunear*, that is, the social act or attitude of minimizing, discounting, slighting, or putting down. Coined from the Spanish pronoun for "nothing" or "nobody," it refers to the treatment meted out to persons whom the speaker literally considers to be "nobody" or "nothing."

Here the I speaker, accompanied by a gender marker that is specifically feminine (cult*a*, viajad*a*), proceeds to analyze the royal "We" (*nosotros*)—not a generic "we" that includes a feminine speaker but a patriarchal WE that excludes a feminine component (*nosotras*). Focusing on negativity itself, in many ways this speaker sums up Castellanos' lucid insights into the links between language, women, and society in Mexico: language is a powerful tool of domination and exclusion.

"Nobodying" confronts this as it frames the poem in an opening reference to the French philosopher Descartes, followed by the statement-of-fact, "I'm not thinking." It immediately activates the reader's association with his dictum on the supremacy of reason, *Cogito, ergo sum* ("I think, therefore I am"), which harks back to a social order of Latin over Spanish, France over Mexico, reason over feelings. The "I" seeks to validate her existence, in the face of the sentence that annihilates her:

> The sentence that reads: "You don't exist."
> It is signed by all those who use the royal
> We to sign: The One who is All;
> the magistrates, the chancelleries,
> the sovereign contracting parties, the
> thirteen Aztec emperors, the legislative
> and judicial powers, the list
> of Viceroys, the Boxing Commission,
> the decentralized institutes,

the United Newsboys Union and . . .
. . . and, solidarily, all the rest of my fellow citizens.

The validating enumeration of the official entities, however, is subverted by juxtaposing the serious with the ridiculous, a tactic that deflates their political, legal, and historical authority. Their convergence with the peer authority of her own "fellow citizens" slams down the final negation of her feminine existence.[30]

Essentially, this is a poem about the negation of the female other, about how the speech acts of official authority codify negation—by subsuming the "I" and "You" into the "We," by coining a new verb to signify the performance of linguistic and social discrimination. The reader first must "fill in the gaps" by making the connection between title and text that produces the whole message. "Put down" is the cultural equivalent but it loses the linguistic pun that in Spanish shapes the central metaphor. "No-bodying" captures the strangeness by attempting a similar neologism and as such is closer to a re-creation of the creative process of the source text. Unless the receptor text transmits the communication context of its usage in Mexican society, the connection will not be made by the reader of the new text. In this case the translator's note is a critical connection in the meaning chain. As the punning title that produces the poem, its social code as well as the lexical one must be transferred to the reader of the translation before the full semiosis of the sign can be realized. Language has the power to oppress as well as to transform and create.

This short poem demonstrates Castellanos' awareness of how that oppression is carried out linguistically; how the authoritarian "We" annihilates a feminine "I." Castellanos' view of how language has shut women out of access to the power structures coincides with one of the major concerns of French feminists like Luce Irigaray, who also argued that women-as-subjects are outsiders to language (*Speculum of the Other Woman*). In the United States, Adrienne Rich wrote about the need for awareness of language as an oppressor at the end of the same decade:

When we become acutely, disturbingly aware of the language we are using and that is using us, we begin to grasp a material resource that women have never before collectively attempted to repossess (though we were its inventors, and though individual writers like Dickinson, Woolf, Stein, H.D., have approached language as transforming power). . . . as long as our language is inadequate, our vision remains formless, our thinking and feeling are still running in the old cycles, the process may be "revolutionary" but not transformative.

Poetry is, among other things, a criticism of language. ("Power and Danger," 247–248)

The examination of Rosario Castellanos' poetry in terms of the complex multiplicity of its speech acts demonstrates how her communication becomes feminized, enabling us to understand the mainsprings of Castellanos' aesthetic creation: the way she is able to make the familiar strange, how she translated her own reality of self, other, body, and language into such powerful poems.

The Appropriation of Signs: Intertexts and Subtexts

Rosario Castellanos' poetry is full of voices, but not all of them originate within her own discourse. On the contrary, she incorporates a wide variety of signs from other texts, weaving an aesthetic polyphony. An examination of how Castellanos appropriates the signs of others to create new ones of her own will elucidate her "networks of meaning" (Díaz-Diocaretz, 71).

At this juncture I should clarify that, in terms of intertextual relations, I will distinguish between two kinds of plurality in Castellanos' writing. Intratexts refer to relationships between texts authored by her, while intertext refers to relationships with texts not authored by her. Subtexts refer to the voice or image of any text as it becomes present in Castellanos' work. In all three there is a transposition of sign systems from one or more texts to another that contributes in some way to the production of meaning in the next text.[31]

We have already observed the existence of a spectrum of intra- and intertextual relationships among Castellanos' individual compositions relating directly to each other across the various genres she practiced. The voice of the woman whose lament we heard in the poem "Malinche" becomes the subject of an essay and, later, a dramatic character in *The Eternal Feminine*. In other words, many texts are siblings within the family of Castellanos' own literary production. In contrast, the texts written by the nineteenth-century Spanish poet Bécquer or the Scotch diarist Fanny Calderón de la Barca are external to Castellanos' work, bringing with them meanings and signs produced in their own traditions and the potentiality to generate new ones in other contexts.

In Castellanos' writing the *source* of the other text is of less concern than how a sign from it, or part of it, *functions* within the new message (Díaz-Diocaretz, 69). In terms of our discussion, Kiril Taranovsky's concept of subtext, an "already existing text (or texts) reflected in a new one" and its four types, is the most useful.[32] I will follow Díaz-Diocaretz' analytical model by focusing on the signs of the textual other as they become present in Castellanos' texts and the ways they contribute to the production of new meanings in her discourse. Toward this end, let us examine the appropriation of signs in four specific poems: the author's use of preexisting discourse formats, the reversal of a nineteenth-century text from the Hispanic tradition, dialogue with a visual text, and, finally, the transformation of multiple images from the feminine literary tradition itself into new signs that speak to and for women.

Formats

The years that Castellanos worked within the Mexican government sharpened her talent for re-creating bureaucratic formats and the officialese of its administrative documents and press releases. These kinds of texts frequently became the vehicle for the metaphors and codes that created some of her most important poems. The title of "Memorandum on Tlatelolco" assigns to it the format of a standard judicial report, the *memorial* used throughout the Hispanic legal system. This poem takes the place of the official report that the Mexican government never rendered about the atrocious massacre that its troops inflicted upon the civil populace in Tlatelolco in 1968. The events themselves constitute another kind of text to which the poem refers directly: a social one.

There are other discursive formats: the chronicle that records public history now serves to inscribe emotional history in "Brief Chronicle"; a postscript serves as poetic afterthought; a scientific survey of male sexual practices becomes a poem about female sexuality in Mexico in "Kinsey Report"; ritual frames of elegies and prayers dominate Castellanos' earliest poetry. The production of irony so characteristic of her poetry stems from the contrasts between these mediums and their messages, resulting, as I have pointed out elsewhere, in subversion. It also produces a kind of discursive parody that is a common strategy in contemporary Latin American testimonial literature where the formats of oppressive governments or sacred ritual are rearranged or reinserted to express protest. It is a way of turning the oppressor's own weapons against him.[33]

A Countervoice: Poetic Punning

If the mere conventions of written formats can contribute significant elements of meaning, a nineteenth-century Spaniard's text and the key phrase in it can generate a contemporary countervoice. "You Are Not Poetry" establishes a polemic with the Spanish Romantic poet Gustavo Adolfo Bécquer, by reversal of his famous line, *"Poesía eres tú"* (Thou Art Poetry). Rather than being directly quoted, Bécquer's line appears to be totally fused into this poem, as there is no marker to detect its presence in the new text, only its complete reversal in the pun that creates its title. Bécquer's poem "Poesía eres tú" is a powerful cliché because it is the catch line for a poem that has become the symbol of Romantic poetry, recited each year in poetry festivals and learned by rote in literature classes throughout the Hispanic world. Thus, the factor of instant recognition in the Spanish-language reader is very high, triggering the production of new meaning in this twentieth-century text. By paraphrasing it, not only does Castellanos negate Bécquer's message, but also from this dialectic her own *ars poetica* emerges. For her, Poetry and Love were not equivalent to the woman reified by Bécquer in poetry. For Castellanos, the self becomes the other where "humanity, dialogue, poetry, begin."

Castellanos' complex punning relies on the fact that the Spanish reader will be aware of this line from male literary tradition. However, the reader of the English translation will not be, posing problems for its reception. First, I have conveyed information about Bécquer's text in a translator's note. Second, I have used English syntax that captures the same flavor of the original communication act to which the poem is at once a counter-reply and the lead into its own new statement. The English syntax with the "You" in the initial position retains some of the emphasis that the Spanish syntax produces, where the normal intonation pattern treats the *tú* as an emphatic one. My earlier version of "Poetry, You Are Not" now seems to be too awkward. This new translation strives to clue the reader to the intertextual duel that has just taken place and to Castellanos' rejection of a traditional male concept and role for women and poetry. In this case a cultural equivalent might be the line, "You *are* a poem," that Will Ladislaw uttered to Dorothea Brooke in George Eliot's *Middlemarch* or John Berryman's more recent "You are the text."[34] However, the more literal approximation better captures the essential negation, which is ideologically truer to the larger body of her ideas and her work. These intertextual techniques prefigure poetic strategies that Adrienne Rich and other North American women poets utilized extensively in the late seventies: "The poet not only creates a diachronic relation between a voice in the past and her own, but also proposes a reversal of values in order to create an internal polemic with the alien text. This specific reformulation of literary tradition, norms, and values is an essential characteristic to describe

the feminist intertextual factor; there is a subversio⁚ of form and content"
(Díaz-Diocaretz, 74).

A *Visual Subtext*

A third way in which a subtext produces meaning in Castellanos' poems is
through the integration of "ideographic elements" whose origin is found
in "a nonlinguistic system, and which consist of an intersemiotic transposition of images from film, photography, painting" (Díaz-Diocaretz,
76). In "Looking at the Mona Lisa," a visual text from the Italian Renais-
sance of reified woman as art object, not creator, is the feminine addressee
who plays the dominant role in shaping this poem. The dramatic scene
and the visual image are set up in the title and first question. "Are you
laughing at me?" one of the "dumb little tourist ladies" asks the Mona
Lisa. Although by her own admission she is an inferior speaker, she uses
the egalitarian *tú* with her prestigious First World addressee. The switch to
"I" enables her to compare herself with a gamut of other Mexican women,
who range from Sor Juana Inés de la Cruz to the Emperor Iturbide's mistress. But equality goes beyond gender problems. The tongue-in-cheek
epigraph, "In the Louvre, naturally," is a condescending interjection to a
reader who has to be instructed where the Mona Lisa hangs. As such it
becomes yet another visual and cultural referent that evokes Paris as the
artistic model for Latin American culture. The perspective of superiority
is reinforced by the equation of the speaker to "a representative specimen / from some social sector of a Third World country." This skillful
creation of scene brings into play the political confrontation between two
women across centuries. It is a critique of art as a consumer product or
sign of upward mobility, and the sense of artistic and cultural inferiority
inculcated in the Mexican middle-class woman on the proverbial trip to
Europe. In its new verbal context, the older visual text becomes a contemporary sign in a dialogue across cultures that criticizes not one, but both
of them.

The poetic confrontation demonstrates that women's problems pertain
to the wider political oppositions between the First and the Third Worlds
and the economic and cultural discrimination that is part and parcel
of them.

Are you laughing at me? You're right.
If I were Sor Juana
or La Malinche . . .
. . . .

you would see me, perhaps, as one observes
a representative specimen
from some social sector of a Third World country.
. . . .
And you smile, mysteriously
as is your obligation. But I can read you.
That smile is mockery. It mocks me and every
one of us who believes that we believe that
culture is a liquid one imbibes at the source,
a special symptom one contracts
in certain contagious places, something
one acquires by osmosis.

Woman as Sign

Castellanos develops poems that draw from women's work and art in the past and reach ahead to their futures. "Metamorphosis of the Sorceress," written about the visual texts of Remedios Varo's surrealist paintings of women, and "Meditation on the Brink" are two examples of those encounters with her sisters' traditions, the exploration of their artistic roots, and ways to turn them forward. In "Meditation on the Brink" multiple subtexts activated by the references to famous women characters, writers, and saints are brought together in a new context that transforms their negative signs into a positive new one—"Another way to be human and free / Another way to be."

No, it's not a solution
to throw oneself under a train like Tolstoy's Anna
or gulp down Madame Bovary's arsenic
or await on the barren heights of Avila the visit
of an angel with a fiery dart
before binding one's veil back over one's head
and starting to act.

Nor to deduce geometric laws by counting
the beams of one's solitary confinement cell
like Sor Juana did. It's not a solution
to write, while company arrives,
in the Austen family living room
or to shut oneself up in the attic
of some New England house

and dream, with the Dickinson's family Bible
under a spinster pillow.

There must be another way that's not named Sappho
or Mesalina or Mary of Egypt
or Magdalene or Clemence Isaure.

Another way to be human and free.

Another way to be.

Each reference to a woman from the past projects "multiple meanings
that are collected and rearranged by the reader" (Díaz-Diocaretz, 13).
These older texts about strong women in patriarchal worlds function as
signs that no longer speak but are spoken about within Castellanos' new
frame. Aligning female tradition that reaches back to Greek and Roman
voices forces us to look for the connections with each other in this modern
text. Each woman named brings her own rebellion into Castellanos'
meditation and urges us to find an alternative to our conflicts. As we readers "rearrange" or "collect" the separate signs, we imagine each woman
standing on the edge of her own abyss, where life as a woman was not
compatible with life as a thinking, independent person. Each name is that
of a woman who, facing that conflict, found herself on the brink of a radical act—suicide, silence, solitude, struggle. If the ways of the past offer
only victims or witnesses, then where can we find the models to avoid our
own pitfalls?

In translating Castellanos' poetry, choices for even a single lexical item
must be made in terms of the author's feminist ideology, or the message
will be skewed. In "Meditation on the Brink," the Spanish word *umbral*
in the original title, "Meditación en el umbral," means "threshold, door-
sill, doorstep" or, figuratively, "threshold, entrance, beginning" (*Simon
and Schuster*, 1563), while *Webster's New Twentieth Century Dictionary,
Unabridged* defines "threshold" as "the place or point of entering or beginning; an entrance; as, on the *threshold* of a career" (1902). But those seem
to be the *wrong* connotations in terms of the ideology of this poem. The
place referred to here is the point of desperation, the edge a woman is
driven to on the verge of a life-or-death act—not a new beginning but the
brink of disaster that offers no way out except the annihilation of intellectual or physical self. *Brink*, with its semantic element of danger, edge,
verge, its figurative use, such as "to be on the *brink* of failure" (*Webster's*,
228), conjures that yawning precipice. As part of the title it provides the

semantic frame for the discourse as a whole where connotations of the original signs are displaced to take on other values in the new text. Women who once signified fame become signs of crisis or annihilation. In this translation an ideological equivalent must take preference over a semantic one.

In terms of that ideology, "Meditation on the Brink" focuses on Castellanos' concern for the conflicts produced in women's lives in cultures where the roles of autonomous thinker or writer and being a woman have not been compatible—cogent testimony to a struggle that still persists, as British poet and critic Anne Stevenson explains:

> [Independence] was bought at the price of what used to be called "woman-liness"—sex, marriage, children and the socially acceptable position of wife. Sometimes I think a woman writer has to pay that price. In my own case, however, I've not been willing, any more than Sylvia Plath was willing, to sacrifice my life as a woman in order to have a life as a writer. Surely, in the 20th century, when society allows so much, it ought to be possible to be a fulfilled woman and an independent writer without guilt—or without creating a bell jar vacuum in which it is impossible to breathe. As I look back over my own experience I see, however, that I have only *just* managed to survive. (163)

Another point is Castellanos' rejection of the canon of established literature imposed upon women by patriarchal society. Literature, like women, must find another way of imagining female creativity, alternative ways of representing female otherness. The poem's closure turns toward the future, leaving negative history behind. The new poetic context has redirected the original negative signs toward a new positive one.[35]

Both these readings focus on yet a larger issue: Castellanos' vision and use of woman as sign: "the extent to which patriarchal representation, by contrast, 'silences' women—the extent to which *woman* or *womanhood*, considered not as an image but as a sign, becomes the site of contradiction and repression" (Jacobus, "The Difference of View," 13). By appropriating signs from other codes, Castellanos has succeeded in transforming patriarchal images of women into new feminist signs. The changes effected when the old codes are inserted into her new contexts bring about changes "in the way in which culture 'sees' the world" (Eco, A *Theory of Semiotics*, 274), mediating its negativity, transforming it into new signs that speak to and for women now.

Fiction: Under a Man's Hand

Rosario Castellanos' fiction centers on two areas of experience long over-looked in Mexican letters: the critique of racial and cultural oppression of indigenous peoples in Chiapas and the status of women in provincial and urban Mexico. The stories translated in this anthology represent those major foci of her prose: a perversion of signs and values in "The Eagle" and women as signs of solitude and conflict under patriarchal rule in "Fleeting Friendships" and "The Widower Román." "Three Knots in the Net" and "Cooking Lesson" are concerned with women's struggle to assert their authentic selves. However, before we turn to the texts, let us consider some of the factors that shaped Castellanos' development as a narrator of social reality in Mexico.

Chiapas and Cultural Oppression

Upon her return from Europe in 1951, Castellanos went straight to Chiapas, where she worked and wrote from 1951 to 1952 and again from 1956 to 1957. Already a published poet, she considered prose the next challenge to her goal of becoming a professional writer. Emilio Carballido suggested that she work on some of her childhood experiences, which she had set down in the earlier short stories[36] and which later became the nucleus of her first novel, *The Nine Guardians/(Balún-Canán)* (1957). Set in the mythic structure of the Tzotzil world of Chiapas, it is narrated through the eyes of a seven-year-old girl. Yet, "more than the life of the Chamula Indians, it relates the solitude of her girlhood," Elena Poniatowska wrote ("Vida," 90).

Between 16 October 1956 and 3 March 1957, Rosario Castellanos wrote three letters from San Cristóbal de las Casas in Chiapas to Elías Nandino, director of *Estaciones*, a magazine that played a key role in the publication of Mexican literature in the fifties. These letters clearly express the break with European symbolism that Mexican writers of that generation carried out. Above all, they attest to Castellanos' consciousness of her own place in this endeavor and the formative role that challenged her own circle of writers: "The postures the Mexican writer has assumed by following European models seem to me to be the most ridiculous betrayal. Betrayal of a reality that is our own—that has not been interpreted by art, defined by science, or tamed by technique. . . . The difficult task is to come to grips with it, with the small or large talent that we may have, with honesty, patience, and perseverance. Knowing that, whatever we

do can be no more than laying foundations" ("Cartas a Elías Nandino,"
20–23). In Chiapas, Castellanos defined the changes that she wanted to
effect in her writing and committed herself to achieving a firsthand knowledge of the Indian culture she had chosen as her subject. "So here I am.
Working with the Indigenist Institute, which allows me a very intimate
contact undistorted by intermediaries, with the mentality, customs, and
hopes of the Indians" ("Cartas a Elías Nandino," 21).

The nine stories in *Ciudad Real* (1960), an old name for San Cristóbal
de las Casas, grew out of those experiences. They are linked to *Oficio de
tinieblas* (1962), the second novel, which used the historical events of
a Chamula Indian uprising in San Cristóbal in 1867 that culminated in
the crucifixion of one of the participants. Castellanos recast them in the
struggle of Catalina Díaz Puijla, an Indian leader who uses her powers as
a shaman against modern colonialism. It is still considered to be one
of the very best examples of neoindigenist writing in Latin America
(Sommers, "*Oficio de tinieblas*," 15–16).

Castellanos' fiction signified an important break with the lurid picture
postcard type of prose that other authors had been writing in the social
realism vein of the thirties and forties, in which regional indigenous cultures were perceived to be exotic worlds where the characters, because they
were victims, were "portrayed as strange, poetic, or good." "I'm not an
indigenist writer," she bristled in an interview with Emmanuel Carballo:

> This simplicity makes me laugh. Indians are human beings absolutely
> equal to whites, except [they've been] placed in circumstances that are
> unique and unfavorable. Because they are weaker they can be worse—
> more violent, more treacherous, or more hypocritical—than white people.
> Indians do not seem mysterious or poetic to me. What happens is that
> they live in atrocious poverty. It's necessary to describe how that poverty
> has atrophied their best qualities. Another detail that indigenist authors
> neglect—or execute very badly—is form. They assume that, since the
> theme is noble and interesting, it's not necessary to take care in develop-
> ing it. Since they nearly always refer to unpleasant events, they do it in
> an unpleasant manner: they neglect language and do not polish their
> style . . . Since my books have different goals, I can't be included in that
> kind of writing. (422–423)

Castellanos' lucid perception of the relationship between indigenous
peoples and the task of her generation of writers links her work with the
ideas and the writing of the Peruvian narrator José María Arguedas.[37] But
the ideological paradigm that explained the relations of domination and

oppression Castellanos found in her reading of Simone Weil on "the attitude of the conquered toward the conquerors, the treatment of the weak by the powerful . . . the current of evil that runs from strong to weak, returning once again to the strong" (Carballo, 420).

"The Eagle" is an excellent example of some of those relationships between races that Castellanos explores in the short stories in *Ciudad Real* and in her essay "An Attempt at Self-Criticism": " . . . the reality wherein descendants of the conquered Indians live side by side with the descendants of the conquering Europeans. If the former have lost the memory of their greatness, the latter have lost the attributes of their strength, and they all conflict in total decadence. The daily social behavior of beings so dissimilar produces phenomena and situations that began by interesting the anthropologists and have never stopped appealing to writers, who struggle to get to the very root of these extreme forms of human misery." In "The Eagle" these conflicts are represented through the perversion of signs. The symbol of political authority, the official stamp of the Mexican republic with its national symbol, the eagle, is used to pervert that same authority for the personal gain of a corrupt *ladino* (a person of mixed Indian-Spanish blood, usually Spanish speaking) by robbing an Indian community. The conflicting perspectives are textually contrasted by the modes of speech representation. In the initial sections, Villafuerte's perspective is represented by free indirect discourse that integrates his prejudices and inner monologues about the Indians. The climax shifts to direct discourse to represent the Indian perception of the stamp with the figure of the eagle as a different kind of sign—a transparent one where the signifier denotes a living bird. Thus it can be read as an allegory about the conflict of signs. At stake is the issue of how their manipulation across cultures may be corrupted into ethnic oppression of Indian communities by *mestizos*, of Spanish-Indian origin.

Daughters and Friends

With the publication of *Los convidados de agosto* in 1964, Castellanos widened the scope of her lens to examine another neglected sector of Mexican society: the life of women in the stifling middle class of provincial Chiapas, whose designated place was "under a man's hand." "Fleeting Friendships" and "The Widower Román" narrate lives of women who are used as pawns to attest to the honor of their fathers and husbands, "this honor that the various structures of male dominance—property, the law, social status, political authority—exist to protect" (Greene and Kahn, 6).

Both stories question parental proprietary by showing its catastrophic negativity—the way it ruins not only women's lives but men's also. But the new element that Castellanos brings to her representation is the focus on women's relationships to each other—her reconstruction of women's perspectives of their experiences that was unique in Mexican prose.

In "Fleeting Friendships," the female adolescent narrator relates the story of her girlfriend who learns to survive under the dire penalties meted out to a young woman who heeds her own impulses to run off with a stranger without benefit of wedlock. However, it is the friendship between the two young women that offers one of them a second chance at living her own life and forces the other to ponder the connections between their lives and her words as a struggling writer. This is an open-ended text that implies alternative scripts for both female characters. Did Gertrudis find a life of her own? Did the narrator find a way to reconcile writing and living?

"The Widower Román" focuses on fathers controlling their daughters' and sisters' lives and sexuality in Comitán, where women are objects of exchange that assure continuity and control of a social community. "At once an object of desire and an object of exchange . . . at the intersection of two incompatible systems, woman appears as the embodiment of an impossible duality, the locus of an opposition" (Furman, 61).[38] Romelia's wedding day is the day she enters this world of women in rural Chiapas:

> From today on Romelia would join the company of women who never say, "I want" or "I don't want," but who always dodge issues by deferring to the man of the house to achieve their aims. This side-stepping may be condensed in a single phrase: "the master wishes . . . the master prefers . . . the master orders . . . one mustn't contradict the master . . . above all one must please the master . . . first I must consult the master"—the master who would exalt her above all to the rank of wife and intimately give her a true image of her body that would finally reach the fullness of knowing, feeling, and performing the functions for which it had been created.

The exploration of women's relatedness to each other through fiction enables Castellanos to explore a literary area that had not been addressed by male writers or critics in Mexico. It is in this sense that her fiction is truly pioneering: the central questions that her work raises about the interdependence of attitudes toward gender and race, and the bonding or absence of it, are the same issues that confront women. The origins of these concerns are found in the acute solitude that Castellanos experienced in

her own life and observed in lives of other women during those years of
growing up in Comitán.

> My earliest experience was individual solitude: I soon discovered that all
> the other women I knew were in the same situation. The single women
> were alone, the married women were alone, the mothers were alone.
> Alone, in a town that was not in touch with other towns. Alone, endur-
> ing harsh customs that condemned love and surrender as an unredeem-
> able sin. Alone in their leisure because that was the only luxury their
> money could buy them. To portray these lives, draw those figures, in-
> volved a process that was autobiographical. I hid from solitude in my
> work, which offered a sense of solidarity with others in something abstract
> that did not hurt me or disturb me as later on love and cohabitation were
> going to hurt me. (Poniatowska, "Vida," 60–61)

Concomitant Readings

Three essays may be read as companion texts to the three stories discussed
above. They begin with biographical details from Castellanos' life that
become springboards to wider issues, a textual strategy characteristic of
her chronicles. "Incident at Yalentay" documents the case of an Indian
daughter whose efforts to escape her tyrannical father were frustrated when
Rosario and her traveling theater team did not use their best negotiator,
the Indian puppet, Petul. It also takes a hard look at how little some bu-
reaucrats knew about communicating with indigenous people in their
own region, a message delivered with considerable impact since Castellanos inscribes herself as one of the actors in this account of a young
woman's failure to free herself from her future as a commodity of her father's property. In this case the theater troupe should have enlisted the
help of the powerful cultural signs transmitted by their puppet Petul—
whose signifying powers for the Indian community reached far beyond the
didactic function used by the Spanish-speaking troupe.

"A Man of Destiny" is probably the best introduction to the world of
Chiapas in which Rosario Castellanos grew up and from which she created the characters and incidents that populate her prose. Written a decade after the first collection of stories, it is a chilling reflection on the
legacy of women under the provincial oligarchy, where "a young lady
married according to her parents' wishes, a fairly close relative . . . ,"
where a bride woke up the next day to discover that "she had become a
respectable married woman after having been an attractive one," and "a
respectable married woman had a child every year and delegated its up-

bringing to the Indian nannies. . . . This was the paradise that I lost out on 'through Cárdenas' fault.'" Through inscription of personal experiences this and other essays form an intimate intratextual relationship with Castellanos' fictional characters, heightening her haunting visions of Mexican women of both races caught in webs of cultural oppression and social change in the microcosm of Chiapas that can be read metonymically for Central America. A third text, "Discrimination in the United States and in Chiapas," provides the historical context for the cultural conflicts that Castellanos transforms into such remarkable prose—reminding her compatriots of the injustices still to be remedied among their own citizens.

Urban Mexico

"Three Knots in the Net" (1961) is a story that was never included in any of the author's collected fiction, remaining practically unknown in Spanish. Yet it is an important bridge text in several respects. It spans the worlds of women between the patriarchal society of Chiapas and the urban Mexico where Castellanos sets the stories published in *Álbum de familia*, ten years later. In addition, it functions as a bridge where biography and writing meet, this time in the moving study of a girl from the provinces caught in the changes between generations and values that urban migration to the capital meant for the provincial families. Now the author focuses on women struggling with the complexities of mother-daughter alienation produced by their changing generations and values. Yet both maintain their dignity and different senses of interior privacy to the end. Patently autobiographical, this story may also be read as an allegory of the transition of power from the old order of provincial landholding Mexico to that of the modern urban capital. With this text Castellanos' inquiry shifts to women in their urban space and to the question of how women's vocations are developed. The four stories in *Álbum de familia* are narrative representations of concepts that the author discussed in her essays written during the same period and had begun to develop for a second play about women.

The Feminization of Discourse

"Cooking Lesson," from that last group of short stories, is the best example of Castellanos' creation of an intrinsically feminine discourse. The form chosen is the interior monologue of a young intellectual bride, who is following a recipe from a cookbook in an attempt to prepare her first meal, a beefsteak for her husband. As she does so, her narrating I is directed to two explicit narratees, one a specifically female reader marked by the formal You (*usted*), "Oh, You, experienced housewife," and the second, an intimate you (*tú*), who is obviously her new husband. Thus, the first and principal receiver of this message is the same "self-sacrificing little Mexican housewife" that Rosario Castellanos is so fond of addressing. This feminine narratee completes a feminine communication frame that ensures Castellanos control of the full impact of her feminist aesthetic message.

This is the feminist context for Castellanos' exposition of a traditional rite of passage, a bride's first cooking lesson, or, better said, a cooking disaster, which Castellanos will employ to build a critique of marriage and the myths that surround it, made all the more devastating by her comic irony. The frozen meat reminds the neophyte cook of her honeymoon and sexual initiation: *"Red, as if it were just about to start bleeding"* (emphasis added):

> Our backs were that same color, my husband and I, after our orgiastic
> sunbathing on the beaches of Acapulco. He could afford the luxury of
> "behaving like the man he is" and stretch out face down to avoid rubbing
> his painful skin . . . But I, self-sacrificing little Mexican wife, born like a
> dove to the nest, smiled like Cuauhtémoc under torture on the rack when
> he said, "My bed is not made of roses," and fell silent. Face up, I bore
> not only my own weight but also his on top of me. The classic position
> for making love. And I moaned, from the tearing and the pleasure. The
> classic moan. Myths, myths.

When the steak turns gray, it reminds her that "I lost my old name and I still can't get used to the new one, which is not mine either." When she thanks her groom for a martini at the bar, she thinks, "Thanks for letting me out of the cage of one sterile routine only to lock me into the cage of another." Later she recalls that more thanks are due, to the second addressee, her new husband: "And what about you. Don't you have anything to thank me for? . . . my virginity. When you discovered it I felt like the last dinosaur on a planet where the species was extinct . . . . I'll stay the same as I am. Calm. When you throw your body on top of mine I feel as though a gravestone were covering me, full of inscriptions, strange names, memorable dates. You moan unintelligibly and I'd like to whisper my name in your ear to remind you who it is you are possessing."

When the meat starts to shrink, it motivates a series of cinematic fantasies. As it turns black on one side, she fantasizes about having an affair with an older man. When it's finally burned to a crisp, it becomes the perfect analogy for reality. "So that piece of meat that gave the impression of being so solid and real no longer exists. So? My husband also gives the impression of being solid and real when we're together, when I touch him, when I see him. He certainly changes and I change too . . . The meat hasn't stopped existing. It has undergone a series of metamorphoses."

The narrator recalls other "recipes" for a successful marriage. Obedience and conformity. "The recipe of course is ancient and its efficiency is proven. . . . it's just that it revolts me to behave that way." The domestic textuality of a recipe does not equate with the sexual or intellectual needs of a modern woman: both the steak and the marriage produced by this conventional cookbook turn out to be unpalatable.

"Cooking Lesson" encodes many of the issues that are characteristic of Castellanos' mature writing in the seventies and displays some of her best ironic humor. The startling analogies that the narrator draws between beefsteak and her own female body, between a shrinking gray steak and the ingredients for successful marriages, encode feminine experience by using specifically feminine metaphors. The analogy between raw flesh, virginity, and female sexuality in the account of the honeymoon transforms Castellanos' vision of middle-class marriage in Mexico into a social catastrophe. With it her critique of marriage comes full circle: first examined in terms of the mesh of reciprocal exchanges that held together the provincial oligarchy, it is now presented in terms of its proprietary constraints on an intellectual woman in urban Mexico.

No text better represents Castellanos' superb command of the feminine metaphor as a vehicle to create literature that is intrinsically feminine in speech act situation, metaphor, and message. Feminine lessons are life lessons and the way to explore them is through feminine metaphors. When these tropes are displaced from their original domestic systems— their cookbook, kitchen, and honeymoon—they acquire powerful new connotations in the context of this story, where they become signs of repression, annihilation, ruin. Their new function of transmitting a message that is exactly the opposite of their original one—in other words, the displacement of traditional sign values to transmit radical messages—is what produces the powerful irony and total feminization of this discourse. Thus, Castellanos achieved at the outset of the seventies a task considered to be one of the most important ones for women writing into the nineties: "deconstructing male patterns of thought and social practice; and reconstructing female experience previously hidden or overlooked" (Greene and Kahn, 6).

Essays: Writing Her Self

Rosario Castellanos was the first Mexican writer to draw the essential connections among sex, class, and race as factors that define women in Mexico. The keys to that ideology are her essays. First written as weekly pieces for *Excélsior* and other newspapers in Mexico City, they constitute a fascinating mosaic of cultural life and thought in Mexico between 1960 and 1974. In touch with her roots, ahead of her time, and laughing at herself, she establishes in these texts an immediate rapport with a wide variety of readers. As part of the lively tradition of the *crónica*, or short creative prose popular in Latin American writing, they are akin to the pieces that her countryman Carlos Monsiváis was publishing during the same decade or the provocative texts that Ellen Goodman presently writes for the *Boston Globe* and the *New York Times*.

Juicios sumarios, the first collection that Castellanos edited, in 1966, passed largely unnoticed. However, her second collection of essays, *Mujer que sabe latín*, which analyzes women's issues and women writers, was avidly read by women all over Latin America, particularly the younger generation of feminists and writers, when it was published in 1971. There had been nothing like it since *Letter in Reply to Sor Philotea*, the intellectual autobiography of the seventeenth-century nun, Sor Juana Inés de la Cruz, in whose extraordinary life and work many patterns coincide with those of her twentieth-century countrywoman.[39] The status of women in Mexico in the fifties and sixties had in essence changed little over the centuries, and the saying on which Castellanos based her title was still popular: *Mujer que sabe latín, ni tiene marido ni buen fin* (A woman who knows Latin will find neither husband nor happy end). Just before her death, Castellanos edited a third collection, *El mar y sus pescaditos* (1975), a compilation of her reviews of other contemporary authors. José Emilio Pacheco compiled sixty-five more chronicles that had first appeared in the editorial pages of *Excélsior*, in *El uso de la palabra* (1974). My own research, conducted in Mexico in 1978, located approximately ninety more uncollected essays that are recorded in my annotated bibliography in *Homenaje a Rosario Castellanos* (134–143).

Although Castellanos' essays constitute a major point of entry to the body of her work, they are her most neglected genre in terms of translation and criticism. The twelve texts in this anthology constitute their first publication in English[40]—and the discussion that follows is the first comprehensive analysis of these texts. The essays can be read as glosses for her poems and fiction, as I have indicated, but above all they are aesthetic creations in their own right. In order for them to take their rightful place in Castellanos' total discourse, it is important to examine the signifying processes they employ to inscribe cultural ideology. The pages that follow begin this critical task.

A Point of Departure

Although Rosario Castellanos began to examine the question of feminine culture when she wrote her master's thesis in philosophy, *Sobre cultura femenina,* in 1950, Beth Miller has shown that she actually used the arguments of Schopenhauer, Weininger, Simmel, Nietzsche, and Freud to establish female inferiority based on biological determinism (*Rosario Castellanos,* 87–88). Even in this early academic project, Castellanos was concerned with women as part of culture as a whole and the tradition and potential of feminine achievement within it. Looking ahead to the directions in which this thesis actually led her, I agree with Miller that "it is actually Castellanos' point of departure" (87). It was clearly an academic exercise that worked through traditional male authorities, whom she soon outgrew. That same year, 1950, study and travel in Europe brought Castellanos into contact with the ideas of Simone de Beauvoir, Simone Weil, and Virginia Woolf, three intellectual and aesthetic mentors who stimulated the development of her own thinking in the decades that followed.

Feminine Mentors

In her essays written during the period 1960 to 1974, Rosario Castellanos' discussion of women in culture anticipated by more than a decade two avenues of inquiry that Franco-feminist critics began developing in the mid seventies: "the deconstruction of magisterial texts, and traditions, and the attention to silences, to what is repressed or only obliquely suggested in women-authored texts" (Jones, "Inscribing Femininity," 96). What is not generally recognized is that Castellanos had focused on both tasks in her essay "Once Again Sor Juana," which she published in 1963, more than a decade before Hélène Cixous and Luce Irigaray began to publish their radical feminist manifestos. Actually, the steps that Castellanos took in *Juicios sumarios* were her authentic beginnings. The book remained out of print for years while the texts collected there were largely ignored until their reappearance in a two-volume set in 1984. Now read with *Mujer que sabe latín* and *El uso de la palabra,* it is clear that Castellanos had been probing the traditions and silences of women in Mexican culture since the early sixties.

In *Juicios sumarios* Castellanos develops her ideas about cultural ideology and gender through exploration of the official *silences* that she finds in her readings of Mexican culture and in the testimony of "magisterial texts": *The Second Sex* by Simone de Beauvoir, the diaries of Simone Weil, and *A Room of One's Own* and *Three Guineas* by Virginia Woolf, which became the touchstones of Castellanos' intellectual development. Their role in the origins of her feminist ideology is evident in the numerous essays to and about them in *Juicios sumarios*, for example, the four long ones that introduce the life and writing of de Beauvoir and Weil to the Hispanic world. In their writing Castellanos learned that "another kind of woman exists: strong women, obstinate ones, the ones who distrust what is preached to them, that shake off the yokes that enslave them; free women. To this kind of woman, pertain two Simones: Weil and de Beauvoir: radically different in attitude but equally productive" ("Simone de Beauvoir o la lucidez," 231–246).

Castellanos' rejection of a biological determinism of women's roles is closely aligned with that of de Beauvoir, who argued that "one is not born, but rather becomes a woman . . . it is civilization as a whole that produces this creature" (*The Second Sex*, 301), that culture determines gender values and roles, and that false myths distort the images of women. Undoubtedly, these readings inspired Castellanos to apply them to her own social reality. "It's not that Rosario was obliged to emulate Simone de Beauvoir, the fact is that the only point of reference was Simone de Beauvoir," Poniatowska explained ("Vida," 45). We have already seen in Castellanos' poems how her concept of the other moves beyond de Beauvoir's masculine/feminine oppositions to transcend gender in humanity.[41]

A second feminine mentor was Simone Weil, whose writings about her experience as a factory worker, iron discipline, and moral code became Castellanos' ethical model. "Her sojourn in Chiapas was carried out under the influence of Simone Weil, and following her thought" (Poniatowska, "Vida," 108). It was her reading of Weil that most helped her to understand the "mechanisms of human relations" between the oppressed and the oppressors (Carballo, 420).[42]

The third mentor was Virginia Woolf, whose *A Room of One's Own* and *Three Guineas* Castellanos reviewed in her essay "Virginia Woolf o la literatura como ejercicio de la libertad" (331–346). Woolf's presence in Castellanos' work is more subtle, but just as substantial. Particularly noticeable are the rhetorical features of Woolf's essays and their "coming together textually of body and mind" (Humm, 136): the British writer's use of the mixed modes of biography and literary analysis, the reader in the text, the imagery of the body to explore sexual differences, and her commitment to writing for and about women (132–143). Woolf's powerful metaphor of the Angel in the House appears as a foil in Castellanos' discussion in "Woman and Her Image," while in later essays, Castellanos, like Woolf, also "made biographies of individual lives to be microcosms of social history" (144).

Castellanos' readings of other feminists are the context for the development of her ideas that gender and sexuality are essentially culture bound,[43] the basis for questioning the ideas that had been preached to her, and the models for many of the textual ways those ideas could be expressed. In translating Castellanos' essays, the translator must read through her readings.

Myths and Mirrors

From de Beauvoir, Castellanos had learned that the study of a culture's myths was a way of decoding its attitudes toward women. "Once Again Sor Juana," written in 1963, presents Castellanos' own ideas on women as myth and as silence in Mexico. "There are three figures in Mexican history that embody the most extreme and diverse possibilities of femininity. Each one of them represents a symbol, exercises a vast and profound influence on very wide sectors of the nation, and arouses passionate reactions. These figures are the Virgin of Guadalupe, Malinche, and Sor Juana." Although Castellanos is looking at exceptional women, this analysis offers a perspective that is historical, not merely biological or literary. It considers the importance of exploring the symbolic value of conflicting national attitudes about the Virgin of Guadalupe, "a woman who sublimates her condition in motherhood," and Malinche, who "incarnates sexuality in its most irrational aspect." In Castellanos' poem, Malinche speaks as a person in her own right, but in the essay Castellanos analyzes her value as a sign at the juncture of sexuality and politics.[44]

However, it is the naïve and curious attitudes toward Sor Juana's intellectuality that Castellanos finds most challenging: "Because she [Sor Juana] was a woman who had an intellectual vocation. Because, in spite of all the resistance and barriers of her environment, she exercised that vocation and transformed it into literary work. A body of work that provoked the astonishment and admiration of her contemporaries not for its intrinsic qualities but because it sprang from a hand whose natural employment should have been cooking or sewing. A body of work greeted by silence, beset by the scorn of centuries now comes to light once again . . ."

Castellanos rejects the Freudian analysis postulated by the German Hispanist Ludwig Pfandl,[45] who labeled Sor Juana a neurotic narcissist. She disputed it for being "a catalog of all the complexes, traumas, and frustrations that can victimize a human being," rejecting the criteria that she had once employed in her thesis: testimony to the changes in her thinking that had taken place over the intervening decade. "A book conceived in this fashion is insulting, not for its partiality but because criteria like these have been superseded by other broader ones. Wouldn't it be fairer to think that Sor Juana, like any other human being, possessed a backbone, that it was her own vocation, and that she chose among all the different kinds available to her—the one she was most able to count on achieving?"

Castellanos' perception of the silences in women's experiences in a world ruled by masculine logic is a pioneering one in American letters. Her essay on Sor Juana is contemporary with Tillie Olsen's classic, "Silences in Literature—1962," and anticipates by more than a decade Adrienne Rich's *On Lies, Secrets, and Silences* (1979). In 1975 the French feminist Hélène Cixous warned against "the snare of silence" in which women, "muffled throughout their history, . . . have lived in dreams, in bodies (though muted), in silences, in aphonic revolts" ("The Laugh of the Medusa," 285, 290). The exploration of silences in Latin American letters comes later in Tamara Kamenzain's book, *El texto silencioso*, in 1983 and Marjorie Agosín's recent proposal that women's discourse in Chile is written in two great metaphors: silence and imagination (*Silencio e imaginación*, 15). In Mexico, the long silences turned women into mute frozen forms, resembling the children's game of statues, which Maria Luisa Mendoza calls "El juego de las encantadas" (Forster and Ortega, 385–390). In Peru the young women poets of the eighties have assumed the task of "recovering the word" from their forerunners of an earlier century. But in 1963 Castellanos was one of the first American thinkers to perceive woman as "a gap or a silence, the invisible and unheard sex" (Jones, "Inscribing Femininity," 83).

The archetypal figures of Malinche, the Virgin of Guadalupe, and Sor Juana provided Castellanos with a rich cluster of metaphors that she used to explore gender, sexuality, and inequality in Mexican life and art. These figures began to function much like Mary Daly's "magnets for feminist ideas" (Humm, 94). In Castellanos' writing they become metaphors for poems, archetypes or signs in her essays, and, finally, actors in a play: three modes of producing meaning in her texts. The women of Mexico are not only a way to explain and understand the cultural myths of their country but a way to write new literature as well.

A Woman Who Knows Latin

In *Mujer que sabe latín,* Castellanos presents the magisterial texts of a wide range of women writers from both European and American traditions and a number of essays that attend to silences in women's lives in Mexico and silences in their texts.

"Woman and Her Image" takes issue with the forces that have kept woman outside history. "In the course of history (history is an archive of deeds undertaken by men and all that remains outside it belongs to the realm of conjecture, fable, legend, or lie) more than a natural phenomenon, a component of society, or a human creature, woman has been myth," Castellanos wrote. She used arguments by Simone de Beauvoir and Virginia Woolf to refute the biological inferiority postulated by male authorities. Scientific arguments for the inferior capacity of the female cranium are reenforced by listing "the inventions that our civilization owes to female talent"—among them rose petal cigarette wrappers, a marker for rubber clogs, and aromatic toothpicks. This parody of scientific report through the enumeration of ludicrous evidence demolishes the scientific hypothesis. It is an example of Castellanos' talent for producing ironic humor by reversal, in this case by using the discourse of scientific reporting as a caricature of itself.

Another principal strategy in this essay is the skillful use of intertextual fragments and references to other feminine figures from texts by or about other women. Virginia Woolf's description of her famous "Angel in the House," the embodiment of woman as the Victorian ideal of "materialism, order, and cleanliness" (Humm, 146), is introduced into the essay as "the model of virtue to which every female creature must aspire." The older text is inserted into the new one by use of quotation marks that enable it to serve as "an image and metonymic device through which a former text in its totality is alluded to" (Díaz-Diocaretz, 73). The results are powerful: first, Woolf's figure reinforces Castellanos' argument through illustration and, second, it produces a new and dual awareness of Woolf's text. The chilling idea that this ludicrous creature from late Victorian England is still alive, sitting in drafts to shield others, that she is still in some way relevant in the twentieth-century world of Hispanic women, revalidates Woolf's metaphor, its relevance to our times, and the tragedies of women who still embody it.

Similar, although more subtle, effects are achieved with the enumerations of female characters from Hispanic and European literatures, among them Melibea, Ana de Ozores, Hedda Gabler, and la Pintada; "each one in her way and in her own circumstances denies the conventional, making the foundations of the establishment tremble, turning hierarchies upside down, and achieving authenticity," Castellanos wrote. These figures are examples of "the road that leads from the strictest solitude to total annihilation," embodying the destructiveness of stereotypes imposed upon the lives of women who dared to struggle for access to their authentic selves. These intertextual mirrors serve to match textual representation with intellectual arguments. In this aspect her work reflects the same features as the writing of her textual mentor, Virginia Woolf, some of which Maggie Humm has analyzed in her illuminating essay on Woolf (123–154). The integration of feminine intellectuality with feminine textuality distinguishes Castellanos' essays. By using the sign systems of other women authors to enrich and feminize her own, Castellanos actually familiarizes their writing, resulting in a new awareness of the network of women writers and thinkers through their relativization in a new context. In this case, the use of female examples for Sartre's "limit situation" prepares the reader for Castellanos' conclusions: "The feat of *becoming what one is* (a feat belonging to the privileged whatever their sex or condition) not only demands the discovery of the essential features beneath the spur of passion, dissatisfaction, or surfeit, but above all the rejection of those false images that false mirrors offer woman in the enclosed gallery where her life takes place."

A *Dialogue with Nineteenth-Century Women*

From the examination of women as national signs in Mexico to the ways that myth keeps women outside history, Castellanos turned her inquiry to women's lives within history in Mexico: "the actual *experiences* of women in the past" (Lerner, 153). Her essay "The Nineteenth-Century Mexican Woman" shares the concerns of historians of women about "the quality of [women's] daily lives, the conditions in which they lived and worked, the ages at which they married and bore children; . . . their relations to other women; their perceptions of their place in the world" (Greene and Kahn, 13–14). When Castellanos inquired about women at the beginning of the republican period in Mexico, she found so few sources written in her own country that she turned to the testimony of another woman of that time, the diary of Fanny Calderón de la Barca, the Scottish wife of the first Spanish ambassador to independent Mexico. Calderón's *Life in Mexico*, first published in Boston in 1843, is now recognized by historians as one of the prime sources for the social history of the independence period, from 1839 to 1841.[46]

Castellanos braids excerpts from this journal into her own essay. The technique consists of inserting extended fragments of direct quotations from Calderón's daily entries, then juxtaposing Castellanos' own commentary. The result is the creation of a dialogue across 170 years of Mexican life, a kind of double window on the images of those nineteenth-century matriarchs, wives, daughters, sisters, and nuns. For example, on the topic of their appearance, Calderón's comparative description prompts Castellanos to reply: "Aristocracy and indolence? Have they not been synonymous among us? To such a point that even the order of courtesy is altered."

In other spheres of feminine life, Castellanos inserts Calderón de la Barca's chilling account of the glittering ceremony a young Mexican girl underwent when she took the veil. This quotation imbeds the direct discourse of the diarist as well as that of another female speaker who together express their horror "at the sacrifice of a girl so young, that she could not possibly have known her own mind . . . but many young girls, who were conversing together, seemed rather to envy their friend—who had looked so pretty and graceful, and 'so happy,' and whose dress 'suited her so well'—and to have no objection to 'go and do likewise.'" Castellanos is quick to deduce: "It is obvious that there is a relationship of cause and effect between these options and the ignorance of the world that is so strongly supported by general ignorance."

The interplay between Calderón's vision of nineteenth-century Mexico transmitted by the actual words of her diaries and Castellanos' twentieth-century comments creates a powerful new one when they are fused in a single frame. By enabling her text to both speak and be spoken about, it takes on renewed life across the centuries. When both perspectives converge, many women's voices generate clusters of meanings centered in their experiences, intensifying the feminization of the discourse. When Calderón's eyes also bear on the same discursive object, the Mexican woman, the clarity and strength of the discursive lens are doubled. It recharges our vision of Calderón, renewing our awareness of the roots of present-day Mexico.

This dialogue among Mexican women and their texts is a cogent example of Castellanos' talent for what Adrienne Rich calls "*re-vision*—the act of looking back, of seeing with fresh eyes, of entering an old text from a new critical direction" ("When We Dead Awaken," 35): Castellanos' skill at creating new verbal meaning from old, her ability to look at a specific case and draw the wider cultural application. Castellanos' grim tongue-in-cheek conclusion produces just such a re-vision: "Devout nuns, impeccable housewives, docile daughters, wives and mothers. The other side of the coin Madam Calderón de la Barca saw in the insane asylums and jails. There most of the cases were madness due to love and murder of the spouse. What a shame that she did not pay a visit to the brothels to make her picture complete!" Rosario Castellanos searched for the silences that must make our understanding of texts complete. As this remarkable closure converts us into *listeners* of women's voices, not only do Calderón's words speak, but so also do her silences.

Other Mirrors

Castellanos' attention ranges beyond Western women for creative motifs. In an essay called "The Liberation of Love," written in 1972, she reflected on the fact that "the example of North American women is impossible to follow in Mexico. Our idiosyncrasies are so different, as well as our history and our traditions! . . . (Sometimes it is a good idea to step into a fun house and see our reflections in the distorted mirrors.) For me, however, this was really a revelation: the attitude that has been adopted in Japan to confront the problem of woman's place in society and the roles that she has to play; an attitude that crystallizes into a Women's Love Movement as opposed to Women's Lib."

That other mirror is Mrs. Kasagi, who opened a "charm school" in Tokyo that passed on the traditional Japanese values of submission, delicateness, and charm: "The training that is acquired at Mrs. Kasagi's institution of learning is so complete that a woman educated there can be intelligent without showing it in the slightest way; she can be ambitious without scaring men away; she can hold important positions, private as well as public, without awakening the competitive spirit of her opponents, but, better yet, she can appeal to their chivalrous spirit to help and protect her." Comparison with Mexico is quick to follow: "As you already know, the Japanese man (like some of your countrymen) is very touchy in these matters. He demands complete submission, and whenever he is opposed he knows how to inflict punishment with an iron hand." The meditation closes on the conclusive evidence of the success of Mrs. Kasagi's strategies: she has obtained permission to travel alone for an absence of five days. "And as for her son, who is now twenty years old, he can choose from among his mother's pupils the one who obtains the best grades."

This is a text that is rich in multiple ironies designed to create an active reader, beginning with the challenge to its double explicit readers: "You, madam, self-denying little Mexican woman, or you, self-sacrificing little Mexican woman on the road to emancipation." Ingrid Muller's perceptive study of this text demonstrates how Castellanos' strategy "is to adopt male rhetoric and to reenact, rather than to point out directly, the manner in which it operates in the social context, letting the reader see for herself where it goes wrong" (1).

> The male perspective is now presented by Mrs. Kasagi as reported by Castellanos. The result of Castellanos' strategy is that not only is she able to add another ironic twist by presenting a woman who is a willing accomplice to her own degradation, but that it removes Castellanos to the "neutral" position of a reporter, which allows her to make her point with considerably greater subtlety, thus making her irony all the more forceful. . . . By turning the discourse over to Mrs. Kasagi then, and allowing her to give free rein to her ideas, Castellanos—and the reader—are able to sit back and watch her getting caught in her trap. Castellanos' strategy thus allows the reader to recognize for herself the insidiousness of Mrs. Kasagi's propositions as they work in the cultural context, in particular, the role of tradition as an ideological tool in a male-dominated society (3–4). . . . The "Liberation of Love," then, has nothing to do with love, and if that were possible, even less with liberation. (5)

A Mad Virtue

Castellanos' inquiry into woman's place and contribution to Mexican culture, ranging from Mexico's beginnings in *La Malinche* or the eloquent silences of the nineteenth century, yields its mature fruit in an essay written in 1971 that was never included in any of the four collections. "Self-Sacrifice Is a Mad Virtue" constitutes Castellanos' mature ideas about the attitudes prevalent among contemporary Mexican women toward a favorite Mexican myth, motherhood, and its relationship to national social problems. The subject is that same "self-sacrificing little Mexican woman" whom we met as the addressee of the tale of Mrs. Kasagi's degradation of love in a male-dominated society. Now Castellanos looks at the idealization of maternity and dependency and their noxious effects upon an entire culture.

For Castellanos, "the essence of femininity does not exist, because what is one thing in one culture is considered to be something else in another, is not considered at all, or is part of the characteristics of masculinity." Culture, not gender, determines our concepts of feminine nature and this has specific connotations: "In Mexico, when we utter the word *woman*, we refer to a creature who is dependent upon male authority: be it her father's, her brother's, her husband's, or her priest's. . . . The Mexican woman does not consider herself—nor do others consider her—to be a woman who has reached fulfillment if she has not produced children, if the halo of maternity does not shine above her." Then Castellanos asks some hard questions about the Mexican children of "these mothers who have done everything for them, sacrificed everything for them." They are dependent, immature citizens whose compensations include alcoholism, macho bravado, and female hypocrisy.

> However, for the Mexican woman's self-sacrifice, children are not enough. This trait is also targeted at other members of the family: at her husband who becomes a domestic tyrant, quickly finding himself stripped of even the most minimal responsibility if he does not succeed in protecting his rights; at her parents with whom an infinitely prolonged relationship, by virtue of its anachronism, is nonfunctioning and morbid; and at her siblings whom she attempts to maintain as eternal minors.

> I insist that, if self-sacrifice is a virtue, it is one of those virtues that Chesterton says have gone mad. And for this madness, the only straitjacket we have is the law . . . to establish equality—political, economic, educational, and social—between man and woman.

But Mexican women have no right to complain, she said, because by practicing the code of self-sacrifice "they refuse to accept what the legal statutes guarantee them and what the constitution gives them: the category of human being." Women themselves, who are in part to blame for their own conditions, must take an active role in their own personal lives to remedy it. Castellanos' concepts of feminism and culture were never compartmentalized—women's problems are essentially social and economic ones that involve and reflect upon their society as a whole.

"Self-Sacrifice Is a Mad Virtue" is, unfortunately, just as current today as it was in 1971. In fact, it can still be read as a basic primer against the same cultural stereotypes that dominate the mass entertainment industry in Mexico, Venezuela, and Argentina. The basic plots of most nightly *telenovelas* (by far the most popular and far-reaching type of entertainment consumed and distributed throughout Latin America and Spanish-speaking regions of the United States) consistently feature variations on the same theme. The principal female character is too frequently a woman who has sacrificed herself for her children or for a man to the detriment of her own life and theirs. It makes for great melodrama on the screen but catastrophic models for real lives.

Servitude

Self-oppression has as its correlation the oppression of other women. "Herlinda Leaves" applies this axiom to Castellanos' own life when she discusses how "servanthood" affects the relationships between women of different social classes in modern Mexico. Using the biography of four women's lives, among them a wrenching confession about her own, Castellanos includes herself as an example of the maternal colonialism which servanthood thrives on and must, therefore, defeat. "There I was off playing Quetzalcoatl, the great white civilizing god, while right next to me someone was walking around ignorant. I was ashamed. I made a promise that the next time (if there was to be a next time) it would be different. My policy in regard to Herlinda Bolaños was totally different. But I would not venture to say that it was more appropriate."

Castellanos is aware, as few women were in her time, that freedom based on the dependence and exploitation of other women and classes is false. Although her stay in the United States coincided with the march commemorating the fiftieth anniversary of women's suffrage in this country, and the demonstrations that dramatized the Women's Liberation Movement throughout it, she thought about them in terms of Mexico. What meaning did these events hold for Mexican women and how were they being interpreted in their own country? How liberated is a woman whose freedom is dependent upon another's servitude?

> We're taking notes on what our cousins are doing, to use whenever we need them. Perhaps not today or tomorrow, because being a parasite (which is what we are, more so than victims) has its own charms. But when industrial development in our country forces us to go to work in factories and offices, take care of the house and the children, and keep up social appearances, etc., etc., etc., then the light will go on. When the last maid disappears, which is the safety net our conformity now rests on, then our first furious rebel will appear. ("La liberación de la mujer, aquí," 59–60)

On Language and Writing

"We have to create another language, we have to find another starting point," Castellanos wrote in "Language as an Instrument of Domination" in 1972. Understanding that our knowledge of the world is through language, Castellanos viewed language both as an instrument of oppression and as a way to combat it—it was the point of access to our authentic selves. While we do not know what the specific qualities of this new language would be, we can speculate that it would look for a way out of the negativity, the false images, and the codified male systems that have excluded women from history and social freedom that Castellanos examines in her poems and her essays. Regina Harrison McDonald has demonstrated that, for Castellanos, "language serves as a codifying system for examining false institutions, antiquated prejudices and iron-clad hierarchies which have been erected in the name of Mexican culture" (41).

"An Attempt at Self-Criticism" and "If Not Poetry, Then What?," written a decade apart, trace the formation of Castellanos' literary vocation, affirming the liberation from traditional literary canons and language that she achieved in her mature writing. These two texts are our critical guides to Castellanos' work, in which writing, identity, and language are linked, not separate, constants. They were her survival, she declared, the way she transformed her reality into memorable material.

Considering the privileged position that language holds in Castellanos' work, we are struck by the many points of convergence with that of the French feminists Hélène Cixous, Julia Kristeva, Luce Irigaray, and Monique Wittig, whose recognition of language as an instrument of oppression, repression, and exclusion and whose call for another language Castellanos clearly anticipates. "Briefly, French feminists in general believe that Western thought has been based on a systematic repression of women's experience. Thus their assertion of a bedrock female nature makes sense as a point from which to deconstruct language, philosophy, psychoanalysis, the social practices, and direction of patriarchal culture as we live in it and resist it" (Jones, "Writing the Body," 248). Clearly, there is a great deal more to say about the points of affinity between this Mexican writer and the wide spectrum of attitudes formulated by these younger French writers five to ten years later, the many coincidences of her writing with their practice of what is now recognized as *l'écriture féminine*, or women's writing. This chapter remains to be written. Yet, even briefly, it is clear that Castellanos' penchant for punning titles, the orality of her discourse, her multiple feminine speakers and addressees, her sarcastic challenges to "you self-sacrificing little Mexican housewives," and the open-ended stories and essays are closely akin to Luce Irigaray's practice of *parler femme*, female writing.[47]

Castellanos' predilection for female body metaphors and the habit of inscribing herself into her discourse in ways I have pointed out in this study relate her writing to Hélène Cixous' call: "Write your self. Your body must be heard" ("The Laugh of the Medusa," 250). Like Castellanos, Cixous saw writing "as one of the sites of resistance or liberation in this phallocentric universe" (Jones, "Inscribing Femininity," 85): "Everything turns on the Word: everything is the Word and only the Word . . . we must take culture at its word, as it takes us into its words, into its tongue . . . no political reflection dispenses with reflection on language, with work on language" (Cixous, "Castration or Decapitation?," 44–45). Castellanos took culture at its word in the many essays that she wrote about language—imbuing it with transforming as well as oppressing powers—revealing its negativity in order to search for "another beginning."

Domesticity as a Discursive Strategy

"My style, as you already know, consists of taking a completely insignificant fact and trying to relate it to a transcendent truth," Castellanos tells her readers in "The Moment of Truth" (*El uso de la palabra*, 256). Reflecting on the tropes that organize her essays, it becomes evident that many that generate some of her best writing are essentially domestic, yet they convey some of her most controversial discussions about women's experiences.

Several strategies fuse domesticity into the discursive organization of Castellanos' essays. Frequently, a text begins with an utterance by an autobiographical I, who tosses out a provocative personal detail or an aside on a domestic event that sets up the discussion of an issue of cultural, political, or artistic importance. "As I was putting on my makeup to attend the dinner that the Israeli government is offering President Nixon and his Secretary of State, Professor Kissinger (I'm not presuming anything, right?), I was thinking about the way things happen" ("A pesar de proponérselo," 269). "A Man of Destiny" begins by mentioning the author's forty-fifth birthday and the fact that she's not interested in ignoring dates as one does gray hairs and wrinkles. Many essays in that same collection, like "Herlinda Leaves," meditate on topics that are intrinsically domestic, such as the relationships between mistress and servants in modern Mexico. By using communication elements from areas of human activity that are intrinsically domestic or feminine, that is, supposedly innocuous, Castellanos enables the reader to initially perceive them to be harmless and non-threatening. But in Castellanos' prose they function either as springboards for a dive into the deep water of controversy that immediately follows or to hold a mirror up to our faces—and follies. In other words, the author uses referents, images, or structures from areas that because they are domestic have been stereotyped as safe, discountable, or insignificant, articulating dialogues or monologues that are just the opposite.

If a woman's body is an object, her image distorted, and language makes her an alien in her own country, little is left for her but the domestic sphere. Domesticity as trope becomes a way of access to the self in Castellanos' writing. As a discursive strategy, it creates a textual sleight-of-hand that is inherently ironic by startling or amusing the reader with a referent from an area not usually permitted or found in the discourse of male writers. When feminine or domestic referents trigger the production of a text, they defuse their topics by bringing them onto familiar ground, engaging the reader's attention and setting the stage for acceptance of the message. Once the analogy is made, it *recharges* or *resemanticizes* the familiar sign with new meaning. Wrinkles and gray hair, putting on makeup, or a charm school metonymically become original, ironic, and appropriate message bearers of significant ideas. Feminine experience converts the ordinary into the relevant and the significant through feminine tropes that articulate spheres of experiences that are usually "devalued or not admitted by the dominant discourse" (Burke, 289).

Domesticity is a sign of dual value in Castellanos' writing. The domestic sphere is a space where women dwell, excel, and create, but it is also a space that may have demeaned or diminished its inhabitants. Perhaps part of that other language that Castellanos was searching for is to be found in those codes that are nearest to us—our bodies, our spaces—the ways and places to invent ourselves as her writing urges us to do.

The Eternal Feminine: Destroying the Myths

In performance Rosario Castellanos found a way to "destroy the myths inside and outside ourselves" (Wittig, 50–51): acting out the stereotypes—and women's collusion with them—that have oppressed women and their lives in Mexico for centuries. Critique of cultural ideology became drama. The quest for the "paradigmatic figures" of a feminine tradition comes full circle in *The Eternal Feminine*, where her "debunking" of La Malinche, Sor Juana, the Empress Carlota, and Adelita, among other Mexican figures, infuses them with new literary and historical life on the stage and in the minds of the audience (Nigro). "It's not good enough to imitate the models proposed for us that are answers to circumstances other than our own. It isn't even enough to discover who we are. We have to invent ourselves" (Act III).

Rosario Castellanos was attracted to writing drama and had even practiced it when she worked with the didactic puppet troupe known as El Teatro Petul that traveled throughout rural Chiapas in the early fifties.[48] Although she often said that she had never been able to master this genre, Kathleen O'Quinn has pointed out that her early play *Tablero de damas* (1952), a one-act satire about women writers entangled in the egos of Mexican literary circles, is a dress rehearsal of the female images and their stereotypes that she perfected more than twenty years later in *The Eternal Feminine*. Without a doubt the latter is one of the most radical plays ever staged in Mexico.

Discussion about the collective writing of a feminist drama began in the fall of 1970 when Castellanos received a telephone call from the actress Emma Teresa Armendáriz and her husband, the director Rafael López Mirnau. As regular readers of her weekly essays in Mexico City newspapers they were convinced that her talent for presenting feminist ideology through humorous language was better suited for the stage than for the printed page (Ortiz, 9). For the rest of that year, until she left for Tel Aviv as ambassador of Mexico to Israel, she met weekly with her new friends to plan a joint creation. Unfortunately, none of the outlines they came up with satisfied them. During a vacation period in the spring of 1973, Castellanos sat down and completed the farce she had been working out by herself over the past year. "Eureka!" she telegraphed her friends, sending the manuscript to them via Raúl Ortiz. Published in 1975, it had a very short run in April 1976. Rafael López Mirnau directed and co-produced it; Emma Teresa Armendáriz was the main actress, playing the part of fourteen different female characters. Reviews published in the Mexico City press were mixed. When financial backing was suddenly withdrawn after only a few weeks of performances, the play was forced to close.[49]

Staging versus Reading

The setting is a beauty salon in a middle-class residential district of Mexico City. A hair dryer that makes the women who sit under it dream into the past, present, or future is the feminine dramatic motif that generates multiple episodes and characters from Mexican history and myth. "Each character projects her present dimension at the same time that she incarnates the symbol of ancestral lies" (Ortiz, 14). It is a devastating satire on "the institutions and stereotyped attitudes which imprison women. . . . an imprisonment in which women are shown to be active collaborators" (Vásquez, 34).

Through experimental staging, Castellanos found ways to combine several centuries of Mexican women into one time frame. The seven dreams in Act I all center around the protagonist, Lupita's, seven possible futures. An example of the innovative dramatic props is the large backdrop screen where the dream sequences that reflected a character's past and present were flashed. When López Mirnau and Armendáriz prepared to stage the play, they realized that the complete script was too complicated to present as it was written, posing many difficulties for the director as well as the actress who must play multiple roles. Act II was omitted. Too long to be included were six radical interpretations of scenes from the lives of various women, extending from Eve in the Garden with Adam to Cortés' mistress, Malintzin. Because these are culturally bound reversals of their accepted versions as recorded in official history or legend, an audience without a working knowledge of Mexican history and legend would find the satire difficult to capture, even with the aid of comprehensive program notes.

The dramatist thought she had found the formula for a dramatic portrayal of her ideas on stage, but in fact the work is as apt for reading, which can include the entire script, as for presentation on stage, where it may be truncated. A reader or spectator must be intimately acquainted with the social and cultural contexts of Mexico in order to capture the full comic catharsis or the ambiguity of her controversial hypothesis. Some of the skits about women are based on unauthenticated gossip about the historical personages, for example, the implication that Sor Juana Inés de la Cruz may have had latent lesbian inclinations. However, this kind of ambiguity allows the play to avoid the scandal that *Tablero de damas* had caused twenty years before.[50]

Drama from Biography: Defusing Negativity

Knowing that *The Eternal Feminine* would be difficult if not impossible to actually stage in a complete version, Castellanos saw it as a powerful vehicle for dramatizing feminist criticism, particularly through humor. To ensure that the play was presented as a feminist message, the playwright created a scene in which she inserted a woman drama critic, who in a lecture to a female audience launches into a diatribe against a Rosario Castellanos and her play entitled *The Eternal Feminine*. Castellanos' capacity for debunking as a critical tool was applied to herself. In fact, this autocriticism constitutes a productive dramatic strategy because it is an effective way of defusing hostility by anticipating the attacks that she knew this play would arouse in Mexican social circles. By turning her talent for ironic humor on herself, playwright and play gain in stature. By enacting acerbic criticism on the stage, it becomes the catharsis that foils negativity. Here then, where biography and drama meet, Castellanos once again proves to be the mistress of the ironic reversal—in complete command of "making literature out of the daily events of her life" (Poniatowska, "Vida," 67). By turning potential negativity into positive drama, the playwright turns it to her advantage before it appears in print. This play is the showcase for Castellanos' awesome talents for ironic humor and the ways that she used it to demolish the myths from within and without women's experiences in Mexico.

Symmetry and Translation

Women speak to and about other women in near perfect symmetry in this play. There are at least seven principal women in each of the three acts, with the third act including a cinematic characterization of five different women in traditionally accepted women's professions. Six dramatic episodes follow, including a scene with a prostitute dependent upon her pimp, and five professional women in jobs usually held by men in Latin American societies. The dramatization of their self-denigrating attitudes becomes a powerful vehicle for Castellanos' ideas about the discounting and dependency inculcated in women by women themselves as well as by men, even in professional positions. The process so aptly identified as "debunking" by Kirsten Nigro in one of the first and best analyses to be written about it operates at many levels and in many forms throughout Castellanos' work. Here, however, enactment confers a power that other literary modes do not achieve. Concentrated within the space, time, and language of the stage, visual dimensions make Castellanos' characters larger than life as they synthesize the images and sign systems of all the author's literary production.

A significant component of the script is Castellanos' implementation of Mexican speech patterns at multiple social and generational levels as an effective tool for the dramatization of feminist ideology. This element posed considerable difficulties for an effective English translation, which Diane Marting and Betty Osiek have resolved through resources provided by their own sojourns in Mexico, diligent research, and a discrete but essential use of notes for the many culture-bound items upon which the ironic humor and contrasts turn. They decided to retain the cultural form of address, señora, in its original Spanish form in order to conserve the cultural and social connotation, which the English equivalents of "madam," "lady," or "Mrs." do not transmit. In most cases the most successful translations were not lexical equivalences but matches of approximate cultural registers or speech situations, as were the choices used to render the exchange of street slang between the prostitute and her pimp. Betty Osiek's rhymed version of the corrido that closes the work simulates the popular music this Mexican folk form expresses. However, this translation of the play, here available in its entirety in the English language for the first time,[51] is the product of collaborative teamwork in the several drafts and revisions that Marting and Osiek worked on jointly over a period of several years. Now that the complete English version is available, it is hoped that it will stimulate new performances and critical readings outside Mexico.

Conclusions

Rosario Castellanos' writing is the place where gender, culture, and textuality meet. In it women occupy the I position—and the You, the We, and the They. They are speakers and hearers, writers and readers. Through the comprehensive imagery of her space, body, myth, and mind, woman becomes the full sign—at once the signifier and the signified. And as sign she acquires creative as well as critical value. In this way Rosario Castellanos made gender a part of the process of writing and with it literature by and about women in Mexico comes into its own.

Notes

1. Modern criticism recognizes the reader's active participation in the meaning process of a text as set out in Holub, 139–189. For the concept of multiple acts of reading and writing in the translation of literary texts, and the translator as mediator, I am indebted to Myriam Díaz-Diocaretz, 10–11 and 25–41.

2. Many anthropological and historical studies document how the region of Chiapas and its people differ linguistically and ethnically from those of central Mexico and point to a feudal social structure that has persisted there since the time of the Spanish conquest. Castellanos' essay "Discrimination in the United States and in Chiapas" speaks to these issues.

3. For a detailed biography of Rosario Castellanos in terms of her total literary production, see the essay by my colleague Mary Seale Vásquez, "Rosario Castellanos: Image and Idea," 15–40. For an intimate account of Castellanos' writing by another Mexican woman writer and close friend, see Elena Poniatowska, "Rosario Castellanos: ¡Vida, nada te debo!," 45–132, which I have drawn on for many insights into Castellanos' personal development.

4. All quotations of Castellanos' words are my translations.

5. Letter to Castellanos' friend Sr. Raúl Ortiz, Mexico City, seen in his collection there in 1978.

6. Poniatowska reproduces this poem as well as the note by Castellanos' teacher Agripino Gutiérrez, which was published with it: "Miss Castellanos is a beginning writer but she will be one of Chiapas' great poets. Her verses hold profound emotion and a note of dreams and illusions" ("Vida," 48). Technically, Castellanos' first publication was a rhyme she sent in to a popular children's magazine (see my translation of her essay "Early Writings" in Doris

Meyer, ed., *Lives on the Line: The Testimony of Contemporary Latin American Authors*).

7. "Muerte sin fin," 1939 ("Death without End").

8. See the poems entitled "Elegy," "Dawn," "Presence," "Dying beyond the Wall," and "Return," the text from which these lines are quoted. Translations of these and other poems that are not included in this anthology are from my unpublished manuscript, "Monologue of a Foreign Woman," an anthology of all of Castellanos' major poems. Earlier versions of some of them were published in Rosario Castellanos, *Looking at the Mona Lisa*, trans. Maureen Ahern.

9. *Apuntes para una declaración de fe* (1948) and *De la vigilia estéril* (1950).

10. *Malinchismo* is a synonym for the behavior of a cultural fifth-columnist, a person who places foreign interests or models before Mexican ones or betrays a cause. It is interesting to note that, while this Indian woman was given the Christian name of Doña Marina, Cortés' association with Malinche earned him the same name from the Aztecs. See Bernal Díaz del Castillo's *Historia verdadera de la conquista de la Nueva España* for a capsule biography of "Doña Marina" and the references to Cortés; an abbreviated English edition is *The Conquest of New Spain*, trans. J. M. Cohen.

11. This was fifteen years before Mary Daly postulated in *Gyn/Ecology* (1978) that the study of myths is important "not simply to *replace* patriarchal myths with feminine versions but to elicit fresh cultural insights by reversing the myths" (Humm, 94–95).

12. "Tillie Olsen's *Silences* and Rich's *On Lies, Secrets, and Silences* teach us about the centrality of silence in women's culture, specifically the ways in which women's voices have gone unheard" (Gubar, 23). See my comments on page 43 about Castellanos' pioneering views on silence and women in Mexican culture.

13. For reader expectations and presuppositions, and how reader response creates meaning, I refer to the concepts formulated by Hans Robert Jauss in his *Aesthetic Experience and Literary Hermeneutics*, 139–189. For the reader as active agent in the creation of meaning, see Eco, *The Role of the Reader: Explorations in the Semiotics of Texts*, 10–19. For the role of Jauss in the development of text-reception theory, see Holub, "From the History of Reception to Aesthetic Experience: Hans Robert Jauss," 53–82.

14. Díaz-Diocaretz has brilliantly demonstrated how speaker/addressee interaction and gender specificity are "paramount" in feminist-identified discourse and how they encompass an entire "spectra" of distinct categories in her chapter "The Speech Situation in Female Identified Discourse" (84–116). I have applied many of the concepts she formulated there to my analysis of the speakers and addressees in the poetry of Rosario Castellanos.

15. "You" can refer to any of the following pronouns in Spanish: *Tú*, familiar singular; *vos*, familiar singular in River Plate and Central American speech; *usted*, formal singular; *vosotros*, familiar plural used in peninsular Spanish or rhetorical address; *ustedes*, third-person plural and throughout Latin America used for the familiar plural. Each has a marked verb form and may signify masculine or feminine genders by the pronouns or adjectives that must agree with it in person and number. "We" may be *nosotros* or *nosotras*, indicating gender. When the reference is to a plural form that includes male and female units, the masculine plural form is used for agreement of nouns and pronouns. Thus, masculine forms obtain grammatical predominance in Spanish.

16. The events associated with the massacre at Tlatelolco are well known in Mexico, but information is supplied for the English reader in order to transmit the reference to this social sign. Tlatelolco refers to a section of Mexico City and its Plaza of the Three Cultures where hundreds of unarmed students were slaughtered in 1968 by government troops who opened fire on them, leaving the plaza strewn with the shoes of the fleeing survivors or the dead. At first no official news of the events was transmitted as the government tried to cover it up (see Elena Poniatowska, *Massacre in Mexico*, and Dolly L. Young, "Mexican Literary Reactions to Tlatelolco, 1968").

17. Castellanos writes her self well before Hélène Cixous' call for women to do that in "The Laugh of the Medusa" in 1975.

18. This point bears exploring in a large number of other Latin American women poets. See, for example, the writing of those translated in Nora Jácquez Wieser, ed., *Open to the Sun: A Bilingual Anthology of Latin American Women Poets*; Doris Meyer and Margarite Fernández Olmos, eds., *Contemporary Women Authors of Latin America*, Vol. 2, *New Translations*; and Mary Crow, ed., *Woman Who Has Sprouted Wings: Poems by Contemporary Latin American Women Poets*.

19. "As traditionally defined and practiced, autobiography has been a congenial form for women. A public act of personal recollection, it poses the problem of welding both private and public experience. But unlike men, who are allowed to move in both spheres, women historically have been relegated to the private realm of home, personal relationships and emotion, a sphere they leave at their peril. Not surprisingly, many have chosen the diary form, which both Mary Jane Moffat and Suzanne Juhasz see as an analogue to women's lives within a patriarchal society: private, amateur, cyclical and concerned with daily experience" (Voss, 226).

20. "The poem is an uttering act. . . . The poet fully takes upon himself his speech act, which becomes an enunciation in the first degree, not represented, without quotation marks" (Todorov, 65). See also Austin and Searle.

21. Cheris Kramarae has pointed out that "the constant attempts made to

silence women mean that women, to be heard by men, try to present themselves in speech forms recognizable and respected by men" (19).

22. I am indebted to Gayle Greene and Coppélia Kahn's discussion of these points in their essay "Feminist Scholarship and the Social Construct of Woman" (12, 26) for the insights they have offered me for this aspect of Castellanos' poetic discourse.

23. "Discourse receives its meaning from the person(s) to whom it is addressed" (Kristeva, "The System and the Speaking Subject," 54).

24. "The language of a particular culture does not serve all its speakers equally, for not all speakers contribute in an equal fashion to its formulation. Women (and members of other subordinate groups) are not as free or as able as men are to say what they wish, when and where they wish, because the words and the norms for their use have been formulated by the dominant group, men. So women cannot as easily or as directly articulate their experiences as men can. Women's perceptions differ from those of men because women's subordination means they experience life differently. However, the words and norms for speaking are not generated from or fitted to women's experiences. Women are thus 'muted.' Their talk is often not considered of much value by men—who are, or appear to be, deaf and blind to much of women's experiences. Words constantly ignored may eventually come to be unspoken and perhaps even unthought" (Kramarae, 1).

25. See Larry M. Grimes, El tabú lingüístico en México: El lenguaje erótico de los mexicanos.

26. The images of female sexuality contrast sharply among different fragments of Nahuatl discourse that have come down to us: devourers of men and children, aggressive sexual conquerors of a king, givers of sexual pleasure, chaste wives and daughters (see Bierhorst; Hellbom; León Portilla). Josefina Muriel documents the biographies and outpouring of mystical and religious writing by women in the viceroyalty of New Spain in her important study Cultura femenina novohispana. For contemporary perspectives, see Nash and Safa, Sex and Class in Latin America. Also to be noted here is Cixous' concept of "woman as the dark continent" that is "neither dark nor unexplorable" ("The Laugh of the Medusa," 288).

27. See, for example, the anonymous bandas, or announcements, that appeared soon after the death of Allende and other texts in Roberto Márquez, ed., Latin American Revolutionary Poetry / Poesía revolucionaria latinoamericana, and, more recently, the underground humor magazines circulated in Argentina during the military governments that carried out genocide by "disappearances," or, in Mexico, the omnipresent jokes about the PRI, the party that has controlled Mexican government for most of this century.

28. See Susan Gubar's brilliant discussion of blood as a major symbol of the female body and its identification with singing or telling: "When the metaphors of literary creativity are filtered through a sexual lens, female sexu-

ality is often identified with textuality" (17). See Hélène Cixous' call for woman to write her body: "Women must write through their bodies, they must invent the impregnable language that will wreck partitions, classes, and rhetorics, regulations and codes, they must submerge, cut through, get beyond the ultimate reserve—discourse . . ." ("The Laugh of the Medusa," 289); "More so than men who are coaxed toward social success, toward sublimation, women are body. More body, hence more writing" (290). For recent critical discussion in English, see Lindsay and Jones.

29. "The childbirth metaphor provides a genuine gender difference in literary discourse as constituted both by the readers and the writers of a given text. . . . Emerging like women themselves from the confinement of patriarchal literary tradition, birth metaphors have celebrated women's birthright to creativity" (Friedman, 50, 76).

30. The contrast with nineteenth-century literary tradition could not be greater. Emily Dickinson, a poet Castellanos translated into Spanish and included in her own collected verse in the section called "Versions," left us a poem about "Nobody" in which she herself, not society, carried out the effacement of identity, whose first stanza reads:

I'm Nobody! Who are You?
Are you—Nobody—Too?
Then there's a pair of us?
Don't tell! they'd advertise—you know!

(Gilbert and Gubar, 554; see also their discussion of this poem, 555).

31. My discussion of intertextuality and subtexts is based on concepts formulated by Díaz-Diocaretz in her discussion "The Intertextual Factor as Feminist Strategy" (67–83) and Kristeva, *Revolution in Poetic Language* and *Desire in Language: A Semiotic Approach to Literature and Art*; also Todorov, "Intertextuality," in his *Mikhail Bakhtin: The Dialogical Principle*, 60–93.

32. "There are four kinds of subtexts: (1) that which serves as a simple impulse for the creation of an image; (2) . . . (borrowing of a rhythmic figure and the sounds contained therein); (3) the text which supports or reveals the poetic message of a later text; (4) the text which is treated polemically by the poet. The first two do not necessarily contribute to our better understanding of a given poem. However, (2) may be combined with (3) and/or (4), and (3) and (4) may, in their turn, be blended" (Taranovsky, 18). All four types as well as combinations of them are present in the four different poems that I analyze in this section, and in other poems in our selection. See also the discussion in Rusinko, 213–235.

33. See n. 27.

34. George Eliot, *Middlemarch*, and John Berryman, *Berryman's Sonnets* (Gubar, 11–12).

35. Díaz-Diocaretz has shown how the redirection of negativity and the search for alternatives to it are issues central to feminist discourse: "The underlying ideological structures in the feminist poet have as target the traditional and patriarchal system of thought still prevalent, and the search for an alternative terrain where to expand the university of discourse by and for women. The ideological displacement of emotional connotations of negativity is undoubtedly a major feminist strategy, and a central clue for the translator" (62).

36. Castellanos set down the experience of the death of her younger brother as told by a first-person narrator in 1950 in her story "Primera revelación," published in *América: Revista antológica*.

37. See, particularly, José María Arguedas' novels *Yawar Fiesta* and *Deep Rivers* and his essay "El indigenismo en el Perú," written in 1965.

38. Nelly Furman, "The Politics of Language: Beyond the Gender Principle?," 60–61. She bases her discussion on Claude Lévi-Strauss' discussion of marriage as a communication device between groups where, "in contrast to words, which have wholly become signs, woman has remained at once a sign and a value" (*The Elementary Structures of Kinship*, 496).

39. Sor Juana Inés de la Cruz, *A Woman of Genius: The Intellectual Autobiography of Sor Juana Inés de la Cruz*, trans. Margaret Sayers Peden (see 1–17); also see Octavio Paz, *Sor Juana Inés de la Cruz o las trampas de la fe*.

40. My translation of another essay, "Early Writings," was published in Doris Meyer, ed., *Lives on the Line: The Testimony of Contemporary Latin American Writers*. An earlier version of my translation of "Woman and Her Image" is included in Marian Arkin and Barbara Shollars, eds., *International Literature by Women*.

41. I refer here to Simone de Beauvoir's statement: "She is defined and differentiated with reference to man and not he with reference to her; she is the incidental, the inessential as opposed to the essential. He is the Subject, he is the Absolute—she is the Other" (*The Second Sex*, xvi). In 1961 Octavio Paz saw woman as essentially alien: "Woman is another being who lives apart and is therefore an enigmatic figure. It would be better to say that she is the Enigma. She attracts and repels like men of an alien race or nationality. She is an image of both fecundity and death. In almost every culture the goddesses of creation are also goddesses of destruction. Woman is a living symbol of the strangeness of the universe and its radical heterogeneity. . . . What does she think? Or does she think? Does she truly have feelings?" (*The Labyrinth of Solitude*, 66).

42. See also Gómez Parham, "Intellectual Influences on the Works of Rosario Castellanos."

43. "While sex is an anatomical fact, sexuality is culturally devised; it is the manner in which society fictionalizes its relationship to sex and creates gender roles. . . . feminism cannot be construed as a separate system of per-

ceptions and values, but can only be conceived as a position one assumes in relation to the cultural construct of sexuality" (Furman, 73–74).

44. For a contrasting contemporary vision of Malinche, see Octavio Paz' discussion of her as the *"Chingada* in person . . . the Mexican Eve" (*The Labyrinth of Solitude,* 86–87).

45. In his *Sor Juana Inés de la Cruz, la décima musa de México: Su vida, su poesía, su psique.*

46. See the critical edition, Fanny Calderón de la Barca, *Life in Mexico: The Letters of Fanny Calderón de la Barca,* ed. Howard T. Fisher and Marian Hall Fisher.

47. For an anthology of texts by Hélène Cixous and other French feminist writers in English translation with a survey of their theoretical positions, see Elaine Marks and Isabelle de Courtivron, eds., *New French Feminisms: An Anthology;* for Luce Irigaray, see her *Speculum of the Other Woman* and *The Sex Which Is Not One;* for Monique Wittig, "One Is Not Born a Woman"; for Julia Kristeva, see her *Desire in Language, Revolution of Poetic Language,* and *The Power of Horror.* Their theoretical positions on language and women as well as their practice of *l'écriture féminine* differ substantially among these writers. For surveys of their thought, see Jones, "Inscribing Femininity: French Theories of the Feminine" and "Writing the Body: Toward an Understanding of *l'écriture féminine";* Lindsay, "Body/Language: French Feminist Utopias." For analysis of different authors, see Burke, "Irigaray through the Looking Glass"; Crowder, "Amazons and Mothers: Monique Wittig, Hélène Cixous, and Theories of Women's Writing"; Nye, "Woman Clothed with the Sun: Julia Kristeva and the Escape From/To Language"; Wenzel, "The Text as Body/Politics: An Appreciation of Monique Wittig's Writings in Contexts."

48. See her uncollected essay "Teatro Petul" and, in this anthology, "Incident at Yalentay."

49. Based on my interview with Emma Teresa Armendáriz and Rafael López Mirnau in Mexico City, August 1978, and Ortiz. I have included reviews by Leñero, Oberfield, and Vargas in the Select Bibliography of Rosario Castellanos Criticism.

50. Allegedly based on the Nobel Prize–winning writer Gabriela Mistral and her literary circle, it is an acid view of women working against each other according to men's rules. When it was published in Mexico City it touched off a polemic that eventually led to the dissolution of *América: Revista antológica.* Castellanos later developed a prose version that became her short story, "Álbum de familia." See her comments on the incident in "An Attempt at Self-Criticism."

51. Another English translation of this play, entitled "Just Like a Woman," was done by Virginia Bouvier as a thesis for the master of arts degree from the University of South Carolina in 1984. Her discussion of her translation and Act II of it were recently published in *Latin American Literary Review.* The

Dabdoub, Mary Lou. "Ultima charla con Rosario Castellanos." *Revista de Revistas*, 11 September 1974, 44–46.

Daly, Mary. *Gyn/Ecology: The Metaethics of Radical Feminism*. New York: Beacon Press, 1978.

Díaz del Castillo, Bernal. *The Conquest of New Spain*. Trans. J. M. Cohen. Middlesex, England: Penguin Books, 1963. Rpt. 1985.

Díaz-Diocaretz, Myriam. *Translating Poetic Discourse: Questions on Feminist Strategies in Adrienne Rich*. Philadelphia: John Benjamins Publishing Co., 1985.

Eco, Umberto. *The Role of the Reader: Explorations in the Semiotics of Texts*. Bloomington: Indiana University Press, 1979.

———. *A Theory of Semiotics*. Bloomington: Indiana University Press, 1976.

Felstiner, John. *Translating Neruda: The Way to Machu Picchu*. Stanford: Stanford University Press, 1980.

Forster, Merlin H., and Julio Ortega, eds. *De la crónica a la nueva narrativa mexicana: Coloquio sobre literatura mexicana*. Mexico City: Editorial Oasis, 1986.

Friedman, Susan Stanford. "Creativity and the Childbirth Metaphor: Gender Difference in Literary Discourse." *Feminist Studies* 13, no. 1 (1987): 49–82.

Furman, Nelly. "The Politics of Language: Beyond the Gender Principle?" In Greene and Kahn, 59–79.

García Flores, Margarita. Interviews. "Rosario Castellanos: La lucidez como forma de vida." In *Cartas marcadas*, 167–177. Mexico City: Difusión Cultural, Depto. de Humanidades 10, Universidad Nacional Autónoma de México, 1979.

———. Interview. "Rosario Castellanos: La lucidez como forma de vida." *La Onda*, supp. *Novedades*, 18 August 1974, 6–7.

Gilbert, Sandra M., and Susan Gubar. *The Madwoman in the Attic: The Woman Writer and the Nineteenth-Century Imagination*. New Haven: Yale University Press, 1979.

Gómez Parham, Mary. "Intellectual Influences on the Works of Rosario Castellanos." *Foro Literario: Revista de Literatura y Lenguaje* [Montevideo] 7, no. 12 (1984): 34–40.

Gorostiza, José. "Death without End." Trans. Rachel Benson. In *New Poetry of Mexico*, ed. Mark Strand, 161–163. New York: E. P. Dutton & Co., 1970.

Greene, Gayle, and Coppélia Kahn. "Feminist Scholarship and the Social Construct of Woman." In Greene and Kahn, 1–36.

———. *Making a Difference: Feminist Literary Criticism*. London and New York: Methuen & Co., 1985.

Grimes, Larry M. *El tabú lingüístico en México: El lenguaje erótico de los mexicanos*. Jamaica, N.Y.: Bilingual Press/Editorial Bilingue, 1978.

Gubar, Susan. "'The Blank Page' and the Issues of Female Creativity." In Spector, 10–29.

Hellbom, Anna-Britta. "The Life and Role of Women in Aztec Culture." *Cultures* 8, no. 3 (1982): 55–65.

Holub, Robert C. *Reception Theory: A Critical Introduction*. London: Methuen & Co., 1984.

Humm, Maggie. *Feminist Criticism: Women as Contemporary Critics*. Sussex, England: Harvester Press, 1986.

Irigaray, Luce. *The Sex Which Is Not One*. Trans. Catherine Porter. Ithaca, N.Y.: Cornell University Press, 1985.

———. *Speculum of the Other Woman*. Trans. Gillian Gil. Ithaca, N.Y.: Cornell University Press, 1985.

Jacobus, Mary, ed. *Women Writing and Writing about Women*. New York: Barnes & Noble, 1979.

———. "The Difference of View." In Jacobus, 10–21.

Jauss, Hans Robert. *Aesthetic Experience and Literary Hermeneutics*. Trans. Michael Shaw. Minneapolis: University of Minnesota Press, 1982.

Jones, Ann Rosalind. "Inscribing Femininity: French Theories of the Feminine." In Greene and Kahn, 59–79.

———. "Writing the Body: Toward an Understanding of *l'écriture féminine*." *Feminist Studies* 7, no. 2 (1981): 247–263.

Kamenzain, Tamara. *El texto silencioso: Tradición y vanguardia en la poesía sudamericana*. Mexico City: Universidad Nacional Autónoma de México, 1983.

Kaplan, Cora. "Pandora's Box: Subjectivity, Class, and Sexuality in Socialist Feminist Criticism." In Greene and Kahn, 146–176.

Kramarae, Cheris. *Women and Men Speaking: Frameworks for Analysis*. Rowley, Mass.: Newberry House Publishers, 1981.

Kristeva, Julia. *Desire in Language: A Semiotic Approach to Literature and Arts*. Trans. Thomas Gora et al. Ed. Leon S. Roudiez. New York: Columbia University Press, 1980.

———. *The Power of Horror*. Trans. Leon Roudiez. New York: Columbia University Press, 1985.

———. *Revolution in Poetic Language*. Trans. Margaret Waller. New York: Columbia University Press, 1984.

———. "The System and the Speaking Subject." In *The Tell-Tale Sign: A Survey of Semiotics*, ed. Thomas A. Sebeok, 47–55. Lisse, Netherlands: Peter de Ridder Press, 1975.

León-Portilla, Miguel. *Literatura del México antiguo*. Ed. Miguel León-Portilla. Caracas: Biblioteca Ayacucho, 1978.

Lerner, Gerda. *The Majority Finds Its Past*. Oxford: Oxford University Press, 1979.

Lévi-Strauss, Claude. *The Elementary Structures of Kinship*. Trans. James

Harle Bell, John Richard von Sturmer, and Rodney Needham. Rev. ed. Boston: Beacon Press, 1969.

Lindsay, Cecile. "Body/Language: French Feminist Utopias." *French Review* 60, no. 1 (1986): 46–55.

Lotman, Jurij. *The Structure of the Artistic Text.* Trans. Gail Lenhoff and Ronald Vroon. Ann Arbor: Michigan Slavic Contributions, 1977.

MacDonald, Regina Harrison. "Rosario Castellanos: On Language." In Ahern and Vásquez, 41–64.

Marks, Elaine, and Isabelle de Courtivron, eds. *New French Feminisms: An Anthology.* Amherst: University of Massachusetts Press, 1980.

Márquez, Roberto, ed. *Latin American Revolutionary Poetry / Poesía revolucionaria latinoamericana.* New York and London: Monthly Review Press, 1974.

Mendoza, María Luisa. "El juego de las encantadas." In Forster and Ortega, 385–390.

Meyer, Doris, ed. *Lives on the Line: The Testimony of Contemporary Latin American Authors.* Berkeley and Los Angeles: University of California Press, 1988.

Meyer, Doris, and Margerite Fernández Olmos, eds. *New Translations.* Vol. 2 of *Contemporary Women Authors of Latin America.* 2 vols. Brooklyn: Brooklyn College Press, 1983.

Miller, Beth. *Rosario Castellanos: Una conciencia feminista en México.* Tuxtla Gutiérrez, Chiapas: Universidad Autónoma de Chiapas, 1983.

———. "Voz e imagen en la obra de Rosario Castellanos." *Revista de la Universidad de México* 30, no. 4 (1975–1976): 33–38.

Muller, Ingrid. Essay on "The Liberation of Love," by Rosario Castellanos, written for graduate seminar SPA 545, Prof. E. Friedman. Arizona State University, 1986.

Muriel, Josefina. *Cultura femenina novohispana.* Mexico City: Instituto de Investigaciones Históricas, Universidad Autónoma de México, 1982.

Nash, June, and Helen Icken Safa. *Sex and Class in Latin America.* South Hadley, Mass.: J. F. Bergin Publishers, 1980.

Nigro, Kirsten F. "Rosario Castellanos's Debunking of the Eternal Feminine." *Journal of Spanish Studies: Twentieth Century* 8 (1980): 89–102.

Nye, Andrea. "Woman Clothed with the Sun: Julia Kristeva and the Escape From/To Language." *Signs* 12, no. 4 (1987): 664–686.

Olsen, Tillie. "Silences in Literature—1962." 1965. In *Silences,* 5–21. New York: Delacorte Press/Seymour Lawrence, 1978.

O'Quinn, Kathleen. "*Tablero de damas* and *Álbum de familia*: Farces on Women Writers." In Ahern and Vásquez, 99–105.

Ortiz, Raúl. Presentación. *El eterno femenino,* by Rosario Castellanos, 7–17. Mexico City: Fondo de Cultura Económica, 1975.

Pacheco, José Emilio. "Rosario Castellanos o la literatura como ejercicio de la libertad." *Diorama de la Cultura*, supp. *Excélsior*, 11 August 1974, 16.

Paz, Octavio. *The Labyrinth of Solitude: The Other Mexico*. 1961. Trans. Lysander Kemp, Yara Milos, and Rachel Phillips Belash. New York: Grove Press, 1985.

———. *Sor Juana Inés de la Cruz o las trampas de la fe*. Mexico City: Fondo de Cultura Económica, 1982.

Pfandl, Ludwig. *Sor Juana Inés de la Cruz, la décima musa de México: Su vida, su poesía, su psique*. Mexico City: Instituto de Investigaciones Estéticas, Universidad Nacional Autónoma de México, 1963.

Poniatowska, Elena. *Massacre in Mexico*. Trans. Helen R. Lane. New York: Viking Press, 1975.

———. "Rosario Castellanos." *México en la Cultura*, supp. *Novedades*, 26 January 1958, 7, 10.

———. "Rosario Castellanos: ¡Vida, nada te debo!" In *¡Ay vida, no me mereces!*, 45–132. Mexico City: Editorial Joaquín Mortiz, 1985.

Rich, Adrienne. *On Lies, Secrets, and Silences: Selected Prose, 1966–1978*. New York: Norton, 1979.

———. "Power and Danger: Works of a Common Woman." In Rich, 247–258.

———. "When We Dead Awaken: Writing as Revision." In Rich, 68–84.

Rivero, Eliana S. "Paradigma de la poética femenina hispanoamericana y su evolución: Rosario Castellanos." In Forster and Ortega, 391–406.

Rusinko, Elaine. "Intertextuality: The Soviet Approach to Subtext." *Dispositio* 11, no. 12 (1979): 213–235.

Searle, John. *Speech Acts: An Essay in the Philosophy of Language*. Cambridge: Cambridge University Press, 1969.

Sommers, Joseph. "Forma e ideología en *Oficio de tinieblas* de Rosario Castellanos." *Revista de Crítica Latinoamericana* 7–8 (1978): 73–91.

———. "The Present Moment in the Mexican Novel." *Books Abroad* 40 (Summer 1966): 216–266.

Spector, Judith, ed. *Gender Studies: New Directions in Feminist Criticism*. Bowling Green, Ohio: Bowling Green State University Popular Press, 1986.

Stevenson, Anne. "Writing as a Woman." In Jacobus, 159–176.

Taranovsky, Kiril. *Essays on Mandel'stam*. Cambridge, Mass., and London, England: Harvard University Press, 1976.

"Threshold." *Webster's New Twentieth Century Dictionary: Unabridged*. 2d ed. 1983.

Torodov, Tzvetan. *Mikhail Bakhtin: The Dialogical Principle*. Trans. Wlad Godzich. Minneapolis: University of Minnesota Press, 1984.

"Umbral." *Simon & Schuster International Dictionary: English/Spanish, Spanish/English*. 1973.

Vásquez, Mary Seale. "Rosario Castellanos: Image and Idea." In Ahern and Vásquez, 15–40.

Voss, Norine. "Saying the Unsayable: An Introduction to Women's Autobiography." In Spector, 218–233.

Wenzel, Hélène Vivienne. "The Text as Body/Politics: An Appreciation of Monique Wittig's Writings in Contexts." *Feminist Studies* 7, no. 2 (1981): 264–287.

Wieser, Nora Jácquez, ed. *Open to the Sun: A Bilingual Anthology of Latin American Women Poets*. Van Nuys, Calif.: Perivale Press, 1979.

Wittig, Monique. "One Is Not Born a Woman." 1979. *Feminist Issues* 1, no. 2 (1981): 47–54.

Woolf, Virginia. "Professions for Women." 1929. In *Women and Writing*, ed. Michele Barrett, 57–63. New York and London: Harcourt, Brace & Jovanovich, 1979.

Young, Dolly. "Mexican Literary Reactions to Tlatelolco, 1968." *Latin American Research Review* 20, no. 2 (1985): 71–85.

Rosario Castellanos: A Basic Bibliography of Her Writing
Poetry

Trayectoria del polvo. Mexico City: Colección el Cristal Fugitivo, 1948.

Apuntes para una declaración de fe. Mexico City: Ediciones de América: Revista Antológica, 1948.

De la vigilia estéril. Mexico City: Ediciones de América: Revista Antológica, 1950.

Dos poemas. Mexico City: Icaro, Impresora Económica, 1950.

Presentación al templo: Poemas (Madrid, 1951). Mexico City: Ediciones de América: Revista Antológica, 1952.

El rescate del mundo. Mexico City: Ediciones de América: Revista Antológica, 1952. 2d ed. Tuxtla Gutiérrez, Chiapas: Gobierno del Estado de Chiapas, 1952.

Poemas (1953–1955). Mexico City: Colección Metáfora, 1957.

Salomé y Judith: Poemas dramáticos. Mexico City: Editorial Jus, 1957.

Al pie de la letra: Poemas. Xalapa: Universidad Veracruzana, 1959.

Lívida luz: Poemas. Mexico City: Universidad Nacional Autónoma de México, 1960.

Materia memorable. Mexico City: Universidad Nacional Autónoma de México, 1969.

Poesía no eres tú: Obra poética, 1948–1971. Mexico City: Fondo de Cultura Económica, 1972. 2d ed. 1975.

Meditación en el umbral: Antología poética. Comp. Julian Palley. Foreword by Elena Poniatowska, Introduction by Julian Palley. Mexico City: Fondo de Cultura Económica, 1985.

Fiction

Balún-Canán. Mexico City: Fondo de Cultura Económica, 1957. 2d ed. 1961.
Ciudad Real: Cuentos. Xalapa: Universidad Veracruzana, 1960. 2d ed. 1982. 3d ed. 1986.
Oficio de tinieblas. Mexico City: Joaquín Mortiz, 1962. 4th ed. 1975.
Los convidados de agosto. Mexico City: Ediciones Era, 1964. 5th ed. 1979.
Álbum de familia. Mexico City: Joaquín Mortiz, 1971. 3d ed. 1977.

Essays

Sobre cultura femenina. [Dissertation, Facultad de Filosofía y Letras, Universidad Nacional Autónoma de México, 1950.] Mexico City: Ediciones de América: Revista Antológica, 1950.
Juicios sumarios: Ensayos. Xalapa: Universidad Veracruzana, 1966. 2d ed. *Juicios sumarios: Ensayos sobre literatura*. 2 vols. Mexico City: Fondo de Cultura Económica, Biblioteca Joven, 1984.
Mujer que sabe latín . . . Mexico City: Sepsetentas, Secretaría de Educación Pública, 1973. Reprint. SepDiana, 1979.
El uso de la palabra. Prol. José Emilio Pacheco. Mexico City: Ediciones de Excélsior-Crónicas, 1974.
El mar y sus pescaditos. Mexico City: Sepsetentas, Secretaría de Educación Pública, 1975.

Theater

"Tablero de damas: Pieza en un acto." *América: Revista Antológica* 68 (1952): 185–224.
"Petul en la Escuela Abierta." In *Teatro Petul*, 42–65. Mexico City: Instituto Nacional Indigenista, [1962].
El eterno femenino: Farsa. Mexico City: Fondo de Cultura Económica, 1975.

A Select Bibliography of Rosario Castellanos Criticism

The following bibliography is designed to acquaint the reader with the major critical studies about Castellanos' writing, including key interviews and reviews contemporary with her work.

A Rosario Castellanos: Sus amigos. Comp. Ma. del Refugio Llamas. Mexico City: Año Internacional de la Mujer/Programa de México, 1975.
Agosín, Marjorie. "Rosario Castellanos ante el espejo." *Cuadernos Americanos* 2, no. 253 (1984): 219–226.
Ahern, Maureen. "A Critical Bibliography of and about the Works of Rosario Castellanos." In Ahern and Vásquez, 121–174.

Ahern, Maureen, and Mary Seale Vásquez, eds. *Homenaje a Rosario Castellanos*. Valencia: Albatros-Hispanófila Ediciones, 1980.

Alarcón, Norma. "Rosario Castellanos' Feminist Poetics: Against the Sacrificial Contract." *DAI* 44 (1983): 1466a. [Indiana University.]

Allgood, Myralyn Frizelle. "Conflict and Counterpoint: A Study of Characters and Characterization in Rosario Castellanos' Indigenist Fiction." *DAI* 46 (1986): 1958a. [University of Alabama.]

Anderson, Helene M. "Rosario Castellanos and the Structures of Power." In Meyer and Fernández Olmos, 1 : 22–32.

Aponte, Barbara B. "Estrategias dramáticas del femenismo en *El eterno femenino* de Rosario Castellanos." *Latin America Theatre Review* 20, no. 2 (1987): 49–58.

Baptiste, Victor N. *La obra poética de Rosario Castellanos*. Santiago de Chile: Ediciones Exégesis, 1972.

Benedetti, Mario. "Rosario Castellanos y la incomunicación racial." In his *Letras del continente mestizo*, 130–135. Montevideo: Arca, 1967.

Bigelow, Marcia Anne. "La evolución de la hablante en la poesía de Rosario Castellanos." *DAI* 45 (1984): 533a. [University of California, Irvine.]

Bouchony, Claire Tron de. "Women in the Work of Rosario Castellanos: A Struggle for Identity." *Cultures* 8, no. 3 (1982): 66–82.

Bouvier, Virginia Marie Danielle. Introduction to "Just Like a Woman." [By Rosario Castellanos.] *Latin American Literary Review* 14, no. 28 (1986): 47–51.

Calderón, Germaine. *El universo poético de Rosario Castellanos*. Mexico City: Cuadernos del Centro de Estudios Literarios, Universidad Nacional Autónoma de México, 1979.

Carballo, Emmanuel. "Poesía de fuera y de dentro." *México en la Cultura*, supp. *Novedades*, 16 June 1957, 2.

———. "Poesía y prosa, imaginación y realidad." *La Cultura en México*, supp. *¡Siempre!*, 11 November 1964, 15.

———. "Rosario Castellanos: La historia de sus libros contada por ella misma." In *Diecinueve protagonistas de la literatura mexicana del siglo XX*, 411–424. Mexico City: Empresas Editoriales, 1965.

Cárdenas, Dolores. Interview. "Rosario Castellanos: La mujer mexicana, cómplice de su verdugo." *Revista de Revistas* [Mexico], 22 (1 November 1972): 24–27.

Castro, Dolores. "El culto a los otros en la obra de Rosario Castellanos." *La Palabra y el Hombre* 11 (1974): 13–16.

Cossé, Rómulo. "El mundo creado en *Oficio de tinieblas* de Rosario Castellanos." In his *Crítica latinoamericana: Propuestas y ejercicios*, 111–137. Xalapa: Universidad Veracruzana, Centro de Investigaciones Lingüístico-Literarios, 1982.

Cresta de Leguizamón, María Luisa. "En recuerdo de Rosario Castellanos." *La Palabra y el Hombre* 19 (1976): 3–18.

Cypess, Sandra M. "*Balún-Canán*—a Model Demonstration of Discourse as Power." *Revista de Estudios Hispánicos* 19, no. 3 (1985): 1–15.

———. "Onomastics and Thematics in *Bahín-Canán*." *Literary Onomastics Studies* 13 (1986): 83–96.

Dabdoub, Mary Lou. "Ultima charla con Rosario Castellanos." *Revista de Revistas*, 11 September 1974, 44–46.

Dauster, Frank. "Rosario Castellanos: The Search for a Voice." In his *The Double Strand: Five Contemporary Mexican Poets*, 134–162. Lexington: University Press of Kentucky, 1987.

de Beer, Gabriella. "El feminismo en la poesía de Rosario Castellanos." *Revista de Crítica Literaria Latinoamericana* 7, no. 13 (1981): 105–112. "Feminismo in the Poetry of Rosario Castellanos." In Palley (1988), 7–16.

Dorward, Frances R. "The Function of Interiorization in *Oficio de tinieblas*." *Neophilologus* 69, no. 3 (1985): 374–385.

Dybvig, Rhoda. *Rosario Castellanos: Biografía y novelística*. [Thesis, Universidad Nacional Autónoma de México, 1965.] Mexico City: Andrea, 1965.

Eidelberg, Nora. "El eterno femenino de Rosario Castellanos." In her *Teatro experimental hispanoamericano, 1960–1980: La realidad social como manipulación*, 164–170. Minneapolis: Institute for the Studies of Ideologies and Literature, 1985.

Fiscal, María Rosa. "Identidad y lenguaje en los personajes femeninos de Rosario Castellanos." *Chasqui: Revista de Literatura Latinoamericana* 14, nos. 2–3 (1985): 25–35.

———. *La imagen de la mujer en la narrativa de Rosario Castellanos*. Mexico City: Universidad Nacional Autónoma de México, 1980.

Forster, Merlin H., and Julio Ortega, eds. *De la crónica a la nueva narrativa mexicana: Coloquio sobre literatura mexicana*. Mexico City: Editorial Oasis, 1986.

Franco, María Estela. *Rosario Castellanos (1925–1974): Semblanza sicoanalítica*. Mexico City: Joaquín Mortiz, 1985.

Frischmann, Donald H. "El sistema patriarchal y las relaciones heterosexuales en *Balún Canán* de Rosario Castellanos." *Revista Iberoamericana* 51 (1985): 665–678.

García Flores, Margarita. Interviews. "Rosario Castellanos: La lucidez como forma de vida." In *Cartas marcadas*, 167–177. Mexico City: Difusión Cultural, Depto. de Humanidades, Universidad Nacional Autónoma de México, 1979.

Gómez Parham, Mary. "Intellectual Influences on the Works of Rosario Castellanos." *Foro Literario: Revista de Literatura y Lenguaje* [Montevideo] 7, no. 12 (1984): 34–40.

González, Alfonso. "La soledad y los patrones del dominio en la cuentística de Rosario Castellanos." In Ahern and Vásquez, 107–113.

Gordillo y Ortiz, Octavio. "Castellanos Figueroa, Rosario. 1925–1974." In his *Diccionario biográfico de Chiapas*, 33–38. Mexico City: Costa-Amic Editor, 1977.

Holm, Susan Fleming. "Defamiliarization in the Poetry of Rosario Castellanos." *Third Woman* 3, nos. 1–2 (1986): 87–97.

———. "'But Then Face to Face': Approaches to the Poetry of Rosario Castellanos." *DAI* 47 (1986): 541a. [University of Kansas.]

Lagos-Pope, María Inés. "Individuo y sociedad en *Balún-Canán*." *Texto Crítico* 34–35 (1986): 81–92.

Leñero, Vicente. "El eterno femenino." *Excélsior*, 15 April 1976, 1-C, 6-C.

Lienhard, Martín. "La legitimación indígena en dos novelas centroamericanas." *Cuadernos Hispanoamericanos* 414 (1984): 110–120.

Lindstrom, Naomi. "Rosario Castellanos: Pioneer of Feminist Criticism." In Ahern and Vásquez, 65–73.

———. "Women's Expression and Narrative Technique in Rosario Castellanos' *In Darkness*." *Modern Language Studies* 13, no. 3 (Summer 1983): 71–80.

Lorenz, Gunter W. Interview. "Rosario Castellanos." In his *Diálogo con América Latina*, 186–211. Santiago de Chile: Ediciones Universitarias de Valparaiso, Editorial Pomaire, 1972.

MacDonald, Regina Harrison. "Rosario Castellanos: On Language." In Ahern and Vásquez, 41–64.

Maíz, Magdalena. "Una aproximación al paisaje cotidiano: Narrativa femenina mexicana." *Cuadernos de Aldeu* 1 (May–October 1983): 347–354.

Mejías Alonso, Almuneda. "La narrativa de Rosario Castellanos y el indigenismo." *Cuadernos Americanos* 260, no. 3 (1985): 204–217.

Mendoza, María Luisa. "Taladrada en el hilo de Rosario." *Excélsior*, 6 April 1958, 3.

Meyer, Doris, and Margarite Fernández Olmos, eds. *Introductory Essays*. Vol. 1 of *Contemporary Women Authors of Latin America*. 2 vols. Brooklyn: Brooklyn College Press, 1983.

Millán, María del Carmen. "Ciudad Real." *Revista de Bellas Artes* 18 (1974): 24–27.

———. "En torno a *Oficio de tinieblas*." *Anuario de Letras* 3 (1963): 287–299.

Miller, Beth. "Historia y ficción en *Oficio de tinieblas* de Castellanos: Un enfoque gramsciano." In Forster y Ortega, 391–406.

———. "The Poetry of Rosario Castellanos: Tone and Tenor." In Ahern and Vásquez, 75–83.

———. *Rosario Castellanos: Una conciencia feminista en México*. Tuxtla Gutiérrez, Chiapas: Universidad Autónoma de Chiapas, 1983.

————. "Rosario Castellanos' Guests in August: Critical Realism and the Provincial Middle Class." *Latin American Literary Review* 7, no. 14 (1979): 5–19.

Miller, Martha LaFollette. "A Semiotic Analysis of Three Poems by Rosario Castellanos." *Revista/Review Interamericana* 12, no. 1 (1982): 77–86.

Miller, Yvette. "El temario poético de Rosario Castellanos." *Hispámerica* 10, no. 29 (1981): 107–115.

"Murió la escritora Rosario Castellanos." *Excélsior*, 8 August 1974, 1, 13a.

Nelson, Esther W. "Point of View in Selected Poems by Rosario Castellanos." *Revista/Review Interamericana* 12, no. 1 (1982): 56–64.

Nigro, Kirsten F. "Rosario Castellanos's Debunking of the Eternal Feminine." *Journal of Spanish Studies: Twentieth Century* 8 (1980): 89–102.

Oberfield, Vicky. "El eterno femenino de Rosario Castellanos." *El Sol de México*, 9 January 1976, D1–D2.

Ocampo, Aurora M. "Debe haber otro modo de ser humano y libre: Rosario Castellanos." *Cuadernos Americanos* 250, no. 5 (1983): 199–212.

————. "Rosario Castellanos y la mujer mexicana." *La Palabra y el Hombre* 53 (1985): 101–108.

O'Quinn, Kathleen. "*Tablero de damas* and *Álbum de familia*: Farces on Women Writers." In Ahern and Vásquez, 99–105.

Ortiz, Raúl. Presentación. *El Eterno Femenino*, by Rosario Castellanos, 7–17. Mexico City: Fondo de Cultura Económica, 1975.

Pacheco, José Emilio. "La Palabra." Nota preliminar. *El uso de la palabra*, by Rosario Castellanos, 7–13. Mexico City: Ediciones Excélsior-Crónicas, 1974.

Paley de Francescato, Martha. "Transgresión y aperturas en los cuentos de Rosario Castellanos." In Ahern and Vásquez, 115–120.

————. "Women in Latin America: Their Role as Writers and Their Image in Fiction." In *Women in Latin America: A Symposium*. Program in Latin American Studies, Occasional Papers, 1:1–14. Amherst: University of Massachusetts International Studies Program, 1979.

Palley, Julian. Introduction to *Meditación en el umbral: Antología poética*, by Rosario Castellanos, 33–72. Comp. Julian Palley. Mexico City: Fondo de Cultura Económico, 1985. "Rosario Castellanos: Eros and Ethos." In *Meditation on the Threshold: A Bilingual Anthology of Poetry by Rosario Castellanos*, 21–46. Trans. Julian Palley. Tempe, Ariz.: Bilingual Review Press/Editorial Bilingüe, 1988.

Peña, Margarta. "La 'Lamentación de Dido' de Rosario Castellanos." In her *Entrelíneas*, 122–126. Difusión Cultural, Textos de Humanidades, 34. Mexico City: Universidad Nacional Autónoma de México, 1983.

————. "*Oficio de tinieblas* o 'La vecindad del cielo.'" In her *Entrelíneas*, 127–138.

Pérez, Laura Lee Crumley de. "*Balún Canán* y la construcción narrativa de una cosmovisión indígena." *Revista Iberoamericana* 50 (1984): 491–503.

———. "La significación del mito indígena en la estructura narrativa de *Balún-Canán*." *DAI* 45 (1984): 853a–854a. [University of Pittsburgh.]

Ponce, Margarita Cadena. "La ironía en la poesía de Rosario Castellanos." *DAI* 42 (1981): 2697a. [University of Southern California.]

Poniatowska, Elena. Prologue to *Meditación en el umbral: Antología poética*, by Rosario Castellanos, 7–27. Comp. Julian Palley. Mexico City: Fondo de Cultura Económica, 1985.

———. "Rosario Castellanos: ¡Vida, nada te debo!" In her *¡Ay vida, no me mereces!*, 45–132. Mexico City: Editorial Joaquín Mortiz, 1985.

Portal, Marta. "*Oficio de tinieblas*." In her *Proceso narrativo de la revolución mexicana*, 212–221. Madrid: Ediciones Cultura Hispánica, 1977.

Rama, Angel. "La generación hispanoamericana de medio siglo, una generación creadora, con un poema 'Toma de conciencia.'" *Marcha* [Montevideo] 24, no. 1217 (7 August 1964): 1–3.

Rebolledo, Tey Diana. "The Wind and the Tree: A Structural Analysis of the Poetry of Rosario Castellanos." *DAI* 40 (1979): 5070a. [University of Arizona.]

Reyes Nevares, Beatriz. *Rosario Castellanos*. Mexico City: Depto. Editorial, Secretaría de la Presidencia, 1976.

Riano, R. Mario E. "Como escribió Rosario Castellanos su obra póstuma 'El eterno femenino.'" *El Sol de México*, 2 March 1976.

Rivero, Eliana S. "Paradigma de la poética femenina hispanoamericana y su evolución: Rosario Castellanos." In Forster and Ortega, 391–406.

———. "Visión social y feminista en la obra poética de Rosario Castellanos." In Ahern and Vásquez, 85–97.

Robles, Martha. "Tres mujeres en la literatura: Rosario Castellanos, Elena Garro, Inés Arredondo." *Cuadernos Americanos* 246, no. 1 (1983): 223–235.

Rodríguez-Peralta, Phyllis. "Images of Women in Rosario Castellanos' Prose." *Latin American Literary Review* 6, no. 11 (1977): 68–80.

Rojas, Lourdes. "La indagación desmitificadora en la poesía de Rosario Castellanos." *Revista/Review Interamericana* 12, no. 1 (1982): 65–76.

Román Riefkohl, Raúl. "Estructura polisémica en 'Lecturas tempranas' de Rosario Castellanos." *Romance Notes* 23, no. 2 (1982): 115–118.

Scherr, Raquel Lorraine. "A Voice against Silence: Feminist Poetics in the Early Works of Rosario Castellanos." *DAI* 41 (1980): 238a. [University of California, Berkeley.]

Schlau, Stacey. "Conformity and Resistance to Enclosure: Female Voices in Rosario Castellanos' *Oficio de tinieblas*." *Latin American Literary Review* 12, no. 24 (1984): 45–57.

Schwartz, Perla. *Rosario Castellanos: Mujer que supo latín*. Mexico City: Editorial Katún, 1984.

Selva, Mauricio de la. Review of *Materia memorable*. *Cuadernos Americanos* 31, no. 6 (1972): 255–262.

¡Siempre! 1105 (28 August 1974). [Issue dedicated to R.C.]

Sommers, Joseph. *After the Storm: Landmarks of the Modern Mexican Novel*, 167–170. Albuquerque: University of New Mexico Press, 1968.

———. "El ciclo de Chiapas: Nueva corriente literaria." *Cuadernos Americanos* 133, no. 2 (1964): 246–261.

———. "Forma e ideología en *Oficio de tinieblas* de Rosario Castellanos." *Revista de Crítica Literaria Latinoamericana* 7–8 (1978): 73–91.

———. "Literatura e historia: Las contradicciones ideológicas de la ficción indigenista." *Revista de Crítica Literaria Latinoamericana* 5, no. 10 (1979): 9–39.

Steele, Cynthia. "The Fiction of National Formation: The Indigenista Novels of James Fenimore Cooper and Rosario Castellanos." In *Reinventing the Americas: Comparative Studies of Literature of the United States and Spanish America*, ed. Bell Gale Chevigny and Gario Laguardia, 60–67. New York: Cambridge University Press, 1986.

Stoll, Anita K. "'Arthur Smith salva su alma': Rosario Castellanos and Social Protest." *Crítica Hispánica* 7, no. 2 (1985): 141–147.

———. "Un analisis de 'Misterios gozosos' por Rosario Castellanos." *Explicación de textos literarios* 16, no. 1 (1988): 48–64.

Vargas, Elizabeth. Interview. "Emma Teresa: Rosario nos incita a inventarnos." *El Sol de México*, 25 April 1976.

Vásquez, Mary Seale. "Rosario Castellanos: Image and Idea." In Ahern and Vásquez, 15–40.

Washington, Thomas. "The Narrative Works of Rosario Castellanos: In Search of History—Confrontations with Myth." *DAI* 43 (1982): 1162a. [University of Minnesota.]

POETRY

With the other
humanity, dialogue, poetry begin.
                    —Rosario Castellanos
                    "You Are Not Poetry"

SILENCE NEAR AN ANCIENT STONE

I'm a woman sitting here with all my words intact
like a basket of green fruit.

The fragments
of a thousand ancient and defeated gods
seek and bind each other in my blood, straining
to rebuild their statue.
From their shattered mouths
a song struggles to rise to mine,
an aroma of burnt resin, some gesture
of a mysterious carved stone.
But I am oblivion, betrayal,
the shell that did not hold an echo
from even the smallest wave in the sea.
I do not watch the submerged temples;
I watch only the trees moving their vast shadows
over the ruins, biting the passing wind
with acid teeth.
And the signs close beneath my eyes like
a flower under the awkward fingers of the blind.
Yet I know: behind
my body another body crouches,
and around me many breaths
cross furtively
like nocturnal animals in the jungle.
I know that in some place,
like cactus in the desert,
a clustered heart of thorns, awaits a name
as the cactus does the rain.
But I know only a few words
in the language or the stone
beneath which they buried my ancestor alive.

M.A.
El rescate del mundo (1952)

TO A TINY MAYAN BADGER

(In the Tuxtla Archaeological Museum)

Covering up your laughter
with your hand
you come hopping down the centuries
in grace and stone.

Let the dark walls that enclose you
tumble down!
Receive the lap
of your mother the earth.

On the wind, on the wind
a happy jingling and
may your childhood join
the children's round.

M.A.
El rescate del mundo (1952)

THE OTHER

Why utter the names of gods or stars,
foam of an invisible ocean,
pollen of the most remote gardens?
If life hurts, if each day breaks
clawing at our gut, if each night falls
convulsed, murdered.
If the hurt in someone else hurts us, in a man
we don't know, who is
present always and is the victim
and the enemy and love and all
we need to be whole.
Never say darkness is yours,
don't gulp down joy.
Look around you: there is the other, always the other.
He breathes what chokes you,
He eats your hunger.
He dies with the purest half of your death.

M.A.
Al pie de la letra (1959)

MONOLOGUE OF A FOREIGN WOMAN

I came from far away. I've forgotten my own country
and I no longer understand the language they
use there for trade or work.
I've reached the mineral muteness of a statue.
Sloth, scorn, and something
I can't distinguish have defended me
from this language, that heavy jewel-studded
velvet that people where I live
use to cover their rags.

This land, like that other one of my childhood,
still bears on her face
a slave's brand,
burned in by fire, injustice, and murder.
As a girl I slept to the hoarse crooning
of a black dove: a conquered race.
I hid beneath the blankets
because a huge animal
crouched out there in the dark, hungry
but as patient as stone.
Compared to him, what's an ocean, a catastrophe,
or the bolt of love
or joy that annihilates us?

I mean
that I had to grow up fast
(before terror devoured me),
go away, keep a firm hand
on things and run my life.

I was still very young
when I spit on places the mob held sacred.
In crowds I was like a dog
that offends with its mange and copulation,
its startling bark in the midst
of a ritual or major ceremony.

So youth,
although serious, was not entirely fatal.
I recovered, healed, and learned to gauge
the pulse of success, prestige,
honor, wealth, with a clever hand.
I possessed what the mediocre envy, the victors
dispute, but only one carries off.
It was mine but it was like eating foam
or passing my hand across the back of the wind.

Supreme pride is supreme renunciation.
I refused to become
a dead star
that takes on borrowed light to come alive.
Without a name or memories
I spin in spectral nakedness
in a brief domestic orbit.

But I still simmer
in the turbid imagination of others.
My presence has brought
a salty gust of adventure
to even this sleepy inland city.

When men look at me they remember that fate
is the great hurricane that splits branches,
uproots tall trees,
imposing merciless cosmic law
—above and beyond the meanness of humankind—
throughout its empire.

The women pick up my scent from afar, dreaming,
like draft animals when they smell
the brutal bolt of the storm.
For the elders
I fulfill that passive role
of the generator of legends.

At midnight I open wide the windows so anyone
keeping watch at night, meditating on death,

suffering the pangs of guilt,
or even the adolescent
(a burning pillow under his brow)
can question darkness through my being.

Enough. I've kept quiet more than I've told.
High mountain sun has tanned my hand
and on my fourth finger, "that points to the heart,"
as they say here,
I wear a golden ring with a carved seal.

A ring used
to identify corpses.

M.A.
Al pie de la letra (1959)

ROUTINE

There's no heaven for love, love, just today,
and this sad strand falling out
when you comb your hair in front of a mirror;
crossing those long tunnels
panting and gasping;
eyeless walls,
a hole that echoes
some hidden garbled voice.

There's no truce for love, love. Night
does not suddenly become breathable.
When a star breaks its chains
it zigzags madly and disappears,
but the law never loosens its talons.
You meet in the dark. A kiss mingles
the taste of tears.
And your embrace encircles
memories of that orphanhood, that death.

M.A.
Lívida luz (1960)

PRESENCE

Some day I'll know. This body that has been
my hostel, my prison, my hospital, is my grave.

Whatever I have joined in a worry,
a pain, a memory,
will desert in search of water, leaf,
original spore, inert matter, and stone.

This knot that I was (bound up in
rage, betrayal, hope,
sudden insight, surrender,
hunger, cries of fear and helplessness,
joy flashing in the shadows,
and words, and love and love and loves)
the years will cut through.

No one will see the ruin. Nobody
will pick up the unfinished page.

Among this handful of disperse
acts, flung to chance,
not one stands out as a precious pearl.

And yet, brother, lover, child,
friend, ancestor,
there is no aloneness, there is no death,
although I forget and though I end.

Mankind, where you are, where you live,
we all abide.

M.A.
Lívida luz (1960)

PASSAGE

I

A blind girl, I touched my face with my hands,
not in order to see but to blot out the line
where the profile says "tomorrow," where
the chin raises its bone opposing death.

With that gesture,
sorrow, presence, memory faded.

(No, I wasn't dying. I never learned
to blot out the name Rosario.)

II

I never knew the law, that constellation
under whose signs my parents conceived me.
I never learned my vegetable destiny, my name
that ends at my fingertips, so
I tried to go one step beyond
where fish drown, where stone shatters.

Beyond the limits. Here,
depth or heights, a place
uninhabitable for my species.

III

I climbed to where man
moved his chess pieces
into a transparent atmosphere of eagles.

(I should have covered my face with a veil
so no one could see this color of jungle
—splendor and catastrophe—
that is still with me.)

M.A.
Materia memorable (1969)

CONSCIOUSNESS

At midnight the wary sentinel
shouts, "Who goes there?" and someone—I, yes, me,
not that mute over there—
ought to answer for herself, for others.

But I'm barely awake and moreover
I don't know their password.

Irritable, sarcastic, shrugging my shoulders
as though it didn't matter, I say that
I only know that I survive
the minor daily tragedies:
a broken fingernail, a spot on the tablecloth,
a run in my stocking,
the balloon that slips out of my son's hands.

I ponder this and don't die. Not because I'm strong
but because I don't understand if what is happening is serious,
irreversible, significant,
or if in some mysterious way I'm trapped
in the snare of events.

The fact is that, still sleepy,
I get up, take a bath and, humming along,
think about other things.

I have breakfast and calmly and soberly read the news
about the old miser whose murderers
slashed open his guts looking for the coins
he had hidden in his stomach.

No, I touch myself and I can't feel the wounds.
I'm still a woman alone.

I drink my coffee and my hand
doesn't tremble when I turn the page,
and there, crouched down in a faraway rice paddy,
shivering with cold and terrified
of an enemy who is also hiding and shivering,
I find a man who is different from me

in color and language but
equal in the lightning illuminating this moment
in which he, his adversary, and I, who can't see them,
come together: we are one single being
and the universe breathes in us.

Darling, sometimes you come to visit me,
stretch out your hand,
or just gaze charitably on how old I'm getting.
You aren't sitting any closer than that man
in the rice paddy or the one long ago
(I can't even remember where)
who gave me a drink of fresh water
on a thirsty, stormy day.
Because now I finally know that I am more than just
a person, a body, and a niche for a name.

I am a wide patio, a great open house,
a memory.

You remain there, the image of a dead man,
the face of someone who left with an easy phrase
on his lips, promising to return.

The members of my tribe and other strangers,
even some animals whose innocence I cherish,
creep close to me at night
as to a bonfire in an open field.

In the midst of this circle of presences
I am myself: matter
that burns, diffuses heat and light.
I snap out the reply, rejoicing: "All's well!"

M. A.
Materia memorable (1969)

METAMORPHOSIS OF THE SORCERESS

For Remedios Varo

Being born, issuing from the mother like the river
that tumbling, thrusting foreign matter, propels
its volume to the end without seeing the sky,
the tree on the bank,
or giving a loving polish to the pebble in its belly.

We call our living vertigo,
devouring whirlpool, algae that traps
whatever tries to rise to the surface.
Between the roaring and its extinction
there is only turbid mire, dark fish, and ceaseless pulse.

So it is for all of us who flow
into the sea before achieving an identity.

For all of us. Not for her. She too was made of water
and lingered in reflected eddies.

What forms we glimpse through her transparency!
Endless corridors, desolate palaces,
complex machinery
transforming the universe
into beauty, into order, into shining laws.
Woman, spinning bolls of light, weaving
nets to catch the stars.

Woman, holding her masks, playing at self-deception
and deceiving others,
but when she saw her own true face
it was a flower of pale
withered petals: love, absence, and death.
On its corolla
a faint scar.

Because of all she knew she was obedient and sad
and when she departed down that street
—the one she knew so well—of good-byes,
beautiful creatures came out to bid her farewell,

the ones she had rescued from chaos, shadow, and
contradiction and made live
in the magic atmosphere her spirit created.

M.A.
Materia memorable (1969)

Note: Remedios Varo, 1913–1963, surrealist painter born in Spain who immigrated
to Mexico in 1941. Varo's paintings are distinctive for their cosmic visions of feminine figures among whimsical beings and objects that make up the creative forces
that propel the universe.

CHESS

Because we were friends and sometimes loved each other,
perhaps to add one more tie
to the many that already bound us,
we decided to play games of the mind.

We set up a board between us:
equally divided into pieces, values,
and possible moves.
We learned the rules, we swore to respect them,
and the match began.

We've been sitting here for centuries, meditating
ferociously
how to deal the one last blow that will finally
annihilate the other one forever.

M.A.
En la tierra de en medio, in *Poesía no eres tú* (1972)

BRIEF CHRONICLE

Between the two of us there was
that which exists between two people who love each other:
blood of a torn hymen. (Can you imagine?
A virgin at thirty! And a poetess! Knock on wood.)
The menstrual hemorrhage in which a child says
yes or no to life.

Then the vein
—mine or someone else's, what does it matter—where the
suicide slash cut just a bit or just enough
to become a tag in the morgue.

Perhaps there were also other fluids:
the sweat of work, of pleasure,
the greenish secretion of rage,
semen, saliva, tears.

Nothing, in short, that a good bath won't wash out.
I wonder
what I'll write our story with then?
With ink? Ah, mere ink
flows from such alien springs.

M.A.
En la tierra de en medio, in *Poesía no eres tú* (1972)

MALINCHE

From the throne of command my mother declared: "He is dead."

And threw herself
into another's arms; the usurper and stepfather
who did not sustain her with the respect
a servant renders to the majesty of a queen
but groveled in their mutual shame
of lovers and accomplices.

From the Plaza of Exchange
my mother announced: "She is dead."

The scale balanced for an instant,
the chocolate bean lay motionless in the bin,
the sun remained at mid-point in the sky
awaiting the sign
which shot like an arrow,
became the sharp wail of the mourners.

"The bloom of many petals was deflowered,
perfume evaporated,
torch flame burned out.

A girl returns to scratch up the earth
in the place
where the midwife buried her umbilicus.

She returns to the Place of Those Who Once Lived.

She recognizes her father, assassinated,
ah, by poison, a dagger,
a snare before his feet, a noose.

They take each other by the hand and walk,
disappearing into the fog."

Thus the wailing and lamentation
over an anonymous body: a corpse
that was not mine because I was sold
to the merchants, on my way as a slave,
a nobody, into exile.

Cast out, expelled
from the kingdom, the palace, and the warm belly
of the woman who bore me in legitimate marriage bed
who hated me because I was her equal
in stature and in rank,
who saw herself in me and hating her image
dashed the mirror against the ground.

I advance toward destiny in chains
leaving behind all that I can still hear,
the funereal murmurs with which I am buried.

And the voice of my mother in tears—in tears!
She who decrees my death!

M.A.
En la tierra de en medio, in *Poesía no eres tú* (1972)

Note: Malinche was the daughter of an Aztec ruler whose family sold her into
slavery to Mayan-speaking peoples to the south. Given as a present to Hernán Cortés,
she became his interpreter and mistress, playing a key role in the rapid Spanish
conquest of Mexico. Her name has become a symbol of betrayal to foreign interests,
ignoring her own original betrayal by her mother.

MEMORANDUM ON TLATELOLCO

Darkness engenders violence
and violence invokes darkness
to jell in crime.

That is why October the second waited until night
so that no one saw the hand that clutched
the weapon, but only its sequel of lightning.

And in that brief livid light, who is it? Who is killing?
Who are in agony, who are dying?
Who are the ones fleeing without shoes?
The ones who will end up in the jailpens?
The ones who are rotting in hospitals?
The ones who keep silent forever, out of fear?

Who? Who are they? No one. The next day, no one.

The plaza dawned swept clean; the newspapers
featured the weather report
and on television, over the radio, at the movies,
there was not a single change of program,
no interrupting news flash or even a
moment of silence at the banquet.
(The banquet continued.)

Don't search for what is not there: clues, corpses.
Everything has been rendered as offering to a goddess:
to the Devourer of Excrement.

Don't comb through the files because nothing has been entered
on the books.

Ah, violence invokes darkness
because darkness engenders dream
and we can sleep dreaming that we can dream.

But here I touch an open wound: my memory.
It hurts, therefore it is true. It bleeds real blood.
Yet if I call it mine I betray them all.

I remember, we remember.

This is our way of helping dawn to break
upon so many stained consciences,
upon an irate text, upon an open grate,
upon the face shielded behind the mask.

I remember, we must remember
until justice be done among us.

M.A.
En la tierra de en medio, in *Poesía no eres tú* (1972)

Note: Tlatelolco refers to a section of Mexico City and its Plaza of the Three Cultures, where on October 2, 1968, Mexican government troops opened fire on hundreds of unarmed student protesters, killing more than four hundred of them, leaving the square strewn with the shoes of the fleeing survivors or the dead. No official news of the events was transmitted as the government tried to cover it up.

SELF-PORTRAIT

I'm a *señora*, a form of address
difficult to obtain in my case, and more useful
in dealing with others than a title conferred
upon me by any academy.

So I brandish my trophy and repeat:
I'm a *señora*. Fat or skinny
according to the position of the stars,
the glandular cycles,
and other phenomena I don't understand.

Blonde, if I select a blonde wig,
otherwise brunette.
(Actually, my hair is getting gray, gray.)

I'm rather ugly. It all depends on
the hand that applies the makeup.

My appearance has changed with time
—although not as much as Weininger says
that the appearance of a genius changes—I'm mediocre.
For one thing this saves me from enemies,
for another it assures me the devotion
of an admirer and the friendship
of men who telephone,
send long letters of congratulations,
slowly sip scotch on the rocks,
and chat about politics and literature.

Women friends . . . hummm, sometimes, rarely,
and in very small doses.
I usually avoid mirrors.
They'd only say the same thing: that I don't dress very well
and that I'm ridiculous
when I try to flirt with someone.

I'm the mother of Gabriel, as you already know, that boy
who will someday become an implacable judge
and perhaps even an executioner.
Meanwhile I love him.

I write. This poem. And another and another.
I deliver the professorial lecture,
contribute to journals in my field,
and once a week a newspaper publishes my column.

I live opposite the Park, but I rarely
ever look at it. I never cross
the street that separates it from me
or walk out, breathe fresh air, or caress
the wrinkled bark of the trees.

I know I should listen to music
but I frequently avoid it. I know
I should see paintings
but I never go to exhibitions,
theater debuts, or film series.

I prefer to stay here, just like now, reading,
or, when I turn out the light, musing a bit
about just anything and other duties.

I suffer more out of habit or tradition
or not to differ from my fellow humans,
rather than for any of the right reasons.

I'd be happy if I knew how.
I mean, if they had taught me the gestures,
the small talk, etiquette.

Instead they taught me how to cry. But crying in me
is a broken-down mechanism;
I don't cry at funerals,
on sublime occasions, or when disaster strikes.

I cry when I burn the rice or when I lose
the latest tax receipt.

M.A.
En la tierra de en medio, in *Poesía no eres tú* (1972)

SPEAKING OF GABRIEL

Like all guests my son disturbed me
occupying a place that was mine,
there at the wrong time,
making me split each mouthful in two.

Ugly, sick, bored,
I felt him grow at my expense,
rob my blood of its color, add
a secret weight and volume
to my condition upon this earth.

His body begged mine for birth, to yield to his,
to give him a place in the world,
the provision of time necessary for his history.

I consented. And when he departed through that wound,
through that unloosening hemorrhage,
the last of my aloneness, of my looking from behind a glass
flowed out.

I remained open, manifest
to visitations, to wind, to presence.

M.A.
En la tierra de en medio, in *Poesía no eres tú* (1972)

HOME ECONOMICS

This is the golden rule, the secret of order:
a place for everything
and everything in its place.
That's how I've fixed my house.

An impeccable bookstand:
one shelf for the novels,
another for essays,
and poetry on all the others.

If you open a closet it smells of lavender
and you can't confuse the linen tablecloths
with the ones for daily use.

There's also the set of china for special occasions
and the other one that's used, broken, replaced
and is never complete.

The clothes are in the right drawers
and the furniture is properly arranged
to make the room harmonious.

Naturally the tops
(of everything) are polished and clean.
And of course
dust isn't hiding in the corners.

But there are some things
I just put down here or there
or tossed into the place for catchalls.

A few things. A cry, for example,
that was never cried,
a distracting nostalgia,
an ache, a pain whose name was blotted out,
a vow never kept, an anguish
that evaporated like perfume in
a partially closed bottle.

And remnants of time lost anywhere.

This discourages me. I always say, tomorrow . . .
and then forget. And proudly show company
a room that shines with the golden rule
my mother gave me.

M.A.
En la tierra de en medio, in *Poesía no eres tú* (1972)

LEARNING ABOUT THINGS

They taught me things all wrong,
the ones who teach things:
my parents, the teacher, the priest.
You have to be a good girl, they told me.

It's enough to be good. Because the good person
gets a piece of candy, a medal, all the love, and heaven, too.

And it's very easy to be good. All you have to do is lower
your eyelids
in order not to see or judge what others do
because it does not pertain to you.

You just don't have to open your mouth not to protest
when someone shoves you because they didn't
mean to hurt you or
they couldn't help it or
because God is testing the mettle of your soul.

But, anyhow, when something bad does happen to you
you must accept it, even be grateful for it
but not return it. And don't ask why.
Because good people
are not curious.

And you have to give. If you own a cape, cut it in two
and give one-half to someone else
—even though that someone else may very well be
a collector of other halves of capes.
That's his business and your right hand must ignore
what your left hand . . . etc., etc.

And you must turn both cheeks. Ah, yes.

They won't always be blows.

It may be a bouquet of flowers that gives you
hay fever. Or the seafood that gives
you an allergy.
Sometimes praise,

which if not false cuts to the quick
and if it is false offends. Forgive,
because that is what good people do.

So I obeyed. For it is known that
obedience is the greatest virtue.

So the years went by
And I was that stumbling block
the absent-minded tripped over or, better yet,
a punching bag
the strong tried out their skill on.

Sometimes at cards I would deal a royal flush
but this cleverness rained indifferently
upon my friends
and my friends' friends,
I mean, my enemies.

So then I sat down to wait for the medal,
the piece of candy, and the smile, in short,
the prize in this world.

But all I saw was scorn for my own weakness,
hate for having been the tool
of others' malice.

Since when did I have the right to want to canonize
myself using others' vices or defects?
Why was I electing myself
the only chosen one?
Why was I that grain of sand in the works
that paralyzes every function?
Paralyzed, the doers were thinking.
And I was the efficient cause of their thoughts.
So for me there was only contempt.

Until I finally understood. So I made myself
into a well-oiled cog with which the machine
now turns perfectly.

A cog. I don't have
any specific name or any attribute
according to which I can classify myself
as any better or any worse or even more or less useful
than any of the other cogs.

If I should have to come up with a justification
for someone (and there isn't anyone—there never was any
witness for what happens)
I would say that I was in my place,
that I spun in the right direction at
the required speed and the required frequency.
That I never tried to get them to replace me
ahead of time or to allow me to continue once
I had been declared useless.

Before I finish I want to make it perfectly clear
that I did none of these things
out of humility. Since when are cogs humble?
Ridiculous! And that certainly
my behavior cannot be attributed to hope.

No, for a long time now heaven is a factor
that doesn't figure in my calculations.

Conformity? Perhaps. Which, in a cog, like me,
is not in any way a merit
but rather, at best, a condition.

M.A.
En la tierra de en medio, in *Poesía no eres tú* (1972)

POSTSCRIPT

My antagonist (who I always am) says to me:
Very simple. You've solved your problem
like Spinoza, *more geometricum*:
a place, a form to last,
and a function, perhaps, to fulfill.

But you've forgotten to say who supervises
the exact coincidence
between the cog and everything else: who signs
the official approval for the deeds. Who . . .
and, in any case, for what? Or why?

Well, obviously, you've never thought about this
but just about getting by
and getting on with living
as though it were necessary. In short, very feminine.

But for God's sake, aren't you ashamed of that crumb
you chew on so laboriously from one day to the next?
Don't you rebel against this circular task
of a mule around a grindstone? At least
put blinders on so you can't see that you're
always in the same place.

You know what? Metaphysics makes everything look good.
It's good adhesive, the same as ethics.
Don't belittle it: you're not so young anymore.
You'll need it, just like religion
or any other drug when
the real moment of dying comes.

M.A.
En la tierra de en medio, in *Poesía no eres tú* (1972)

YOU ARE NOT POETRY

Because if you existed
I too must exist. And that is a lie.

There is nothing more than us: the couple,
sexes conciliated in a child,
two heads together, but not looking at each other
(so that no one is turned into a mirror),
rather staring straight ahead, toward the other.

The other: mediator, judge, balance
between opposites, witness,
knot that binds up all that had broken.

The other, muteness begging a voice
from the speaker,
claiming an ear
from the listener.

The other. With the other
humanity, dialogue, poetry begin.

M.A.
En la tierra de en medio, in *Poesía no eres tú* (1972)

Note: In one of the famous *Rimas* by the ultraromantic nineteenth-century Spanish poet Gustavo Adolfo Bécquer the beloved asks, "*¿Qué es poesía?*" (What is poetry?), to which the poet in the next line responds to her, "*Poesía eres tú*" (You are poetry). This poem is Castellanos' counterreply to that same question.

RE: MUTILATIONS

One day you say: A fingernail. What's a fingernail?
A corneous excrescence
that needs to be cut off. So you cut it off.

You cut your hair to be in style
and there's no diminishment or pain.

Another day Shylock comes along and demands
a pound of flesh, from your flesh,
to pay the debt you owe him.

And afterward. Oh, afterward:
words they extract from your mouth,
skull trepanation
to extirpate that tumor that grows
when you think.

At the sight of the tax collector
you hand over your paralysis as an offering.

A casket is superfluous for your death
because you never kept anything of your own
that would not fit into a nutshell.

An epitaph? On what stone?
Not a single one is small enough to write
the letters that were left in your name.

M.A.
Otros poemas, in *Poesía no eres tú* (1972)

MEDITATION ON THE BRINK

No, it's not a solution
to throw oneself under a train like Tolstoy's Anna
or gulp down Madame Bovary's arsenic
or await on the barren heights of Avila the visit
of an angel with a fiery dart
before binding one's veil back over one's head
and starting to act.

Nor to deduce geometric laws by counting
the beams of one's solitary confinement cell
like Sor Juana did. It's not a solution
to write, while company arrives,
in the Austen family living room
or to shut oneself up in the attic
of some New England house
and dream, with the Dickinson's family Bible
under a spinster pillow.

There must be another way that's not named Sappho
or Mesalina or Mary of Egypt
or Magdalene or Clémence Isaure.

Another way to be human and free.

Another way to be.

M.A.
Otros poemas, in *Poesía no eres tú* (1972)

Note: Clémence Isaure was a fifteenth-century French woman whose name was synonymous with poetry celebrating the Virgin.

KINSEY REPORT

1

Am I a married woman? Yes, I mean
somebody made out a license in some office,
in time it turned yellow,
and there was a church ceremony
with sponsors and everything. And a banquet
and a whole week in Acapulco.

No, I can't wear my wedding dress anymore.
I've put on weight with the children
and the problems. As you can see, there's enough of those.

At a rate I can regularly predict
my husband makes use of his rights,
or, as he likes to say, he pays the conjugal
debt. Then he turns his back on me and snores.

I always resist. Out of decency.
But then I always give in. Out of obedience.

No, I don't like anything special.
Anyhow I'm not supposed to like it.
Because I'm a decent woman; and he's so gross!

Besides, I worry about getting pregnant again.
And the panting and the squeaking of the
bedsprings might wake up the children,
who won't go back to sleep until dawn.

2

Single, yes. But not a virgin. There was
my cousin when I was thirteen.
He was fourteen and we didn't know about anything.
I got very scared. I went to a doctor
who gave me something and nothing happened.

Now I'm a typist and sometimes I go out
with my men friends.

To the movies or to dinner. We end up spending
the night at a motel. My mother ignores it.

At first I was ashamed, it humiliated me
to have men look at me that way *afterward*.
To deny me the right to say no when I didn't feel like it
because they had me tagged as a whore.

I don't even charge. I can't even
get a few kicks in bed.

They're all s.o.b.'s. What do you mean, why do I do it?
Because I feel lonely. Or I get fed up.

Because, can't you see? I'm getting old.
I've lost hopes of getting married
and I'd rather have a couple of scars
than a memory like an empty hope chest.

3

Divorced. Because he was stupid like all the rest of them.
I know a lot of other men. That's why I can compare.

Once in a while I go on a fling
so I won't get hysterical.

But I have to set a good example
for my daughters. I don't want them
to repeat my luck.

4

I've offered this abstinence up to God.
Please, let's not go into details.

Sometimes I dream. Sometimes I wake up all wet
and it's really hard to tell my confessor that
I've sinned again because the flesh is weak.

I don't go to the movies anymore. The darkness
and the crowds in the elevators make it worse.

They thought I was going to go crazy
but a doctor is treating me. Massages.

And I'm feeling better.

5

You can just throw the indispensable sex
(as they like to believe themselves)
out into the garbage, the way we did.

My girlfriend and I get along very well.
The one who dominates is tender, in compensation;
and the one who obeys
is a flirt and gets her revenges.

We go to a lot of parties, we travel a lot,
and at the hotels we ask for
a single room with one bed.

They laugh at us but we laugh at them, too,
so we're even.

When we get bored with being by ourselves
one of us is going to get a baby from an agency.

No, not that way! From an artificial
insemination lab.

6

Miss. Yes, I insist, Miss.

I'm young. They say I'm not bad looking. Easy-going
disposition. And one day
my Prince will come, because I've prayed to Saint Anthony
to get him for me. Then
we'll be happy. Sweethearts forever.

What does it matter if we're poor? If he drinks
I'll cure him of it. If he chases women
I'm just going to keep myself always so attractive,
so attentive to his tastes, such a good housewife,
such a prolific mother,

and such a great cook
that he'll become faithful as a prize for my merits,
among which the greatest is patience.

We'll celebrate our golden wedding anniversary
with a solemn high mass
just like my parents and my husband's parents.

No, I've never had a boyfriend. No, none
yet. Tomorrow.

M.A.
Otros poemas, in *Poesía no eres tú* (1972)

LOOKING AT THE MONA LISA

(In the Louvre, naturally)

Are you laughing at me? You're right.
If I were Sor Juana
or La Malinche, or, not to depart from national folklore,
some incarnation of the Güera Rodríguez
(as you can see, extremes are my lot, just like Gide),
you would see me, perhaps, as one observes
a representative specimen
from some social sector of a Third World country.

But I'm only one of those dumb little tourist ladies,
one of those who gets a travel agency
to set up a tour for her—
and a monolingual to boot!—
who's come to contemplate you.

And you smile, mysteriously
as is your obligation. But I can read you.
That smile is mockery. It mocks me and every
one of us who believe that we believe that
culture is a liquid one imbibes at the source,
a special symptom one contracts
in certain contagious places, something
one acquires by osmosis.

M.A.
Viaje redondo, in *Poesía no eres tú* (1972)

Note: La Güera Rodríguez was the mistress of Augustín de Iturbide (1783–1823),
Mexican general in the struggle for independence from Spain and self-proclaimed
emperor of Mexico, 1822–1823.

NOBODYING

In the land of Descartes, close to the stove
—since it's snowing and I'm shivering—
I'm not thinking, because thinking is not my forte, and
I'm not feeling, because feeling is not my specialty;
I'm just staring and saying
(because a word is a stare):
What the devil am I doing here in the City of Lights
putting on the airs of a cultured and well-traveled woman
but simply postponing the execution of a
sentence that has been pronounced upon me?

The sentence that reads: "You don't exist."
It is signed by all those who use the royal
WE to sign: The One who is All;
the magistrates, the chancelleries,
the sovereign contracting parties, the
thirteen Aztec emperors, the legislative
and judicial powers, the list
of Viceroys, the Boxing Commission,
the decentralized institutes,
the United Newsboys Union, and . . .
and, solidarily, all the rest of my fellow citizens.

M.A.
Viaje redondo, in *Poesía no eres tú* (1972)

Note: The title in the Spanish text is *Ninguneo,* a Mexican term coined from the adjective and pronoun for "nobody, no one, nothing," referring to the act of verbally slighting, discounting, or putting down someone.

NAZARETH

Going down into the cave where the Archangel
made his announcement, I think
about Mary, that chosen vessel.

Like all vessels, fragile.
Like all vessels, too small
for the destiny poured into it.

M.A.
Viaje redondo, in *Poesía no eres tú* (1972)

SHORT FICTION

I'm a wide patio, a great open house,
a memory.
                              —Rosario Castellanos
                                 "Consciousness"

The Eagle

In his youth he acquired the profile of a bird of prey: eyes close together, receding forehead, and shaggy eyebrows. The stance of a fearless man: feet apart and firmly planted, massive shoulders, hips made for carrying a weapon. And, above all, the name: Héctor Villafuerte.

What was to be done with that seething in his head, in his blood, in his very being, living in a town like Ciudad Real? And a widow's son, besides.

The childhood home smells of quince, of incense. The pots bubble, the little pots of rump, the timid pots of stew upon the hearth. The starched petticoats rustle in the wind along the corridors and on the patios.

How incongruous Héctor looked in his altarboy's cassock! Twisting it into his waistband, he climbed trees, jumped over hedges, and got into wild scuffles with other little Indian urchins. A week later he had to return it in sorry shape to Father Domingo, who had been nurturing the hope of turning that unruly boy into an enthusiastic priest, a missionary with guts.

Héctor's schooldays were stormy: pranks in class, bad grades, and a boisterous final expulsion "for being the instigator of a riot that broke all the windows in his classroom [besides destroying doors, walls, and furniture]."

To learn a trade was a stigma for the family. They kept titles of nobility, signed by the king of Spain, in a large old chest, and over the front doorway was a coat of arms that time had erased. Poverty is no crime, but a vulgar job . . .

A kind of natural selection that separated Héctor from church, school, and work left him smoking arrogantly and spitting contemptuously in the streets with his friends. They led him to the squalid prostitute's bed, to the rough table of the barroom, and to the sordid atmosphere of smoke and artificial light in the pool halls.

Héctor hung around no-account musicians. Wherever the marimba was played, there he would be, helping to load and unload the instrument with the same care he would have given a dead body. His loud cheering became indispensable to those who were paying for the serenade. And at dawn he would fire shots into the air with someone else's pistol, his defiant impulses trusting the needless explosions—that untamed colt prematurely bridled by custom.

He acquired petty bits of knowledge: how a gamecock strikes, and which hunting dog is best. To be a gentleman, Héctor needed only money.

Héctor could not afford to be idle. His mother began pawning her jewels to free him from the dishonor of a gambling debt. Afterward, it was easy to part with paintings, dinnerware, and clothing. Pawnbrokers do not want old junk. They haggle, they hand money over reluctantly, and, as if to get even, tip with a harsh word and a warning that can hardly hide the smug inner smile at a piece of useless advice.

The widow struggled till the end to save the altar saints from her son's squandering, but when the altar was empty, the old woman lost her will to live. Her death was courteous: no surprise and no fuss. Distant relatives and charitable ladies took up a collection to pay for the funeral expenses.

In his first months of life as an orphan, Héctor became the compulsory patron of celebrations and fiestas. He kept a discreet distance in order to respect the mourning period, and from there he would watch the others eating or having fun. He would watch them with a distant look, because, in him, contempt was an attitude, not a state of mind.

When the knees of his pants began to shine disgracefully and when he had to step carefully to prevent his soles from completely detaching, Héctor thought it was time to settle down.

He announced his intentions everywhere. He let his status as available bachelor be known, sure that his wares were the kind that are always in demand. The women looked at him longingly and Héctor responded to all of them—equally, so as not to make a commitment—with the same smile of expectant cynicism and indifferent sensuality.

If only Héctor had a horse to streak down the cobblestoned streets, creating sparks of pride and rivalry. Patience. It will come. There will be a fine table, bills in his wallet, greetings of respect and humility from those who now shun him or look down upon him; a wife who must provide him with comfort and show him respect . . . It could be any girl. In the dark all broads look alike. Héctor would fulfill his duties as a husband, keeping her pregnant year after year. Between pregnancies and raising children, she would quietly keep her place.

But it so happens that women in Ciudad Real do not walk out and about the streets alone. Perhaps, if the choice were theirs, they would, but there are fathers, brothers, walls, and customs that protect them. And it is not simply a matter of suddenly pouncing like a wildcat. One's elders always win in the end, or they disinherit one.

Héctor's attempts at getting married did not succeed. The man wore out the sidewalks, whistled on street corners with the calculating air of a braggart, and ventured any one of a number of flattering remarks while passing in front of windows. The girls escaped him with a deafening slam of the shutters and behind the panes they made fun of Héctor's advances, perhaps a little sad that they could not take pleasure in them.

There was, however, one woman with no relatives, not even a dog to bark at her; only an older woman to keep up the house and appearances— but otherwise unattached. She was somewhat past her youth and already an old maid. She had a solemn frown, and lips that were gathered in bitter creases. No man had ever approached her, because, although she was known to be wealthy, she was better known as a miser.

The suitor figured that when a woman in Emelina Tovar's situation falls in love, she will open her hand. Getting her to fall in love with him will not be difficult; just wave a red cape in front of her and she will charge, blind with passion and longing.

Contrary to all of Héctor's calculations, Emelina did not charge. She watched her suitor frequenting her balconies and gathered her brows more tightly in a supreme effort of attention. That was all. Not even an impatient flutter or hopeful sigh in that spinster's shriveled bosom.

When Héctor managed to speak with her for the first time, Emelina listened to him, blinking as if a glaring light were bothering her. She did not know what to say to him. And by this silence, the suitor understood her acceptance.

The wedding was not what one would call lavish. A handsome bridegroom, yes, but without even the wherewithal to support a flea. A squandering nature, that he had in excess.

Holding tightly to Héctor's arm, Emelina walked down the aisle of the Church of Mercy (because she had made a vow to that Virgin, who had performed so many miracles, to get married in front of her altar). She was fearful, even though in the midst of this precarious triumph and at the end of a long and humiliating solitude her destiny had been brightened.

Emelina supported herself by making sweets. Insects were constantly buzzing around the backyard, where she had almond delights, candied citron, and pastries stretched out to dry in the sun. The work did not yield much, but a methodical and careful woman is able to save. Not enough to amass a fortune, but enough to meet an emergency, an illness, or hardship. And she would get plenty of these from this younger untamed husband of hers who was concerned only for his own comfort.

If Emelina had not been in love with Héctor, she would, perhaps, have been happy. But her love was an ever-open wound that bled at his slightest gesture or action. She wallowed in jealousy and despair in her frequently abandoned bed. A caged bird like Héctor is not content with birdseed alone. He breaks the cage open and flies away.

The new husband did not manage to see all this clearly. And his wife's money? He would turn trunks inside out, lift mattresses, and dig holes on the grounds. Nothing. That cunning woman had it well hidden, if she had it at all.

The certainty is that her savings were exhausted in the first few months and they had to resort to using the capital. All of it was used up on Héctor's carrousing, fancy meals, and lost bets.

It was over. Emelina could not withstand a difficult childbirth that her age had made impossible, and Héctor was left alone, miraculously free again. And flat broke.

What are friends for? Precisely for hard times such as these. Yesterday's merrymaking companion today has a responsible job and can recommend someone to the bigshots.

"Do you know how to write, Héctor? A little. Well, your handwriting is terrible and you can't spell. If only you had learned something when your mother, may she rest in peace, was paying for your schooling! But this is no time for regrets. Yes, you can read cursive. And math? Just average. I can't promise you anything but, well, we'll see what can be done."

A few months later Héctor Villafuerte held before him the nomination for city clerk in the town of Tenejapa.

A wretched town! The town hall, the parish church, and a few houses are made of adobe. The rest are huts of plaited cane and mud. Mud in the roads, undergrowth, open fields beyond the first corner; there is garbage everywhere; farm animals and naked children roam freely.

"This is just where I pictured you!" said Héctor to himself. Nobody to talk to, all alone, since the ladinos[1] around here are nobodies, and the Indians aren't even people. They don't even understand Spanish. They hang their heads to say yes, master, yes, ma'am, yes, *ajwalil.*[2] They don't even raise them when they get drunk. Drink after drink. And they don't shout with joy or snort with pleasure. They go turning around like stones and as a result they just fall over. I don't want to mix with them, not with any of them. Because, as the saying goes, he who goes among wolves

---

1. White people or educated mestizos.
2. In Tzotzil, a Mayan language spoken in Chiapas, a term of address, meaning boss, master, protector.

learns to howl like one. There's no hope of my getting out of this rat trap. The miserable salary I earn goes for paying my board and for cleaning my clothes. There's not even a chance to make a deal. It looks like around here the only way to make a buck is in selling liquor. All the ladinos put their stands in the entrance way on holidays or market days. The Indians enter very courteously and stumble out drunk. You can't even walk, there are so many bodies sprawled in the streets. Maybe I'd earn more being a recruiter, but where would I get the money to get started?

City clerk. Pretty title! One might even think that Héctor was performing an important job, but he only took care of insignificant matters: stolen chickens, sheep, cows at best. Crimes of witchcraft and passion, drunken brawls, private vendettas in which people felt they had no right to interfere. But, ah, yes indeed, every single event required an officially registered report.

"What a stingy government this is!" Héctor complained to himself. They expect you to live on air. The dignity of the nomination means nothing to them because a city clerk should be respectable for these ignorant people. And who's going to take me seriously if I go around looking like a beggar? I have to work, eat, and sleep in the same room. And you'd be amazed at the furniture! A leather cot and a table and a few chairs made for looking but not touching. Even the town seal is so old it doesn't leave an imprint. And these miserable wretches want all their correspondence to bear this great big seal. What a nuisance!

After this soliloquy Héctor refused to continue writing up the documents. "There's no seal," he would say grudgingly to the Indians. "So, without a seal, whatever I write is worthless."

Silently, the delegation of "leaders" walked out. They stood awhile whispering in the corridor of the city hall and then returned to Héctor's office. The eldest of the group spoke: "We want to make sure, *ajwalil*, that it's true what you said about the seal coming to an end."

"What seal is that?" asked another old man humbly.

"It's the eagle," answered the clerk arrogantly.

The Indians understood. They had all seen its picture at one time or another on the national coat of arms. And they thought that its wings were meant to carry complaints and allegations to the feet of justice. And look how the town of Tenejapa was drowning in crimes among a backlog of documents that were now incapable of taking flight.

"How did the eagle come to an end?"

The questioning was taken up by everyone with the same astonishment that large-scale natural disasters create. Héctor Villafuerte shrugged his shoulders to avoid an answer, which, in any case, these ignorant Indians would not have understood.

"Can't you get another eagle?" someone cautiously proposed.

"Who's going to pay for it?" interrupted Héctor.

"That depends, *ajwalil*."

"How much does it cost?"

Héctor scratched his chin in order to calculate better. He wanted to impress the others with the value of the tools he used. He answered: "A thousand pesos."

The Indians looked at each other, frightened. And, as though the number possessed a stunning effect, a great silence filled the room. It was broken only by Héctor's outburst of laughter. "Well, how about that! You're dumbfounded, right? A thousand pesos."

"Isn't there a cheaper eagle?"

"What do you think, you ass of an Indian? That you're going to bargain just like you're buying a yard of cloth or a drink? The eagle isn't just any old thing; it's the *nahual*, the spirit of the government."

What a ridiculous conversation! If it dragged on it was due to Héctor's boredom and his insistence on maintaining the infallibility of his judgment.

"All right, *ajwalil*."

"Until tomorrow, *ajwalil*."

"Have a pleasant evening, *ajwalil*."

The Indians left. But the next day, early in the morning, they were there again.

"We want to file a petition, *ajwalil*."

"How dense you are! The petition is useless without the eagle seal."

"Doesn't the paper speak?"

"It doesn't speak."

"All right then, *ajwalil*."

"Good-bye, *ajwalil*."

The Indians left again. Not very far from the city hall they milled about outside, arguing.

"What are they scheming?" Héctor asked himself, worriedly. He had heard stories about ladinos whose homes they had burned, and whom they chased through the mountains brandishing their machetes.

But the "leaders" appeared to have peaceful intentions. Toward the end of the afternoon they dispersed.

The next day the group was back again, clearing their throats, not venturing to speak. Finally, one of them approached Héctor.

"How is the little bird this morning, *ajwalil?*"

"What little bird?" inquired Héctor, sourly.

"The one that goes on the paper."

"Oh, the eagle. I already told you; it's dead."

"But surely you have another one."

"I do not."

"Then where can you get one?"

"In Ciudad Real."

"When are you going?"

"When I damn well feel like it. And, besides, where will the dough come from?"

"How much are you going to want?"

The insistence of the Indians had already gone beyond stubbornness. It was a sign of real concern. Suddenly Héctor realized that the opportunity he had dreamt about for so long was right there to grab hold of by the tail. Casually, even though he could hardly contain the excitement that his revelation produced, he decreed, "I want five thousand pesos."

"You said one thousand the first time."

"That's a lie! Who should know more about this, you or me? It says here" (and feverishly, Héctor opened a random book in front of the Indian): "the eagle costs five thousand pesos."

The Indians were crestfallen. Without saying a word, they all left together to deliberate outside. Villafuerte watched them withdraw; he was worried.

If you're too greedy you could lose everything. I lost my self-control in asking for so much money. Where are these poor wretches going to get it? But, in the long run, what difference does it make to me? Let them work, let them sell themselves into hard labor on the coastal plantations, or ask for a loan, or dig up their pots of money. I'm not one to take pity on them. What a nuisance! As if I didn't know how generous they are with their shamans and fiesta celebrations for their saints; for that they'll throw away fistfuls of money. For the church, oh, yes, very generous: a three-priest mass, a jubilee. Why should the government get any less?

This line of thinking convinced Héctor that the purchase of the seal was indispensable, and the price he had put upon it, fair. He resolved not to compromise his decision.

But these Indians are stubborn. They come and go, harping on the same subject.

"How about two thousand pesos, *ajwalil?* We can't collect any more than that."

"What's the eagle for? My benefit?"

"We're very poor, master."

"Don't come crying to me, you vermin."

"How about three thousand pesos, sir?"

"I said five thousand."

They continued haggling mechanically. The Indians knew that in the end they would have to give in.

That night Héctor counted up his treasure by the light of a paraffin lamp. Old coins, kept for who knows how many centuries; ancient statues, inscriptions now illegible. The possessor's devotion had never allowed him to part with them even when faced with the anguish of misery, or pangs of hunger. And now they would be used to buy the picture of a bird.

Héctor went off to Ciudad Real followed by the convoy of "delegates." When he tired of riding his horse, his peons, or *tayacanes*, had his hand-carried chair ready. Héctor spent the most dangerous parts of the road on Indian shoulders.

The Indians yielded humbly to this demand. It was a role that would make them worthy of carrying the seal on the way back. Because, Villafuerte had lectured them, the seal is a very highly prized object. In order to keep it safe from thieves, one must travel under false pretenses. If they pretend that the trip has some other purpose, business for instance, nobody would bother them.

Thus, in Ciudad Real, Héctor bought huge quantities of merchandise: foodstuffs, candles, and, especially, liquor. Inside one of the many bundles that the Indians were carrying went the famous seal.

Back in Tenejapa, Héctor Villafuerte succeeded in finding a site on which to open his store. Those five thousand pesos (four thousand nine hundred and ninety, to be exact, for the seal had cost him ten) were the foundation of his fortune.

Héctor prospered. He was able to marry again, this time according to his taste. The girl was young, and submissive, and brought with her some livestock as a dowry. Héctor, however, did not give up his post as city clerk. It gave him prestige, influence, and authority in his relationships with other businessmen.

And, besides, seals don't last forever. The one that he was using was already showing signs of wear. The features of the eagle were already almost unrecognizable. It already looked like a blur.

Translated by Laura Carp Solomon
Ciudad Real (1960)

Three Knots in the Net

Águeda's birth turned out to be a disappointment—upsetting and at the same time gratifying a fulfilled prediction—among the members of the Sanromán family.

After Juliana's first three successive maternal failures, it was not only expected but also right that she give birth to a boy. But who can trust these women from just any part of town, with no breeding or pride? She had a female, and, as if that were not enough, the fastidious woman allowed herself the privilege of not conceiving again.

At their Sunday gatherings the Sanrománs, drowsy after a hearty meal, would sigh and ask, what is going to become of Esteban's beautiful cane fields, the enormous herds of cattle, the highland and lowland estates? They would fall into the hands of a stranger, if they should be so lucky, because Águeda, judging from appearances, was not going to be easy to marry off.

Esteban was not too concerned about his daughter's future. He just figured that the dowry he had set aside would have to be larger. After all, she was an only daughter, since bastards did not count. Juliana, on the other hand, had confidence that the girl would, in time, fill out. Furthermore, she would take it upon herself to make sure that Águeda resorted to all the feminine wiles. If she went to great lengths to take care of her appearance, take an interest in household matters, and appear lighthearted, she would not want for someone to take notice of her and marry her. After all, that is our destiny: marriage and death.

But, as Águeda was growing up, her parents found fewer and fewer points to support their illusions. Esteban's fortune dwindled to near extinction when the government redistributed the land and the Indians rose in rebellion, refusing to continue working for nothing. The state of his finances was neither unusual nor secret. Now he could certainly admit, unabashedly, that his daughter was turning out to be a bit strange.

Whom did she take after, dear Lord in Heaven?

During their sleepless nights, Esteban and Juliana, each from his or her own matrimonial brass bed, would go over accounts of their respective ancestors to get at the root of the matter, to find the explanation.

"Maybe it's that distant cousin of yours, the one from Tabasco, the one who went crazy."

"And what would you have expected from her? Carranza's troops raped her right in front of her fiancé and then finished him off with a bullet."

Disturbed, Juliana sighed. It was one of the tragedies that had darkened her youth, one in which she would like to have been heroine. The fact that her husband didn't understand her irritated her. To get back at him, she said, "And how about your great-grandmother? They say she used to sleep in a coffin that she had ordered for herself for when her time came."

"Mamá Gregoria was always well prepared."

"She certainly outdid herself."

"On the other hand, there are some who prefer to leave everything up to the gods so they don't have to think about tomorrow."

Juliana felt the indirect jab. Esteban had, of course, alluded to her mother, the widow who never knew how to add, poor thing, or save a cent. She had not even been capable of making good matches for her daughters. There was Juliana, for example, tied to a man twenty years her senior and twenty thousand times more cunning, with nothing left but his rich man's airs. And as for the other daughter . . .

As if their thoughts had converged by way of different routes, her husband would ask with feigned innocence, "Did they finally find out what caused your sister Elena's death?"

"They didn't poison her to get her inheritance, like they did yours."

What had begun in a tenuous whisper continued gathering the intensity and volume of a violent argument. The insults, recriminations, and reproaches bounced off the high roofs, thick walls, and expansive rooms of the houses of Comitán.

Águeda, in the next bedroom, would awaken with a start: "They're talking about me."

She could make out her father's voice: massive like his body, solemn like his footsteps, precisely aimed like the sharp point of the mahogany cane that would always hit its mark on the very spot where it came to rest. On the other hand, her mother's words were an impulsive stream. She gave the impression that nothing could contain her. And suddenly the wavering would begin, as if they were turning drawers inside out looking for something that they had already forgotten. Finally, a total silence would come over them.

What Águeda never knew was that what silenced her mother was not her husband's justifications, nor caution, but terror. Not of anger, not of punishment, not of retaliation, but the terror of reconciliation.

Águeda trembled, too, but from other terrors: terror of the dark where a ghost was always lurking, where a ferocious beast was always lying in wait. But, above all, she trembled at the terror of her parents' sudden voices that covered her with painful festering wounds; wounds of guilt, whose name she never precisely understood, a guilt that was within her bones rotting them, within her heart strangling it, within her head where it was the only echoing ring.

Guilt, moreover, without atonement. The child frequently dreamed that she had died and that her empty place was occupied by someone else, someone who really belonged there; that the gulp of air she had been stealing before now supplied strength to its rightful owner.

Upon awakening, she would never altogether regain the certainty of being alive, nor did she want to. She slipped noiselessly through the corridors—avoiding mirrors—and hid in the far end of the back patio. There she would stay until someone brusquely came to get her at mealtime.

In front of the adults there was no way to get her to speak, *because she was not there.*

As for Esteban and Juliana, they paid no attention to anything other than their own hostility and rancor. They sarcastically asked each other to pass the salt; they caustically thanked each other for the dessert. But they would not waste a single extra word in conversation.

Águeda would run from the dining room as soon as possible to find her favorite distant refuge. There in the late afternoon she would entertain herself twisting the necks of birds, who, as the sun began to set, would fly lower and more slowly until they were within the reach of preying hands. Afterwards, with the little cadaver hidden between her blouse and chest, Águeda would go into the garden and dig a shallow hole along the edge in which to bury it. On top of the refilled earth she would place a flower as a sign of mourning.

She also took pleasure in stripping lizards of their green skin covering. Beneath the fat and roughness appeared a whitish membrane almost transparent enough to observe the violent palpitations of its viscera. Águeda would patiently watch its rhythm diminish until it became still. Then she would carefully place the animal on a stone and set it free. The little lizard would remain immobile for an instant and then dash off to be lost in the bushes.

On one occasion Juliana caught the child in the act. Her first impulse was to rush at her impetuously and strike her, interrupting the cruel game. But a kind of ancestral veneration restrained her. Águeda is a Sanromán, she told herself. How could Juliana fight an immutable hierarchy? She's a Sanromán, she repeated, walking away. Therefore, whatever evil and compulsion she had within her was inherited from the former torturers of slaves and floggers of Indians. From herself, humble embroiderer of San Sebastián parish, Águeda had inherited nothing. Juliana breathed a sigh of strange relief, that of her own innocence.

The impunity made Águeda idle and rebellious. She didn't know where her parents' weakness toward her came from, but she had concluded that neither of the two would dare to give her an order or deny her a whim. They must feel sorry for me, I suppose. When I say something is so, they answer "yes, yes," just as they would to madmen or imbeciles.

Juliana once tried, through a game, to interest her in the household activities. Águeda, noticing that a trap had been set for her, answered, "That's servants' work."

Nevertheless, sometimes she lowered herself to water the plants, or swept out a corner until a sneezing fit made it impossible for her to finish the job. And the one time she went into the kitchen, she fainted from disgust at the sight of raw food.

When Juliana wanted to adorn her daughter with all the graces of young ladies, she ran up against a stubborn stupidity that could be considered no less than perverse. At the piano keyboard Águeda was incapable of distinguishing one note from another, and if at the beginning her fingers were clumsy, the whole lesson went badly. She sewed and unraveled pieces of cloth that never turned out to be anything useful. And as for her painting, it never went beyond scribbling on papers that were scornfully thrown away.

We mustn't ever leave her alone, Juliana reflected. But, for Águeda, friendship didn't come easily, either. Through her family and social class she had belonged to a certain select circle since birth. She was accepted. But they soon began to avoid her on one pretext or another. Why spend time with someone who got bored with every game? For she did not like making mudpies or changing dolls' diapers or gossiping with any of them.

Juliana had to resort to the young Indian nannies and bribe them in spite of the fact that they left at the slightest provocation. The fact was that they were frightened by the passive way that Águeda arranged for them to entertain her. Songs, dancing, stories, anything that could be watched from a distance and anything in which she did not specifically have to participate. But the poor little maids never knew at what point Águeda would turn on them and try to pull their ears because they had not answered some question of hers correctly.

This certainly goes beyond all limits, decided her mother. She must be in league with the devil.

And she went to consult with her spiritual leader.

The priest—a classic profile, stirring voice in the pulpit, the town's idol—advised her, "Bring her to me. We must tear out the roots that torment her. I myself will indoctrinate her."

Juliana enjoyed a fleeting moment of triumph. Her sisters-in-law seethed with envy. The priest would not have deigned to do this for anyone but Águeda.

With Father Ripalda's catechism in one hand and a ruler in the other, the classes began in the parish locutory. The questions were easy, quick, and mechanical. The answers should be likewise. But Águeda, after pondering with a wrinkled brow, would come out with a new question, applying the rule to a specific case where it became counterproductive, demanding that the nuances be well defined, to avoid mistakes, posing endless scruples.

The priest threw up his hands. The catechism was not explicit nor the rod just. He secretly called in Doña Juliana to tell her that her daughter's case was so unique that he did not dare administer the sacred host to her for fear of committing a sacrilege.

What should be done in the face of such a disgrace, which her sisters-in-law immediately took upon themselves to spread around town? Escape someplace where no one knew them or singled them out by poking pitiful fun at them. To Mexico City.

Once in the capital city, Juliana could not find any way to untie Águeda from her apron strings. Was she going to let her wander the streets so that, in her distraction, she would get run over by a car? Was she going to enroll her in a public school so that she would have to contend with a band of insolent scheming little boys? Because Águeda might be everything they thought, thank God, but she was not malicious.

So there was no alternative but to find a very decent, reputable, and, above all, expensive parochial school. Yes, the most expensive. That was the only guarantee.

When Esteban arrived in Mexico City, after liquidating his interests in Chiapas, he found his family already settled.

The surprise was unpleasant. The apartment that Juliana had rented was extremely small and the furniture secondhand. Furthermore, in order to compensate for school expenses, there were no servants.

Esteban consented to the questionable merits of each of Juliana's arrangements. However, he felt homesick for his hemp hammock on the porch, for space that he had never lacked until now, and air that was not thick with the smell of fried food and burnt garbage.

Águeda was the cause of this upheaval and it was not going to be easy for Esteban to forgive her. But when he saw her return from school in her gray uniform and heavy schoolbag, with, for the first time, an eager and wide-awake look on her face, he almost did not recognize her.

"She's getting very good grades," boasted Juliana. "Do you want to see them?"

Águeda was already opening her schoolbag when her father's negative gesture made her freeze. She stood there perplexed, looking at him. How incongruous it appeared to her, the face of this stranger, into whose arms she was about to throw herself! How ridiculous he was in his vest, his gold watch chain, his mahogany cane, and his dark greenish hat!

Without a word they went into the dining room. Juliana bustled about noisily in the kitchen and came in with a platter of steaming soup, stewed meat, and beans. Águeda hardly ate anything while Esteban picked at this and that, grumbling because it was not seasoned properly, or it was so hot it burned his tongue, or it was so cold he lost all sense of taste.

Juliana sat at the table until the end of the meal and placed her folded hands (red from lye and work) on the oilcloth that served as a tablecloth. Here, next to her were the two beings to whom she was bound by duty and closest kinship. As though by the light of a lightning bolt, she saw them, distant and alien. She had never understood them or even loved them. This last revelation disturbed her, and she silently recited a little prayer to exorcise it.

The days took on the pattern of an unvarying routine. Águeda and Juliana would get up early so that the girl would get to school on time. Around noon Esteban would dress up in the finest clothes in his closet and go downtown, where he would conduct some business, the vagueness of which he never bothered to explain. He had influential friends; it was only a matter of weeks before they would be sending in his nomination.

This version was valid only for a few days. After some long and fruitless delays Esteban decided to spend his mornings in a more pleasant place. He selected Alameda Park. He looked for a convenient bench and ceremoniously unfolded his newspaper. On certain occasions, such as the celebration of a particularly important event, Esteban would tap his feet in time to the fast rhythm of a bolero. Sometimes he chatted with another habitué of the park. He never let his partner in conversation overstep the bounds of comments on the weather or complaints about politics. In that way he kept his distance and his dignity, which he was losing little by little, because, first, he had to dispense with his cane, which was a nuisance on public transportation; later on, while he was dozing on the way home in the streetcar next to the window, a thief snatched his hat. As a precaution he hid his watch and chain so that the only shine on his vest was the shine of age and wear.

Juliana sniffed out an affair in these absences. "I wouldn't even tolerate that from the Holy Father himself," she would repeat, furiously scrubbing the dinner dishes.

At night, on the most trivial pretext, the fights began. Torrents of vulgar words and vile adjectives would flow from her mouth. Águeda would calculate the time it would take for the anger to subside and repentance to take its place. Esteban accelerated this period by not responding to any of the accusations, hiding behind the wall of the newspaper's classified section.

Already dawn (Juliana suffered from insomnia) she cautiously slipped to her husband's bed to ask his forgiveness. Esteban turned toward the wall and, almost asleep, repeated several times: too late . . . too late.

This was the beginning of the silence. The three of them were always absorbed in their own thoughts. No one had anything to share with anyone else.

At the beginning Juliana thought that taking on the household tasks would only be temporary. But Esteban considered this arrangement to be satisfactory, and permanent. He liked seeing her wax the floor, clean the windows, and make the beds, from a special easy chair he had acquired for his exclusive use.

Now she's making up for the years of idleness in Comitán. After all, what would she have become without my name or my money, except a maid?

His money. With his money he had at one time acquired youth, beauty, and a semblance of love that had vanished. With his money he was assured of Juliana's fidelity and self-sacrifice forever. He considered it to be the only instrument of authority, the only backbone that could keep him standing above those who surrounded him. That is why he held onto it tightly with a compulsive grasp, so as not to let it go.

Every morning he would watch for the moment to arrive when his wife would come to him and ask him for it. He would observe her hesitations in the doorway, her pretenses at looking for something near the easy chair, her deliberate rubbing of a nearby piece of furniture. Finally, the words would come out of Juliana's mouth, choked and tremulous. Esteban would pretend not to hear her and she would have to plead all over again. Spurred on by her anguish, Juliana enunciated clearly and distinctly now: "I need ten pesos for expenses."

Esteban would look at her with an expression of infinite compassion. Had she suddenly gone mad? Because money doesn't grow on trees to squander like that. "What do you want it for?"

"For food."

"Is it for some special banquet? We have guests and you want to impress them with pheasant or truffles?"

Without any sign of humor or impatience, as if the question were completely normal, Juliana answered: "It's just that everything is very expensive."

"It says in the newspaper that the measures taken to lower the cost of living are producing excellent results."

"If you don't believe me, come with me to the marketplace."

"Why shouldn't I believe you? You're my wife, and a wife should never lie to her husband."

"Then give me the ten pesos."

"First tell me what you're going to buy."

"Two ounces of rice."

"Doesn't that seem extravagant to you? Yesterday more than half the soup was left over."

"It doesn't go to waste. It's used later for supper."

"All right, here's the money for the rice. What else?"

"A pound of meat."

"A pound of meat! And why not a whole cow?"

"You eat most of it. Águeda and I barely taste it."

"Choose it carefully then. Tender, without gristle. The best. Is that all?"

"We need vegetables and beans."

"You certainly can't tell me that those aren't cheap."

"No."

"Then you'll manage with seven pesos. Here."

"But you won't do without your fruit, and your sweets, and your coffee."

"If you know how to ration sensibly, you can get it all out of this."

As if she hadn't been listening, Juliana would persist. "I also need to buy soap, sugar, . . ."

"But you bought that barely a week ago."

"It's already gone."

"I don't understand. Unless they're not giving you the full amount in the store."

"Maybe."

"Well, insist on it. You have the right."

Juliana would make one last gesture of consent and stretch out her hand to receive the remaining three pesos that Esteban would hand her with a magnanimous gesture. Immediately afterward her steps would be heard rushing outside, the noise of the door closing.

Águeda would interrupt her schoolwork to look at the characters in the scene. Greed, subservience. Is that what marriage was? No, it wasn't possible. She was sure that her schoolmates' parents lived differently. They loved each other.

She thought about this word without having the slightest idea of what it meant. She had never loved anybody, much less this pair of strange beings, stingy and vulgar, from whom she had never managed to detach herself. Everyone was sure that Esteban and Juliana were her parents, but she rejected this affirmation with all her might. The whole world was lying in order to hide who knows what infamous sham. Some day her real parents would come and rescue her from this hell, the ones who, in an act of surrender and pleasure, had given her life.

She delighted in imagining them. He was elegant and beginning to age with dignity. He was well traveled and well read. He held a very important position and his time was filled with useful and prominent business. But when he came home he was just a simple and affectionate man who respected her mother and spoiled his daughter.

As for her mother, she was charming. Tall, very elegant, with hair smoothly pulled back, and no makeup on her serene and sweet face.

When they came to claim Águeda neither Esteban nor Juliana would dare to stop them. They would let her go off to a most luxurious house where every detail revealed the attention and good taste of its mistress.

During the first few nights they wouldn't sleep. They had so many things to tell each other! Later on, when Águeda finished her studies, with honors, they would reward her with a tour of the most beautiful cities in Europe. Upon returning, *he*, a young associate of her father, would be waiting for her. Everyone predicted a wonderful future for them . . .

Suddenly Águeda came to. The door had slammed shut. It was Juliana returning from market, red and out of breath.

The year Águeda finished high school, there was a big ceremony at the end of classes. All the graduates would attend in cap and gown to receive their diplomas. The parents would occupy the place of honor to applaud the capping of their daughters' efforts.

Águeda decided from the very first not to notify either Esteban or Juliana. To make sure they would not attend, she gave as a pretext an illness from which she did not recover until the event was over.

The scheme would not have had any consequences if it had not been for the concern of the principal, who sent a message to Juliana asking her for an appointment.

Juliana became very nervous; she begged Esteban to go in her place but he steadfastly refused. So there was nothing else she could do but search her bureau for the least-outdated dress that, in her judgment, was the most appropriate one for the occasion. One of her neighbors provided her with a pair of gloves and another loaned her a hat and a pocketbook that did not match. She could not solve the shoe problem so she had to wear her everyday ones.

Inside of this unaccustomed finery, Juliana felt as though she were seasick, and the condition was accentuated as she passed through the intense silence of the courtyards during vacation. When she reached the waiting room, she was breaking out into a cold sweat of nausea.

The principal looked her over quickly and uncertainly, inviting her to sit down, although she herself remained standing behind her desk, a gold crucifix its only adornment.

"I consider it my duty, madam, to speak to you about your daughter Águeda. To begin with, we have nothing to complain of as far as her diligence in her schoolwork is concerned. It is a gift that the Lord has given to her and that she does not waste. But there is something about her that has always disturbed me: her behavior."

Juliana remembered the twisted necks of the birds, the little flayed lizards, and gave a sudden start, which did not interrupt the speaker.

"It is not that she is undisciplined; to the contrary, she obeys the rules in a manner that I would consider excessive. But there is no enthusiasm, no feeling in anything she does, just a kind of fury, as if by carrying out her duties she were destroying an obstacle or taking revenge on something, or someone."

"Forgive my slowness in understanding, Sister. But what you're telling me is so strange . . ."

"I'm not aware of the nature of Águeda's attitude toward her family at home, but here, during the years she has been with us, she did not develop a single friendship among her schoolmates. She never had an admiring attachment for any of her teachers, nor burn with one of those intense emotions so common in adolescent girls. She never even chose a regular confessor. It made no difference to her if she went to one priest or another. And when she was told to persevere, she obeyed without protest.

"She has always seemed very unloving, very indifferent to everyone. The thing I am not sure about is whether it is a matter of character or of the treatment she has received from those who should have shown her more concern, more affection. Why didn't she come to the graduation exercises? She knew she was going to receive her diploma and several prizes."

"When was it? We didn't know anything about it."

"It doesn't matter now. But that confirms my suspicions. Águeda didn't come because she knew no one was going to accompany her on this solemn and special occasion. Perhaps it hurt her too much to be there alone."

Mechanically, Juliana began to remove her gloves, which were causing a painful pressure on her hands. What was this woman talking about? And she didn't let up. She went on, and on . . .

"I understand that your husband couldn't neglect his business. But you, madam, couldn't you have given up some engagement, perhaps some not very important engagement, when your daughter needed you?"

Suddenly Juliana understood the truth. Águeda had deliberately kept everything from them because she didn't want either Esteban or her to attend a ceremony where her schoolmates' parents would be gathered. She kept them at a distance because she was ashamed of them.

Juliana had often suspected it in little ways. Whenever she and Águeda were together on the street, the girl would walk ahead as if to deny her relationship to this unattractive woman who was painfully running to catch up with her. She was always ready to refuse any outing or good time that her parents would also attend. And now she had preferred to miss her graduation party so that she wouldn't have to introduce them to anyone.

The evidence was so glaring that Juliana felt an enormous weight lifted from her. She finally had reason enough to give Águeda her freedom to go off alone or with whomever seemed worthy of her! What a relief to stay at home, her apron on, her hair down, shuffling around in her old slippers, while the radio played a vulgar song!

" . . . now your daughter is going through a dangerous age, full of temptations and pitfalls. If she can't confide in her mother, whom else could she confide in?"

No, not a song. Better yet, one of those soap operas that were popular now. If she didn't hurry she wouldn't get there in time. Juliana abruptly jumped to her feet, and, without noticing whether the principal's speech was coming to an end or not, she came up to her and took her hand to kiss it.

"Thank you, Sister. Thank you for everything."

The contact with Juliana's hands—calloused hands, hands cracked from lye—although fleeting, made the principal think again. No, the woman who had just left was not a social butterfly nor an expert canasta player. As for her appearance, now that she thought about it, it seemed rather depressing. Could Águeda be from a poor family? She never, however, got behind in her tuition payments. At any rate, it was better that she had already finished her studies. Crossing herself in front of the crucifix and bowing slightly, the principal also left.

While Juliana was on her way back to the apartment under the cold and distant March sun, she took off her hat and fluffed out her hair to let the breeze blow through it. She felt neither humiliated nor sad because of what she had just found out. She simply thought once more: Águeda is a Sanromán. As such, she had a right to scorn her. And the funny thing was that this scorn made her feel lighter, irresponsible, free. Inside she sympathized with her husband who would now be worrying about Águeda's future. He didn't know that it was unnecessary, that the girl was stronger and more ruthless than anybody.

At mealtime, the only time that Esteban regained his position as head of the household, he started a long defense of chemistry as a career. It was the most appropriate one for a young girl in his opinion. As soon as she got her degree she would easily earn good money just by letting the pharmacies, who wanted someone visibly responsible, display her registration number.

Águeda agreed with everything. What her father said was true. But she had just finished going through the process of registering in the Law School. Some obscure instinct pushed her in that direction without consulting with anyone. She suspected that a familiarity with the law would provide her with a justification for her existence, whose worth had been repudiated since birth, and give her destiny a legitimate direction that would assuage her anxieties and queries.

When she casually let them know of her decision, Esteban's face took on the solemn look of a martyr, defenseless and wounded, and he did not direct his words again to Águeda, other than to allude to the lack of children's gratitude, their lack of respect for the experience and advice of their elders, and that death was preferable to reaching the age at which one became a nuisance.

Águeda would listen to him with fixed attention, as though it were necessary to classify the species to which this man belonged, this man who had reached old age without ever having come in contact with any form of love or understanding. She finally classified him with a contemptuous name and paid no more attention to his moaning.

All in all, a semblance of peace and harmony reigned in the house, which was enough for Juliana's liking. She gave up (and it was high time!) all efforts to appear presentable; she threw her girdle into the garbage can and bought herself some housedresses at the market.

She had more free time since Águeda had obtained work in a law office and ate downtown. Now she could devote her time, accompanied by the indispensable radio, embroidering a never-ending tablecloth that she would donate to the High Church of Comitán in thanksgiving for the blessings she had received, and as an offering that her luck not change.

But her luck did change, however, and very suddenly. One night Esteban woke up with a sharp pain in the middle of his chest, in his left arm, and in his ribs. The doctor diagnosed it as a pending heart attack, prescribed some medicine, and recommended plenty of rest.

And then Esteban attained something he thought he would never have during his lifetime: happiness. From that day on he no longer had to invent pretexts about business and meetings, nor waste his mornings frying or freezing, depending on the season, on an uncomfortable park bench. His easy chair was now his throne; sitting back in the perfect position, he devoted himself assiduously to watching over his heartbeat, his pulse, and the sudden irregularities of his chest.

Confronted with the new emergency, Juliana resorted to the sacraments to renew her faith and bear her cross with resignation. She provided her husband with all the comforts imaginable: cushions, wraps to cover his legs, magazines and games to entertain him, from simple card games to the incomprehensible chess. Águeda would come and go to her classes and her work, always finding the couple deeply engrossed, with a passion that she could only find contemptible, in an endless and savage competition.

Moreover, Juliana would surprise her husband with little delicacies. So many efforts converged to establish a kind of cordiality between the two. But when Juliana wanted to find out where she stood, she immediately met with that very peculiar Sanromán gesture which meant: everything that others do for me they do out of obligation and because of my merits. Everything I receive is mine by right.

The deception, perhaps the fatigue as well, made Juliana begin to display a certain detachment from the invalid. He would complain in vain

Fleeting Friendships

> . . . *we come to this earth*
> *only to meet*
> *one another, we are*
> *just passing through.*
> —Anonymous Nahuatl poem

My best friend during my adolescence almost never spoke, something that made our closeness possible. For I was possessed with a kind of frenzy that compelled me to talk incessantly, to make up secrets and plans, to define my every mood, and to interpret my dreams and memories. I did not have the slightest idea who I really was or who I would turn out to be; and I was eager to make order out of my life and to define myself, through words, if not yet with deeds.

Gertrudis, wide-eyed, listened attentively while I plotted ways to distract the vigilance of the nuns at school so that she could meet with Oscar.

Their pleasant, uneventful courtship displayed all the signs of leading to marriage. Oscar was serious and respectful, and he took correspondence courses in electronics. Gertrudis was sensible, and her early orphanhood had thrust into her hands both the management of the household and the care of her younger brothers and sisters. As a result she became skilled at all the feminine duties. Apart from this, her talents as a scholar never surprised anyone with the slightest inclination for study. Her continued residence at the school could be attributed to other reasons. Her father, Don Estanislao Córdova (Don Tanis), who had been widowed in his prime, engaged in a lifestyle best left unwitnessed by his children.

In order to avoid shocking his neighbors in Comitán, he had moved down to the hot country where he owned property. In this unwholesome climate, he ran some cattle ranches and operated the best-stocked store in the town of La Concordia and the surrounding region.

He needed a woman to help him, so he took one mistress after another, but none of them ever suited him. He sent each one packing in turn, always with the greatest civility and the most splendid gifts. Finally, he decided to abandon the headache of it all and remarry. With a legitimate wife, it was possible to gather his scattered family back together.

When Gertrudis learned the news, she commissioned me to compose a sad farewell poem to Oscar for her—not too sad because her absence was to be a short one. Oscar had nearly finished his studies, and he would open up his shop immediately after graduation. Once it began to show a profit, they would get married.

How slowly time passes when one must wait! Besides, arguing with her stepmother and listening to the constant bickering of her brothers and sisters added to Gertrudis' impatience. Her only company was Chickie, the baby of the house. Chickie followed her like a little lap dog to the garden, where Gertrudis checked to see that everything was weeded; to the barn, where she collected the milk; and to the store, where Gertrudis' father had put her in charge.

The clientele was varied, ranging from the mule driver, who needed quantities of salt or blanket fabric, to the Indian, who pondered for hours before deciding between a large red kerchief for catching the sweat of the fields or a brand new machete.

They also served liquor. Gertrudis screamed the first time she saw a neighbor fall dead to the floor, his fingers still clasped around his empty glass. No one else even batted an eyelash. The authorities came with their customary slowness, filled out a report, and interrogated the witnesses. Gertrudis regained her composure when she found out that such unfortunate occurrences were commonplace. If the death was the result of a personal vendetta, no one had the right to interfere. And if it was caused by liquor manufactured by the alcohol monopoly (which used chemicals, whose known toxic properties were not accounted for, to accelerate the fermentation process), well, there was really nowhere to complain.

Gertrudis began to get bored the moment they took the corpse away. None of the deaths that followed even came close to the excitement of the first. Moreover, the letters she received from Oscar were copied word for word out of *Letters for Lovers*, of which she also owned a copy. If, on the one hand, she enjoyed the advantage of knowing exactly how to answer them, it took away her expectations since she was able to foresee their contents. There was not a word about the workshop, about a wedding date, even less. It was not easy to interject such topics amid the hearts and flowers of nostalgia. I was the one who kept her posted on what was happening. Oscar had begun to recover from his grief. He played billiards with his old gang, attended evening services on Sundays, and went to serenades on Tuesdays and Thursdays. He remained faithful. He was not seen in the company of a single girl, not even to escort the occasional "odd girl out" with his friends. He went to dances and other affairs, always with an appropriately decent air of sadness. But rumor had it that he was not investing his savings in materials to set up his shop, as expected, but in preparations for a trip to Mexico City, for reasons which were not entirely clear.

I liked writing those letters, giving form to Oscar's shadowy figure, the ambiguities of his character, his feelings, his intentions. It was because of those letters—and my lack of an audience—that I found my true vocation.

Gertrudis fanned herself with the paper, not changing her position in the hammock. The heat was sapping her, stripping her of any impulse to suffer or rebel. Oscar . . . how odd it seemed all of a sudden, that name! How difficult to place it in her new surroundings, amid the merchandise and the crowds and the mangy dogs! Who could remember the tone of his tender words if all one ever heard was a stepmother's grumbling, a father's warnings, the servants' chatter, or the orders of the customers? Gertrudis herself was different, no longer the girl who had lived in Comitán. In school, her future had been predictable. "A place for everything, and everything in its place"; that was the motto of home economics classes. But here she found neither stability nor focus. Objects—always provisional—seemed to find their places at random. People were liable just to take off. Relationships were fragile. Nobody cared, in this heat, what anybody else did. People assumed responsibility for their actions only if they felt like it. Oaths, even promises, lost meaning. Oscar, an inhabitant of colder climes, would not have recognized his fiancée. Fiancée! What a namby-pamby, hypocritical term! Gertrudis laughed as she walked to her favorite bathing spot. In La Concordia, people bathed their whole bodies, completely nude—not the way it was in Comitán, where they dabbed their eyelids with warm water, taking care not to splash any on the rest of their faces.

Gertrudis assured me, in messages penciled on any available scrap of brown wrapping paper, that she had no time to answer my letters more extensively. Her chores . . . The truth was, she was lazy. She spent the hottest hours of the day behind the store's counter, amusing herself by watching how the hordes of flies ate themselves silly on the trays of sweets. And if some unlucky person should interrupt her for some trifling thing, she would shoot him a terrible hostile glance, saying brusquely: "We're out of it."

One day at noon, the sound of a galloping horse disturbed her drowsiness. The rider, sweaty and tense, dismounted, walked into the store and ordered a beer. His throat was so parched with thirst that Gertrudis had to serve him three bottles before he was in any condition to speak. When he finally did say something, it was not about himself. "A person could get pretty bored around here," he said, looking at Gertrudis.

She shrugged her shoulders with indifference. What did it matter?

"Haven't you ever thought about leaving?"

"To go where?"

"Anywhere."

Gertrudis leaned toward him and said in a low voice, "I don't like to come back."

The man made a gesture of agreement and ordered another beer. He seemed to be thinking about something. Finally, he proposed something: "What if we left together?"

Gertrudis quickly glanced out at the road. "You have only one horse."

"Can't you ride behind?"

"We have horses that are rested in the stable. It's just a matter of having one saddled for me."

The man nodded. Having solved the problem, he couldn't understand why this woman continued to stand there like a stone, without moving. But Gertrudis was thinking about the details. "I have to get my clothes together."

"It's not good to carry too much."

"You're right."

Gertrudis served the man another beer before disappearing inside the house. She told the stable attendant that she was going to bathe in the river but was too tired to go on foot. As she raced around the room, packing up her things, Chickie appeared. In spite of her bad timing, she was well received.

"Where are you going?"

"To the river."

"Take me with you."

"All right."

Gertrudis had answered automatically. What would the man think? After all, if he didn't like it, he could go on by himself. But . . . what would *she* do? She hurried back to the store with a bundle under her arm and Chickie hanging on to her skirts.

"Who's the clinging vine?"

"My little sister. She's very attached to me. I can't leave her."

"Can she stand the ride?"

"We'll see."

"How much do I owe?" the man asked.

Gertrudis made a quick count of the empty bottles. "Twenty pesos."

The man put his money on the counter. "It won't do for them to see us leaving together. I'll wait for you by Iguana Pond."

Gertrudis agreed. After he was gone and she and Chickie were there alone, she began filling a saddlebag with crackers, cans of sardines, and her purse containing the proceeds from the day's sales.

The stableman poked his head out. "Your horse is ready, Miss."

"Stay here and take over the store until I get back."

Gertrudis mounted sidesaddle, holding Chickie in a tight embrace. No one saw them pass through the corral gate. In a few minutes they had reached the meeting place. The man decided which road to take and they followed him.

They went fast, faster. As night fell, they arrived at a tiny hamlet.

"I'll go look for a place to stay," the man said.

Gertrudis dismounted, careful not to wake Chickie. Where could she put her? Her arms ached from carrying her.

There was a clearing in the woods and Gertrudis put her down to sleep. "I hope she doesn't get covered with ticks."

No longer burdened with the child, Gertrudis set about opening one of the tin cans. She was hungry. She was wiping off the oil that had dripped onto her hands when the man came back.

"I found somewhere for us to spend the night. Come on."

It was so close that they walked the distance on foot, pulling the horses by their halters. The man condescended to carry Chickie.

The proprietors of the house appeared in the doorway with an oil lamp, guiding them through the dark with friendly conversation. In the kitchen they gave them a cup of coffee and then led them to the room.

Its dimensions were small, it had a dirt floor, and its only furniture consisted of a small cot and a hammock. They put Chickie in the hammock, tying her in to keep her from falling. The two of them lay down on the cot.

Gertrudis never thought about Oscar even once. Nor was she thinking about this stranger who was possessing her and to whom she yielded, without resistance or enthusiasm, sensuality or remorse.

"Aren't you afraid I'll get you pregnant?"

Gertrudis shook her head. A baby was such a remote possibility!

They slept almost until dawn. Then they were awakened by the furious yelping of dogs, the commotion of a group of men on horseback, and the alarming exclamations of the owners of the house.

The man got dressed right away. He looked pale. Gertrudis thought she had been dreaming until her father stood before her, shaking her violently by the shoulders.

"You ought to be ashamed! You had to go screwing around! What did you ever need that I didn't give you? Couldn't you have asked me for anything you wanted?"

He gave Gertrudis a hard slap across her bare cheek. She kept herself from crying aloud so as not to wake Chickie.

Don Tanis turned toward the door and called his companions into the room.

"Here's the one you've been looking for," he said, pointing to the man. "I've heard of him. His name is Juan Bautista González."

The man hung his head. There was no use denying it.

"OK, my lawyer friend, don't just sit there like a fool. Read the list of allegations."

The man thus addressed came forward. First he had to put on a pair of reading glasses; then, clearing his throat with authority, he read: ". . . for attempting to destroy the lines of communication."

"What was all that?" Gertrudis wanted to know.

"That prize catch of yours has been amusing himself by cutting the telegraph wires."

"In so many words, young lady."

"Young lady . . . ," muttered Don Tanis, holding up the blood-stained sheet. "Put this on the list of charges, too."

The lawyer was about to consult a copy of the legal code that he wouldn't let go of to clarify something when Don Tanis cut him short. "Skip the technicalities and just put it down."

The lawyer, trembling and trying not to miss anything, put down every word that applied to the case. "Abduction, sexual relations under false pretenses, rape . . ."

"And robbery. Don't forget to add the 200 pesos that are missing from my cashbox or the supplies that disappeared."

"What's the punishment?" the man demanded to know. He didn't seem too worried about it. He must have had some pretty good connections.

"Well, according to law . . ."

"Do me the favor of keeping your mouth shut, Lawyer. The punishment is that you're going to rot in jail for the rest of your life. And if you use any tricks to get out of there, I'll personally track you down on the first street corner."

"Thanks for the information," said the man, without losing his composure.

"The sentence would be shortened," the lawyer suggested timidly, "if the accused were to make restitution for some of the damages. Returning the money, for example."

Gertrudis felt under the pillow and handed the purse over to her father. "Count it. It's all there."

The success of his first suggestion inspired the lawyer to make another. "You could also make amends for the loss of the young lady's honor by marrying her."

"Which young lady?" asked the man.

"Listen, you son of a bitch, don't try to tell me you didn't find my daughter just exactly the way God made her! I have proof, proof!"

And as if he were a tree, Don Tanis hung the sheet from his arms again.

"No, that's not what I was referring to," the man continued. "It's just that before I went to La Concordia, I ran away with another girl."

Chickie woke up crying. She didn't recognize her surroundings. Where was she? Why was everybody making all this noise? Gertrudis covered herself up with her dress and went to console her.

The lawyer scratched his ear meditatively. "Do you remember the name of the injured party?"

"We didn't have time to talk, you understand, since I was on the run . . ."

"The person you have to marry is my daughter."

"Even though the other one has priority?" the lawyer asked, regretting his question as soon as he saw the expression on Don Tanis' face.

"Don't give me any petty criticisms, Lawyer, just marry them right this minute. Gertrudis, come here."

Gertrudis obeyed. She was uncomfortable because the dress that was covering her kept slipping. And Chickie was heavy, besides.

"Put that Indian brat down somewhere and get your dress on right. Don't be immodest."

When his orders had been carried out, Don Tanis added, "Now the bride and groom clasp hands—isn't that right, Lawyer?"

"Yes, naturally. May I be allowed to look for the nuptial written by Melchor Ocampo? It's right here in my lawbook."

"No, no useless ceremonies. These gentlemen," said Don Tanis, pointing to the riders who had gathered at the door, "will serve as witnesses that you pronounce them man and wife."

"I want a ring," sighed Gertrudis.

There was a silence all around. Everybody looked at each other. The proprietor's wife wiped away a tear with the corner of her apron.

Don Tanis handed Gertrudis the purse. "Your dowry," he said.

"Thanks, Papa."

The couple let go of each other's hands, which had begun to sweat and get sticky.

"Don't you want to drink a little toast?" The proprietor's wife had brought a tray of half-filled glasses of chocolate liqueur from Comitán. Nobody refused. She even gave one to Chickie, who went into spasms of choking and had to be slapped on the back.

"Long live the newlyweds!"

Don Tanis took Gertrudis aside to give her his blessing. "I always thought you would be a chip off the old block. . . . not quite like this, but what can we do about it now? You know something?" he concluded, stroking her nose softly with the edge of his whip. "Today you reminded me of your mother. You look alike. Yes, you look very much alike."

Gertrudis had heard stories about her parents' marriage—Don Tanis had gone to ask for a girl's hand on behalf of a friend; while the elders deliberated, he and the girl had warmed up to one another and ran off together. What a scene! The things people had said about them! But they had been happy. Why wasn't she going to be?

"All right, ladies and gentlemen, time to go home. I'm taking Chickie. And you, which way are you going?"

The lawyer nearly choked. "We're going to municipal headquarters, Don Tanis. There your . . . your son-in-law will be charged."

"You better hurry up and get started. It's a long way."

"Don't you understand what I mean, Don Tanis? Your son-in-law is going to jail. And your daughter . . . does she know anybody in San Bartolomé, excuse me, in Venustiano Carranza?"

"No," replied Gertrudis.

"Then her situation is going to be somewhat difficult."

"We all have our trials in life, Lawyer. One must meet suffering square in the face, with strength and courage. If Gertrudis hadn't left my custody, I'd protect her, I swear. But now she's in a man's custody and meddling in-laws are an abomination."

Gertrudis discovered the truth of this when she went to live with her own in-laws. The old man was a monster, and the old woman, a powder-keg. The two of them never agreed on anything except to complain about their daughter-in-law, and they made her work in exchange for her room and board.

Meanwhile, Juan Bautista had not been able to extricate himself from jail. His wife visited him on Thursdays and Sundays, always bringing him a snack, a magazine, a songbook . . . and a body whose docility was gradually turned to pleasure.

The visits hardly gave them time to discuss the progress of the trial. They never spoke about what they would do once Juan Bautista gained his freedom.

So the news of his release caught them unprepared. The first day was one of parties and family celebrations. But when their marriage had settled into a routine, Juan Bautista began to show signs of restlessness.

"What's the matter?" Gertrudis asked, out of courtesy.

Juan Bautista pretended to think for a moment and then he suddenly made a decision. He took his wife's hands in his own and looked into her eyes. "I had a girlfriend from before, Gertrudis, ever since we were little. She hasn't let me down. She's waiting for me."

Gertrudis withdrew her hands and lowered her eyes.

"Besides, our marriage isn't really legal. There's no certificate, no records . . ."

"But my father will be mad. He provided the witnesses."

"All right, we can get divorced to keep from hurting his feelings. Luckily, you haven't been burdened with children."

"Am I barren?" Gertrudis asked herself.

"God doesn't like deceitful people like us. That's why we haven't had any babies."

"That's good, because it's sad to be barren."

"This way you'll be free. And I'm going to help you any way I can. Where do you want to go?"

"I don't know."

"To La Concordia? Or Comitán?"

Gertrudis said no, she never wanted to go back there. "To Mexico City."

"But how is a little thing like you going to find her way around a great big city like that?"

"I have a friend who lives there. She still writes me long letters. I'll go look for her address."

And that's how Gertrudis and I came to see each other again. My parents blinked their eyes in amazement when they heard her story. No, they would absolutely not allow me to contaminate myself by being around such a bad example. Nor was I to think for one minute that she could stay with us, either. A job and a place to stay would have to be found for her. That was the Christian way. But to let her into the house? For God's sake, no. Charity begins at home.

In vain, I argued, I cried, I pleaded, but my parents were completely inflexible.

Somehow, Gertrudis got ahead. We met each other secretly on Sundays. I had become a little more reserved and she was more talkative. Our conversations were pleasant and more evenly balanced than before. We were happy—it was as if we didn't realize we were cut from entirely different cloth.

One Sunday I found Gertrudis, all dressed in black, sobbing her eyes out. "What's the matter with you?"

"They killed Juan Bautista. Look, it says so right here in this telegram."

I smiled, relieved. "You scared me. I thought something serious had happened to you."

Gertrudis gave me a questioning look. "Isn't being left a widow serious enough?"

"But you aren't a widow. You were never married."

She dropped her head in resignation. "That's just what Juan Bautista said. But you know what? We lived together just like man and wife; sometimes he was very affectionate toward me. I would have to be heartless not to cry for him!"

I decided to go along with her. When she had calmed down, I started asking about the details. "How did they kill him?"

"They shot him in the back."

"My God!"

"Well, they were chasing him."

"What was he doing?"

"The same as usual, cutting down telegraph wires. I don't know where he picked up that trick."

"Really. That is strange."

We were quiet for a minute. Then I broke the silence. "Did he ever get married?"

"Yes, to his old girlfriend." Gertrudis said this with a kind of admiration for their faithfulness and constancy.

"Then it's her job to mourn him, not yours."

At first she gave me a wild, unbelieving look; then her expression turned to one of agreement.

"Take off those black clothes and let's go to a movie."

I heard her humming in the bathroom while she was changing. "Is there anything good playing?"

"Good enough to pass the time. Hurry up."

"I'm ready."

Gertrudis looked at me with a face from which all memories seemed to have been erased; her eyes were unclouded by any desire to look back. She seemed only to be happily anticipating an entertainment whose title was yet unknown to her.

In the darkness of the theater, next to Gertrudis' incessant chomping (she had a terrible sweet tooth, which she had generously supplied with popcorn and caramels), I suddenly felt very sad. If circumstances had not thrown us back together again, Gertrudis, would she have even remembered my name? What an absurd question from someone who has built her life on human memory and the permanence of words!

"Wait here for a minute. I won't be gone long."

I never did find out if Gertrudis heard that last sentence, because we never saw each other again. When I got home, I took out my notebook and opened it . . . For a long while I sat absorbed in thought in front of the blank page. I tried to write, but I couldn't. What for? It was so hard! Maybe, I repeated to myself, my head in my hands, maybe it's simpler just to live.

Translated by Lesley Salas
Los convidados de agosto (1964)

The Widower Román

Doña Cástula always served Don Carlos Román the last coffee of the evening in the room her master called his study, originally furnished as a doctor's office. But the unused examination and operating tables and the cabinets for surgical instruments had gradually been removed, leaving behind only a faded framed diploma, a now illegible Hippocratic oath, and a small reproduction of the famous picture of a doctor who, in surgical attire, battles a skeleton for possession of a young woman's body bearing no visible sign of disease.

Though the study was the part of the house where Don Carlos spent most of his time, it nevertheless had the impersonal atmosphere of hotel rooms. Not because it lacked concessions to luxury, not to mention comfort, but because the furniture (reduced to a leather chair and a mahogany desk with three drawers, only one of which contained papers and was always kept locked) bore none of the prints man gradually leaves on objects used daily. No charred mark appeared on the wood for Don Carlos did not smoke; nor was there a scratch from sharpening a pencil with a blade or an inkspot since Don Carlos never wrote. Perhaps the only visible traces were a chair slightly worn in the seat from the weight of his body and some bookcases containing volumes never opened, bookcases whose presence he did not enjoy but tolerated.

Doña Cástula placed the tray with the coffee pot and cup on the desk. For some time now Don Carlos had denied himself sugar, maintaining that no precaution was too great at his age. While her master savored the first hot aromatic sips, she drew the list of the day's expenditures from her apron pocket to submit for his approval.

Don Carlos examined it carefully, pausing at times for her comments about a detail, ready to reproach a needless extravagance or make an exasperated comment about the increased cost of an item. Finally, grumbling, he added the figures and with a resigned gesture stored the paper in the customary folder. Doña Cástula waited for this last gesture, which concluded the ritual, before withdrawing. This evening, however, to her respectful "Good night," Don Carlos did not respond with his usual patronizing "Good night"; instead he made a casual remark about the weather. "Bit chilly out, isn't it?"

"Would you like me to light the brazier, sir?"

"No, it's not that cold. Besides, it makes me feel good. What about you? Don't you like it?"

Disconcerted, Doña Cástula shrugged her shoulders. It had never occurred to her that the weather was a question of likes and dislikes, let alone hers.

"Perhaps because the hacienda where you grew up is more toward the hot country."

"Yes, sir. But now I don't even remember. They took me away when I was a tiny thing. And I have always worked in Comitán."

"You mean always in my house. Why, you started as my nanny!"

"The whippings your blessed mother, may she rest in peace, used to give me with a leather strap when she found us talking familiarly! 'Uppity,' she used to say, 'you'll be a bad influence on him.' And then, so that you'd become refined, they sent you to roam the world."

"Meanwhile, you seized the opportunity and had yourself a fling, didn't you?"

Doña Cástula covered her blushing face with her apron. "Oh, Master, that comes from being stubborn and from having had instincts. Everyone kept nagging me: 'That man will be the death of you.' But talking to me was like talking to a stone wall. When he said, 'Let's go,' I didn't pretend to beat around the bush or stop to ask for a priest or judge. I just tied up my suitcase and at the crack of dawn slipped away with him."

"To the plantations on the coast."

"Where else can the poor go, Master? There they had offered him happiness, a dream come true, but when the time came, the poor fellow ended up in jail because they accused him of God knows what crimes."

"And you?"

"Me? I went to the hospital. I had caught a chill, I was on my last legs, and on top of that I had a miscarriage. Oh, how I cursed. There I was stretched out on the floor. I wasn't even entitled to a cot, there was no one to bring me a glass of water, and I was as flat as a flounder. When they put me out of the hospital because it no longer had room for so many sick folk, I looked like I had consumption. People ran from me in fright. They tossed me coins from a distance so that no harm would come to them."

"And your husband?"

"No, he wasn't my husband, Master Carlos. He was just a man. Being a fast talker, he soon got out of jail; he then went to seek his fortune at the border. There he met some of my kin who asked for news of me. 'She's already dead,' he told them. 'There's a cross with her name on it right in the Tapachula cemetery. I bought it for her myself,' says the big shot. They swallowed it whole. Then out of the blue I turned up in Comitán. 'It's a ghost!' shouted the Indians, and the women made the sign of the cross at me; even the men turned white."

The housekeeper guffawed as she recalled these scenes. She couldn't go on.

"Could you forgive all that, Cástula?"

"They were simple folk, Master. How were they to know? Not until they reached out and touched me were they convinced that I wasn't a soul from the other world."

"I'm not referring to the people," Don Carlos explained, with a tinge of impatience in his voice, "but to the man who ran out on you."

Doña Cástula became serious and made an effort to consider the matter from the viewpoint suggested by Don Carlos. After reflecting momentarily, she said, "I wasn't his legal wife, Master. I ran off with him asking no one's consent; my own nanny cursed me."

"But surely he must have promised you, must have sworn . . ."

"Ah, Master, since when don't birds fly! Like a fool, I believed him. You know how it is with a young girl." She sighed, excusing herself for her folly, sorrowful perhaps, yet longing for the man. "God knows where he's wandering now and the hard times he's been through. I came to take shelter with you again, and since then you have not forsaken me."

Doña Cástula would have liked to recount how she had gradually risen by her own merits from parlor maid to cook, then to housekeeper, and finally to the rank of her mistress' confidante. And when his mother died, Doña Cástula inherited her position—in matters of authority, of course, not in appearances. Yet with guile and tact Doña Cástula permitted no one else to take the reins of the house. When Don Carlos married, his wife could have been a rival, but . . .

"What would you do if you saw him again?"

"If I saw him again . . ."

The truth is that if Doña Cástula had suddenly met him she wouldn't have recognized him. His features had faded from her memory many years ago. His name meant no more than any other man's. She did not dare confess as much, however, to a gentleman who from the moment he became a widower had never put off his mourning.

Don Carlos refilled his cup and stared hard at it as if concentration would help him word his question. "If you could get your hands on him and punish him to get even, what would you do, Cástula?"

Frightened, the housekeeper drew back. "Master, I'm a woman. Revenge is for men, not for me."

"But it was you he mistreated, not your relatives, who aren't going to lift a finger to wipe out the affront. Don't you realize, you fool, what that man did to you? Not only did he dump you in the hospital to manage on your own with only God to help you, but he declared you dead so others would not worry about you. And there you are, happy as you please, with no hard feelings toward him . . ."

Doña Cástula knew she deserved the scolding but did not know how to answer. Hard feelings—when in the world could she have felt them? From morning to night there was nothing but work. "Cástula, sweep the corridor. Cástula, water the plants. Cástula, go to the market early so you can pick out the choice meat. Cástula, you didn't mend the clothes. Cástula, be on the watch for the man who sells charcoal; it's getting low. Cástula . . . Cástula . . . Cástula." At night she collapsed, exhausted, dead for sleep, when there was nobody sick to watch over.

But were these reasons enough to excuse her? To Don Carlos, her behavior proved nothing but her abject acceptance of her station. For him, a gentleman educated abroad who had returned with a degree, the ritual of his widowhood was a serious matter. To observe it properly he had not needed to become an idler. He oversaw the management of his ranches better than most other owners. For him it was not enough to go only during branding and harvesting, but he also kept up with births and deaths, during dog days and downpours, marketing and storing. And he never permitted his foremen to abuse their power in representing him, or to render bad accounts. In Comitán, where he also owned lots and houses, he did not use intermediaries to deal with his tenants. He had the reputation of being just; he did not fleece his renters, but neither did he ever forgive a debt.

Immediately after Estela's death Don Carlos abandoned the practice of his profession, but that, according to Doña Cástula, lacked importance. For a rich person a title (of doctor or whatever) served only as an ornament to be worn. So there it was, hanging on the wall; yet who was going to admire it? For Don Carlos—and this confirmed the depth and tenderness of his feelings—no longer associated with anybody. He deliberately refused to receive anyone, even his mother-in-law, who called on him from time to time. He attended no social gathering, entertainments, or fiestas.

And he secluded himself longer and longer in his study. Some days he even refused to leave it for his meals.

Though he was clearly a gentleman, and a gentleman who knew how to bear his grief gracefully, Doña Cástula thought he was beginning to show signs of fatigue. He kept her near him under any pretext. Examining the accounts provided an easy one; he lingered over them and asked about vegetables in season, for he would sometimes have a special whim. Or he insisted that they had overcharged her, thus giving her the opening to describe at length her haggling with the vendors. Gradually the sort of people with whom she chatted became more varied, so that Don Carlos again caught up on the goings-on in town, thanks to his housekeeper.

Their conversations thus became more leisurely, and their familiarity often erased the boundaries that usually separate master and servant. From the very beginning, however, they tacitly agreed never to make the vaguest reference to anything concerning the past, which was extremely painful to Don Carlos.

What words sufficed to describe Estela's beauty, the bridegroom's love, the pageantry and gaiety of the wedding? How to recall the sudden nameless misfortune which struck like lightning their very first night together? Then the disconsolate, hopeless months of Estela's agony. And the final outcome to which no one could ever be resigned. Yet now Don Carlos, for no apparent reason, broke the barriers he himself had set up and ventured questions as vehement as if something vital depended upon their answers.

"So you hold no grudge," he concluded. "Well, the angels will reward you for it. Surely they're already rewarding you by allowing you a deep, long, undisturbed, good night's sleep. Am I right?"

Embarrassed, Cástula, who at times had heard her sleepless master roaming the corridors at ungodly hours of the night, hung her head and replied, "The cock crows early for me, Master."

"And here I am delaying you with all this nonsense. Go on, get some sleep."

But before she crossed the threshold, Don Carlos detained her with one final order, "Tell the man who comes by the week to clean out the stable thoroughly and stock it with fodder and corn. Tomorrow they are going to bring a horse I just bought. It's a fine one and must get good care."

That night Doña Cástula could not enjoy her long, deep, undisturbed sleep. Time and again the figure of Don Carlos appeared to her being thrown by a spirited, fiery horse—he who on his visits to his plantations always used only sure-footed mules. Or she saw him galloping away from the house, his refuge for so many years, to meet rich men who on wild drunken sprees lit their cigars with hundred-peso bills or gambled away on one card, one throw of the dice, their wives or daughters after they had already lost whatever else they owned.

Doña Cástula awoke troubled. Why would Don Carlos insist on getting mixed up with such dangers? He was not a man like others who spend their time in cantinas and whorehouses. He was a doctor, even if nobody seemed to remember it. He had studied abroad and polished his manners and should frequent the casino, where young ladies and gentlemen played forfeits while mothers chaperoned and fathers discussed business and politics. Perhaps the presence of someone who had kept aloof for so long would astonish them at first. When Don Carlos walked along the streets of Comitán, shut-ins quickly parted the window curtains to catch a glimpse of his face and bearing. The passersby yielded him the right of way on the sidewalk as he deserved, though they did not speak, for they were no longer apt to recognize him. Who was going to shake hands with him when he had not one single friend? His friends before his trip to Europe had taken different paths and were unable to hold a conversation with one so learned as he. Those he met upon his return . . . well, upon his return Don Carlos had eyes for no one but Estela and time only to woo her and hasten the preparations for the wedding. And then . . .

With the tolling of the first bell for early Mass, Doña Cástula automatically got up. Urgent chores kept her from other worries.

Though quiet, having been broken by harsh discipline, the horse turned out to be a noble animal with well-rounded buttocks. The stable boy saddled him very early for the master's exercise, limited according to his own prescription but indispensable if he was to do justice to the breakfast which had been prepared with such careful attention.

On his ride Don Carlos soon detoured from the main streets, crowded at that hour with Indians down from the hills to sell vegetables and clay cooking ware, with servants carrying to the mill pots of corn to grind for tortillas, and with sanctimonious women muffling their piety and decrepitude in black woolen shawls, and took a road to the outskirts. He rode at a trot in front of the thatched huts, following the winding paths where grasses lay in wait before sprouting and engulfing the recently beaten track. His final destination on these excursions was usually a slight rise from which one could take in the entire town of Comitán at a glance.

While the horse, loosely tied to a bush, browsed among the branch tops around him, Don Carlos leaned against a tree trunk and contemplated the uniform rooftops darkened by rain and time. His eyes lingered thoughtfully upon the smooth unpretentious, unevenly whitewashed walls, upon the brusque, forbidding doors, and upon the windows that promised but disclosed nothing.

In this distant contemplation, in which he did not dare penetrate beyond the surface of what he saw, from the depths of the past Don Carlos resurrected the innocence, eagerness, and perhaps happiness of his childhood, the nostalgia of his youthful years abroad, the fervor of his return, and the sorrow and catastrophe of his mature years.

Gradually, however, in a way even Don Carlos was unaware of, his grief began to subside. Perhaps the break started with the first superfluous word he directed to Doña Cástula. Presently the venting of his anguish became less concentrated and more moderate, like a lament that modulates from one mode to another. His imagination strove to free itself from certain images which had formerly obsessed him and to admit others, then still others.

This was a sort of apprenticeship: to become once more acquainted through his senses with objects from which he had been long estranged. By careful observation he discovered in the thick, lofty foliage of a tree an infinite range of greens. He discovered a stone fallen by chance, rough to the touch, defiant with its edges. He discovered a rolling contour of land where one might detect nature's willingness to show its benevolence and hospitality to man. Don Carlos became more and more aware of his gradual recovery. Not only were objects no longer hostile to him, they were not even strange. They had become friendly, cordial presences. He met them with anticipated pleasure and enjoyed them fully.

The most difficult part of the transition was still to come: that which would lead him again into the world of human beings. He began by trying to choose his routes without considering the risk of meeting an old acquaintance. The alternative of stopping to greet him or riding by without turning his head no longer tormented him. If the other were communicative and amiable, why shouldn't Don Carlos respond to the friendliness? And if he were not, why try to breach others' diffidence when it was much less rigid than his own?

After so many years of being vulnerable, the widower relished his new self-mastery. Isolation had been his solution to problems that had seemed intolerable. Proximity to others aroused in him a restlessness no logic could suppress. He feared their compassion as much as he disdained their curiosity, but he could not have pardoned their indifference. He was disgusted by the knowing wink with which men let him realize they were in on the secret of the means he used to bear his loneliness. For it was inconceivable that Don Carlos, a man in the prime of life and virility, should remain continent when even priests, champing at the bit of a religion in which they did not believe, were not always chaste. He was annoyed by the gauche solicitude of matrons eager to put an end to his unorthodox state by offering him what nature requires and God's law commands: a female companion. Like spiders motionless in the center of the web, they called attention to the daughter, the niece, the cherished ward embellished with every ornament, sum total of all virtues, whose only mission in this life consisted in making Don Carlos happy, his home hospitable, and his progeny numerous.

But lo and behold, suddenly Don Carlos ceased to fear the encounters and to flee the snares. There was no reason why others' feelings should determine his moods. If others made plans involving him, that was their problem. Don Carlos was free, master of his fate.

Though now ready for sociability, Don Carlos was not in so great a need as to go in search of it. As he had learned throughout his years of solitude and meditation, time is what brings things to maturity. To rush headlong, plunge into events that are hardly germinating and whose development may miscarry and cannot be hastened, winds up useless, tiring, and self-defeating.

His contact with other people turned out very different, however, from what he had imagined or maybe planned. It so happened that one morning his meditations were suddenly interrupted by the appearance of a group of children, the eldest among them not even twelve. They came running, shouting, and pushing. The presence of an older person paralyzed them momentarily. But the tolerant manner of Don Carlos, on the one hand, and the children's numerical superiority, on the other, threw them again into a kind of collective frenzy surely dictated by some secret rule no outsider could fathom.

They were all barefooted and wore filthy rags. They shouted lewd curses and made obscene noises. Purposeless at first, they gradually concentrated all their activity upon one child, the smallest, weakest, poorest, who presently became the enemy incarnate. He had a nickname, of course, and during the clamor of the fight others were improvised. Each invention was greeted with uproarious laughter which fired the group, egging it on to new boldness, and further terrified the little one.

As he observed the scene, a brief spark of interest flickered in Don Carlos' eyes. With their amoral spontaneity the children's actions and reactions reminded him too much of those he had witnessed in animals for which he had no love. But an element of danger one could smell in the air kept him alert to the game's progress, in which insults only fore-shadowed more violent action, namely, throwing things—orange peels, peach stones, and rocks. Assailed on all sides, the target turned this way and that and tried to protect himself by covering his face with his forearm, until a rock struck him in the temple and he fell bleeding to the ground.

Stunned, the children stared at him for a moment. One of them even sneered as if the beaten child had broken the rules of the game. But as soon as they fully realized that something completely beyond their under-standing had happened, they scattered in all directions.

Seeing them flee, Don Carlos made no attempt to stop them or shout any harsh reproach. Unhurriedly, calmly, he stood up and went to the wounded child with a kind of automatic professionalism that resurfaced, intact, after having lain dormant for many years.

A careful look at the wound revealed that though painful it was not se-rious. With his handkerchief Don Carlos improvised a bandage to stop the bleeding. The child submitted to treatment with the same big frightened eyes with which he had previously submitted to persecution.

Don Carlos regretted not having a piece of candy, something sweet to console the child. Nor did he know how to get close to him to gain his confidence. He made an effort to give his voice a touch of tenderness and asked: "Do you live far from here?"

The child pointed to the nearest cluster of houses. At the same time he made motions of leaving, but Don Carlos held him back. "No, I'll go with you to explain to your mother what has happened. Because if she sees you arrive like this, she'll be frightened."

"She hits me, too."

Filled with determination to get revenge in the future the child's words reflected only the helplessness he was reduced to at the moment. As soon as he grew up . . .

Don Carlos took him by the hand, and together they arrived at a patio of trampled earth where a woman sitting on a straw mat, surrounded by children of various ages, carded wool.

Seeing the newcomers, she abandoned her work and suddenly cried out. The neighbors emerged immediately, whispering among themselves, airing the most unlikely versions of what had happened. From so many accounts only one fact remained clear: that Don Carlos was kind and skilled, though his skill might not be considered a virtue. He was a trained doctor who could cure not only the boy's slight scratch but also internal ailments that suddenly crop up, like that of poor Enrique Liévano, who for months now had been stretched out on his bed, unable to move.

Wouldn't the nice doctor be kind enough to see him—just a quick look? What's more, Enrique was an orphan cared for by his sister, who earned her living ironing and would not be able to pay him for the consultation. But since he was already here and Enrique lived only a few houses away, what difference did that make? Come on, for the sake of whatever soul he held most dear.

Don Carlos did not know how to ward off these collective pleas, faltering yet vehement. How was he to explain to them that it had been ages since he had scanned a medical text, that he had forgotten even the most rudimentary techniques of listening to the heart and of diagnosis, and that he had not brought with him any instrument that could help him? Nevertheless he nodded and let them escort him.

As he crossed the threshold of an extremely small room, feebly lit by one window and poorly protected from the weather by sparse shingles, what first repulsed Don Carlos was the odor—the stench of a motionless body, of bodily functions, of stale ointments and poultices.

Don Carlos would have liked to retreat, to breathe again the uncontaminated country air, but onlookers blocked the door of the hovel. When he tried to leave, he felt a hand firmly grasp his arm to prevent his escape and to lead him to the sick bed; it was the hand of one of those women whose misfortunes congeal hideously on their faces.

The patient lay upon a cot, a skeleton wrapped in a worn-out, dirty wool blanket, his head resting upon a bundle of clothes serving as a pillow. His cheeks were flushed from fever, and in his sunken eyes shone that glimmer which bonfires emit before flickering out.

The stranger's presence and the intrusion of so many neighbors upset the patient. He wanted to do something—to sit up, perhaps to hide, but his movement turned into a coughing attack, that useless tubercular cough, feeble from repetition, without relief.

Don Carlos was not afraid of being contaminated, and as for the others, who had until then been around Enrique without taking precautions, it seemed useless for them to do so now. The weakest would have succumbed months ago, and the others evidently knew how to protect themselves.

Enrique's sister, Carmen, whose hand had until then gripped Don Carlos' arm, now released him in order to draw up a chair from which the doctor could observe the patient, take his pulse, listen to his breathing, perform, in short, all the ritual without which no cure is deemed possible.

Don Carlos asked her to make the intruders leave and to withdraw herself but only to a distance from which she could remain on call.

Left alone facing Enrique, Don Carlos did not quite know how to begin his questions. In medical school he had learned how to formulate them precisely but from lack of practice had forgotten them, and today his memory went blank in this emergency, perhaps paralyzed by his conviction that any effort would be futile.

What could Enrique say that Don Carlos could not assume? Judging from the advanced stage of the illness, the first revealing symptoms should have appeared months ago. The causes were not difficult to guess: hunger, exhausting work, and malaria. As for the treatment, why even consider it? Neither of the two hospitals in Comitán (one run by the government, the other by nuns) had a ward for contagious diseases. There remained, of course, the possibility of moving him to Mexico City. But who would pay for the move? Don Carlos, in a burst of generosity, could offer to, but such a trip would only serve to hasten the end.

Don Carlos and Enrique talked at length, however, for nothing obsesses a patient so much as the chance to describe his sensations, the more so when the listener is informed and apt to understand what the healthy do not know and cannot even imagine. So Enrique hurriedly amassed details, ventured suppositions, and wanted to make this listener the depository of his secret so that Don Carlos would give him health in return.

Don Carlos did not just listen passively to a story where so many old familiar symptoms of his student days were appearing: Euphoria, the forerunner and inseparable companion of the first stages of the illness; the unpredictable yet persistent fever; the night sweats like those suffered when one awakens from a nightmare. And the cough. Compulsive at first, racking. Later diminishing but obstinately serving to remind the patient perpetually of his condition, that he is not to get excited, that he should be more careful when swallowing, and that air is a rare gift that could be snatched away from him at any moment.

As if lassoing a wild yearling, subduing it, and branding it with its owner's iron, Don Carlos gave technical names to Enrique's descriptions, which were vivid and less awkward than what we might expect from a country person. Gaping, Enrique took in this performance and repeated the magic words which lent an aura of importance to his ailment over which the ignorant would do well to pause and meditate.

Don Carlos could not say good-bye without promising to return the following day. This time he would come provided with instruments and medicines, unlike today, when he had come unexpectedly and without his paraphernalia.

Carmen helped the doctor onto his horse, holding the stirrup without asking a single question or demanding the least reassurance. She would have liked to know only how long, when it would all end. She was tired of always watching a face that each day became more haggard and emaciated. Her invalid tied the steps of the healthy just as a piece of string restrains the flight of a bird. What was she to do with her life, her life that was running away like water through her fingers, her life that found outlets in neither marriage nor religious exercises, in working as a servant, in travel to Mexico City, or as a last resort in becoming a whore, because first and foremost she had to fulfill her duties as a sister?

Without a word, even the customary show of gratitude, Carmen watched Don Carlos leave and envied him being the one to depart at a brisk pace from that hopeless case, from that miserable shack. She watched him leave with the additional certainty that if Don Carlos were a clever man—and he should be, for gentlemen always are—he would never come back.

She was wrong. He did return the following day, and the next, and the next. In his bag, which by now had become part of his person, he brought along some potions that relieved Enrique's pain, fatigue, and choking spells. To prevent him from talking, from wasting his breath, which steadily became more labored, Don Carlos undertook to carry on the conversation all by himself. He recounted his trips abroad, his student adventures, his burning zeal to master his lessons; his first unforgettable amazement when he watched truths from the textbooks become reality in the world of facts; the passion, like a hunter's, with which he tracked down the cause of malfunction in that most complex and perfect of mechanisms, the body; the cold detachment with which, once the cause was discovered, he chose the quickest and most efficient means to eliminate his enemy; his pride in a victory which he would have preferred to attribute to justice rather than to science.

At times, carried away by his eloquent discourse, the doctor failed to notice that Enrique was unable to follow him and to understand. He also realized, belatedly, that the patient's interest waned along with his strength. From then on, Don Carlos' visits were silent. Under the pretense that he was taking the dying man's pulse, he held one of his hands between his own as if he wanted to show his empathy through the light pressure of his fingers. For, perhaps, of all Don Carlos had learned as a doctor, the only lesson he would never forget was that the dying long for help from those who surround them, those from whom they are separated more and more by an inexorably widening gulf, and that they dread this final severance more than their entrance into the valley of the shadows.

During Enrique's final moments, Don Evaristo, a priest from the

Templo Mayor, came deferentially to assist. He heard Enrique's confession, absolved him from his sins, and anointed his feet with the holy oils. While this solemn ceremony that required privacy was being performed, Carmen gave way to her despair by wailing in the patio. Solicitous neighbors offered her tin cups full of steaming water and linden infusions which, by waving her arms, she spilled on the ground in her refusal to let them reach her lips. Thanks to the sedative with which Don Carlos injected her, she sank into a profound sleep. Consequently, all the negotiations to obtain the coffin, including, needless to say, payment for it, and the supervision of the wake and burial were presided over by the doctor, the only man respected among the motley crew of onlookers, some of whom—the men—seized the respectable pretext to get drunk, others—the women—unleashed their hysteria, and the children ran wild.

Don Evaristo sprinkled holy water over the moist, just tamped dirt of the grave and over some bunches of wild flowers lying on it, the kind one picks when sauntering beside stone walls.

When the mourners departed, Dr. Román shook the priest's hand to indicate pleasure at having met him, gratitude for his help in lightening the burden of the recent ordeals, and finally as a sign of farewell. But while Don Evaristo acknowledged the gesture, he refused to grant its parting implication.

"Are you heading home, Doctor? We can walk together part of the way. I live just a few blocks from here. That is, if you don't mind my joining you."

"On the contrary. If I didn't suggest it first, it's only because I've become so unused to people that . . ."

"No one would have thought so seeing you behave with such aplomb when faced with difficult circumstances."

"That's my specialty, Father. If you remember something that occurred long ago, though there was no particular reason why it should have impressed you—I'm referring to my wife's death—you'll recall that I didn't do such a bad job."

They stopped. Don Evaristo was disconcerted by the tasteless, unnecessary remark. Don Carlos stared down as he pensively poked the ground with the metal tip of his cane. All the while his head was bent, he endeavored to make his face expressionless.

"Forgive the poor taste of my comment. One who has grown used to talking to himself says things that shock others."

They started walking again.

"What kind of things do you suppose I hear in the confessional? Precisely those that people say to themselves and conceal from others. I, too, am a specialist, if I may use the term. Many have compared our respective trades, Don Carlos."

"To my knowledge, I practice none."

"Then what do you call what you did for Enrique?"

"It all depends. If we are to judge by the results, I wrought no cure."

"What more could be done for a man already on the brink of death? Yet you're wrong, Don Carlos; there was a cure: yours. At long last you've been rescued from isolation and misanthropy. Unless I'm greatly mistaken, the humble people from this neighborhood, all who have closely observed your selflessness and charity, will never abandon you again."

Don Carlos shrugged his shoulders, resigned. "That's what I'm afraid of: the entrance to my house packed day and night, crowded with worm-infested children, pregnant women, rheumatic old men . . ."

"And since they have nothing to pay you with, they are bound to arrive with a little something for your cooking pot, as they do for mine."

"I'll refuse to accept it."

"I did the same at first. Until I understood that their feelings get hurt. Now the problem is my cook's who is at a loss for new ways of preparing chicken so I can continue to put up with it."

"Mine, Doña Cástula, who knows her way around and knows her business, has some recipes that might provide variety. Why don't you take a chance and come for dinner with me tomorrow evening?"

And so in this casual manner Don Evaristo received and accepted his first invitation to visit Don Carlos' house—an invitation followed by so many others that habit made them unnecessary. Now Don Carlos' house, no longer forlorn, was moreover besieged constantly by the needy, who dirtied it, made a show of their sores, and took advantage of the least opportunity to steal. Doña Cástula would have resigned had she not seen the priest's sacred presence pass through the same door that admitted the rest.

His pastoral duties had given Don Evaristo enough experience not to be misled by first impressions. He had often wondered about Don Carlos Román and inwardly ventured explanations for that strange temperament. But in contrast to the other townsfolk chance drew him sufficiently close to the object of his curiosity to allow detailed observation.

Until now Don Evaristo had known only one trait of Dr. Román: that which he had revealed in his relationship with Enrique Liévano and the attitude he adopted toward those who now came to him for help. He was generous with his time, skill, and money; yet something within Father

Trejo prevented him from considering Don Carlos truly generous. Was it that his actions did not stem from a Christian motive; or did an almost daily visit disclose characteristics in Don Carlos' behavior which, if they did not contradict what is commonly recognized as generosity, were at least ambiguous? Certain biting expressions and cruel mocking forced the priest to withhold judgment, a judgment that, in any event, nothing obliged him to pronounce.

One evening, after a supper Doña Cástula had prepared with special care, subtly mating food and wine, and producing the antique gold-monogrammed china, a set of goblets of the finest crystal, and a tablecloth of the whitest linen, Father Trejo could not help commenting, "Had someone told me you're a bon vivant, Don Carlos, I wouldn't have believed him, not even under oath. But now I must surrender to the evidence. You certainly know how to enjoy the finer things life offers us. And really I don't blame you. They are so few."

"But you're wrong, Don Evaristo. It's not that I'm an expert wine taster, let alone a candidate for hellfire for having indulged in the deadly sin of gluttony. I can give up what the masses call the pleasures of the table (and the pleasures of other household furnishings as well, to be more explicit) without, well, let's not say a sacrifice, but without the slightest effort."

"And so?"

"The clue lies elsewhere. I'm a man ruled strictly by logic. If you are to understand the effects, we must go back to the causes. And to your remarks that some changes have been made in the dining room."

True. The wallpaper had been redone and the ceiling embellished with fine wood paneling. In one corner a brisk, cheerful fire blazed.

"Excuse me, Don Carlos, but first of all I'm astonished by how miraculously fast the work was finished. I'm familiar with the workmen in Comitán, and they're no more industrious than those in the biblical vineyard."

"It's easy to explain. I offered to raise their salary proportionately to the speed with which they finished the job. What's more, Doña Cástula never took her eyes off them for a second. Consequently, while you were on one of your parish rounds, the surprise was readied."

"And can you explain the second miracle as easily?"

"I see no other miracle."

"Your decision to undertake this work."

"Oh, that you'll understand easily. It concerns Doña Cástula. My recent comeback as a doctor has annoyed her. She has overwhelmed me with reproaches, all of them telling that I have prudently and completely ignored them. But once she began to complain of not feeling well, reflecting that a sojourn at the thermal baths of Uninajab would do her good, and opining that the time had come for her to retire and live with her family, etc., etc., I understood that danger was imminent. She was threatening me with nothing less than leaving. On the other hand, I couldn't acknowledge her threats, let alone plead with her to stay on. To offer a raise in salary would have been unforgivably tactless. Obliged to proceed with much more subtlety, many nights I lay awake thinking about what would give Doña Cástula a really deep and, above all, lasting satisfaction. After wracking my brains, I realized that the house, which in the long run is more hers than mine, ought again to be what it once was in the good old days. It should be renovated and resplendent again with the choicest treasures gradually collected by my ancestors one by one and handed on from generation to generation, treasures which augmented not at all and which I did not even allow to be of use. Finally Doña Cástula would be able to show off her talents as a hostess."

The priest smiled gently at Don Carlos' adroit, lengthy explanation of his motives.

"The only prerogative I have fully retained is the selection of my guest: namely, you. To your health, Don Evaristo!"

They raised their glasses and drank. Father Trejo was now laughing heartily.

"Left to my imagination, I'd have attributed all these changes to—how should I word it?—more lofty motives. Such as the ones I assumed in Enrique Liévano's case. I then thought you were trying to draw near to God through charitable works."

Don Carlos' tone, while grave, remained nonetheless cordial. "We have always been very frank about religion, Father. You're not unaware that I respect and admire God, and should our paths ever cross, I won't fail to greet Him with all the consideration due His high rank. Meanwhile, however, I prefer not to meddle in His business, bound to be so much more important and complicated than my own."

"Which boils down to remaining in good standing with your housekeeper. In my ingenuousness, I would have sworn that behind all the recent transformations you and your house have undergone there was a woman."

"Doña Cástula is a woman, Father, even though her age and station prevent you from conceding the title Mother Nature bestowed upon her."

"Let's not joke about it, Doctor. In mentioning a woman, I meant someone your heart might have fancied."

"Fancied?"

Deep in thought, Don Evaristo held his glass between his cupped hands as if uncertain whether to go on. Finally, he said abruptly, "To be united in the Holy Sacrament."

Don Carlos made a gesture to stop him. "Come now, Father, forget the jargon, for a doctor's is far more exact and blunt. Let's use everyday terms. Did you really think I was willing to marry again?"

"Why not? The Scriptures say that it is not good for a man to be alone."

"Vox populi, which after all is vox Dei, affirms that it is better to be alone than in bad company, and I stick to the popular saying rather than to the Scripture."

"Must the company necessarily be bad? Why, the virtue of the women of Comitán is proverbial."

"And you, Father, who know them deep down, since the screen of the confessional is the sieve through which all secrets filter, would you put your hand in the fire for them?"

His answer was a categorical "Yes."

"Well then, let's have a toast that such virtue still persists, and may those who cherish it live forever and a day."

"You don't count yourself among them, do you?"

"I'm no expert in the matter. As far as women are concerned, you could say I've been out of the fray for many years."

Faced with a comment which Don Evaristo interpreted as reflecting a wound still requiring some care, the priest thought it tactful to keep silent. Yet Don Carlos' tone allowed other implications, difficult to define, to shine through. Don Carlos himself explained: "At my age . . . and with my reputation of being an ogre, . . . no, really, there are things one no longer has the right to think about . . ."

Don Evaristo considered it premature to contradict Don Carlos at the moment. Had he done so, he would only have strengthened the position Don Carlos adopted, or claimed to have adopted. Eventually he would find out which during future conversations.

Don Evaristo did not bring up the subject, naturally. By remaining passive, however, he forced Don Carlos to refer to his widowhood once more, and Don Carlos did so as if he were dealing with a state worth mentioning only because of the extreme loneliness and long isolation it had led him to.

"I'll be frank with you, Father. What paralyzed me all those years, to the point of secluding myself and seeing no one, wasn't sorrow. At least, not sorrow alone, though that was part, a large part of it, too. But there was something my mind ran up against day and night: the absurdity of it all. For if you examine it closely, my story has neither rhyme nor reason. I love someone, and at the very moment I'm about to attain that love (what, for you, though you might consider this blasphemous, would be tantamount to getting to heaven) I lose that love forever. Why, just why? For if the love was so deep, it should have been possible. And if it wasn't possible . . . all these years I haven't remained alone merely to weep to my heart's content, rend my garments, and sprinkle ashes over my head, as many have believed. All I've tried to do is understand."

"That's your mistake. The ways of Providence are not ours to understand."

"Enough of that! Remember, Don Evaristo, I'm a man of limited vision and simple motivations. Remember my decorating the dining room. In order to understand my misfortune, I didn't intend to go back to the original causes. No, not at all. I was going to reconstruct all the elements involved in my predicament. I was going to arrange and rearrange them until each fitted into its proper place, like the pieces of a puzzle, until all became coherent and meaningful before my eyes. As I have already told you more than once, Father, my main passion is logic."

"Did it help you at all in this case? Did it at least comfort you?"

"More than that. I nevertheless don't owe everything to logic, but to persistence and patience as well. I ended up freeing myself from an obsession in which time was meaningless. Now that the obsession has vanished, I must admit it's too late."

"How old are you?"

"Thirty-nine. And in excellent physical health. But age and health don't count when you consider the inner turmoil I have suffered. As a result of it, I'm finished."

"That's not the impression you give. Your obvious concern for those who come to consult you can be explained only as a result of affection . . . or vanity."

"For some months now, I've been suffering from a thyroid condition which compels me to keep on the move."

"Morality, physiology, who cares? This appetite for activity, manifested as a kind of sympathy, can also be applied to relationships other than those between doctor and patient."

"And what about our friendship, Father?"

"It's not very satisfactory because of its exclusiveness, and then I'm not a worldly man. Besides, there's a higher level of spiritual and physical communion."

"I suppose you are referring to love."

"Marriage, to use a term embracing both the moral and physiological. I want to corral you."

"I give up. But please, a truce. The idea, the very idea of . . . it still seems so unbearable, so hard to swallow."

Because marriage was an abstract idea, Don Evaristo knew that the best way to overcome his friend's resistance was not to argue, but to put before his eyes names, figures, living embodiments, as it were, of such a possibility.

From his childhood as an orphan, when he had been entrusted to the seminary's impersonal care, Don Evaristo, whom Divine Grace had until then preserved from the sins of a concupiscent eye without any great effort or deserving on his part, had confined his feminine ideal to the Virgin Mary under the advocation of our Lady of Perpetual Succor. Her purity, resplendent in its beauty, was enhanced by her inaccessibility. It was easy to be moved to tears by merely contemplating her perfections. It was easy to remain faithful, above all if one considered that Don Evaristo was not surrounded by women of flesh and blood apart from his more or less close relatives, more or less impertinent with their whimsical notions, or his more or less assiduous parishioners, or his more or less sincere penitents. On the other side of the fence—that side upon which, to avoid endangering his everlasting salvation he would never dare trespass—ranged the serpent's disciples, Satan's allies, the repositories of all evil secrets.

As a result of his set ways and limitations, had someone suddenly asked Don Evaristo to describe the features of one of the ewes in his flock, to match a name with a body, to indicate the traits of a personality, he would have been at a loss. Thanks to his resolve to find Don Carlos Román a wife, Father Trejo began paying attention to the eligible girls' features, noticed their words, clothes, and attitudes, and remembered peoples' comments about them. Thus he learned, with no less surprise than compassion, of the desperate fight maidens put up from the very moment of their becoming eligible against the years which others counted inexorably; in secrecy he heard disclosures about every family's faults; he discreetly inquired into the size of fortunes and dowries. After a most careful winnowing, he finally decided to show Don Carlos his trumps.

The session was not held in the dining room or study, for neither the masons nor the carpenters had finished their work, but in the parlor, where the furniture had been stripped of its protective coverings and where the mirrors, relieved of the mourning crepe that had shadowed them for many years, reflected ornaments of porcelain, gold, and ivory, the meticulous detail of the woodcarving, and the austere chiaroscuro of pictures from which peered the faces of stern men, prim ladies, and muted children, all surveying the present, from whose bustle they had been removed.

The first candidate Don Evaristo offered Don Carlos was Amalia Suasnávar. She made up for her lack of lineage and meagre wealth with the unselfishness of a character tempered by adversity. Her behavior during her mother's long, painful illness showed how patiently, sweetly, and cheerfully a person whose moral conscience fully reigns over human selfishness can bear a cross.

Don Carlos paid the expected tribute of admiration to Miss Suasnávar but expressed certain objections, unimportant ones, needless to say. Why should someone who may choose total perfection be content with what is only half satisfactory? Miss Suasnávar, if Don Carlos had not been misinformed, had carried her humility to the extent of allowing her brothers, who showed up only at the moment of the distribution of their mother's estate, to snatch away her inheritance. Miss Suasnávar carried her modesty to the point of dressing freakishly and her shyness to the extreme of not entering into conversations except to blunder. Wasn't she the girl who became notorious during her late mother's novena for complaining before the mourners of a stubborn insomnia from which, when she managed by some kind of miracle to induce a moment's sleep, she had bucked about so that she immediately awoke in moral anguish. When people found out what Miss Suasnávar meant by "bucking about" they realized she had supposed that the only creature given to bucking about was a colt.

Unable to counter this, Don Evaristo moved on to candidate number two, Soledad Armendáriz, called Cholita by everyone because of the warmth she inspired spontaneously and immediately among those privileged to know her. She was very young, of course, almost a child, but for Don Carlos this meant being able to mold and shape her according to his taste. Her innate goodness became evident when her beauty, justly praised by acquaintances and strangers alike, not only did not swell her with pride, but she did not even try to enhance it with cosmetics or show it off at outings and parties. Far from it, she tried not to attract attention, so that, if she sinned from overdoing anything, it was in the modesty of her attire and attitudes. So much so that those closest to her came even to suspect some mystical bent, which, as experience proves, is a very good ingredient in happy marriages.

"Cholita Armendáriz . . . Cholita Armendáriz . . ." Don Carlos drummed the arm of his chair with his fingertips as if trying to recall something. Until at last he arose with a triumphant gesture. Why, of course! Wasn't she the one who played the angel at all gatherings and who, suffering from tonsilitis, had once to be replaced in the role by her sister in order not to cancel the performance? Faced with such a prospect, Cholita, driven by a religious zeal that surpassed her sisterly affection, saw the perfect opportunity to reveal her sister's unworthiness to wear garments made sacred by what they represented, to cover a body that had abandoned itself to the lowest passions. Cholita mentioned with surprising accuracy the accomplices' names, the places, times, and number of acts, of which she had kept a careful record. The parish soirée did not take place, of course, but the inhabitants of Comitán savored a juicy scandal instead. The sister was banished to one of her father's ranches, and Cholita enhanced the attractiveness of her own appearance with the virtue of an implacable, fiery finger ready to point at corruption wherever it might be, even among those she cherished most.

Like his fellow townspeople, Don Carlos applauded this quality, though it was preferable to contemplate it from afar rather than run the risk of sometime becoming the object of Cholita's accusation. For the flesh is weak, the righteous man falls seventy times a day, and no one is free from temptation.

Candidate three, Leonila Rovelo, was rich and aristocratic and enjoyed excellent health . . .

"Please, Don Evaristo, don't go on. I know her and I think she's a splendid example of a Swiss cow. While she might be good for nursing the entire town, she is incapable of stringing two words together. Do you know why she broke off with Ramiro Albores, the suitor she was about to marry?"

Don Evaristo had to admit he did not.

"Well, it so happened that, with the wedding imminent, Leonila's relatives looked the other way to let the couple talk alone for a few moments. The setting could not have been better: a bench in the park surrounded by jasmine trees, whose aroma, as the poets say, scented the air. From the bandstand the marimba emitted its sweetest melodies, and the moon shone softly in the sky. It was one of those opportunities one doesn't enjoy twice. Ramiro, though certainly no poet, summoned up enough eloquence, however, to speak about his love, his hopes, the happiness they would achieve together. Leonila listened to him enraptured, but when it was time for her to say something, she began to tie knots in her handkerchief. Ramiro insisted, politely at first, then more firmly, but always tenderly. He finally dared to take her hand, but she remained speechless. When at long last she decided to speak, it was to say, 'What time is it?'"

"She must have had something urgent to do."

"No, nothing urgent, and besides right in front of her loomed the enormous town clock with all its numbers so that, if she had to, in the last resort she could have glanced at it. But, no, she only tried to say one short everyday sentence that she herself could understand."

Don Evaristo was not deterred by Don Carlos' victory. "You should have said so before! What you really want is a brain. Well, then, there's Elvira Figueroa: she invents acrostics to Saint Caralampio, the patron of her neighborhood and performer of countless miracles . . ."

"Not including the marriage of that young maiden, of course."

"Men fear her and run from her because they don't care to compete with her. She knows by heart the names of the capitals of Europe and can solve even the most complicated crossword puzzles."

"And meanwhile the house comes tumbling down."

"No, you're not going to catch me on that point. Home economics holds no secrets for her. And as for her culinary talents, suffice it to say that even the nuns of the Convent of the Merced ask for her recipes and advice when they want to show off every time they entertain the bishop."

"But I doubt that she can beat Doña Cástula."

"In other areas as well, she's a most consummate artist. She embroiders, does charming woodburnings, embosses velvet, paints in water colors . . ."

"And plays the piano."

"With such bravura that no man could possibly match her."

"So that explains the moustache!"

"Doctor, what you have just said is indelicate, to say the least. One never mentions that kind of shortcoming in a young lady. Even if she does shave."

"Mea culpa, Don Evaristo. Let's proceed."

"I can't think of anyone else."

"How come? Could you possibly have failed to notice your neighbors across the street?"

"Whom do you mean? The Orantes girls?"

"That's right. For unless I've offended you by what I have just said about Miss Figueroa's moustache—I take it all back and from now on, I shall refer to it as a downy shadow—I can't really fathom why you haven't put one of the three on your list. From among the three of them, any taste is apt to be pleased."

"Not yours, which is so demanding. The eldest, Blanca, is a lady of the Sacred Heart of Mary and Warden of the Holy Sacrament."

"As far as I know, she's never had a suitor."

"No, and unfortunately she doesn't have the calling of a nun either. Hence she has to content herself with the lukewarmness of spinsterhood."

"What about the next one?"

"Yolanda? She's scared that if she even goes near the church her sister's fate will overtake her. And so she lives only for a good time and has made a play for every man in Comitán. Except you—she's too smart to bark up the wrong tree. At this stage after having tried her hand with every man, only traveling salesmen remain available. She attracts them, but as soon as they find out what the score is they either try to take advantage of her or pull up stakes. That's what life is like for her. Now take the youngest, Romelia, who thinks she's the cat's meow though she has barely put on an evening dress for her first ball, and now no day passes when two or three young whippersnappers don't swarm like gnats to her balcony or a night when they don't serenade her."

"Is she very pretty or merely flirtatious?"

"How do I know? How do you expect me to look at her after the marimba her suitors serenade her with keeps me awake all night long and I have to get up at the crack of dawn for my first mass?"

"It'd be worth taking a look, Father, even with sleepy, bloodshot eyes. I saw her once. And she impressed me as a person with a thirst for life. Not with a thirst that debases, no, but rather with a longing that exalts. What shines on her face is not hunger but an urge for fulfillment."

"Aha! So we've been playing dirty, have we? While I was painstakingly scrutinizing souls, you've had an ace up your sleeve."

"Father, I've seen her only from a distance and that's all. Just once. I know nothing about her and haven't wanted to inquire."

"And yet, you know all about the others. Thanks to Doña Cástula, I suppose."

"Doña Cástula is no longer my only contact with the world. I now have my patients, Father. And you know how freely people can talk, I mean really talk, with only their priest or doctor."

"So it's the patients. For some time now I've noticed that mainly the well-to-do have stayed on. There are no longer so many poor ones in the hall, and instead you've had to spruce up the waiting room with comfort-

able armchairs, flower vases, and tables with magazines on them. . . .
No, this isn't a reproach. Merely the observation of a natural law. Water
seeks its own level."

"I've become popular among the well-to-do. They come to see a queer
duck at close hand."

"And what about you? How do you treat them?"

"I give them their due."

"Well, then, they're going to keep coming. Have you managed any
cures?"

"Spectacular ones. As if by incantation I've made imaginary ailments
disappear, though of course I've never promised a permanent cure. The
rich need a hobby, and it's not right to deprive them of their whims."

"Hmm. Not a bad tactic. By now you've become famous. One of these
days, Don Rafael Orantes, the father of the girl who has caught your eye,
will end up coming to see you. He is somewhat advanced in age and suffers certain discomforts. His family worries. What's to become of them all
when they are no longer sustained by the respect now paid to the man of
the family? Who's to administer the money Don Rafael has made driving
herds of cattle to Guatemala to sell?"

"But he has a son. I remember him well; we were schoolmates. He was
called Rafael after his father."

"He died a while back."

"How strange I never knew. It must have happened when I was away
from Comitán."

"No. It was about the same time your wife died. A few days later."

"Oh, that explains it then. I lost touch with everything but my misfortune. But what did he die of?"

"A hunting accident. His gun went off and blew his brains out."

"Rafael must have been quite young, well, as young as I thought I was.
Twenty-eight more or less."

"Yes, more or less."

"Was he single or married?"

"He gave his parents many a headache. He liked to run around and
chase girls. There he'd go, sampling here and there. But he never really
went steady with any girl."

Don Carlos smacked his thigh sharply like one who has just remembered something. "Why, yes, it's true. Estela herself told me something
about his having courted her."

"Why should she be the exception?"

"The affair became somewhat complicated because Estela's mother objected to the relationship and forbade them, in no uncertain terms, to see each other or to write. In short, her mother behaved as if marriage was really what she was after. No mention was ever made of it. Not even of an engagement."

Don Carlos capriciously changed the subject. "So for lack of a male heir, Don Rafael Orantes leaves three women behind. Oh, Don Evaristo, it's in cases like these I regret not being a Muslim."

"That's sacrilegious as well as hypocritical. You've already given one girl the eye. And the other two might just as well be erased from the face of the earth."

Don Carlos assumed a grave expression before answering. "Now remember, Don Evaristo, I know nothing about Romelia. And now, thanks to you, I'm anxious to find out all I can."

Hardly against his will Don Carlos had, however, another continual source of reliable information: Doña Cástula, who from her vantage point perceived details that, though trivial and simpleminded, revealed much more than the vague generalities Don Evaristo used in trying to define Romelia's personality. Doña Cástula grew wary as she noticed how her domain was being endangered. For now some of the farm hands who worked by the week were turning the earth in the garden to plant new seeds, old trees were being pruned, corridors were being filled with rare orchids, and imported vines were growing around the pillars.

That Don Carlos should be in a mild quandary concerning women would have seemed natural and completely reasonable to Doña Cástula, whereas the contrary would have seemed altogether abnormal. But that he should remarry she considered untimely, risky, and even slightly ridiculous. The more so when one considered that the favorable winds were blowing in the direction of the youngest Orantes daughter, a member of a family whose servants never stayed on, who lived in a house whose service one entered out of curiosity and left with enough material to entertain all the other Comitecan ladies during their idle hours.

From all she heard about Romelia, Doña Cástula gathered that her birth was a miracle performed by Saint Anne since it occurred long after her parents had given up hope of more offspring. For this very reason, and on account of the great age difference between her and her older brother and sisters, Romelia became the pet. She was cuddled in the arms of one person after another, and they quarreled over who was to lull her to sleep, amuse her, and give her sweets. The affection of the family was so pervasive that Romelia quite naturally came to regard herself as the center of the universe. Since no one needed to be persuaded of this fact, she did not have to resort to tantrums, stubbornness, or imaginary illnesses because no one ever forgot who Romelia was and her importance.

Under such propitious circumstances her character therefore became pleasant, even lively and outgoing. She knew herself to be the bestower of happiness and was herself happy in being able to supply it to others.

She was not expelled from this childhood paradise by school discipline, for year after year the adults postponed her registration, nor by the indifference of those surrounding her, nor by the disloyalty of someone engrossed in more urgent matters or more demanding affections. It was death that finally destroyed Romelia's world. Unable to understand death, she could not face it.

Death not only snatched away her brother, Rafael, perhaps the most devoted of her worshippers, at least the one who came up with the nicest surprises, most varied diversions, and most exciting excursions; it also changed those who had previously loved her into profoundly strange, inscrutable, and hostile beings.

Full of rancor, she still remembered that on the day the Indians brought Rafael's body on a litter from the ranch no one looked her way or made a move to shield her from the horrible sight. Nor did anyone during the preparations for the burial notice whether Romelia ate or not. During the nights of the novena Romelia, her teeth chattering with fright, shut herself up in her bedroom where not even sleep kept her company. She lost track of the number of times fever came and went with no loving hand to touch her forehead or offer some remedy to her lips. Why should she cry if there were no witnesses? To whom could she turn? In a wide-eyed stupor Romelia watched what was happening around her.

Hysterical, her mother, Doña Ernestina, wandered unkempt and dirty about the house. Neither her husband's authority nor her daughters' pleas sufficed to bring her to her senses. When she agreed to stay in her room, she conjured up, screaming in the dark, the presence of her departed son. She took advantage of the slightest negligence of those guarding her to summon fortune tellers, soothsayers, and women suspected of witchcraft. She even dared to defy Don Rafael's anger as well as public opinion by attending a séance from which she was thrown out for having violently tried to force the medium to materialize her dead son.

Don Rafael bore the tragedy differently. He kept on tending to his business with great care. He did not stop seeing his friends, and he continued to preside at the family table where the places of Rafael and Doña Ernestina were now vacant. But no one remembers seeing him laugh, let down his reserve, or relax the conscious control over his own actions which might otherwise have gotten out of hand. When alone he broke down and wept over the ruins of a life he no longer cared to preserve now that it had lost its reason for being. As a consequence, he readily surrendered to the first indications of sickness and decrepitude, though not to the point of changing the habits he had managed with such heroic effort to keep intact.

As for Rafael's sisters, their youthful energy and hope for the future tempered their suffering. Disconcerted by their mother's clamorous, irrational grief, they suspected that this event, which after all was natural and which many of their friends bore matter-of-factly and with resignation, veiled a mystery that their feminine nature prevented them from understanding. And they could not imagine any reason for involving themselves directly.

Blanca vaguely suspected some sin—suicide?—which she felt obliged to expiate. Yolanda, ashamed of Doña Ernestina's eccentricities, accepted them as a challenge to which she responded by exaggerating her efforts to please. Thus, one sister became devout, the other coquettish. And to realize their desires, both were counting on an inheritance which had suddenly taken on a magnitude that their minds could not conceive.

As for Romelia, at first she tried to show her intense grief in every possible way to attract the others' wavering attention. She fainted in public and was melancholy in private. But her mother was a genuine competitor; besides, she was much too expert so that Romelia was forced to retreat. She chose persistence rather than showiness. She not only refused to come out of mourning long after the prescribed period was over but even to relieve it with a swatch of color. She always wore a locket where she kept neatly folded the only note her brother ever wrote her. He had written on the occasion of the first peach crop at the ranch. The note said simply, "I hope you enjoy them."

Though in the eyes of the Comitecans Romelia's displays turned her into a legendary figure, they did not succeed in drawing her parents and sisters out of their self-absorption. In desperation she sought out substitute affection to compensate for all she had lost in the catastrophe. She clung to the maids' skirts, to the seamstress who came to mend the family's clothes, and to the chocolate-grinder.

The help paid attention to her because after all as the master's daughter she was bound to deserve it. But each inhabited a world apart in which Romelia did not fit.

When she began school—for in a lucid moment her parents noticed that Romelia was twelve years old and did not even know the rudiments of reading—she painfully discovered that being named Romelia Orantes meant nothing and that though her family name was good there were others equal or better with which she had to compete. If she wanted to win her teachers' and classmates' approval, she had to be deserving. She could succeed by applying herself to her studies, acquiring skill in games, and being loyal under difficult circumstances.

Romelia's first reaction to school showed both pride and rejection. She refused to accept the rules and wanted to return to her childhood omnipotence and invulnerability. But her will came into conflict with her father's and was crushed under his final orders, which forced her to keep attending classes with extreme punctuality.

Humiliated, Romelia strove to adjust to her new circumstances; she did so somewhat ineptly and with little success. She earned the tepid sympathy of this nun or that, but never the exclusive, impassioned favoritism enjoyed by others whose behavior was more exemplary than her own. She managed to have one or two conversations with girls whom, given the choice, she would have repudiated. She never shared a secret, swore an oath of friendship like those the others exchanged, or received an invitation to see someone outside the classroom.

Living in such an unsatisfactory present, Romelia turned to the past to idealize the image of her dead brother, the only faithful one, and to preserve a ritual that his family, becoming indifferent and oblivious with time, was beginning to abandon. The symbol of that ritual was the locket always shining upon her breast even on the most insignificant occasions and to the exclusion of all other jewelry.

Meanwhile, Romelia was contriving plans for future revenge. Some time, in a manner still vague to her, she was going to recover her privileged position. She was going to be raised to heights inaccessible to others; in sublime exaltation she was going to be proclaimed the favorite.

The instrument to achieve these ends began to become apparent to her with the dawning of puberty. It was to be her body. Beneath the schoolgirl's dark, severe uniform, men divined contours that promised to be magnificent.

Romelia, far from being embarrassed by lascivious stares, once more felt the electrified atmosphere of her childhood. But now she knew something she had previously ignored: that power is always fragile; since any circumstance can destroy it, you must take advantage of it while you have it in your hands, use it intelligently to get what really counts.

What really counted for her was love, a form of love that would fill her emptiness and not need to be reciprocated, though of course she was not so naïve as to be unwilling to make necessary concessions for the sake of appearance.

Next came position, for love must descend toward the chosen like light from a distant, powerful star, not rise like a cloud of incense. Romelia would exchange Orantes only for a better name.

Then came fortune. Though used to the security wealth offered, she needed to develop to the point of enjoying luxury. She was endowed not with the crass instinct inevitably to prefer the gaudiest, but with the perceptiveness to discern the most expensive.

While Romelia was arriving at the final stage of her ambition, she had to be content with such minor triumphs as being elected queen of the National Holidays and appearing in all the ceremonies escorted by a representative of the governor himself, receiving daily homage from some admirer to whom she would not deign to show the slightest gesture of kindness, discovering her friends' envy and watching it closely, so closely that she exasperated her sisters, especially Yolanda.

These episodes satisfied Romelia for a day, a while. At times, for reasons she could not fathom, she felt at peace for months. But the other, the real, the definite was slow in jelling.

When it did jell, it exceeded all her expectations, even the wildest and most ambitious. A man like Don Carlos met the required conditions to the utmost perfection and added to them one more trait, that of having been considered unconquerable.

How many girls had tried to lure and attract him but had been forced to abandon the venture as impossible! Then suddenly a girl not only uninterested in Don Carlos but even unaware of his existence unhinges him, forcing him to seek her out, pursue her, frequent places previously scorned, and adopt attitudes lowering him in everyone's eyes in order to woo her with all the guile of the art.

Don Carlos, who had not set foot in church since the day of his wedding, now attended early mass daily just to wait for Romelia's arrival, observe her from afar during the ceremony, and follow her at a distance as she returned home.

She felt his stare, which made her tremble, with a feeling of triumph. Some time that man, so strong and complete, so much a master of himself yet intimidated by her mere presence, was going to dare to approach her, speak to her, tell her that he loved her, beg that she condescend to be his fiancée and wife. She would feign bewilderment, surprise, and would sweeten the prescribed initial rejection with false modesty. How could a distinguished person of Don Carlos' cultivation and experience (no, she would not allude to his age; he might be offended) possibly have come to notice a girl as insignificant as Romelia? Of course it was possible that he had let himself be dazzled by appearances.

But how long does a pretty face last? And what is it good for if virtue and sobriety are not also present? Romelia, who to say the least was frank and open to everyone, should confess her defects, some of them serious and others merely annoying. The man who wanted her would have to accept her just as God made her. And since this would not be easy, nothing less than love, true love, was imperative.

Though this confession had all the appearance of a rejection, it would be so cunningly worded that Don Carlos, no matter how obtuse he might be, would finally detect in her some hope encouraging him to prove his love to be as true as the love she required.

Once set within this framework, Romelia would gradually concede that at her age no character is definitively formed and that under able direction and wise counseling she could mend her ways. For like all young girls, Romelia enjoyed flattery and delighted in parties and relished them when-ever they were to be had, though naturally she of course relished them within the limits of decency so that no one could accuse her of indiscre-tion, slips, or folly. Her purity, already tested occasionally, had proved to her that some kinds of temptation are not so easily resisted. But Romelia was not going to cling to these habits because she understood that what attracted her to promenades and parties was nothing more than what a married woman finds abundantly in her own home: namely, company, support, protection, and love. Having these, one feels calm and peaceful, and the world outside seems less appealing.

Though her frivolous side seemed to make light of such a state, Romelia had never dreamed of more than a tranquil, secure affection. She dis-trusted the passions, feared adventures, and longed for nothing more than to find a worthy man to whom she could dedicate herself unconditionally and faithfully. Unfortunately, Romelia was one of those women who keep their word, single-mindedly pursuing what she wanted.

Her imaginary confession so moved her that it brought abundant tears to her eyes. With the fingers of her right hand she convulsively clutched the locket, symbol of her steadfast affections.

From the way Don Carlos endured his widowhood Romelia sensed that he above all would know how to appreciate what her keeping the locket meant. Veneration due the dead might become their first area of agree-ment; later they might discover astonishing affinities of tastes based on the present was well as the past. Romelia was willing to be instructed and initiated into his interests, whatever they might be, or to show contempt for people who waste their time in trivialities in case Don Carlos had no interests.

Romelia decided to respect Don Carlos' past as sacred and not refer to it without previous authorization; and when she did, she would speak of it in the tone of someone who understands that the reality she confronts exceeds her own merits.

For example, she had heard that Don Carlos had turned one of the main rooms of his house into a sort of museum where he kept Estela's belongings intact, scrupulously looked after and clean. Well, then, Estela's successor would serve as the most zealous guardian of the veneration that this—not museum, but altar—deserved until Don Carlos himself would beg her not to overdo it, and she would obediently let cobwebs grow, mildew spread, and mold multiply. No one would again remember the closed room when so many open ones would require attention and care. Time would breed inevitable complications, pregnancies and births, for instance. The moment would come when there would not be sufficient room for herself and the newborn. Could Don Carlos oppose storing the useless objects in a trunk and converting the room into a nursery? Then afterward, she could put it to other uses, for the sewing room she had always dreamed of and had planned exactly how to decorate.

According to rumor, Don Carlos was melancholy; so Romelia would adjust to his mood at first. But, gradually, solicitous for her husband's welfare, she would try to gather a select circle of friends around them both. They would organize parties, trips to the country, and maybe . . . maybe even balls.

What place would Don Evaristo, now Don Carlos' only friend, find in this circle? Probably none because it would comprise primarily young married couples, and the presence of a bachelor, a priest moreover, is always awkward, inhibits others, and kills the liveliness and spontaneity. They would reserve special days, farther and farther apart, for receiving Don Evaristo until he and Don Carlos would understand simultaneously that their worlds had drifted apart and try to avoid agonizing visits during which no topic of conversation flourishes, no interest is shared, and no statement meets with approval.

Romelia was sure that Doña Cástula, considering herself lady and mistress of the house, would certainly put up a fight, not surrendering readily to being dethroned by a newcomer; the newcomer, she must therefore treat the indispensable Doña Cástula carefully, for Romelia wanted to unload all the tedious routines of housewife and mother upon her. But her tactics would involve a kind of reeling in and letting out, generous concessions and arbitrary refusals, strict vigilance to keep her from overstepping her bounds and forgetting her inferior station combined with extreme benevolence and acts of absolute confidence.

In general terms, this could be an effective line of action. But here, as in everything else, Romelia was prepared to improvise along the way, change her attitudes according to circumstances, and even revise them altogether if necessary.

For example, in the case of the engagement. Her calculations proved useless from the moment Don Carlos failed to discuss this matter with her directly but instead, under the pretext that he would be unable to bear a refusal, sent Father Trejo as his emissary to the Orantes family.

Thus, the arrangements were carried out on a level where one's presence, Romelia's at least, did not count. Before consulting her, her parents weighed the pros and cons of such a match, and Don Rafael had the foresight to call on Doña Clara Domínguez, Estela's mother, to ask for references concerning the man who had been her son-in-law.

Though Doña Clara could never forgive Don Carlos for not inviting her as a widow, also alone, to stay in his house, where she had attended her daughter when sick and her wake when dead, and to remain there permanently as his housekeeper but had preferred to place his trust in a servant, she had to admit that as a husband he was flawless.

From the very beginning he recognized the seriousness of Estela's illness and did what he could to cure her. He spared no expense and had famous specialists come from Mexico City; he also let the humblest local healers give opinions. The means were not important to him. What mattered was Estela's life. And he fought at first to save it, then to prolong it, never betraying a sign of impatience or weariness until nothing more was possible. For God determines a man's last breath and man takes not another; Estela's fate was sealed.

Encouraged by these disclosures, Don Rafael felt inclined to consent to the wedding. He accordingly transmitted to Romelia through Doña Ernestina not a recommendation but an order which the girl obeyed with the docility of a model child, the only role which at this moment she was allowed to assume.

During the brief engagement Don Carlos and Romelia were systematically prevented from seeing each other alone, for such is the custom. But when, by tacit agreement, the chaperones should grow negligent for a moment, she would lower her eyes and blush, waiting for the romantic phrase she had read in a novel, the languid look like the one issuing from the eyes of a picture postcard model, and the brutal, clumsy attempt to get close that she would heroically resist.

But Don Carlos seemed not to notice the opportunity presented to him and wasted the fleeting moments talking of clothes ordered from Mexico City, of the carpenters' delay in delivering the furniture, of the need to get the certificate of baptism.

How was Romelia to interpret her fiancé's behavior? He did not act out of clumsiness, needless to say, for he was a man of the world; nor from lack of love because when a man does not love a woman he does not marry her, and this man seemed to be devoured by a feverish anxiety that the event be consummated. Therefore he must be acting out of tact. That was all. She should feel flattered and grateful.

At long last the wedding ceremony, a solemn mass sung by three priests with Don Evaristo Trejo as the chief officiate, was celebrated in the main church. The nave blazed with lights and flowers supplied by every possible vendor in Comitán.

In the background the organ and children's choir struck up the moment the bridal party entered. Dressed in antique brocade, with no jewelry save the famous locket, the bride, at her father's side, advanced along a red carpet with deliberately slow steps so that her beauty could be observed down to the smallest detail of her attire. Her expression reflected the seriousness appropriate to the act whereby she was committing her life, her blush seemed essential to the nature of that act, and her budding smile foreshadowed happiness.

Next came the groom escorting Doña Ernestina, wondrously lucid. She walked with a sprightly step, proud of her tasteful, elegant attire, bejeweled as always on grand occasions with diamonds inherited from her great-grandparents as if in all the years since Rafael's death she had done nothing except appear in society.

Romelia's sisters, the bridesmaids, had in no way been able to agree on the colors and style of their dresses. Blanca chose a dark gray fabric with a severe nunlike cut. Yolanda had to give in to the entreaties of her future brother-in-law and adapt a dress that had captured her fancy—a bright red silk with an unduly low neckline and sleeves much too short. To keep the peace she had to compromise by reducing its intense color to a moderate shade with an inoffensive opaque tier which softened the brightness of the fabric. A veil concealed the plunging neckline, and long gloves almost came up to the sleeves.

The guests paid little attention to the men. Don Rafael's bearing was that of an old man who by the force of his will stands steadfast but upon whom life has already turned its back. Don Carlos, still youthful and well set up, with a jaw that openly hinted at stubbornness and a frown revealing remoteness, expressed nothing but the poise, self-assurance, and self-control of one who has passed through hardships and thanks to his courage emerged victorious to reach at long last a safe harbor.

When the protagonists knelt on the bench, music flooded every recess of the church with the chords of Gounod's *Ave Maria*. At the reading of the Gospel silence prevailed, and the guests, standing, listened to the words with which the priest pronounced them man and wife.

Don Evaristo spoke easily and enthusiastically of the perfection of Christian matrimony, the earthly symbol of the mystical union of the church and Christ, of the duties their new status imposed upon the wedded couple, and of their obligation to form a family based solidly on faith and obedience to the Divine Commandments.

Through lowered eyes Romelia managed to glance about quickly. Yes, there in the closest pews were her friends, who tomorrow and perhaps always would still be called señoritas; who were not to be initiated, as she was to be this evening, into the mysteries of life; who would not attend outings, social gatherings, or burials supported by a man's strong arm; who would not hide behind a husband's person to avoid the annoyance of petty decisions and the responsibility of important ones; who would not use a husband's name to deny a favor and refuse hospitality; who would not incur debts backed by a husband's credit; who would be unable to invoke a husband's authority to dismiss a maid or punish a child.

From today on Romelia would join the company of women who never say, "I want" or "I don't want," but who always dodge issues by deferring to the man of the house to achieve their aims. This side-stepping may be condensed in a single phrase: "the master wishes . . . the master prefers . . . the master orders . . . one mustn't contradict the master . . . above all one must please the master . . . first I must consult the master"—the master who would exalt her above all to the rank of wife and intimately give her a true image of her body that would finally reach the fullness of knowing, feeling, and performing the functions for which it had been created.

The musicians burst forth in a Gloria in which the thousand different sounds of a crowd preparing to disperse soon joined. Bumping into each other, smiling, mutually yielding the way, the guests, up to the brim with their impatience to comment on the events, began to whisper in short, abrupt phrases. Behind perfumed handkerchiefs they concealed their smiles but allowed amusement, derision, and envy to show in their eyes. Considering the newlyweds' destiny, they shrugged their shoulders with a skepticism which seemed unfounded, for everything, love, youth, and wealth, favored the alliance. And yet . . .

The reception was held in the evening at the house of the bride's parents. The only incident worth mentioning apart, of course, from the abundant, exquisite food, plentiful wines, and attentions lavished upon the guests was that at the very moment when the bride and groom posed for the traditional photograph, a black butterfly came flying in through an open window and lit upon the train of the wedding dress. Before anyone had time to chase it away, a whisper had already passed through the crowd: "It's the soul of Estela!"

Romelia turned pale with humiliation, anger, and fear. Her heartbeat so quickened that her locket slipped from its center position to the side opposite her heart. The bride cast a pleading look at the man beside her, now her husband whose duty it was to protect her. She expected him to rescue her from this predicament and define her rightful place before everyone's eyes. Don Carlos responded with a quick, decisive movement that brushed the butterfly away, while others, following his example, finally chased it out of the room.

Romelia sighed with relief and half closed her eyes to prevent others from detecting a gleam of triumph that might dazzle them. Until then she had been uncertain of what place she held in Don Carlos' affections. Her vanity bristled at the very thought of playing second fiddle, though common sense convinced her that Estela would retain first place at least during the initial days of the marriage. But now Romelia knew that she was walking on conquered territory and that her rival had no more substance than a ghost.

This revelation climaxed a day during which, in one unique, privileged, miraculous instant, her childhood paradise converged with the overflowing present. This moment, which realized her dream not only of happiness but also of restitution and justice, led her through the doorway to the wide-open path of maturity as much as it returned her to her remotest origins and roots.

Even so, when she bade her family farewell to follow her husband, she wept and clung to her mother. The two men, the one who had watched over her maidenhood and the one who was going to shelter her unto death, had to persuade her tenderly to leave the embrace custom prescribes and without which parents would feel offended by their daughter's ingratitude and ease in leaving them and the husband would distrust the apparently loose character of the woman in whose hands he had just placed his honor.

Meanwhile, all was ready in Don Carlos' house to receive him and his new wife. The bride's belongings, sent beforehand, were now put away in wardrobes, chests, dressing tables, and jewelry boxes. Her bridal night-gown was spread upon the bed, and the dim lamps were but a prelude to darkness.

With these preparations over and a cold supper and some uncorked bottles of champagne set on the table, Doña Cástula, annoyed by it all, discreetly withdrew to her bedroom, now at the back of the house.

Romelia crossed the threshold gently supported by Don Carlos. He courteously inquired whether she wanted to see what, from that moment, was to belong to her forever. To demonstrate her disinterest, she replied that she was exhausted from the commotion and excitement of the day. Don Carlos upbraided himself aloud for not having grasped such an obvious fact and led her straight to the bedroom. After showing her where she could find things she might need, he left her alone to move about freely.

Romelia explored a bit, pondered the value of objects, and then quickly and adeptly took off her wedding dress and its accessories. Before slipping into her nightgown, she briefly studied herself in the mirror and smiled approvingly at her nakedness. She hesitated over which side of the bed should be hers and decided on the one closer to the dressing table. She made herself comfortable, gracefully spread her hair over the pillow, and waited for Don Carlos to arrive. He did not make her wait long and, in the same motion with which he leaned over to kiss her, turned off the light.

Romelia woke up upon hearing someone brusquely draw the window curtains. Closing her eyes tightly to protect them against the violent intrusion of morning light, she muttered a protest.

For a few moments she continued to be seemingly confused, unable to decide where she was or recognize her surroundings. Then Doña Cástula's respectful but not servile voice made her suddenly realize her location. Instinctively she covered herself with the sheets—a useless gesture since the housekeeper had not deigned to look at her but went about performing other, more practical duties. Setting the breakfast tray down near Romelia, Doña Cástula went to the wardrobe and as she opened it asked what clothes madam was going to wear.

Romelia was puzzled by this awakening, so different from what she had anticipated, next to a tender, solicitous man in love. Unhappy with herself for giving the family she had just joined a first impression of laziness and irresponsibility or at least of ignorance or lack of respect for the household customs, she answered one question with another: "Did the master get up a long time ago?"

"At six, as usual. He went riding."

"What time will he get back?"

Doña Cástula shrugged her shoulders to indicate that she did not know.

"Because I could wait so that we could have breakfast together."

"As you please, ma'am. But before departing, Don Carlos asked me to inform you that he wanted to find you dressed ready to go out, for you're going to pay a visit."

"A visit?"

Romelia began to feel alarmed. She expected to encounter peculiar, eccentric habits in her husband, but not so soon nor one of such a humiliating nature. By now, all the time she had been sleeping on, the entire town knew she was alone while her husband rode about to prove to everyone that whatever had occurred the night before was neither exhausting nor worth continuing the next morning. With what pity would they comment that poor Romelia had been unable to keep him at her side, so soon had the novelty worn off.

True, her caresses had been clumsy. But isn't gaucheness natural to virgins? Any response other than resistance or fear, any surrender not apparently forced, would have aroused a husband's doubts about his wife's purity, suspicions about the authenticity of her innocence. But Romelia thought that she had found the perfect balance to keep her reputation untainted and satisfy her husband as well. Now, however, she did not know what to think. On the one hand, Don Carlos had not been very expressive; on the other, she had been so obsessed with herself, her fear, and the ritualistic gestures expected of her that she could not study him, or even see him. During those moments they had been two characters acting their respective parts. To her Don Carlos had existed merely as the antagonist, judge, owner, and male but had had no face and she had not heard his voice.

Was it then possible that to offend her he had abandoned her at dawn to appear alone in the streets of Comitán as he had done when he was a bachelor? And now he wanted to plunge the sword deeper by forcing her to accompany him on a visit.

For a visit would display to the public the aching gait of a freshly deflowered virgin; the circles under her eyes would betray her fatigue and the difficulty and discomfort with which she assumed her new wifely condition; and everything would lend itself to crude jokes. That is why it was the custom for Comitecan newlyweds to remain cloistered during the first few days until people became used to thinking of them as just another couple, until the newlyweds acquired the habit of being together and behaving with the matter-of-factness of those who have shared a common existence for many years.

But what did Don Carlos know of such refinements? Spiteful tears filled Romelia's eyes, but she nevertheless forced herself to conceal her vexation in front of an imperturbable Doña Cástula still waiting for an answer.

"Which dress should I get ready, ma'am?"

Making sure that her voice would not tremble, Romelia emptied her cup of humiliation to the very dregs.

"Didn't the master explain what kind of call? A formal one with nice people, or with his friends from the outskirts?"

Irony and contempt pervaded the question so that the maid should learn that her new mistress was proud and know that even if she obeyed her husband this was the last time she would tolerate orders conveyed through inferiors.

"I don't know, ma'am. Don Carlos told me nothing."

"Then get out the white piqué dress."

When Doña Cástula did not budge, Romelia had to add: "It's cool today, and since it's not very fancy it can also be used for . . ."

"It's white, ma'am."

Only then did Romelia realize how inappropriate her choice had been. Why, that was just the detail needed for Comitecans to cook up some juicy gossip at the expense of Don Carlos' virility. Impatient, she conceded, "Then whatever's there. It's all the same to me."

Doña Cástula persisted with the serenity of someone who is right. "A choice must be made. And it's the mistress, not the servant, who always chooses."

"Thanks for the lesson, Cástula. I'll have the chance to reciprocate. Then I'll wear the peach-colored crepe. I had that special collar made to show off my locket."

With a mechanical gesture repeated thousands and thousands of times since childhood, Romelia raised her hand to her breast and immediately shrieked, "My locket! Where is it?"

It amounted to an accusation of theft, a petty revenge on someone who had witnessed Romelia, unsure of herself, blunder and ridiculously flounder about. But Doña Cástula ignored the implication. "It's there on the dresser, ma'am. Isn't this it?"

She handed the locket to Romelia, who recognized her uncalled-for alarm as one more blunder. As she fastened it around her neck again, she tried to remember the moment when she had taken it off. True, the night before she had been bewildered and nervous, maybe even giddy from the toasts. At any rate, what did it matter that she had taken it off when now it was back in its place and stood out attractively on the collar of her peach dress?

When Don Carlos returned, he found no reason to be upset. His wife had followed his instructions to the letter and was now ready to go out with him. Moreover, she had managed to calm down, forget her displeasure, conceal her curiosity, and receive him with smiles and without questions.

Don Carlos, walking over to her, ceremoniously kissed her hand. "Did you sleep well, madam?"

They continued to address each other formally. Romelia nodded and wanted to justify herself. "I must have been exhausted, for I didn't wake up until Doña Cástula came in to give me your message."

"Then may we go now?"

"Yes."

The perfect wife began to walk behind her husband not knowing where she was headed. Just yesterday—at this very hour?—she had sworn to follow him to the end of the earth if need be with no comforting right to ask where or to demur. Yet Don Carlos, a civilized man, did not abuse his power and condescended to reveal his intentions. "We're going to your parents' house."

Romelia's face lit up with happiness. But she did not want to add any further sign to the one that had burst forth freely and spontaneously. Affection for her kith and kin ought by now to have yielded to her new duties as wife.

At the Orantes' house the newlyweds were received with vague apprehension masked by an exaggerated show of courtesy and joyful outbursts.

As there had not yet been time to clear away the remnants of the celebration and the drawing room was being tidied up and cleaned by a horde of servants, the visitors were received in the sewing room. Were they not after all intimates? Why, more than that, they were part of the family.

They were offered refreshments, sweets, a drink. Politely but firmly

Don Carlos refused each offer, and Romelia dared not differ from her husband, who now said, "It's not worth going to all the trouble. I'll be here only a few minutes, just long enough to communicate to you, Don Rafael, and to you, Doña Ernestina, a matter of utmost importance."

Uneasy, the parents looked at each other. Blanca and Yolanda stood up in order to withdraw. Romelia turned pale. "Should I go, too?"

"No, madam, for the matter concerns you as much as us."

When they were left alone, the silence became agonizingly intense and prolonged. No one knew how to break it. Finally, Don Rafael understood that his age and position as father obliged him to take the initiative, so he cleared his throat and said, "Well, Don Carlos, we're ready to listen."

"What I have to say, believe me upon my honor, is more painful to me than to anyone else. But there is no other way. I have come to return to this house a woman unworthy of living under my roof."

Stunned, Romelia gaped, unable to grasp the meaning of this man's words. Don Rafael clinched his jaw, and Doña Ernestina fastened the pin of her ribbon.

"Do you realize the enormity of what you're saying, Don Carlos?"

"I swear that it's as serious for me as it is for you. The step I am taking means dishonor for us all."

Romelia stiffened; her eyes flashed and her cheeks turned purple with rage. "Dishonor—why?"

Don Carlos looked impassively at her, and when he addressed her his tone was almost benevolent. "Don't make me go into details which as a physician are easy for me to express but as a deceived husband are painful to acknowledge. If you have any decency left, madam, don't subject your parents to the humiliation of hearing in the crudest, ugliest words how the confidence they placed in your chastity was betrayed."

The last phrases were almost drowned by shocking outbursts of laughter from Doña Ernestina, whereupon Romelia had to shout, "How, when, and with whom could I have committed such a sin? Someone always watched over me; no man ever came near me, and I was never alone with anyone before you."

"I don't care how, when, or with whom. The fact is that I found you were not a virgin."

"It's a lie, father, tell him to shut up. He's lying. I have proof."

Don Carlos answered before Don Rafael could reply. "What proof?"

Romelia's voice faltered. She found it difficult to pronounce a word always repulsive to her. "The blood . . . the sheet was stained with blood. Father, you shall see it. I'll show it to you."

Doña Ernestina, speechless, pulled herself together and now contemplated the scene from such a distance that she showed no perceptible sign of deep interest.

"Don Rafael, I'm not so naïve as to suggest that you take my word only. After all, I'm merely a stranger and Romelia's your daughter. But I'll gladly repeat what I've said and prove it on any grounds you demand."

"Is this a challenge to a duel, Rafael?" asked Doña Ernestina with a show of interest prompted by good manners.

Without addressing anyone in particular, Don Rafael admitted, "Don Carlos has given his word of honor that he is a man of honor. Therefore I must believe him."

"And what about me?" Romelia broke in passionately. "Aren't you even going to take the trouble to inspect the sheets?"

Don Rafael shook his head.

Romelia, kneeling before her father, her head hard upon his chest, repeated, "Remember, father, how we've lived, how you've reared us, always pent up, with a sharp eye on us."

Don Rafael looked around and fixed his wife with a cold, accusing glare. She did not notice it. She was absent-mindedly analyzing the lace pattern on her handkerchief.

"Tell me with whom, father, with whom could I have committed the sin you all accuse me of!"

While Don Rafael was hesitating between compassion for his daughter's helplessness and obedience to a code of honor that made him, as a man, join forces with Don Carlos, the sewing room door opened noiselessly to reveal, on the threshold, the silhouettes of Blanca and Yolanda, momentarily frozen.

Obviously both had been eavesdropping. Shaking violently, Blanca stepped forward. Though she made an effort to speak, only confused, strangled sounds issued from her throat. But her movements were sure, bold, and precise. She went straight to where Romelia was still kneeling before her father and with one shove pushed her away and sent her rolling on the floor. Still panting, Blanca finally was able to get some words out. "And the hussy dares to ask with whom! Don't you remember your brother, Rafael? Have you forgotten that you used to sleep in the same bed with him? Or did you think we were all so blind and deaf around here as not to realize what was going on?"

"For God's sake, Blanca. You're insane," said her father. "When Rafael died, Romelia was a mere child."

"Yes, a child he had defiled. I used to lurk around, day and night, to catch them red-handed . . . I couldn't sleep from imagining . . . ridden with remorse from thinking about them . . . and then I had to go to confession and do penance the priest imposed on me, only to fall again into temptation because they never let me rest."

Romelia had gotten up and faced her sister. "You're jealous. You never forgave him for loving me most of all, and now you take revenge by debasing the memory of one no longer able to defend himself. Why, if you were more than suspicious, if you were so sure, why didn't you expose us? Because you prefer to wallow in your obscene fantasies than to know the truth."

"The truth is here, right now, and since a man asserts it, his testimony is beyond question."

"No, no, Don Carlos," Yolanda broke in. "Please don't believe it. I, too, witnessed the whole thing, and both were innocent. God has already judged Rafael, but Romelia . . . have mercy on her. Think of what life here with us will be like for her—with Blanca around repeating the same words to torture her constantly and with me, unable to forgive her ever, since because of her no man will ever look at me without a sneer, without contempt, and I'll never marry, have children, or be able to leave this rathole because I'm the sister of a prostitute."

Violently seizing Yolanda's arm, Don Rafael ordered, "Shut up."

Meanwhile Blanca had emerged from a profound meditation, now fully aware of a sudden insight: "I was never able to understand why he killed himself. But now I know, I'm sure; Rafael killed himself out of shame and remorse. As if he had been the only guilty one!"

With a smile, Doña Ernestina took Blanca's hand between hers and patiently, as one explains the most obvious things to a child or imbecile, said to her, "But Rafael didn't kill himself, child; we all know it was an accident. How could he deliberately hurt us like that? He was so good! Don't you agree, Don Carlos?"

Instead of answering, Don Carlos prepared to leave. "Not only am I not entitled to voice an opinion, madam, but I really don't care to hear all this talk."

"Absurdities," cried Don Rafael with surprising energy. "That's enough, girls; your mother doesn't feel well. You must take her to her room and look after her."

"Me, too, father?" Romelia wanted to know with one last glimmer of hope.

"You, too. Don Carlos and I are about to discuss men's affairs."

The women gone, Don Carlos proceeded to clarify the only matter pending, Romelia's belongings which, he went on, would be scrupulously returned as promptly as possible. He rose. At Don Rafael's insistence, however, Don Carlos, unable to disregard someone whose sole persuasive force was age, sat down again.

"Don't worry, Don Carlos, I'm not going to ask anything that might affront your dignity, for I esteem my own rather highly and want to keep it above and beyond all this catastrophe. Women, as you have just seen, plead, swear they are innocent, and are quite capable of resorting to any means to avoid the consequences of their actions. What else can be expected from the sex whose nature is weak, hypocritical, and cowardly? But as long as there is a man in this house, that man will answer for them and pay the price. I personally assume full responsibility for what has happened. Your good faith has been duped and you have suffered an irreparable moral damage without my knowledge, let alone my consent, I can assure you. To give you the public satisfaction you demand I am willing to do whatever you consider proper, however."

As Don Carlos stood up, he reached out to shake the old man's hand. "Had the other man been endowed with your integrity, this disaster would have been avoided." And turning on his heel, Don Carlos left.

At the time of the afternoon when matrons doze in hammocks as a young servant, much too young to perform a more difficult or complicated chore, massages the soles of their feet or brushes their hair; when the schoolgirl dallies over her notebooks without deciding to begin her homework; when the lonely adolescent gropes for the pornographic book under his mattress and locks himself in so as not to be discovered while he reads it; when the embroiderer pauses an instant, her needle dangling, hears footsteps outside, and waits with bated breath for someone she expects to come to her in loneliness; when the kitchen servants banter amidst the rattle of half-washed dishes; when the tailor, leaning on a wooden yardstick as if it were a cane, stops in the middle of the sidewalk in front of his workshop; when the shopkeeper unbars the doors of his store getting ready to handle customers slow in coming; when the candy vendor declares a truce in her fight against flies; when hunger born of idleness demands prey to devour—the belongings of Romelia Orantes were conveyed from Don Carlos Román's house to her parents'.

The entire town watched the procession of porters carrying trunks full of clothes, crates full of items about whose use there was much speculation, jewel cases, and trinket boxes.

The woman who discreetly refrained from opening her windows nevertheless peered out through the blinds; one man interrupted his billiard game, while another left a piece of half-measured fabric on the counter in order to take in such an unusual spectacle.

Almost immediately whispers swelled into comments out loud. From balcony to balcony, from sidewalk to sidewalk, questions put directly to the carriers somehow elicited answers that seemed to be vague. Then the most prominent people started making assumptions that were at times daring, insolent, or pitying but invariably humorous. Ridicule hovered like a halo over the protagonists of the affair. Who was Carlos Román? A deceived groom? An impotent husband? What about Romelia? Was she a loose woman, a victim? As for the Orantes, had they deliberately foisted off on their son-in-law a fake instead of the genuine article? Or had an apparently sound apple deceived them, too, by harboring a worm inside?

There were those who swore up and down that the heart of the matter lay in the dowry, a dowry which once the marriage was consummated, Don Rafael refused to make good. Plenty of people stated that the late Estela's spirit had appeared to the newlyweds and haunted them all night long, driving them early out of their minds with fright. And that they were able to appease the ghost only by promising they would part forever.

The flood of words surged, then subsided, mixed with ancient legends, and reached even to the retreat of Don Evaristo Trejo, who at first refused to believe his ears. But, later, confronted with the evidence of his own eyes, he had no alternative but to rush to the house of his friend Don Carlos.

Doña Cástula welcomed him like a breath of spring air. She had spent the entire morning packing what yesterday she had scarcely finished storing in chests. Since her household status denied her the right to question any order, unable to understand what had happened except that it must be due to something very grave, she feared for her master's health, even for his life. Since his return from the Orantes' house, after leaving orders that Romelia's belongings be returned, he had shut himself up in his study, forbade anyone to enter, and refused to eat.

"Prohibitions just don't apply to me," Don Evaristo said. Having thus absolved Doña Cástula beforehand of the sinful disobedience which she was about to commit, Father Trejo headed toward the room where, he assumed, he could enter only by forcing the door. At his first knock, though, Don Carlos' calm, even voice answered, "Come in."

Studying him, the newcomer saw no alarming sign in his expression. So Don Evaristo made himself comfortable in his customary armchair while Don Carlos locked the door. As he was doing so, he said, "I was waiting for you, Father. I was beginning to worry about your delay."

"I just found out. . . . What is this atrocity they tell me? Is it true Romelia's no longer here . . . that she has gone back to her parents' house?"

"Yes, I took her there myself this morning."

"You say it as if you had taken her out for a stroll. I still don't know your reasons. But regardless of who is at fault, you have, between the two of you, broken an oath taken only yesterday. Do you realize that? Only yesterday, before God."

"And to think you vouched for us."

"So what does that matter?"

"What really matters is that for us to be forced to commit such a—does one call it sacrilege?—you ought to consider that very powerful causes and insurmountable obstacles existed."

"Of course man's haughtiness and pride are shattered by the first little thing."

"Is it a little thing to discover that one's wife had made use of her body before matrimony?"

"No. But nothing, not even that, justifies your monstrous lack of charity. Oh, don't imagine I'm so dense as to believe that you're inclined to be charitable to her; rather you'll be so only to yourself. What great grist for the scandal mill you have given the people! And not only at the expense of that poor woman, whose life has been ruined, but also at your own. Everything concerning you, even your virility, has become the talk of the town. But that doesn't worry you. You didn't hesitate before making such a decision, did you?"

Don Carlos calmly listened to the excited speech of Don Evaristo, and, when he responded, he did so almost reproachfully. "Why, Father, I thought you knew me better than to believe me capable of acting rashly, driven by impulses to the point of destroying myself. Oh, no, Father, I always plan ahead, think, and can wait as long as I must. What has just happened is only the denouement of a long story, so long I don't know whether you have either the patience or desire to hear it."

"For God's sake!"

"As it is, I don't care to impose upon you as a friend, so I appeal to the priest. I'm going to ask you to hear my confession, Father."

"Confession? When I asked you to confess before the wedding, you flatly refused."

"The time wasn't ripe then. Now it is."

For the first time Don Evaristo looked at him warily. He suspected a joke, maybe a blasphemy. Don Carlos, aware of the other's scruples, smiled.

"You have no right to deny me what you allow any pious spinster just because what for her is nothing more than a mechanical habit long since devoid of meaning is for me a free, spontaneous act of the will."

Don Evaristo put on the stole he always carried with him and, head between his hands, murmured the opening prayers that the penitent, who had been ordered to kneel before him, couldn't follow. Finally he looked up and said: "Confess your sins. Without omitting or minimizing anything. In the name of the One and Only who can absolve you, I want the truth."

Instead of obeying, Don Carlos insisted until he was certain: "What I may say now falls under what you call the secret of the confessional? That inviolable secret priests must keep even at the cost of their lives?"

"Certainly."

Don Carlos stood up and drew a deep breath of relief. The tone of his voice and attitude changed. He was no longer concerned about feigning a reverence he did not feel or maintaining needless reserve. Pacing back and forth across the room, he began to speak.

"No, you can't imagine—how can you if you've never fallen in love?—what it means to fall head over heels in love. How you anxiously wait for the moment when the loved one is going to be yours and belong to you forever. I swear when I opened the door to let Estela, my new wife, enter, I trembled with happiness, with fear. For to be alone the very first time with a person you love is not easy. There is, urging and paralyzing us, a desire to possess and at the same time a need to worship."

"Save the rhetoric," Don Evaristo curtly interrupted. "From my readings of the Mystics, I'm quite familiar with all that."

"Very well. When we entered, she asked to be excused for a moment. She needed to change clothes, comb her hair, do some of the things with which women like to remind us that sublimity is not their forte and that to love them just as they are and want to be loved, one must stoop to their level."

"Again we digress."

"You're right. At any rate, she went where she said she was going—that's if, after all this, I can still believe some of what she said—and I decided to wait for her here, right where we are now, in the study. I was in a very strange mood, nervous, impatient, ill at ease, when Doña Cástula came in carrying a package in her hand. She said a stranger had just given it to her and had urged her to deliver it to me immediately. That it was a gift of some sort and that the only thing that mattered, besides its intent, was the timeliness of its arrival. I remained alone with the package, and, since my bride took more time, I mechanically, almost unconsciously began to open it. It was letters. These letters. Read them."

With these last sentences Don Carlos went to the desk, opened the only drawer he always kept locked, and took out a bundle of yellowing papers, handled thousands of times, with ink faded by the years. The words on the surface were still quite legible, however. The handwriting was regular, clear, impersonal, obviously learned and practiced from longhand models of a convent. The spelling was capricious, the style simple and direct, naïve and passionate.

The letters were not addressed to a specific name; instead, they contained affectionate nicknames with some jesting and much tenderness commingled. Then followed long paragraphs typical of lovers avowing their constancy and musing upon the intensity of their feelings, where they cry out jealousies, lament absences, clear up suspicions, and promise and promise and promise.

Nor were the letters dated, but a lapse of time was indicated by the increasing intimacy tinging them. Physical intimacy, references to embraces in which all restraint surrendered slowly but inevitably to passion. And later the unavoidable. The languorous surrender, pangs of remorse, alarm over possible consequences, threatening fear of their secret's being found out, the first glints of distrust, complaints of the lover's desertion, the discovery of the frailty of their promises, and the horror of seeing in the eyes of the beloved, not only one's image vilified but, on occasion, even emptiness.

Suddenly there appeared a name: Dr. Don Carlos Román—at first mentioned with a hint of petulance. But what woman is not flattered at being loved and does not use the love she arouses in another against the lover who begins to tire of her? Don Carlos was useful as an incentive, as a rival. Gradually, he acquired another role, a concrete role her family bestowed on him in agreeing unanimously that he was the best match the girl could aspire to; and if his intentions were serious, as everything seemed to indicate, on no account should the opportunity be wasted. Perhaps the girl sometimes dared disagree with others' opinions, but she was so severely scolded and punished that there was left her no other course than to feign submission. Unless her correspondent prevented it, she was doomed to marry Dr. Don Carlos Román.

Oh, what fits of despair, what sarcasm in portraying this man whose power (money, profession, name) crushed her. How ruthlessly she judged his shortcomings, how cannily she spotted his quirks, how blind she was to his good qualities, how cruelly she mocked his feelings, how implacably critical she was describing his visits, his conversations, how contemptuous of his gifts. She summed up all her hatred and helplessness in one phrase: the Brute. She never again referred to Don Carlos by any other name.

She mentioned it only to seek help from the other, the disdainful one, who from the context of the letters encouraged the marriage of convenience, not as a sacrifice of his pleasures but rather as the prerequisite to continued enjoyment of them freely and safely.

There the correspondence ended. Why? Did the authoress of the letters react to cynicism with silence? Or did she agree to the pact in some secret rendezvous? On the last page a man's hand had written a phrase: "I hope you enjoy them."

Don Evaristo looked up astonished. He had read the signature thirty, fifty times and still could not believe his eyes: "But these letters are Estela's!"

"How careless of her, don't you think? He suppressed all the evidence except what pointed to her. Oh, for God's sake, Don Evaristo, take that shocked look off your face; otherwise I'll have to laugh. My expression when I first held these papers in my hands must have been worse. I mean, when Estela came into the room and saw me, she stood there petrified. Full of fear. But when she saw the letters, her expression changed. I swear I have never seen such a pained look on anyone's face. Yet it wasn't distress for me, you must understand; she didn't care a fig for my contempt, which could never match her own. Her initial fear turned to joy; and I caught in her eyes her wish to die right there by my hand. I believed that what hurt her most was the other's betrayal. But there, too, I was mistaken. The other, even though she had yielded to his demands to the extent of marrying me, had gradually become more irascible, more elusive, to the point of not going to the meetings and returning her letters unopened. She assumed that he no longer loved her, and it so happened that suddenly she had before her eyes undeniable proof of his spitefulness, to which she had clung desperately as a sign of love. No, she couldn't stay here a minute longer. She tried to dash out into the street to find him, perhaps to thank him for the vile deed he had just committed—who knows? The fact is I didn't let her go. I stopped her forcibly, and we spent the entire night fighting. I talked like a madman; I swore, I pled, I promised. She didn't stop crying; she shivered from cold, from fever, and cowered before my blows, yet she would not utter his name, that name which she never wrote and which I was subsequently never to get out of her because from that moment on she was never again able to talk."

"With her silence she was defending his life, and maybe even your own as well, Don Carlos, because in your frenzy, you would have been capable of murder."

"No, it wasn't like that. I loved Estela exactly with the same lack of pride with which she loved him. I would have forgiven her . . ."

"That's what you say now."

"I swore so then. I proposed that we burn the letters, that we forget the nightmare we had lived that night; I promised never again to question her. But she wouldn't even listen to me. She just wanted to die."

"Poor child."

"Yes, in the midst of my own suffering, I felt sorry for her, too. But she would have nothing to do with me, least of all with my pity. Since she didn't allow me to go near her, not even to take care of her, because by then she had become very ill, I had to depend on her mother, on outsiders. We watched over her day and night. I did everything humanly possible to save her. But it was useless. Estela refused to eat, to take medicine, to follow directions. Whenever we turned our backs, she pulled out the needles with which we tried to keep her alive and the tubes we used to feed her. I was always by her bedside, hoping that during an unconscious moment, in her delirium, she would call for him. But she didn't. When I offered to bring him so that she could see him for the last time, she shook her head so vehemently that she exhausted the energy she had left. Thus, she died as she had once proposed to do: for his sake."

Pausing, Don Carlos took a deep breath so as to continue. "I was left alone; I refused my mother-in-law's company and avoided my friends' solicitousness. I needed to think. Who could he have been, the man for whom Estela had sacrificed herself? Anyone, in principle. Perhaps the friend who came to offer me his sympathy, to express regrets. But when, only a few days after my wife's burial I learned of Rafael Orantes' death, I began to see clearly."

"Why? It could have been a simple coincidence."

"Because Rafael did not die in a hunting accident as we were led to believe; full of shame and remorse, he committed suicide. And I'm not making that up. Blanca, his sister, vouches for it."

"That woman is out of her wits. She finds guilt where none exists."

"Then what can the poor soul do if she's missing the basic facts? But I who have always had them at hand tied up the loose ends bit by bit. Why should I hurry now that Rafael had deprived me of every possible revenge plus proof that my suspicions were true."

"What were they based on?"

"On the fact that Rafael and Estela had been sweethearts. The relationship seemed unimportant; it didn't even lead to engagement. He was fickle, and she obeyed her mother's prohibition; but they continued to see each other on the sly. Judging from the letters, they didn't just *see* each other. Without realizing it, my mother-in-law furnished many clues in seemingly trivial conversations. But I needed the last, definitive unique fact that could serve as irrefutable proof. Then I found out about Romelia's locket."

Don Evaristo had by now covered his face with his hands. "Oh, my God!"

"No, Father, it'll do you no good to shut your eyes to the matter. Here is the paper. Look at it, compare what this man wrote to his sister with what he wrote to me: the same sentence, the same handwriting!"

Don Evaristo, now violently urged on by Don Carlos, was endeavoring to find the similarity apparently so obvious to his friend. But the characters had been effaced by time, disfigured by folds in the paper.

"No, this evidence is insufficient."

"How do you mean? It's perfectly clear, beyond any doubt. Only he who does not want to see it, won't. And you don't want to."

"You do, and you see only what you want."

Don Carlos' face glowed with fury. Gesticulating wildly, he brandished the two sheets of paper and compared one handwriting with another until Father Trejo gave up.

"But even if you're right and Rafael didn't die in an accident but committed suicide . . ."

"As his own sister asserts."

"Even supposing this to be true, didn't his blood suffice to atone for his guilt? Why did an innocent girl have to pay, too?"

"What innocent girl?"

"The victim of this entire plot: Romelia."

"Ah, yes, poor Romelia. Well, one cannot safely be an assassin's pet, possess evidence of a murder, and not run some risks. Remember the locket was hers and under no circumstances would she take it off."

"And to get hold of it, you set up this infamous strategem?"

"Are you talking about the wedding?"

"I'm talking about everything. About our accidental meeting at the bedside of Enrique Liévano! About your hospitality when you received me at home. About your cunning in directing our conversations toward marriage. I recommended it, of course. You were so lonely! I strove to guide you. But my suggestions were always rejected for one reason or another. It's obvious; by then you had already drawn up your plan."

"You overestimate my ability, Father."

"Rather I'm acutely aware of my own obtuseness. Though ability isn't the word for what you have done."

"If you want to get it out of your system by calling me names, go ahead. I promise I won't be affronted."

"That's the limit. Nothing can spoil your smugness over your success. Not even the memory of that innocent girl whose life you have ruined."

"What makes you so certain of Romelia's innocence? Because she doesn't write letters? Or if she does write them, her correspondent is discreet? No, Don Evaristo. You can have the wool pulled over your eyes once but not twice."

"And, to justify yourself, you accused her of not being a virgin."

"What does it matter whether she was a virgin or not? For a layman virginity is a guarantee of virtue, but not for a physician. There are second hand, third hand, *n*th hand virginities. In my profession there are those who specialize in patching up maidenheads."

"Your tone and words are not those a confessor can listen to, but before you finish just tell me this: what would you have done if you had found the locket empty or the handwriting different?"

Don Carlos was startled by the question, but he reacted quickly. "It so happens the locket did contain the paper and the handwriting was the same. I had no other alternative."

"And, for me, there's no alternative except to deny you absolution unless you repent what you have done and restore to the Orantes family the honor you have wrenched from them."

"What I have done, Father, is merely restitution. Don't forget that someone in that family dishonored me first."

Don Evaristo started to remove his stole. "I don't understand such a vindictive compulsion."

"We no longer need to understand each other, Father, inasmuch as we shall not be speaking any more."

"I haven't withdrawn my friendship, Don Carlos."

"Really. I know that trap, and I'm not about to fall into it. Your apostolic zeal will force you to come, night after night, to talk with the stray lamb. To soften him up until he repents and gives his victims complete and public satisfaction. But I fear, Don Evaristo, our plans don't coincide. After having struggled so many years, I think I deserve a rest. As of today, I've therefore already canceled my consultations, and your visit will be the last I receive."

"You are going then to immure yourself once more with the fine company of those papers?" By now Don Carlos had begun to straighten out the letters with a deftness acquired only through practice. Then he placed on top of them, as if crowning them, the slip of paper Romelia had kept in her locket for so long. Who knows whether one day she was destined to discover its disappearance?

Translated by Ruth Peacock
Los convidados de agosto (1964)

Cooking Lesson

The kitchen is shining white. It's a shame to have to get it dirty. One ought to sit down and contemplate it, describe it, close one's eyes, evoke it. Looking closely, this spotlessness, this pulchritude lacks the glaring excess that causes chills in hospitals. Or is it the halo of disinfectants, the rubber-cushioned steps of the aides, the hidden presence of sickness and death? What do I care? My place is here. I've been here from the beginning of time. In the German proverb woman is synonymous with *Küche, Kinder, Kirche*. I wandered astray through classrooms, streets, offices, cafés, wasting my time on skills that now I must forget in order to acquire others. For example, choosing the menu. How could one carry out such an arduous task without the cooperation of society—of all history? On a special shelf, just right for my height, my guardian spirits are lined up, those acclaimed jugglers that reconcile the most irreducible contradictions among the pages of their recipe books: slimness and gluttony, pleasing appearance and economy, speed and succulence. With their infinite combinations: slimness and economy, speed and pleasing appearance, succulence and . . . What can you suggest to me for today's meal, O experienced housewife, inspiration of mothers here and gone, voice of tradition, clamoring secret of the supermarkets? I open a book at random and read: "Don Quijote's Dinner." Very literary but not very satisfying, because Don Quijote was not famous as a gourmet but as a bumbler. Although a more profound analysis of the text reveals etc., etc., etc. Ugh! More ink has flowed about that character than water under bridges. "Fowl Center-Face." Esoteric. Whose face? Does the face of some one or something have a center? If it does, it must not be very appetizing. "Bigos Roumanian." Well, just who do you think you're talking to? If I knew what tarragon or *ananas* were I wouldn't be consulting this book, because I'd know a lot of other things, too. If you had the slightest sense of reality, you yourself or any of your colleagues would take the trouble to write a dictionary of technical terms, edit a few prolegomena, invent a propaedeutic to make the difficult culinary art accessible to the lay person. But you all start from the assumption that we're all in on the secret and you limit yourselves to stating it. I, at least, solemnly declare that I am not, and never have been, in on either this or any other secret you share. I never understood anything about anything. You observe the symptoms: I stand here like an imbecile, in an impeccable and neutral kitchen, wearing the apron that I usurp in order to give a pretense of efficiency and of which I will be shamefully but justly stripped.

I open the refrigerator drawer that proclaims "Meat" and extract a package that I cannot recognize under its icy coating. I thaw it in hot water, revealing the title without which I never would have identified the contents: Fancy Beef Broil. Wonderful. A plain and wholesome dish. But since it doesn't mean resolving an antimony or proposing an axiom, it doesn't appeal to me.

Moreover, it's not simply an excess of logic that inhibits my hunger. It's also the appearance of it, frozen stiff; it's the color that shows now that I've ripped open the package. Red, as if it were just about to start bleeding.

Our backs were that same color, my husband and I, after our orgiastic sunbathing on the beaches of Acapulco. He could afford the luxury of "behaving like the man he is" and stretch out face down to avoid rubbing his painful skin . . . But I, self-sacrificing little Mexican wife, born like a dove to the nest, smiled like Cuauhtémoc under torture on the rack when he said, "My bed is not made of roses," and fell silent. Face up, I bore not only my own weight but also his on top of me. The classic position for making love. And I moaned, from the tearing and the pleasure. The classic moan. Myths, myths.

The best part (for my sunburn at least) was when he fell asleep. Under my fingertips—not very sensitive due to prolonged contact with typewriter keys—the nylon of my bridal nightgown slipped away in a fraudulent attempt to look like lace. I played with the tips of the buttons and those other ornaments that make whoever wears them seem so feminine in the late night darkness. The whiteness of my clothes, deliberate, repetitive, immodestly symbolic, was temporarily abolished. Perhaps at some moment it managed to accomplish its purpose beneath the light and the glance of those eyes that are now overcome by fatigue.

Eyelids close and behold, once again, exile. An enormous sandy expanse with no juncture other than the sea, whose movement suggests paralysis, with no invitation except that of the cliff to suicide.

But that's a lie. I'm not the dream that dreams in a dream that dreams; I'm not the reflection of an image in a glass; I'm not annihilated by the closing off of a consciousness or of all possible consciousness. I go on living a dense, viscose, turbid life even though the man at my side and the one far away ignore me, forget me, postpone me, abandon me, fall out of love with me.

I, too, am a consciousness that can close itself off, abandon someone, and expose him to annihilation. I . . . The meat, under the sprinkling of salt, has toned down some of its offensive redness and now it seems more tolerable, more familiar to me. It's that piece I saw a thousand times without realizing it, when I used to pop in to tell the cook that . . .

We weren't born together. Our meeting was due to accident. A happy one? It's still too soon to say. We met by chance at an exhibition, a lecture, a film. We ran into each other in the elevator; he gave me his seat on the tram; a guard interrupted our perplexed and parallel contemplation of the giraffe because it was time to close the zoo. Someone, he or I, it's all the same, asked the stupid but indispensable question: Do you work or study? A harmony of interests and of good intentions, a show of "serious" intentions. A year ago I hadn't the slightest idea of his existence and now I'm lying close to him with our thighs entwined, damp with sweat and semen. I could get up without waking him, walk barefoot to the shower. To purify myself? I feel no revulsion. I prefer to believe that what links him to me is something as easy to wipe away as a secretion and not as terrible as a sacrament.

So I remain still, breathing rhythmically to imitate drowsiness, my insomnia the only spinster's jewel I've kept and I'm inclined to keep until death.

Beneath the brief deluge of pepper the meat seems to have gone gray. I banish this sign of aging by rubbing it as though I were trying to penetrate the surface and impregnate its thickness with flavors, because I lost my old name and I still can't get used to the new one, which is not mine either. When some employee pages me in the lobby of the hotel I remain deaf with that vague uneasiness that is the prelude to recognition. Who could that person be who doesn't answer? It could be something urgent, serious, a matter of life or death. The caller goes away without leaving a clue, a message, or even the possibility of another meeting. Is it anxiety that presses against my heart? No, it's his hand pressing on my shoulder and his lips smiling at me in benevolent mockery, more like a sorcerer than a master.

So then, I accept, as we head toward the bar (my peeling shoulder feels like it's on fire) that it's true that in my contact or collision with him I've undergone a profound metamorphosis. I didn't know and now I know; I didn't feel and now I do feel; I wasn't and now I am.

It should be left to sit for a while. Until it reaches room temperature, until it's steeped in the flavors that I've rubbed into it. I have the feeling I didn't know how to calculate very well and that I've bought a piece that's too big for the two of us—for me, because I'm lazy, not a carnivore; for him, for aesthetic reasons because he's watching his waistline. Almost all of it will be left over! Yes, I already know that I shouldn't worry: one of the good fairies that hovers over me is going to come to my rescue and explain how one uses leftovers. It's a mistake, anyhow. You don't start married life in such a sordid way. I'm afraid that you also don't start it with a dish as dull as broiled beef.

Thanks, I murmur, while I wipe my lips with a corner of the napkin. Thanks for the transparent cocktail glass, and for the submerged olive. Thanks for letting me out of the cage of one sterile routine only to lock me into the cage of another, a routine which according to all purposes and possibilities must be fruitful. Thanks for giving me the chance to show off a long gown with a train, for helping me walk up the aisle of the church, carried away by the organ music. Thanks for . . .

How long will it take to be done? Well, that shouldn't worry me too much because it has to be put on the grill at the last minute. It takes very little time, according to the cookbook. How long is little? Fifteen minutes? Ten? Five? Naturally the text doesn't specify. It presupposes an intuition which, according to my sex, I'm supposed to possess but I don't, a sense I was born without that would allow me to gauge the precise minute the meat is done.

And what about you? Don't you have anything to thank me for? You've specified it with a slightly pedantic solemnity and a precision that perhaps were meant to flatter but instead offended: my virginity. When you discovered it I felt like the last dinosaur on a planet where the species was extinct. I longed to justify myself, to explain that if I was intact when I met you it was not out of virtue or pride or ugliness but simply out of adherence to a style. I'm not baroque. The tiny imperfection in the pearl is unbearable to me. The only alternative I have is the neoclassic one, and its rigidity is incompatible with the spontaneity needed for making love. I lack that ease of the person who rows or plays tennis or dances. I don't play any sports. I comply with the ritual but my move to surrender petrifies into a statue.

Are you monitoring my transit to fluidity? Do you expect it, do you need it? Or is this hieraticism that sanctifies you, and that you interpret as the passivity natural to my nature, enough for you? So if you are voluble it will ease your mind to think that I won't hinder your adventures. It won't be necessary—thanks to my temperament—for you to fatten me up, tie me down hand and foot with children, gag me on the thick honey of resignation. I'll stay the same as I am. Calm. When you throw your body on top of mine I feel as though a gravestone were covering me, full of inscriptions, strange names, memorable dates. You moan unintelligibly and I'd like to whisper my name in your ear to remind you who it is you are possessing.

I'm myself. But who am I? Your wife, of course. And that title suffices to distinguish me from past memories or future projects. I bear an owner's brand, a property tag, and yet you watch me suspiciously. I'm not weaving a web to trap you. I'm not a praying mantis. I appreciate your believing such a hypothesis, but it's false.

This meat has a toughness and consistency that is not like beef. It must be mammoth. One of those that have been preserved since prehistoric times in the Siberian ice, that the peasants thaw out and fix for food. In that terribly boring documentary they showed at the Embassy, so full of superfluous details, there wasn't the slightest mention of how long it took to make them edible. Years, months? And I only have so much time . . .

Is that a lark? Or is it a nightingale? No, our schedule won't be ruled by such winged creatures as those that announced the coming of dawn to Romeo and Juliet but by a noisy and unerring alarm clock. And you will not descend to day by the stairway of my tresses but rather on the steps of detailed complaints: you've lost a button off your jacket; the toast is burned; the coffee is cold.

I'll ruminate my resentment in silence. All the responsibilities and duties of a servant are assigned to me for everything. I'm supposed to keep the house impeccable, the clothes ready, mealtimes exact. But I'm not paid any salary; I don't get one day a week off; I can't change masters. On the other hand, I'm supposed to contribute to the support of the household and I'm expected to efficiently carry out a job where the boss is demanding, my colleagues conspire, and my subordinates hate me. In my free time I transform myself into a society matron who gives luncheons and dinners for her husband's friends, attends meetings, subscribes to the opera season, watches her weight, renews her wardrobe, cares for her skin, keeps herself attractive, keeps up on all the gossip, stays up late and gets up early, runs the monthly risk of maternity, believes the evening executive meetings, the business trips and the arrival of unexpected clients; who suffers from olfactory hallucinations when she catches a whiff of French perfume (different from the one she uses) on her husband's shirts and handkerchiefs and on lonely nights refuses to think why or what so much fuss is all about and fixes herself a stiff drink and reads a detective story with the fragile mood of a convalescent.

Shouldn't it be time to turn on the stove? Low flame so the broiler will start warming up gradually, "which should be greased first so the meat will not stick." That did occur to me; there was no need to waste pages on those recommendations.

I'm very awkward. Now it's called awkwardness, but it used to be called innocence and you loved it. But I've never loved it. When I was single I used to read things on the sly, perspiring from the arousal and shame. I never found out anything. My breasts ached, my eyes got misty, my muscles contracted in a spasm of nausea.

The oil is starting to get hot. I let it get too hot, heavy handed that I am, and now it's spitting and spattering and burning me. That's how I'm going to fry in those narrow hells, through my fault, through my fault, through my most grievous fault. But child, you're not the only one. All your classmates do the same thing or worse. They confess in the confessional, do their penance, are forgiven and fall into it again. All of them. If I had continued going around with them they'd be questioning me now, the married ones to find things out for themselves, the single ones to find out how far they can go. Impossible to let them down. I would invent acrobatics, sublime fainting spells, transports as they're called in the Thousand and One Nights—records! If you only heard me then, you'd never recognize me, Casanova!

I drop the meat onto the grill and instinctively step back against the wall. What a noise! Now it's stopped. The meat lies there silently, faithful to its deceased state. I still think it's too big.

It's not that you've let me down. It's true that I didn't expect anything special. Gradually we'll reveal ourselves to one another, discover our secrets, our little tricks, learn to please each other. And one day you and I will become a pair of perfect lovers and then, right in the middle of an embrace, we'll disappear and the words, "The End," will appear on the screen.

What's the matter? The meat is shrinking. No, I'm not seeing things; I'm not wrong. You can see the mark of its original size by the outline that it left on the grill. It was only a little bit bigger. Good! Maybe it will be just the right size for our appetites.

In my next movie I'd like them to give me a different part. The white sorceress in a savage village? No, today I don't feel much inclined to either heroism or danger. Better a famous woman (a fashion designer or some-

thing like that), rich and independent, who lives by herself in an apartment in New York, Paris, or London. Her occasional *affaires* entertain
her but do not change her. She's not sentimental. After a breakup scene
she lights a cigarette and surveys the urban scenery through the picture
window of her studio.

Ah, the color of the meat looks much better now, only raw in a few
obstinate places. But the rest is browned and gives off a delicious aroma.
Will it be enough for the two of us? It looks very small to me.

If I got dressed up now I'd try on one of those dresses from my trousseau
and go out. What would happen, hmmmm? Maybe an older man with a
car would pick me up. Mature. Retired. The only kind who can afford to
be on the make at this time of day.

What the devil's going on? This damned meat is starting to give off horrible black smoke! I should have turned it over! Burned on one side. Well,
thank goodness it has another one.

Miss, if you will allow me . . . Mrs.! And I'm warning you, my husband is very jealous. . . . Then he shouldn't let you go out alone. You're
a temptation to any passerby. Nobody in this world says passerby. Pedes-
trian? Only the newspapers when they report accidents. You're a temptation for anyone. Mean-ing-ful silence. The glances of a sphinx. The older
man is following me at a safe distance. Better for him. Better for me, because on the corner—uh, oh—my husband, who's spying on me and
who never leaves me alone morning, noon, or night, who suspects everything and everybody, Your Honor. It's impossible to live this way, I want a
divorce.

Now what? This piece of meat's mother never told it that it was meat
and ought to act like it. It's curling up like a corkscrew pastry. Anyhow, I
don't know where all that smoke can be coming from if I turned the stove
off ages ago. Of course, Dear Abby, what one must do now is open the
window, plug in the ventilator so it won't be smelly when my husband gets
here. And I'll so cutely run right out to greet him at the door with my best
dress on, my best smile, and my warmest invitation to eat out.

It's a thought. We'll look at the restaurant menu while that miserable
piece of charred meat lies hidden at the bottom of the garbage pail. I'll be
careful not to mention the incident because I'd be considered a somewhat
irresponsible wife, with frivolous tendencies but not mentally retarded.
This is the initial public image that I project and I've got to maintain it
even though it isn't accurate.

There's another possibility. Don't open the window, don't turn on the
ventilator, don't throw the meat in the garbage. When my husband gets

here let him smell it like the ogres in all the stories and tell him that no, it doesn't smell of human flesh here, but of useless woman. I'll exaggerate my compunction so he can be magnanimous. After all, what's happened is so normal! What newlywed doesn't do the same thing that I've done? When we visit my mother-in-law, who is still at the stage of not attacking me because she doesn't know my weak points yet, she'll tell me her own experiences. The time, for example, when her husband asked her to fix coddled eggs and she took him literally . . . ha, ha. Did that stop her from becoming a fabulous widow, I mean a fabulous cook? Because she was widowed much later and for other reasons. After that she gave free rein to her maternal instincts and spoiled everything with all her pampering . . .

No, he's not going to find it the least bit amusing. He's going to say that I got distracted, that it's the height of carelessness and, yes, condescendingly, I'm going to accept his accusations.

But it isn't true, it isn't. I was watching the meat all the time, watching how a series of very odd things happened to it. Saint Theresa was right when she said that God is in the stewpots. Or matter is energy or whatever it's called now.

Let's backtrack. First there's the piece of meat, one color, one shape, one size. Then it changes, looks even nicer and you feel very happy. Then it starts changing again and now it doesn't look so nice. It keeps changing and changing and changing and you just can't tell when you should stop it. Because if I leave this piece of meat on the grill indefinitely, it will burn to a crisp till nothing is left of it. So that piece of meat that gave the impression of being so solid and real no longer exists.

So? My husband also gives the impression of being solid and real when we're together, when I touch him, when I see him. He certainly changes and I change too, although so slowly that neither of us realizes it. Then he goes off and suddenly becomes a memory and . . . Oh, no, I'm not going to fall into that trap; the one about the invented character and the invented narrator and the invented anecdote. Besides, it's not the consequence that licitly follows from the meat episode.

The meat hasn't stopped existing. It has undergone a series of metamorphoses. And the fact that it ceases to be perceptible for the senses does not mean that the cycle is concluded but that it has taken the quantum leap. It will go on operating on other levels. On the level of my consciousness, my memory, my will, changing me, defining me, establishing the course of my future.

From today on, I'll be whatever I choose to be at the moment. Seductively unbalanced, deeply withdrawn, hypocritical. From the very beginning I will impose, just a bit insolently, the rules of the game. My husband will resent the appearance of my dominance, which will widen like the ripples on the surface of the water when someone has skipped a pebble across it. I'll struggle to prevail and, if he gives in, I'll retaliate with my scorn, and, if he doesn't give in, I'll simply be unable to forgive him.

If I assume another attitude, if I'm the typical case, femininity that begs indulgence for her errors, the balance will tip in favor of my antagonist and I will be running the race with a handicap, which, apparently, seals my defeat, and which, essentially, guarantees my triumph by the winding path that my grandmothers took, the humble ones, the ones who didn't open their mouths except to say yes and achieved an obedience foreign to even their most irrational whims. The recipe of course is ancient and its efficiency is proven. If I still doubt, all I have to do is ask my neighbor. She'll confirm my certainty.

It's just that it revolts me to behave that way. This definition is not applicable to me, the former one either; neither corresponds to my inner truth, or safeguards my authenticity. Must I grasp some one of them and bind myself to its terms only because it is a cliché accepted by the majority and intelligible to everyone? And it's not because I'm a *rara avis*. You can say about me what Pfandl said about Sor Juana, that I belong to the class of hesitant neurotics. The diagnosis is very easy, but what consequences does the assumption hold?

If I insist on affirming my version of the facts my husband is going to look at me suspiciously; he's going to live in continual expectation that I'll be declared insane.

Our life together could not be more problematic! He doesn't want conflicts of any kind, much less such abstract, absurd, metaphysical conflicts as the one I would present him with. His home is a haven of peace where he takes refuge from all the storms of life. Agreed. I accepted that when I got married and I was even ready to accept sacrifice for the sake of marital harmony. But I counted on the fact that the sacrifice, the complete renunciation of what I am, would only be demanded of me on The Sublime Occasion, at The Time of Heroic Solutions, at The Moment of the Definitive Decision. Not in exchange for what I stumbled on today, which is something very insignificant and very ridiculous. And yet . . .

Translated by Maureen Ahern
Álbum de familia (1971)

ESSAYS

We have to laugh. Because laughter, we already
know, is the first evidence of freedom.
                    —Rosario Castellanos
              "If Not Poetry, Then What?"

Incident at Yalentay

We used to direct a traveling theater troupe that we had named after its main character: the puppet Petul. His adventures of an Indian boy in the process of learning to live the way other Mexicans lived served as entertainment and instruction for his Indian compatriots whom we used to visit even in the most remote spots of the Highlands of Chiapas.[1]

Our team consisted of seven persons: six Indians, whose native language was Tzotzil but who were all bilingual, and myself, who only spoke Spanish.

I was in charge of writing the scripts, a kind of handy guideline for the comedy sketches that owed so much to improvisation. I used to write them by following the instructions of the technical teams in agriculture, education, or highways, whose goal was to carry out some enterprise for which Indian collaboration was indispensable.

Once I had inserted a strategic dosage of propaganda within the simple plot (which to the degree possible was supposed to capture the audience's interest) the seven of us would get together to proceed to translate it from Spanish into the other two languages, assign the parts, and prepare the puppets that we needed.

When everything was ready, we would go out into the countryside. Our visit to the Indian towns never met with indifference. Petul was loved everywhere and it was not unusual for the children (or the elderly, who were perhaps the wisest of all in their astonishment) to come up to offer him an orange to quench the thirst of the road or invite him to stay at an Indian home or beg him the honor of becoming the godfather of some newborn infant.

But let it be clearly understood: this response was due to Petul, not ourselves, the flesh-and-blood human beings, who, like any others, were capable of committing an evil deed. Petul, on the other hand, gave them

---

1. See also Rosario Castellanos, "Teatro Petul," *Revista de la Universidad de México*, January 1965, 30–31, and *Teatro Petul*.

advice for their own good, knew many of them by name, was always in a good mood, and managed to get out of all the tight spots scot-free. Furthermore, Petul was an Indian like themselves. You could not tell the difference in either his speech or his clothes. On the other hand, his masters, didn't they dress like the mestizos? Didn't they speak Spanish as though it were their own language? No, it wasn't easy to make friends with us. On the other hand, with Petul, dialogue, cordiality, empathy were all possible.

One time a girl came up to Petul in Yalentay, a village surrounded by fog, in whose very high thin air it was difficult to breathe.

When the skit was about to end, the girl (who from the first had occupied one of the places closest to the stage) took advantage of the noise of applause to ask our hero if she could be admitted as a student to the boarding school that the National Indigenist Institute had established in the city of San Cristóbal? Petul told her that he was going to find out and promised to answer her as soon as possible.

While my companions took down the stage props and put away the puppets in their chest, I looked for a chance to chat with the girl. She spoke a little Spanish, thanks to having worked as a maid for a family in San Cristóbal. But that wasn't enough for her and she was ready to learn to read and to write her name. She had hopes of living somewhere besides Yalentay, where her only future was exhausting work and a father who brutally mistreated her.

We were very happy when we returned to San Cristóbal. People like this girl were the ones we needed in order for the work of the institute to bear fruit: persons with ability, willpower, nerve. What if there wasn't any room at the institute? But what an absurd concern! Room is somehow made when it's needed.

We went to speak with the director of the Education Section, Professor Montes, proud of our find and ready to place it in his hands immediately.

He told us that, as far as he was concerned, there was not the slightest obstacle to accepting the girl among the boarding students but that we could not take her out of her village without her father's consent. And Chamula fathers were not easy to handle.

But what more does he want, I argued. They were going to give his daughter a home to live in that was much better than her own and clothes. And food. And they were going to teach her useful new things. All this without costing him a cent.

I would have gone on indefinitely about the benefits of the boarding school if I had not seen the looks on my audience's faces. On Professor

Montes' face there was a kind of gentle, mocking condescension. On my companions' faces the same seriousness as when they meditated on eternal truths.

A few days later, we returned to Yalentay in the company of Professor Montes. The girl was waiting for us anxiously and she had gotten especially dressed up to meet us. It surprised and somewhat bewildered her not to see us loaded down with all the gear that is required for the theater presentations. Today it wasn't a matter of theater, it was a private matter: to put Professor Montes in contact with her father and to manage to get both of them to agree about the girl's admission to the boarding school.

The old man was sitting on a log in the doorway of his hut. He didn't appear to be expecting us and did not make the slightest gesture of welcome when he saw us approaching. He didn't even chase off the dogs— mangy, skinny, hungry ones—that barked furiously around us. We finally managed to reach the place from which the old man had not moved and to make ourselves heard amid the barking, to which was added the squawking of chickens, grunting of pigs, and clucking of the neighbors, who had gathered to observe the scene.

The old man allowed the interpreter to speak for Professor Montes and then answered that he was not going to turn his daughter over to strangers. Who was going to guarantee to him that they were not going to pervert her? And even if that did not happen, how were they going to return her to him? Turned into a Spanish-speaking Indian that put on airs, scornful of her family and the men whom she would have been able to marry. He opposed all our arguments with stony mistrust. When we considered ourselves beaten and were about to leave, he suggested an arrangement. If the people at the institute were so rich they would pay him something for the girl . . . let's say a couple thousand pesos . . . or at least five hundred . . . it could take her wherever it felt like, if that's what it wanted.

It's not possible to discuss it on that basis—cut in Professor Montes— and we set out on our return journey. We could still hear at our backs the words of bartering, then the insults, and then the threats to punish the girl who ran after us, her hair coming unbraided and sobbing.

Why didn't you bring Petul? she reproached us—He was the only one that could have convinced my father.

July 22, 1963

Translated by Maureen Ahern
El uso de la palabra (1974)

Once Again Sor Juana

There are three figures in Mexican history that embody the most extreme and diverse possibilities of femininity. Each one of them represents a symbol, exercises a vast and profound influence on very wide sectors of the nation, and arouses passionate reactions. These figures are the Virgin of Guadalupe, Malinche, and Sor Juana.[1]

Only positive elements seem to converge in the Virgin of Guadalupe. In spite of her apparent fragility, she is the sustainer of life, the one who protects us against danger, the one who comforts our sorrows, presides over the most pompous events, legitimizes our joys, in short, the one who saves our body from sickness and our soul from the devil's stealth. How can we but help loving her, revering her, converting her into the dearest, most beloved core of our emotional life? That is precisely what Mexicans

---

1. The Virgin of Guadalupe, Patroness of Mexico and Latin America, who first appeared to the Indian Juan Diego in 1531 at Teypeyac, a hill outside the city of Mexico that had been the shrine of the Aztec goddess, Tonantzin. The popular devotion that developed to this virgin spiritually unified the conquered and the conquerors, becoming a national cult that is celebrated each December 12 at the basilica in La Villa dedicated to her. Malinche, born near Veracruz around 1500, was the daughter of the local Indian ruler whose family sold her into slavery to Mayan-speaking peoples to the south. Given as a present to Hernán Cortés in 1519, she became his interpreter, counselor, and mistress. As the voice who spoke for Cortés, she played a key role in the rapid Spanish conquest of Mexico and Central America. Her name has become a symbol of betrayal to foreign interests, a stereotype that ignores her original betrayal by her own mother. Sor Juana Inés de la Cruz (1648–1695), the most brilliant intellectual of colonial Mexico, author of baroque poetry, plays, and scientific studies of philosophy, astronomy, geometry, and music. Her *Letter in Reply to Sor Philotea* was the first document in the New World to defend women's rights to study, write, and teach. See *A Woman of Genius: Sor Juana Inés de la Cruz*, trans. Margaret Sayers Peden (Salisbury, Conn.: Lime Rock Press, 1982), and Octavio Paz, *Sor Juana Inés de la Cruz: The Pitfalls of Faith*, trans. Margaret Sayers Peden (Cambridge, Mass.: Harvard University Press, 1988).

do—even to the point of separating their religious beliefs from the personality of the Virgin Guadalupe in order to safeguard her, in the event these
beliefs conflict with each other, undergo crisis, or must go into hiding due
to circumstantial pressures. A classic example is the case of our atheists,
who suffer no pangs of conscience when they make their annual pilgrim-
age to her shrine at La Villa.

Malinche incarnates sexuality in its most irrational aspect, the one least
reducible to moral laws, most indifferent to cultural values. Because sexuality is a dynamic force that is projected outward and is manifested by
deeds, Malinche has become one of the key figures of our history. Some
call her a traitor, others consider her the foundress of our nationality, according to whatever perspectives they choose to judge her from. Because
she is not dead, she still wails in the night, crying for her lost children
throughout the most hidden corners of our land, just as she still makes her
annual appearance disguised as a giant at Indian festivals and she continues to exercise her fascination as a woman, a female, and a seductress
of men. Before Malinche, consciousness remains alert, vigilant, and
forced to qualify her and understand her in order not to succumb to her
power, which like Antheus' is always renewed whenever she comes into
contact with the earth again.

The attitudes toward the Virgin of Guadalupe or Malinche are clear
ones because their figures are also very clear-cut: the former, a woman
who sublimates her condition in motherhood, the latter, a woman of our
roots, uninterested in the process of its development, indifferent to the results. But Sor Juana? The initial enigma she poses for us is not her genius
(sufficient to worry many doctors) but her femininity. She speaks of it in
different passages of her writing, not in terms of a consummated and assumed fact but rather as a hypothesis that perhaps cannot be proven. She
states, for example, in a ballad:

> I don't understand these things,
> I only know that I came here.
> So that if I be woman
> No one can truly say.

Such explicit confession and evident purpose constitute the stumbling
block for scandal among Sor Juana's admirers. Either they look through
her, or they prefer to ignore evidence that in the long run has the value of
being first hand and prefer to continue to construct her according to their

own tastes: frivolous damsel of the viceregal court, a bird that allows herself to be caught in the snare of an impossible love from which her only escape is to beg asylum behind the consecrated walls of a convent. There she finds the solace of solitude and drowns her sorrows in sonnets and other minor matters. Like all the chosen of the gods, Sor Juana dies young and fee fi foe fum our story is done.

There's a paragraph written by Sor Juana in her *Letter in Reply to Sor Philotea* that is a type of autobiography, in which she spoke of the many doubts that assailed her before she took the veil. She knew her own character very well, her preference for solitude, how difficult it would be for her to submit to the discipline of a community life. In the end she chose the convent because the only other alternative was marriage, for which she felt an unconquerable aversion.

That paragraph has not prevented many persons from praising her monastic vocation, finding her obedience to the orders of the several superiors that she endured to be irreproachable, her zeal in the fulfillment of her vows excessive, and her final sacrifice and her charity toward her suffering sisters nothing less than saintly. For all of these reasons there has been no lack of those who, carrying their admiration to the utmost, have begged the pertinent authorities to canonize her. Naturally, the cause has not advanced. The Church straddles the Rock of Ages and resorts to very painstaking procedures before elevating anyone to its altars.

However, the attitudes that we have just described are, in the final instance, naïve and thus inoffensive. There is another attitude that takes on all the trappings of science, placing the curious specimen under the microscope in order to classify it.

Why so curious? Not because she chose the convent, a very commonplace deed in the New Spain of her time. Not because she wrote somewhat charming verse, because it was already a saying that in this newly founded metropolis there were more poets than fertilizer (and fertilizer was very abundant). No, it was because it was a woman who wrote those poems. Because she was a woman who had an intellectual vocation. Because, in spite of all the resistance and barriers of her environment, she exercised that vocation and transformed it into literary work. It was a body of work that provoked the astonishment and admiration of her contemporaries, not for its intrinsic qualities but because it sprang from a hand whose natural employment should have been cooking or sewing. A body of work greeted by silence, beset by the scorn of centuries, now comes to light once again, thanks to the research of scholars, among whom first place goes to Father Alfonso Méndez Plancarte.[2]

Thus, Sor Juana returns to the present, not only as an author but as a person. We see her dissected by the instruments of psychoanalysis, thanks to the Germanic curiosity (and being Germanic it is thorough and solemn) of Ludwig Pfandl.[3]

His diagnosis does not do her any favors. Moreover, it is a catalog of all the complexes, traumas, and frustrations that can victimize a human being. Naturally, in her relationship with her family there are all those ambiguities that are explained, thanks to the dummy card of Oedipus. Naturally, due to her beauty and her talent, she was a narcissist. Did she confess an eagerness to know more? She's a neurotic. Does she use symbols? Was she effusive to someone? Careful! That's either mistaken affection or an unconscious urge to kill.

A book conceived in this fashion is insulting, not for its partiality but because criteria like these have been superseded by other broader ones. Wouldn't it be fairer to think that Sor Juana, like any other human being, possessed a backbone, that it was her own vocation, and that she chose among all the different kinds available to her, the one she was most able to count on achieving?

26 October 1963

Translated by Maureen Ahern
Juicios sumarios (1966)

---

2. A reference to Alfonso Méndez Plancarte, editor of the complete works of Sor Juana, *Obras completas de Sor Juana Inés de la Cruz*, 4 vols. (Mexico City: Fondo de Cultura Económica, 1951–1957).

3. A German Hispanist who wrote *Sor Juana Inés de la Cruz, la décima musa de México: Su vida. Su poesía. Su psique*, ed. Francisco de la Maza, trans. Juan Antonio Ortega y Medina (Mexico City: Instituto de Investigaciones Estéticas, UNAM, 1963).

An Attempt at Self-Criticism

To say that I have made the transition from poetry to prose (narrative and critical) is to suppose that readers, that species we writers want to believe are not extinct, are acquainted with my book. But experience tells me that such a supposition is very risky, false, to be exact; that readers, if they still exist, will have exercised their profession on other texts and that my works have not been distributed as widely as I would have liked. Thus, the shortest explanations are to the point.

My first publication dates back to 1948: an extremely long poem in which I wanted to embrace and give meaning to the entire universe, thanks to the only permanence possible, which was, to my way of thinking, that of aesthetic creation. I used free verse and abused imagery to such an extent that any train of thought was often lost. To sum it up, *Trayectoria del polvo* was as ambitious as it was frustrating.

It taught me neither brevity nor sobriety. All of its excesses and defects were repeated in the following poem: *Apuntes para una declaración de fe*. As an original touch, I deliberately added clichés and the commonplace in order to paint a black picture of the contemporary world, in order to end in a hopeful, but completely unfounded, apotheosis of a better future, envisioning its development (and why not?) on exceedingly fertile American soil.

I still blush with embarrassment at the critics' reception of such a monstrosity with all the insults that it deserved. From that time on I was finally able to end a poem when it was finished and not go on writing through inertia, dragged along by the force of adjectives. The second book—*De la vigilia estéril*—in spite of its unfortunate title, made a certain amount of progress. The poems were less rambling, more modest in subject matter, and tighter in form (I was beginning to discover my individuality and validity which, in poetry, has to express the moods of the soul).

Ah, but dead wood still covered the better part of my discoveries and only my closest friends continued to have confidence in me, even though they advised me, at the same time, to try to cultivate other genres. In theater, for example, I perpetrated a "high drama," which, protected by the title of *Tablero de damas*, did me the favor of demonstrating that I did not know how to handle dialogue and that my characters were as rigid and fragile as though they were made from cardboard. But if *Tablero de damas* was a complete disaster from a literary point of view, from a social point of view it helped me to make enemies of my women-writer colleagues, who felt that I had alluded to them in the farce (and I must confess, some of them were right) and did not find their portraits flattering. The conflict grew way out of proportion until it reached the magazine's editors, who had taken my text under their protective wings. The outcome was that such generosity had as its reward the extinction of a magazine that until then had been a forum for beginners, a place of honor for the successful, and a refuge for fossils.

Studies, travel, and the systematic practice of criticism helped me to overcome the most obvious difficulties that my intellectual work had stumbled over until then. I am talking about 1952, the year I wrote two poems, for which I hold myself fully responsible: "Joyful Mysteries" ("Misterios gozosos") and "Splendor of Being" ("El resplandor del ser"). The series of influences to which I paid tribute fit into place and came together harmoniously for the first time: I was able to integrate and transmit a coherent vision of things, and an authentic relationship was established between them and myself.

If the poems mentioned above were basically constructed from fragments whose unity was thematic and formal, in "Lamentación de Dido" I tried to use the wide rhythmical verse line to retell a story already told by Virgil. I did not aspire to add any perfection or new beauty to it, but rather a deep personal experience. I believe that in no single moment have my goals and my achievements better coincided; for me poetic language has never been so flexible or so precise. I have never again reached such fulfillment even though I recognize the partial success of some of the poems in *Al pie de la letra* and *Lívida luz*.

It is not easy to let go of the vantage point one has chosen in order to contemplate life lyrically, or the linguistic habits that we have relied on for years to translate these contemplations. So when I tried to write a novel for the first time—*The Nine Guardians* (*Balún-Canán*)—I was not armed with rigor, only profuseness. Metaphors glittered everywhere, but I saved myself from condemnation, arguing that I had intended to retrieve a lost childhood and a world presided over by magic and not by logic. But the balance would be thrown off each time this world required an understanding and an explanation from me, and not merely simply a description.

I have gradually yielded to this demand in my subsequent narratives.

Oficio de tinieblas is a novel that is based upon a historical period, which is reconstructed along the lines that the imagination traces according to its laws. The coincidences between both planes are not forced, but their discrepancies could well be classified as differences in levels, where the deepest would correspond to the novelist.

In *Ciudad Real,* the prose—which attempts to be a precision instrument placed at the service of intelligence—necessarily strips away a great deal of its adornment. Unfortunately, by the same token, it did not strip away certain rhetorical obsessions and certain quite obvious and simple techniques that detract from its quality. In spite of that, this book compiles an inventory of the elements that make up one of the components of Mexican national reality: the reality wherein descendants of the conquered Indians live side by side with the descendants of the conquering Europeans. If the former have lost the memory of their greatness, the latter have lost the attributes of their strength, and they all conflict in total decadence. The daily social behavior of beings so dissimilar produces phenomena and situations that began by interesting the anthropologists and have never stopped appealing to writers, who struggle to get to the very root of these extreme forms of human misery.

As far as I'm concerned, *Los convidados de agosto* exhausts that vein of archaic provincial life which served me so richly. After "Ritos de iniciación," a still-unfinished novel, I am venturing into other fields, tackling other problems and, consequently, trying out a style that I feel I have not as yet completely mastered.

Translated by Laura Carp Solomon
Juicios sumarios (1966)

Discrimination in the United States and in Chiapas

When faced with the violence (always latent, sometimes exacerbated, later repressed) of racial friction in United States territory, the grand master of the Ku Klux Klan took it upon himself to declare to a reporter from a mass circulation magazine that the main goal sought by him and his proselytes was to keep alive the sacred fire of the purity of the white race, avoiding any kind of contamination or mixture, particularly, of course, with its extreme opposite in the human chromatic scale, that is, with the blacks.

It is not an original attitude but immediately refers us to its Nazi predecessors, which only manages to elevate our feelings of justice and inflame our certainty regarding the absolute equality of all people, equality for which all distinctions artificially imposed by custom, circumstance, and prejudice lose their validity.

To what degree is this certainty abstract and to what point would it support the proof of a prolonged coexistence with human population groups of an economic and cultural level very different from our own?

Let's not hurry to put our hand into the fire, confident that we will never find ourselves at such a juncture, because even within the borders of our own country and our own times we might happen to find ourselves confined to some region in which the indigenous inhabitants constituted a majority, even though the advantage of numbers should be amply outweighed by the disadvantages of poverty and ignorance.

It is possible that during the first months we would assume an attitude of benevolence and even of generosity and would respond with help for the needy. But we would soon be disappointed to find out that our efforts were not enough, as a solution to the need that shocked us but also as the cause of gratitude among our beneficiaries.

Indifference would allow deception, scorn would follow indifference. And if this process takes place in the course of a few months, or, at latest, after a few years, why should it not happen with the passing of generations and centuries?

Our moods, our interests, our experiences would harden in a series of attitudes and convictions that would not be very far from the racist ideologies that we so loudly condemn.

But this evolution is not fatal and can be guided by a watchful conscience, which detains the irrational impulses of fear, pride, and hate for the sake of harmony and moral standards. This is the case of the declaration of principles made in San Cristóbal de las Casas, at the critical point when, more than integrity, the existence of this town had been placed in danger (for the fifth time since the time of the Conquest) by the rebellion of the Indian communities surrounding it.

The conflict occurred in the year 1867 when the Chamula tribe, headed by Pedro Díaz Cuscat, took up arms against their masters in the area and advanced, victory after victory, to the very gates of the main city.

An eyewitness informs us about the amazing events that occurred then— the lawyer Vicente Pineda, a native son of San Cristóbal to the very marrow of his bones, who takes advantage of this lesson that history offers to propose measures guaranteeing the effective and definitive hegemony of white peoples, without causing alarm.

Mr. Pineda finds only three alternatives for putting down the Indians: education, assimilation, and fusion.

The first one is a task that is incumbent on the government, who in order to carry it out must resort to as many "men of science and experience" as are available. It is essential that the Indians be spoken to in their own language "in order to make oneself understood, and to be understood about everything concerning the political and administrative rule of the people . . . because it requires real scruples to punish persons for deeds or omissions commanded or prohibited by the law, laws no one has taken the trouble to explain or make known. The ministers of religion will be useful for teaching dogma and moral maxims, to make obvious the advantages of their open-handed and loyal acceptance of them. Violence is absolutely prohibited. For all these cases it is indispensable to use persuasion. How can results be obtained if the one who persuades does not possess the vocabulary of the person he is trying to convince? On the other hand, no one can deny that ideas are comprehended more clearly and concisely in the native tongue than in any other language, no matter how well one may command it."

The knowledge that can be instilled in the Indian must lend to his improvement as a farmer, an activity "to which he is very inclined and from whose dedication it would not be prudent to distract him, because farm labor requires many hands and the Spanish-speaking persons of mixed blood are not very fond of the fatigue connected with this profession."

There is another sure, although slow, method to balance the numbers of savages and civilized people. This could be achieved, according to Pineda, by sending only two judges of the first instance so that all Indian orphans be appointed a civilized person to act as their guardian, one capable of appropriately instructing them and training them for the job for which they demonstrate most aptitude.

The fusion of races would also produce acceptable results, "because the moral and physical ties would join together the inhabitants of the state in such a way that, after a certain period of time, it would not be easy to distinguish their different origins. In order to put this project into practice, we need only for our Honorable Congress to award a prize to the civilized men and women who contract matrimony with natives. Granting them a dowry would increase these unions—which already take place without any incentive—which would benefit society in general, gradually destroying odious caste distinctions."

Don Vicente Pineda—and the gentlemen of his class—passed their trial by fire, because it has been a long time since anyone preached the extermination of those who threaten their privileges, their properties, and their lives and even longer since anyone was repulsed by interbreeding with the serfs. Fray Bartolomé de las Casas sowed his seed on fertile ground. The act of plunder and domination has not been abolished. But neither has it been justified by any doctrine.

September 4, 1965

Translated by Maureen Ahern
El uso de la palabra (1974)

A Man of Destiny

You may not be ready to hear about it but I'm ready to tell you about it—about them, better said. I'm exactly forty-five years old today. I never attempted to subtract a single one or ignore a date as one ignores a gray hair or a wrinkle. No, every single day has been worth what it cost me many times over.

Because I've often resisted the frivolous temptation of an artificial youth and because frequently I've had to struggle to keep on going and be responsible for at least my age, I can now assume it publicly and fully. If you should ask me which has been the most important fact, or the decisive event of my life, I couldn't answer with a book that I've read or written; a love come true; a vocation discovered; maternity in full bloom; the horizons of travel or meeting exemplary men and women.

Yes, it's true that all that has been given to me, and I don't discount its importance and solemnity a single iota. But it was extra. Most important were the opportunities offered to me, windows opened by a government leader, by his idea of justice and the persistence of his will for the law to be applied. I refer to Lázaro Cárdenas.[1]

His was the first name that I heard my elders pronounce with fright, rage, and powerlessness. Not only because his policies were damaging to their economic interests—when he ordered the distribution of land throughout Mexico and made no exception of the state of Chiapas—but also because he was stripping them of all that certainty which had upheld them for centuries.

The world they inhabited, not only as though it were legitimate but also as though it were eternal, suddenly collapsed. The dogmas that had resisted the most ironclad arguments suddenly became prejudices and sophisms that any lay person could successfully refute. The norms of con-

---

1. President of Mexico from 1934 to 1940, who championed the rights of peasants and workers, carried out agrarian land reform that broke up the large ranches owned by old families, and nationalized the foreign oil companies' holdings.

duct affirmed as something more than just the valid ones—as the only ones—became the object of censure and even ridicule.

The landowners emigrated, pressured not so much by poverty (because prudent administration placed them safely out of the reach of fortune's whims) but because the very symbol that they had embodied was annihilated. Back there, on their lands and their properties, on their realms, they were the ancestral masters whose forefathers had made history and whose descendants would preserve their privileges.

The peasants obeyed them, their equals respected them, the powerful sought their alliance and their counsel. But here in the city they had no status, they were lost in the crowd, they were no different from other people. When someone noticed them it was to smile at their bizarre clothes, their old-fashioned sayings, their timidity, their rustic awkwardness.

Anonymity was at once the bitterest cup and the safest refuge. If their pride was terminally, irrevocably, wounded, then their vanity, at least, remained intact.

Now that all hope was lost the elder generation turned to us, their children. What was to become of our future that once had stretched before us like the precise steps of ritual succession, that was now exposed to attack from the unforeseen, a stroke of luck, a brush with adversity?

What was to become of me? Before Cárdenas there would never have been a doubt. As a child I would have gone to school in a "lady's" home to learn the rudiments of the alphabet and basic arithmetic steps. When the first signs of puberty could be noticed, a colored map of the world on a sheet of cardboard was hurriedly ordered and I was addressed as young lady.

A young lady went out for walks in the company of her girlfriends watched over by a "respectable person." She received burning glances from timid suitors, rejected the package of chewing gum that the boldest one tried to give her, and hid the letter from her favorite one (copied word for word from *The Sweetheart's Secretary* with here and there an accidental misspelling) in her brassiere.

A young lady went to dances after offering up a novena to the most miraculous local saint, San Caralampio, to grant her the favor not to let her sit out dances when the marimba played the slow pieces, because that would have been an unbearable humiliation and an ominous sign of susceptibility to spinsterhood.

A young lady married according to her parents' wishes, a fairly close relative who owned a ranch whose boundaries abutting on the property that she was to inherit constituted a reason for even more rejoicing over the right choice of a partner.

A newly married woman woke up the next day and put on low-heeled shoes, a shapeless shift, and not a trace of makeup on her face and tied on a black scarf to make her new civil status apparent to all eyes. Overnight she had become a respectable married woman after having been an attractive one.

A respectable married woman had a child every year and delegated its upbringing to the Indian nannies just as she delegated the domestic chores to a horde of servants that swarmed over the kitchen, patios, bedrooms, and parlors.

The mistress, whose eternal pregnancies did not allow her to exercise and whose progressive obesity gradually reduced her to complete immobility, dictated orders, decreed punishments, and meted out reprimands from a hammock (when the weather was nice) or from her bed (when she needed more warmth).

The mistress, who could not accompany her husband in the work out on his lands, resigned herself to being substituted there by some woman whose condition was so lowly that it made her practically nonexistent. As the matriarch, the mistress took in the children that resulted from those illegitimate and more or less lasting unions and took charge of getting them a job or a station—subordinate, of course, but secure—within the society that she ruled.

The mistress, in time, kept watch over the education of the male children, the marriages of the females, and the fair division of the inheritance. In good time she became a grandmother, and widowhood enabled her to dedicate herself entirely to the Church and to die in the aroma of sanctity.

This was the paradise that I lost "through Cárdenas' fault." This was the legacy that I was never able to enjoy. Perhaps, O dreadful fate, I was going to have to work, and in spite of how bad we felt about it, it was better to start studying something useful, but something that did not excessively detract from my femininity. Secretarial? Chemistry? At any rate, something that would enable me to earn my living without acquiring the reputation of a know-it-all because not even the most self-sacrificing of my cousins or the snobbiest of the social climbers—to whom Cárdenas gave wing—would pardon me for that.

And, quite definitely, they never did. Now when I weigh the two kinds of lives (the one that Cárdenas made impossible and the one Cárdenas made possible), I couldn't say which would have been the happiest, most peaceful, least stressful life. But I do know that the one I had was the most responsible, the fullest, and the most human. And I also know that I have him to thank for it.

May 30, 1970

Translated by Maureen Ahern
El uso de la palabra (1974)

Woman and Her Image

In the course of history (history is an archive of deeds undertaken by men, and all that remains outside it belongs to the realm of conjecture, fable, legend, or lie) more than a natural phenomenon, a component of society, or a human creature, woman has been myth.

Simone de Beauvoir affirms that a myth always implies a subject that projects its hopes and fears toward a transcending heaven. In our case, man converts whatever is feminine into a receptacle of contradictory moods and places it at a distance from which we are shown a figure that, although varying in form, is monotonous in meaning. And the cumulative mythmaking process manages to conceal its inventions with such opaque density, insert them so deep in the recesses of consciousness and at such remote strata of the past, that it obstructs straightforward observation of the object or a direct knowledge of the being that has been replaced and usurped.

The creator and the spectator of the myth no longer see a woman as a flesh-and-blood person with certain biological, physiological, and psychological characteristics; much less do they perceive in her the qualities of someone who resembles them in dignity but is distinct in behavior. Rather, they perceive only the incarnation of some principle, generally sinister and fundamentally antagonistic.

If we look back at the primitive theogonies that attempt to explain the emergence, existence, and structure of the universe, we find two forces. Instead of complementing each other in harmonious collaboration, they oppose one another in a struggle in which consciousness, willpower, spirit—in short, masculinity—subjugate the feminine, which, being imminent passivity, is inertia.

The sun breathes life and the sea reaps its bounty; winds scatter the seed and the earth opens to germination; in a world that places order above chaos, where form saves matter from its inaneness, conflict is inevitably resolved by the triumph of man.

But absolute victory would require the banishment of his opponent. Because that demand has not been met, the victor—who plants his heel on the cervix of the vanquished enemy—feels in each heartbeat a threat; in each gesture, the imminence of flight; and in every move, an attempt to revolt.

Fear creates hideous new deliriums: delusions of the sea devouring the sun at sunset; the earth feeding on offal and corpses; chaos unchained in an enormous surge that arouses the license of the elements, unleashing powers of annihilation that turn the staff of plenty into empty shadows. Fear breeds actions that simultaneously foment its cause and do violence against it.

Thus, throughout the centuries, woman has been raised to the altar of the gods and has breathed the incense of the faithful. That is, when she is not locked up in a boarding school or a harem to share the yoke of slavery with her own kind; when she is not confined to the courtyards of the unclean; when she is not branded with the mark of the prostitute; crushed by the servant's burden; expelled from the religious congregation, the political arena, or the university classroom.

This ambivalence of male attitudes is merely superficial. If we examine it closely, we will find an indivisible and constant unity of purpose that is disguised in a multiplicity of ways. For example, suppose that a woman is praised for her beauty. Let us not forget that beauty is an ideal composed and imposed by men, which by strange coincidence corresponds to a series of qualifications that when fulfilled transform the woman who possesses them into a handicapped person; that is, without exaggerating, we might more accurately state, into a thing.

Big strong feet are ugly, they say, but they are good for walking and maintaining an erect posture. In a man, big strong feet are more than permissible, they are obligatory. But, in a woman? Even our tritest local troubadours surrender to "a foot as tiny as a thimble." With that foot (which in the China of the mandarins was bound so that it could not develop to its normal size, and in the rest of the civilized world was never subject to any exercise) one cannot go anywhere, which evidently is what it was all about.

A beautiful woman stretches out on a sofa, exhibiting one of the attributes of her beauty, her small feet, for male admiration, exposing them to his desire. They're covered by a shoe that some glittering fashion mogul has declared to be the expression of elegance and that possesses all the characteristics that define an instrument of torture. At its widest part it pinches to strangulation; the front ends in unlikely points to which the toes must submit; the heel extends thanks to a spike heel that does not sufficiently support the body to stand on, making balance precarious, a fall easy, and walking impossible. But who, except the suffragettes, dares to use comfortable shoes that respect the laws of anatomy? That's why the suffragettes, in just punishment, are unanimously ridiculed.

There are peoples, like the Arabs, the Dutch, and some Latin Americans, who only concede the title of beautiful to the obese woman. Her food and her sedentary customs earn her that title, at the price, of course, of her health and her ease of movement. Clumsy, easily tired, she deteriorates from sloth to paralysis.

But there are other more subtle and equally efficient methods to reduce woman to helplessness: those who would transform her into pure spirit. As long as this spirit does not keep the company of angels in heaven, she is lodged, alas, in the prison of her body. However, in order for the heaviness of this transitory state not to overcome its victim, the body must become as fragile, vulnerable, and nonexistent as possible.

Not all women possess the ethereal condition they are supposed to have. Therefore, one must camouflage abundant flesh with choking corsets and eliminate it with extenuating diets. After all, the weaker sex is incapable of picking up the handkerchief she drops or of opening a book that closes or of pulling back the lace curtain through which she contemplates the world. Her energy is used up in exhibiting herself to the eyes of the man who applauds her wasp waist, the shadows under her eyes (which if not caused by insomnia or illness can be produced by belladonna), her pallor that reveals a soul sighing to heaven, or the fainting spell of one who cannot bear contact with the brutal realities of everyday life.

Long fingernails prevent the use of hands for work. Complicated hairdos and makeup take up an enormous amount of time and require the appropriate setting to be properly shown off: one that protects her against the whims of the weather—the rain that ruins the shape of her eyebrows so carefully drawn with a pencil; that erases the rouge so painstakingly, so artistically applied to her cheeks; that dissolves the beautymarks distributed according to a calculated strategy into ridiculously arbitrary blotches that accent the imperfections of her skin. Or the wind that blows out curls, irritates her eyes, rumples her clothes.

The countryside is not the habitat of a beautiful woman, nor is the open air or nature. It's the salon, a temple where she receives the homage of her faithful admirers with the dauntlessness of an idol, an expressionless visage that cannot even demonstrate the single crack of a vain smile because any movement in her face could break into a thousand wrinkles revealing the decline of a star that is, after all, subject to the rigors and ravages of time.

The antithesis of Pygmalion, man does not aspire, by means of beauty, to convert a statue into a living being, but rather a living being into a statue. What for? To adore her, even though it may be for a brief time, or so we are told. But also, according to what we are not told, in order to immobilize her, to convert any plan of hers into unachievable actions, to avoid risks.

Womankind, in her natural state, does not lose her link with the dark powers, irreducible to reason, untamed by technology, that still circulate on this planet, disturbing the logic of events, disorganizing the structured, satirizing the sublime. Woman not only preserves her link with these dark powers, *she is* a dark power. Nothing will make her change her sign. But she can be reduced to impotence, at least, as we have seen, on the aesthetic level and, as we will see, on the ethical level.

Here we are dealing with the concept that Virginia Woolf called "The Angel in the House," the model of virtue to which every female creature must aspire.[1] This same English writer defines and describes her in this way: "She was intensely sympathetic. She was immensely charming. She was utterly unselfish. She excelled in the difficult arts of family life. She sacrificed herself daily. If there was chicken, she took the leg; if there was a draft she sat in it—in short she was so constituted that she never had a mind or a wish of her own, but preferred to sympathize always with the minds and wishes of others. Above all—I need not say it—she was pure. Her purity was supposed to be her chief beauty—her blushes, her great grace."[2]

What connotation does purity have in this case? Of course it's a synonym for ignorance. A radical ignorance of everything that happens in the world, but particularly about matters that have to do with "the facts of life" as one so euphemistically alludes to the processes of copulation, reproduction, and perpetuation of the sexual species, among them the human one. But, above all, it's ignorance of what the woman herself is.

Thus, a rigorous and complex morality is elaborated to protect feminine ignorance from any possible contamination. *Woman* is a term that acquires an obscene nuance and that is why we should cease using it. We

---

1. Castellanos borrowed the term "The Angel in the House" from Virginia Woolf's essay "Professions for Women," first published in 1929 (Virginia Woolf, *Women and Writing*, ed. Michèle Barrett [New York and London: Harcourt, Brace & Jovanovich, 1979], 57–63). Woolf developed her concept from the name of the heroine of a popular Victorian poem of idealized domestic life by Coventry Patmore (1823–1896).

2. Virginia Woolf, "Professions for Women," 59.

have other much more proper terms available: lady, madam, miss, and, why not, "The Angel in the House."

A lady is not acquainted with her body by reference, touch, or even sight. When a married woman bathes (that is if she bathes) she keeps her body covered with some modest tunic that is an obstacle to cleanliness and also to vain and pernicious curiosity. A monster in her own labyrinth, an unmarried woman becomes lost in the meanders of a capricious and invisible intimacy, ruled by principles that "the other sex" knows to the point of exactly locating and naming each spot, each turn, predicating the function, importance, and limitations of each shape.

An unmarried woman gropes blindly with an anatomy about which she has mistaken notions, stumbling across surprises, terror, scandal, in dark hallways and basements whose secret name belongs to "the other sex"; she does not understand, nor should she understand, the form that contains her, the function of that which serves as her dwelling, nor is she able to find her way out into open space, light, freedom. This situation of confinement, which is commonly called innocence or virginity, is apt to last for many years and sometimes for an entire lifetime.

The courage to inquire about herself: the need to become aware of the meaning of her own bodily existence or the unheard of pretention of conferring meaning upon her own spiritual existence is harshly repressed and punished by the social system. This has dictated, once and for all, that the only legitimate feminine attitude is that of waiting.

This is why, from the time a woman is born, education works on the given matter in order to adapt it to its destiny and convert it into a morally acceptable entity, in other words, a socially useful one. Thus, woman is stripped of her spontaneity of action, forbidden the initiative of decision, taught to obey the commandments of an ethic that is completely alien to her and has no more justification or basis than that of serving the interests, goals, and ends of others.

Sacrificed like Iphigenia on the patriarchal altars, womankind does not die: she waits. The expectation is that of the transition from potential to action: the transformation of moth into butterfly, events that will not take place through mere patience.

Like asceticism for the saints, which is nothing but a prerequisite that does not oblige divine grace to reward it, patience does not oblige chance to dispense or deny the agent that is the active principle and the catalyst of the natural processes: man. Not just any man but rather one anointed by the sacrament of marriage, thanks to which the cycle of development sublimates its profane origin and attains the required validity. Thus, the possibility of fulfillment, sinful in conditions that may not be the ones prescribed, is fulfilled in an atmosphere that renders it acceptable and desirable.

Through the male mediator, woman finds out about her body and its functions, about her person and her obligations, only that which is suitable for her and nothing more. Sometimes less. It depends on the generosity, the skill, or the knowledge available to whomever initiates her in the rites of passage.

Moreover, in either a tacit or explicit way, she is thus offered the chance to surpass her limits in a phenomenon that, while it does not erase, at least mitigates the negative signs that mark her, fulfill her needs, and incorporate her into the human nucleus with a letter of genuine citizenship. That phenomenon is maternity.

If motherhood were nothing more than physical birthing, as among animals, it would be anathema. But it is not merely a physical burgeoning because that would imply uncontrollable euphoria, something very distant from the spirit with which society has imbued the perpetuation of life.

In the maternal cavity, a mysterious event takes place, a kind of miracle that, like all miracles, arouses astonishment: it is witnessed by the attendants and experienced by the protagonist "in fear and trembling." Careful. One sudden move, carelessness, an unsatisfied whim and the miracle will not happen. Nine unending months of rest, of dependence upon others, precautions, rites, taboos. Pregnancy is a sickness whose outcome is always catastrophic for whomever suffers it.

You will deliver in pain, the Bible dictates. And if pain does not occur spontaneously, it must be forced out. Repeating the traditional advice, recalling examples, preparing the spirit to provide more room for suffering, inciting moaning and crying; requiring their paroxysmal repetition until that huge cry erupts that splits the neighbors' eardrums even more than the innards of the birthing woman by the newborn.

Is the price paid? Not quite yet. Now the child will become the implacable creditor. Its helplessness will arouse the total abnegation of its mother. She will watch over it while it sleeps; she will eat for it; she will weather the storm in order to shelter it.

Magically, the selfishness that we assume to be characteristic of the human species is rooted out of women. With unbounded pleasure, we are assured, a mother outdoes herself for her offspring. She proudly bares the deforming results to her body; she wilts away without melancholy; she hands over what she has stored up without thinking, oh, no, not for a single moment, of reciprocity.

Praise be to those dear old gray heads! Eternal glory "to the one who loved us before she knew us." Statues in the squares, days dedicated to her celebration, etc., etc. (Sometimes, like a fly in the ointment, we read on the crime page of the newspaper that someone—and herein follows an appropriate rending of vestments—that some unnatural being has committed the crime of infanticide. But it is a teratological case that does not jeopardize any basic principle. On the contrary, it is the exception that confirms the rule.)

We have mentioned the annulment of women in the realms of the aesthetic and the ethical. Need we allude to something as obvious as the intellectual arena? If ignorance is a virtue, it would be contradictory that, on the one hand, society praise her as it should and yet, on the other, provide the means to destroy her.

Feasibility is reinforced or derived from concepts. The heart of the argument is that women do not receive instruction because they are incapable of assimilating it.

Leaving aside Schopenhauer's vulgar diatribes, Weininger's esoteric outpourings, and Simmel's suspicious equanimity, let us only cite Moebius, who, with Germanic tenacity, organized an impressive amount of data in order to prove scientifically, and irrefutably, that woman is "physiologically retarded."

It is not an easy task to explain, one laments, exactly what constitutes mental deficiency. It is something that lies equidistant from imbecility and normality, although for the purpose of designating the latter we do not have an appropriate word at our disposal.

In everyday life, two opposing terms are used: intelligent and stupid. The person who discerns well is intelligent. (In relation to what? But it's rude to interrupt this speech.) The stupid person, on the other hand, is lacking in critical capacity. From the scientific point of view, what is usually called stupidity can be considered as much a morbid anomaly as a great reduction in the capacity to discern.

Now, that capacity is linked to bodily characteristics. A small cranium encloses, obviously, a small brain. And a woman's brain is minuscule. Not only are the weight and volume less if we compare them with those of the masculine brain, but the number of circumvolutions are also less. Always. Fatally. Sometimes exaggeratedly. Rudinger (who might this illustrious gentleman be?) found a Bavarian woman who had a kind of brain identical in all respects to that of wild animals. So, why waste ammunition and attempt to impart culture where it is impossible and superfluous!

But M. A. de Neuville, another gentleman as illustrious as Rudinger, takes the podium, to contradict him by making a catalog of the inventions that our civilization owes to female talent: "Mlle Auerbach has manufactured a comb that allows liquid to reach the scalp directly, simplifying the work of the hairdresser and the maid and permitting elegant persons to possess combs of different essences; Mlle Koller, thinking of smokers and the ladies who imitate them, invented a new wrapper for cigarettes prepared with compressed rose petals; Mlle Doré discovered a new prop machine for the dance with streamers performed by animals: dogs, monkeys, bears; Mlle Aernount, taking pity upon the unfortunate cyclists who ran over rabbits on badly laid cobblestone streets, planned a home velodrome system; Mlle Gronwald discussed the possibility of an aromatic and antiseptic toothpick with a soluble outer coating. Mme Hakin introduced a kind of tie for rubber clogs that prevents confusing and mismatching of the pairs; Mlle Stroemer . . ."

Enough! We agree with Luis Vives that no one looks for originality of thought, memory, or liberality in women. Because if you search you'll find extravagant cases like the ones we have just listed or the ones that feminists are ready to carry out at a moment's notice.

Let us not allow ourselves to fall into the old trap of trying to change, by a syllogism or a magic spell, the mutilated man—who according to Saint Thomas is woman—into a whole man. Rather, let us insist on another problem, which is that, in spite of all the domestic techniques, tactics, and strategies used in all latitudes and in all eras by all men, a woman always tends to be a woman, to spin in her own orbit, to govern herself according to a peculiar, untransferable, irrenunceable system of values.

With a strength that bends to no coercion and a stubbornness that no argument can persuade, with a persistence that does not diminish in the face of disaster, woman breaks the models that society proposes and imposes upon her in order to achieve her authentic image and consummate herself—and be consumed—in it.

In order to select oneself and place oneself before others one needs to have reached vitally, emotionally, or reflectively what Sartre calls a "limit situation"—a situation that due to its intensity, its dramaticism, or its raw metaphysical density is a point of ultimate desperation.

Nuns that tear down the walls of their cells, like Sor Juana or the Portuguese sister; maidens who scorn the guardians of their chastity in order to burn in love like Melibea;[3] lovers who know that abjection is a mask of true power and that domination is a disguise of incurable weakness like Dorotea and Amelia; married women whom boredom leads to madness like Ana de Ozores or to suicide like Anna Karenina, after passing fruitlessly through adultery; married women like Hedda Gabler or the Marchioness de Marteuil, who cold-bloodedly destroy all that surrounds them and destroy themselves since nothing is forbidden to them because nothing matters; generous prostitutes like la Pintada; old women to whom time has not added hypocrisy like Celestina; lovers whose impetus overcomes their objective like . . . like all lovers. Each one in her way and in her own circumstances denies the conventional, making the foundations of the establishment tremble, turning hierarchies upside down, and achieving authenticity.

The feat of *becoming what one is* (a feat belonging to the privileged whatever their sex or condition) not only demands the discovery of the essential features beneath the spur of passion, dissatisfaction, or surfeit, but above all the rejection of those false images that false mirrors offer woman in the enclosed gallery where her life takes place.

Smashing to bits the facile composure of features and actions; tossing our reputations to the dogs; affirming our authority over disgrace, scorn, and even death, such is the road that leads from the strictest solitude to total annihilation.

But there was a moment, a decision, and an act in which woman managed to conciliate her behavior with her most secret desires, with her truest forms, with her ultimate substance. And in that conciliation her existence was inserted at the point in the universe befitting her, proving herself to be necessary, and resplendent with meaning, expression, and beauty.

Translated by Maureen Ahern
Mujer que sabe latín (1973)

---

3. Female characters in Spanish and Portuguese literary works who defied the traditional codes of behavior that their societies prescribed for standard female behavior.

The Nineteenth-Century Mexican Woman

The gallery of feminine portraits is neither very abundant, varied, nor profound if we heed the literary manuals written in Mexico. On the whole, females simply serve as a backdrop so the main figure can be highlighted. He is the military boss, or *caudillo*, the man of action, the one who executes enterprises, plots, intrigues, dreams of a better future, fails, and suffers. As for a backdrop, a few lines are enough to trace an outline, a stereotype: the mother, with her unending capacity for sacrifice; the wife, stolid, loyal; the sweetheart, chaste; the prostitute, ashamed of her condition and willing to accept the worst humiliations as long as she redeems herself; the "other" woman, who surrenders alternately to pride and to remorse for having given in to the mere impulses of love without heeding the requirements of society; the camp follower, rough and mannish; the mother-in-law, a meddler; the spinster, bitter; the servant, a gossip; the Indian woman, timid.

Are we like that? We must be, because this is the image that we project. Only in this image the nuances are missing, as well as more careful and studied elaboration, including psychological analyses. Our search in books written by women does not entirely satisfy us. It's true there are more details, but they are so tainted with narcissism and self-complacency that it is not possible to assume them without an ironic grain of salt or mistrust.

Therefore, it is valid to resort to other sources, to other testimony. And if they are not contemporary, better yet. Because our roots are fixed and nourished in the past. Because many of our actions and many of our customs can only be explained when we remember.

Here, then, is that clever, "midwife of the soul," the Marchioness Calderón de la Barca, who added to her cultural formation a curious, inquisitive, alert spirit; a gift of insatiable charm and a capacity for observation that managed to discriminate very well between the trivial and the significant.

Madame Calderón de la Barca, one need not repeat, was the wife of the first Spanish ambassador to independent Mexico and remained among us in this diplomatic post for two years, from 1839 to 1841, time enough to penetrate our ways of being and expressing ourselves, of living and cohabiting, of beginning to demonstrate the first features of our own physiognomy that will only grow sharper in time and smoother in history.

Nothing escapes Madame's attention, not even the peculiarities of the climate, nor the characteristics of the landscape, the colorful garments, nor the customs of a society that had transplanted European fashions by adapting them to its own needs and demands.

It is natural that the marchioness, who enjoyed a privileged position due to her husband's rank and her English background, would establish comparisons between what she, as a woman, was accustomed to practice as proper conduct and the standards of conduct that she found prevalent among the representatives of her own sex in the country in which she found herself.[1]

The first matter that comes to mind is appearance. Is the Mexican woman beautiful? On first sight, no. The Mexican woman lacks the brilliant complexion and slim figure of the Englishwoman, the finely sculptured features of the Spanish woman, the grace and wit of the French woman. But gradually it is revealed that "the beauty of the women here consists in splendid black eyes, fine dark hair, a beautiful arm and hand, and very small, well-made feet. Their defects are that generally speaking

---

1. Fanny Calderón de la Barca, née Fanny Erskine Inglis, a Scotswoman (1804–1881), first published her compilation of her journals and letters under the title *Life in Mexico* in Boston in 1843 and very shortly afterward in London, where it was very well received throughout the English-speaking world. "In Mexico, where serialization in Spanish was begun shortly after a few copies of the book arrived on the local scene, the effect was a violent front-page newspaper storm of protest" (xxi). Over the years it has become a classic prime source for nineteenth-century Mexican history, and today it is highly regarded in Mexico itself. The first full-length published translation into Spanish was that executed by Enrique Martínez Sobral, issued in two volumes in 1920. In 1944 the Mexican government published excerpts of this translation issued by the Secretaría de Educación Pública and a subsequent complete Mexican edition of the same translation, accompanied by a preface by Artemio de Valle-Arizpe. "In June 1959 there appeared in Mexico a new Spanish translation by Felipe Teixidor—soon reissued as a large two-volume edition with a prologue and many illustrations. The first to be annotated, it constituted a landmark in the history of the book" (636). Rosario Castellanos' quotations are apparently taken from the 1959 Teixidor translation. The quotations in our English version of her essay and the information regarding translations are taken from *Life in Mexico: The Letters of Fanny Calderón de la Barca*, ed. Howard T. Fisher and Marian Hall Fisher (Garden City, N.Y.: Doubleday & Company, 1966), and the pagination indicated for them corresponds to this edition.

they are too short and too fat, that their teeth are apt to be bad, and their complexion not the clear olive of the Spaniards, nor the flowing brown of the Italians, but a bilious-looking yellow. Their manner of stuffing the foot into a shoe half an inch shorter ruins the foot and destroys their grace in walking, and consequently in every movement."[2] For this reason the marchioness prefers them to be sedentary although she laments their lack of affection for walking that so helps English women to keep in shape. "In the Alameda, it is very agreeable to walk; but, though I have gone there frequently in the morning, I have met but three ladies on foot, and of these, two were foreigners. . . . After all, everybody has feet, but only ladies have carriages, and a mixture of aristocracy and laziness prevents the Mexican dames from ever profaning the soles of their feet by a contact with their mother earth."[3]

Aristocracy and indolence. Have they not been synonymous among us to such a point that even the order of courtesy is altered? A lady is important and for that reason she takes care of her assets. But a gentleman is even more so, and that must be made evident in all possible ways. For example: "men may sit on chairs or benches in church, but women must kneel or sit on the ground. Why? '*¿Quién sabe?* Who knows?' is all the satisfaction I have ever obtained on that point."[4]

But perhaps this phenomenon can be related to others that are described in the following pages when the marchioness finds that feminine coquetry is not applied to conceal the ravages of time or make productive "that desire to enter upon the cares of matrimony which is to be observed in many other countries. . . . I have seen no courting of the young men either in mothers nor daughters: no matchmaking mammas, nor daughters looking out for their own interests. In fact, young people have so few opportunities of being together that Mexican marriages must be made in heaven, for I see no opportunity of bringing them about upon earth! The young men, when they do meet with young ladies in society, appear devoted to and very much afraid of them. . . . As for flirtation, the name is unknown, and so is the thing."[5]

In contrast, how enthusiastically do women take the veil here! This is how the brilliant ceremony is conducted: the future spouse of Christ "was arrayed in pale blue satin with diamonds, pearls and a crown of flowers.

---

2. Calderón de la Barca, 154–155.
3. Ibid., 168.
4. Ibid., 202–203.
5. Ibid., 230.

She was literally smothered in blonde and jewels; and her face was flushed as well it might be, for she had passed the day in taking leave of her friends at a *fete* they had given her, and had then, according to custom, been paraded through the town in all her finery. . . . Beside her sat the *madrina*, also in white satin and jewels; all the relations being likewise decked out in their finest array. . . . Then the organ struck up its solemn psalmody, and was followed by the gay music of the band. Fireworks were set off outside the church, and, at the same time, the *madrina* and all the relations entered and knelt down in front of the grating which looks into the convent. . . . Suddenly the curtain was withdrawn. . . . Beside the altar, which was in a blaze of light, was a perfect mass of crimson and gold drapery—the walls, the antique chairs, the table before which the priests sat, all hung with the same splendid materials. The bishop wore his superb mitre and robes of crimson and gold, the attendant priests also glittering in crimson and gold embroidery. . . .[6] Suddenly and without any preparation, down fell the black curtain like a pall, and the sobs and tears of the family broke forth. . . . Water was brought to the poor mother. . . . 'I declare,' said the Countess . . . to me, wiping her eyes, 'it is worse than a marriage!' I expressed my horror at the sacrifice of a girl so young, that she could not possibly have known her own mind . . . but many young girls, who were conversing together, seemed rather to envy their friend—who had looked so pretty and graceful, and 'so happy,' and whose dress 'suited her so well'—and to have no objection to 'go and do likewise.'"[7]

It is obvious that there is a relationship of cause and effect between these options and the ignorance of the world that is so strongly supported by general ignorance. "Generally speaking, then, the Mexican señoras and señoritas write, read and play a little—sew, and take care of their houses and children. When I say they read, I mean they know how to read; when I say they write, I do not mean that they can always spell; and when I say they play, I do not assert that they have generally a knowledge of music. . . .[8] But if a Mexican girl is ignorant she rarely shows it. They have generally the greatest possible tact, never by any chance wandering out of their depth."[9]

---

6. Ibid., 261–262.
7. Ibid., 267.
8. Ibid., 286–287.
9. Ibid., 288.

Devout nuns, impeccable housewives, docile daughters, wives, and mothers. The other side of the coin Madame Calderón de la Barca saw in the insane asylums and jails. There most of the cases were madness due to love and murder of the spouse. What a shame that she did not pay a visit to the brothels to make her picture complete!

Translated by Maureen Ahern
Mujer que sabe latín (1973)

Language as an Instrument of Domination

When the Hispanist attempts to justify the conquest of America (as though it were not sufficient that a historical event had been necessary or *had simply existed*), he reminds us that, among its positive aspects, the arrival of the discoverers to our continent reduced the diversity of dialects of the Precolumbian tribes to the unity of the Spanish language.

But Hispanism does not stop to specify how many and who were the beneficiaries of the gift that came to us "from over the ocean blue" and what use was made of it, how it was applied, to what subjects, with what intentions, and with what results.

After that one still would have to distinguish the value of Spanish in the regions densely populated by Indians, with their own cultural tradition still in force, and the significance of Spanish in places where nature had not yet ceded its turn to history.

In the first case we could say that language—like religion or race—constitutes a privilege that, paradoxically (or at least apparently), tends to cease to be one when it is divulged, communicated, extended.

The efforts of the missionary fathers to incorporate huge masses of the native population into European culture are notable, among other things, for their lack of success. Once the first apostolic impetus was past, things that had been settling into their rightful hierarchy tended to make that hierarchy persist: the Indian in submission; the mestizo in a no-man's-land of conflict; the *criollo*, or American-born Spaniard, at his ease; and the Spaniard in power.

The most important thing then was to display signs of distinction that demonstrated at first glance, and in the eyes of any passing stranger, the rank that one held in society. The color of one's skin said a lot but not everything; one had to add the purity and antiquity of faith and something else: the command of the oral means of expression.

That command perhaps was understood, at the beginning, as linguistic correction; but very soon this concept was changed to one of possession. This restriction then gave way to abundance. Speaking was an opportunity to exhibit the treasures that one owned, to display luxury, to arouse envy, applause, the will to compete and to emulate.

But to whom did one speak? Or with whom? One spoke to the servant to dictate an order, which if it was barely understood was poorly executed, which only gave grounds for scorn. One spoke to the neophyte in order to preach a dogma that did not ask for his understanding but rather his total acquiescence; to the vassal so that he would obey a law, which although undecipherable was still obligatory; to the audience who attended the spectacles where matters of honor, love affairs, and doctrinal problems were settled. The same audience appreciated that moment of ecstasy, although going beyond oneself did not imply, by any means, reaching another level of reality of any kind. To go into ecstasy was simply to become absent, not to be pursued on the trail of force, persecuted in the terrain of terror, subject to the realm of punishment.

To those long, florid, emphatic monologues corresponded (never responded—it was not possible to respond) that ancient custom of falling silent, which, according to Larra, makes the tongue stumble. And the Indian's tongue was heavy enough already, due to his ignorance, and the mestizo's because of his timidity.

People who talked, spoke with their equals. Leisure offered the *criollo* the chance to refine, polish, embellish himself with all the adornments that wealth offers and cleverness can procure: the decorative quality of language, skillful word matches, verbal fencing. Virtuosity is practiced and, in order to demonstrate the multiplicity of recourse, difficulties are also invented. The sentence curls and breaks from its own subtlety. It is the height of the Baroque.

Here the word is not an instrument of intelligence or the storehouse of memory but rather the "fair covering" with which the terror of the void is appeased, a talisman to ward off anguish. That is why the word will cross the threshold of the ladies' theater boxes to reach the jail where *The President*[1] walls up his enemies.

"Speak, keep on talking, don't keep quiet, no matter what, because silence frightens; I'm afraid, it seems to me that a long hand in the shadows is going to grab us by the neck and strangle us!"

---

1. Nobel Prize winner Miguel Asturias' (Guatemala, 1899–1974) first novel, *El Señor Presidente*, about terror and corruption in a dictatorship. It is characterized by his innovative use of poetic prose.

The hand that stretches out to strangle does not need the accomplice of darkness. It operates in full daylight and it has many names: Oppression, Poverty, Injustice, Dependence.

It has names; it is not named. The chatterers are too absorbed in the play of words that, to avoid the wind blowing them away, are pinned down, like butterflies, with the pin of writing. Here are the clerks busy at the task of constructing a sonnet that can be read from top to bottom, and bottom to top; from left to right and right to left; an acrobatic acrostic; a metric in which the jungle is petrified in Hellenic marbles. It doesn't matter that the forest explodes or the stone rots. Words have not been vulnerable, because they were separate from and beyond the reach of stone or jungle. It was an eternal chipping away in the realm of pure sound.

Language as Possible Liberation

Meanwhile, this world that never ceases being discovered awaits its baptism. Things, as García Márquez says, happened in Macondo, are pointed to with a finger, not by any name that defines, illuminates, or locates them.

The usufructors of language perverted it over the course of three or four centuries; they sacked it. It is not worth the trouble to appeal to the local court because the treasure, that treasure, is irrecoverable.

We have to create another language, we have to find another starting point, search for the pearl within each shell, the pit beneath the peel, because the shell holds still another treasure, the peel another substance. Word is the incarnation of the truth, because language has meaning.

In view of this, what does it matter if the princesses are sad?[2] The Harmony Fairy has ceased in her functions of deceiving fools, "crooning to sorrow and rocking pain."

Now the word travels from mouth to mouth, from hand to hand like a coin that is used to barter ideas, to change opinions, to purchase good will.

But just as happens with coins, words wear out and lose that sharpness that makes them valuable, words become mistaken, polyphonic. Handled and spit upon, they must be bathed in purity in order to recover their pristine qualities.

This pristineness consists in exactness. The word is the arrow that hits its mark. To substitute it with another is to betray the thing that it aspired

---

2. A reference to the poem "Sonatina," by Rubén Darío (1867–1916), and the elitist aspects of the Modernist movement (1880–1915) in Spanish American letters, with its penchant for medieval emblems and personae, as well as exotic motifs.

to represent fully and faithfully with sharpness, precision, and not to be roughly outlined with the wide brush strokes of a painter of farces.

The word, which is unique, is at the same time and for the same reason gregarious. When it occurs it convokes the presence of all the others that are in tune with it, the ones linked by blood ties, legitimate associations, forming families, constellations, structures.

They may be complex, they may be governed by an order that produces pleasure in the beholder. What is not permitted them is to once more become gratuitous. Words have been endowed with meaning and a person who handles them professionally is not permitted to strip them of that meaning but, on the contrary, promises to bear witness to it to make it evident at every moment.

The meaning of a word is its addressee: the other being who hears it, understands it, and who, when he answers, converts his questioner into a listener and understander, establishing in this way the relationship of dialogue that is only possible between beings who consider themselves and deal with each other as equals. And that is only fruitful between those who wish each other to be free.

Translated by Maureen Ahern
Mujer que sabe latín (1973)

If Not Poetry, Then What?

Justify a book? It's easier to write another one and leave to the critics the task of transforming confusion into something explicit, vagueness into precision, erratic matter into a system, arbitrariness into substance. But, in my case, when all my books of poetry are collected in a single volume that opens to a first line that affirms

the world cries out sterile, like a mushroom,

there's nothing left to do but quickly proceed to explain. Well, as commentators made me see in their good time, the mushroom is the antithesis of sterility since it proliferates with shameless abundance and nearly a total lack of stimulation. Actually, what I wanted to say then was that the world had a genesis as spontaneous as that of the mushroom, that it had not sprung from any divine plan, that it was not the result of the internal laws of matter, nor was it the *conditio sine qua non* for the development of the human drama. That the world was, in short, the perfect example of fortuitousness.

If this was what I wanted to say then why didn't I say it? Simply because I don't want to do so. And I must add that inertia more than conviction dragged me into taking up the banner of faith that declaimed an America more rhetorical than real. I was not an optimist in those days but pessimism seemed to me to be a private and mistaken attitude, the product of childhood traumas and a difficult adolescence. Neither did I have the slightest notion of what that "continent that lies dying" was, but I had thought about it so little that it had not been lost together with all my other beliefs, after a serious crisis of values that had left me in the most absolute of Cartesian winters.

But (now I realize it) I've moved from cover to cover of the book without stopping to look at it. There's a title there—(*Poesía no eres tú*) *You Are Not Poetry*—that merits a separate paragraph. Is it a reaction at this stage of the game, against the Spanish romanticism that Bécquer so well embodied? We're anachronistic but not that much. Is it a contradiction, in more recent terms, of Rubén Darío when he decides that one cannot exist without being romantic? It's not that either. What happened is that I developed very slowly from the most closed subjectivity to the disturbing discovery that the other existed and, finally, to the rupture of the pattern of the couple to integrate myself into the social sphere that is the one in which the poet defines, understands, and expresses herself. The *zoon politikon* does not achieve such a category unless it be composed of a minimum number of three. Even in the Gospels, Christ assures us that wherever two persons meet in His name, the Holy Spirit will come to rescue them from their solitude.

Well, then, is it triangles in the French style? Naughty vaudeville? Nothing could be further from my intentions. At least the link between the related parties does not have to be an amorous one. But if it is, I have always conceived of love as one of the instruments of catastrophe. Not because it doesn't achieve fullness or permanence. That's a minor matter. The major matter is that, like St. Paul, it takes the blinders off our eyes and we see each other as we are: needful, mean, cowards. Careful not to risk ourselves in our giving and not to commit ourselves in our reception of gifts. Love is not a consolation, declared Simone Weil.[1] And she added something terrible: It is light—that light from which the soul draws back so that its crevasses cannot be illuminated, that clamor for us to dive into them, that will annihilate us and then . . . the promise is not clear. Afterward it might be the void that is not conceivable for our intelligence even though it may be desirable, due to the sensitivity that strives for the definitive cessation of suffering. Or perhaps rebirth on another plane of existence, marvelously serene, that paradise that Jorge Guillén condenses to a single line: *"where love is not anguish."*

So it seems that, after so much hopping about and comings and goings, I am only a poetess ("poetriste" or "poetresse," Mejía Sánchez proposed as alternatives) who *also* writes about love! Shades of Delmira Agustini, Juana de Ibarbourou, and Alfonsina Storni,[2] be still! It is not precisely the

---

1. Simone Weil (1909–1943), French philosopher and mystic. Originally Jewish, she was attracted to Christianity in 1940, believing that Christ on the Cross was a bridge between God and mortals, and became a practicing Roman Catholic. Most of her works published posthumously are notebooks and collections of religious essays and have been translated into English. The influence of her thought on Castellanos' work is strong and deserves an essay in its own right.

2. Three Latin American women poets best known for their erotic, romantic, and vanguard poetry based on passionate love affairs. Delmira Agustini (1886–1914), Uruguayan; Juana de Ibarbourou (1895–1970), Uruguayan; Alfonsina Storni (1882–

same thing. I would not want to resign myself to its being the same. It is true that I read them with the application of an apprentice. It is true that I admired Agustini's sumptuous imagery and Storni's ironic similes and in both of them the oblique and direct suicidal impetus. It is true that from Ibarbourou I learned that everything of hers was alien to me. But my problem sprang from other sources and consequently demanded other solutions.

At the time when one discovers one's vocation, I found out that mine was one of understanding. Until then, unconsciously, I had identified this need with that of writing. Whatever came out. And rhymed, eleven-syllable lines are what came out. Four by four and three by three. Sonnets. Their composition offered me some relief from the anguish, as though, for a moment, I had been emancipated from the dominion of chaos. Order reigned, laughable perhaps, certainly provisional, but order at last.

Someone revealed to me that what I was doing was called literature. Later I found out that there was a college at the university where one studied its history and techniques. I went to register for it, simply to convince myself that the list of dates and names, the catalogs of styles, and the analysis of the techniques did not help me in the least in understanding anything. The programs of studies in humanities not only were lacking answers to the major questions but they also didn't even ask the main questions, which are, for example, Why? What for? How? And, naturally, I am referring to everything.

My Guardian Angel made me see that next to the classes of literature they were giving philosophy classes, where, yes, they asked all those questions. And I refer again to everything.

I changed classrooms. "Happy, unwarned, and confident," I began to receive instruction about the pre-Socratics—who wrote, if I remember correctly, poems. Parmenides and Heraclitus gave the body of an image to their conception of the world. Plato, too, although he already struggles to draw a dividing line between the two ways of knowledge and expels poets from his Republic because by nature they contain the undesirable germ of dissolution. Aristotle came later and the separation between philosophy and letters was consummated.

1938), Argentinean. See Nora Jacquez Wieser, ed., *Open to the Sun: A Bilingual Anthology of Latin-American Women Poets* (Van Nuys, Calif.: Perivale Press, 1979), for selections of their poetry in English translation.

When I realized that philosophic language was inaccessible to me and that the only notions within my reach were those disguised as metaphors, it was too late. Not only was I just about to finish my degree but I also no longer wrote hendecasyllables or rhymed verse or sonnets. Now it was something else. Amphibea. Ambiguity. And like the mating of different species, it was sterile.

Evidence? A lot of destroyed manuscripts and the first two poems of the book that we've been talking about, "Apuntes para una declaración de fe" and "Trayectoria del polvo." (Which, in parenthesis, maintain a chronological order distinct from that of their location in the book. It is not obvious, there is so little development from one text to the other.) The unforgivable sin of both poems is the abstract vocabulary that I used in them. It was indispensable for me to substitute for it another vocabulary that would refer to objects at hand, with which themes could acquire a consistency that could be felt and touched.

I could find no better way out of this blind alley than to place a model or example in front of me and then laboriously copy it as faithfully as possible. I chose Gabriela Mistral,[3] the Gabriela of "Matter," "Creatures," and "Messages," the reader of the Bible, a reading which I then of course also applied. The image of such exemplary models casts its shadows and some of its substance over the pages of *De la vigilia estéril.*

An unfortunate title that enabled my friends to make plays on words. Sterile or hysterical? I was still single against my will and the drama of rejection of the most obvious aspects of femininity was genuine. But who could guess that, if I covered it up with so much clutter and rubbish? I had arrived at the same conclusion as the sculptor: the statue is what remains after you have removed the excess stone.

So my goal was, then, simplicity. I advance much more quickly to *Rescate del mundo.* And, nearly weightless, I get carried away with "Misterios gozosos" and "El resplandor del ser."

But as St. Augustine said, it is the heart that is heavy. It is similar weight that upsets the balance of a poem. *Eclipse total,* yes, briefly. Suffering is so enormous that it spills over the vessel of our bodies and goes in search of

---

3. Gabriela Mistral, Chile (1889–1957). Winner of the first Latin American Nobel Prize for Literature in 1945, her poetry is based on themes of a collective love for humanity in its more universal aspects, of children, people, places, and things that she encountered, as well as the expression of her personal tragedy and loss and an abiding concern for social justice.

more capable vessels. It finds the paradigmatic figures of a tradition. Dido, who raises the triviality of an anecdote (is there anything more trivial than a scorned woman and an unfaithful man?) to majestic heights where the wisdom of centuries resounds. "Dido's Lament" ("Lamentación de Dido"), in addition to being the story of individual misfortune, is the convergence of two readings: Virgil and St. John Perse. One gave me matter and the other form. And from that privileged moment of felicitous intercourse the birth of a poem took place!

It immediately rose up before me like a barrier. I was afraid to write again and I was afraid not to write again, until I decided to ignore it and to start from zero in *Al pie de la letra*.

Among so many echoes I begin to recognize my own voice. Yes, I'm the one who writes "La velada del sapo" as well as "Monologue of a Foreign Woman." Three cardinal points to follow: humor, solemn meditation, and contact with my carnal and historical roots. And everything is bathed in that *livid light* of death that makes all matter memorable.

I say that I was detained at this stage because I don't like to recognize that I'm stagnating. There has to be a very strong jolt from outside in order for perspective to change, style to be renewed, in order to open up to new themes, new words. Some of them are vulgar, crude. What can I do about it? They are the ones that are useful to say what I have to say. Nothing important or transcendent. A few insights into the structure of the world, some guidelines to some of the coordinates that help me locate myself in it, the mechanics of my relationships with other beings, which are neither sublime nor tragic. Perhaps, a bit ridiculous.

We have to laugh. Because laughter, we already know, is the first evidence of freedom. And I feel so free that I can begin with "dialogue of the most honorable men," I mean, with other writers. On an equal basis. On a first-name basis. A lack of respect? A lack of culture, if culture is what Ortega defined as a sense of hierarchies? It could be. But let us give ourselves the benefit of the doubt. Let the *reader-accomplice* go to the bother of elaborating other hypotheses or other interpretations.

Translated by Maureen Ahern
Mujer que sabe latín (1973)

Self-Sacrifice Is a Mad Virtue

W oman's contribution to culture in Mexico has been very important
if we consider it from a qualitative point of view alone. Sor Juana's
genius spans three centuries of colonial life. Her rich expression, varied
means of creativity, depth of thought, and universal appeal cause us to be
unaware of the silence that surrounds her, the void from which she
emerges, and the inadequate environment in which she develops.

But one swallow does not a summer make. In the nineteenth century
even that swallow was missing. And in the twentieth century, in which we
live, successive Pleiades of dazzling figures appear, only to shine one moment and burn out the next. None of them are close enough to provide us
with sufficient perspective to judge their value and speculate on their
permanence.

At any rate, statistics, not exceptions to the rule, are what we use to
measure the cultural index for a sector of the population. And the statistics
that refer to the education of women in Mexico cast out some very sorry
figures. If culture is not assimilated, how can it be produced?

The comparative percentages of elementary school education of men
and women do not show much difference among sectors of peasants, ar-
tisans, and skilled workers. But if we refer to other groups and look at
higher education, the differences are more than appreciable: an alarming
85 percent of professionals are men compared to 16 percent women.

Among the latter, how many of them actually exercise the profession
they studied? How many of these women would rather keep their diplomas tucked away in the attic, after having wasted years of effort and irre-
trievable sums of money that the country has invested in people who turn
out to be unproductive? These phenomena (scarcity and waste) must have
an explanation and it is this explanation that we propose to look for.

Let us not yield to the simple sophistry of the antifeminists who pro-
claim an inferiority attributable to sex. Sex, as well as race, does not constitute any biological, historical, or social predetermination. It is simply a
collection of conditions, a frame of concrete references within which hu-

mankind makes the effort to attain fulfillment in the development of its creative potential.

The first argument that comes to the lips of feminists who are more angry than they are reflective—comparing their own situation with that of men—is the demand for equality. A demand, that, much as it is metaphysical, logical, and practically impossible to satisfy, provides a false starting point, dragging along with it a series of undesirable consequences. Furthermore, in the final analysis, it is no more than an acknowledgment of masculine life style and behavior as the only feasible ones, the goal that must be attained at any cost.

No, indeed. If we intend to build an authentic but, above all, efficient feminism, we must start out from other premises. The first would be diligent research, the most exact and pure knowledge that can be attained from the complex of qualities and defects, deficiencies and attributes, aspirations and limitations that define womankind.

This investigation will lead us to a very important discovery: that the essence of femininity does not exist, because what is one thing in one culture is considered to be something else in another, is not considered at all, or is part of the characteristics of masculinity.

However, if the essence of femininity does not exist, we must admit that what do exist are the concrete personifications of femininity. It has become difficult to compare the strong woman of the Gospel to the Soviet woman astronaut or to the matriarch of Kuala Lumpur. If this is so, it becomes clear that we must focus our attention upon the problems of the contemporary Mexican woman.

What do we find? At first glance we are confronted with apparently irreducible diversity. Does the young Indian girl who tends the sheep grazing on the Chiapas plains belong to the same species as the girl who is a science student at the university? Does the provincial girl who still wears "her blouse up to her ears and her skirt down to her ankles" live in the same century as the sportswoman who water-skis at Acapulco or other fashionable beaches, barely covered by a skimpy bikini? What is there in common between the servant girl who has just discovered the miracle of the automatic blender and the airline hostess for whom a jaunt around the world is merely routine?

It is true that each one of the examples we have mentioned (and there are many more that are equally antagonistic) includes different economic, cultural, and even temporal strata. But they are all interrelated, at least in the following ways: they are all subject to the rights and obligations of the same legislation; all of them have inherited the same wealth of traditions, customs, standards of conduct, ideals, and tabus; all of them are endowed with the same degree of liberty to demand their rights if they should be diminished, to fulfill or not fulfill the obligations imposed upon them, to opt between following tradition or breaking with it, to accept or reject the archetypal way of life that society presents them with, and to expand or reduce the horizons of their expectations; to ignore prohibitions or obey them.

Yes, now we know what we are talking about. In Mexico, when we utter the word *woman*, we refer to a creature who is dependent upon male authority: be it her father's, her brother's, her husband's, or her priest's. She is subject to alien decisions that dictate her personal appearance, her marital status, the career she is going to study, or the field of work she is going to enter. Trained from infancy to be understanding of and to tolerate abuse from those stronger than she is, she, in turn, in order to reestablish her inner balance, treats those over whom she has power with an iron hand. The Mexican woman does not consider herself—nor do others consider her—to be a woman who has reached fulfillment if she has not produced children, if the halo of maternity does not shine above her.

Love for one's child supplants or substitutes for all other kinds of love, which qualify as less perfect because they presuppose reciprocity—which in the maternal realm seems to be relinquished. Love for one's child is superior to all the feelings of frustration that surge from interrupted studies, from training that is not put into practice, from the inability to earn one's living, from the precarious ways she tries to satisfy her needs, from being cooped up in a house—and sometimes in one room—with no other stimulation than the child's demands (that are, alas, as diverse as they are inexhaustible). To sum it up, love for one's child allows one who feels it to ascend, among clouds of incense, to the highest peaks of self-denial.

Self-sacrifice is the Mexican woman's most famous virtue. But I am going to be presumptuous enough to say something that, worse than a question, is a doubt: is self-denial really a virtue?

I hasten to explain that my doubt is not groundless. I have observed in self-sacrificing women excessive self-complacency, an obvious enjoyment of the situation, which clearly supposes that these efforts are not directed as precisely and completely toward the welfare of the other person as much as they are toward their own self-satisfaction. This premise is confirmed when we see the results. What are they like, children of these mothers who have done everything for them, sacrificed everything for them?

To begin with, they are children who are less able to solve their own problems, become self-sufficient, handle emergencies, and overcome obstacles than those who have not always had someone hovering over them. This naturally makes them less sure of themselves, slower to develop, and less motivated to attain independence and maturity. It is not unusual that these persons remain in a perennial childhood with the resulting loss of contact with reality, and also a resulting pursuit, not to establish this contact but rather to find ways to evade it or compensate for it. The sad ways that our people use for evasion or for compensation: alcoholism, bragging macho behavior, female hypocrisy, from the crudest lie to the most subtle fabrication, attitudes that tend to protect us from a world that, because we cannot control it, acquires extraordinary proportions (or disproportions) relative to our size.

However, for the Mexican woman's self-sacrifice, children are not enough. This trait is also targeted at other members of the family: at her husband, who becomes a domestic tyrant, quickly finding himself stripped of even the most minimal responsibility if he does not succeed in protecting his rights; at her parents, with whom an infinitely prolonged relationship, by virtue of its anachronism, is nonfunctioning and morbid; and at her siblings, whom she attempts to maintain as eternal minors.

I insist that, if self-sacrifice is a virtue, it is one of those virtues that Chesterton says have gone mad. And for this madness, the only straitjacket we have is the law.

All the legal regulations that we have been developing throughout history tend to establish equality—political, economic, educational, and social—between man and woman.

It is not just—and therefore neither is it legitimate—that one of the two persons who make up the couple gives all, yet does not expect anything in return.

It is not just—thus it is not legitimate—that one of them has the opportunity to develop intellectually, while the other has no alternative but to remain subject to ignorance.

It is not just—and for the same reason it is not legitimate—that one of them finds not only a source of wealth through work, but also the joy of feeling useful, of becoming a participant in the community, of being fulfilled through creativity, while the other carries out duties not worthy of remuneration, that barely reduce the feeling of superficiality and isolation: duties, which by their very nature are short-lived and never-ending.

It is not just—and opposes the spirit of the law—that one of them has every freedom of movement while the other is reduced to paralysis.

It is not just—therefore it is not legal—that one of them is master of his own body and disposes of it at will, while the other reserves her body, not to derive benefits, but to unwillingly have it acted upon.

It is not just, the way men and women are treated differently in Mexico, but we allow ourselves the luxury of violating the law in order to continue circling like mules around a draw well, out of habit, even though the law exists (and we are aware of it) to correct whatever custom retains that is obsolete, defective, and unjust.

If injustice still affects Mexican women, they have no right to complain. That is the choice they have made. They have scorned the legal recourses they have at hand.

They refuse to accept what the legal statutes guarantee them and what the constitution gives them: the category of human being.

But we must not be discouraged. Every day, a woman—or many women—(who knows exactly how many, since what happens is often anonymous, done modestly without showing off) wins a battle to obtain and preserve her personality. Winning the battle requires not only lucidity of mind, determination of character, and moral courage, which is a serious matter, but additional resources like astuteness and, above all, persistence. It is a battle which, when victorious, develops more complete human beings, happier marriages, more harmonious families, and a country made up of conscientious citizens for whom liberty is the only atmosphere one can breathe; justice, the ground in which they take root and prosper; and love, the indestructible bond that unites them.

Mexico is a young country; therein lie the roots of its strengths and hopes. That is why the best efforts of our leaders are directed toward guiding young people along the road of ideals and truth. The enormous potential that Mexican youth, with all its concerns and passions, signifies for the increasing stability and progress of our country is the task that Professor Aurora Arrayales Sandoval—the untiring president of the Social Service and Cultural Committee, A.C.—will propose to us.

February 15, 1971

Translated by Laura Carp Solomon
Diorama de la Cultura, Excélsior February 21, 1971, 5, 14.

The Liberation of Love

You, madam, self-sacrificing little Mexican woman, or you, self-sacrificing little Mexican woman on the road to emancipation: what have you done in the last few months on your own behalf? I can imagine the obvious answer: you have reviewed Simone de Beauvoir's now classic text, either to disagree or support your own arguments or, plainly and simply, to become informed. You have kept abreast of the books that are published, one after the other, in the United States: Betty Friedan's exhaustive descriptions, Kate Millet's aggressiveness, and Germaine Greer's lucid scholarship.

Of course you closely follow the events that document the existence of Women's Lib. Of course you pretended not to understand when you learned about that symbolic act of burning underwear, because this lent itself to any number of good jokes. You held onto your own, vaguely recalling the Spaniards' cry under the reign of Ferdinand the VII: "Long live chains!" and it never occurred to you that it applied in the least to the situation that concerns us now.

Perhaps you felt like an accomplice to the women who kidnapped the director of a pornographic magazine because it portrayed women as mere sex objects, but, in any case, you deeply regretted that the example of North American women is impossible to follow in Mexico. Our idiosyncrasies are so different, as well as our history and our traditions! The fear of being ridiculed paralyzes us and we well understand that French poet when he confesses that "he has lost his life because of sensitivity."

For whatever it may be worth, I am going to give you, free of charge, a piece of information that perhaps you already have. (Sometimes it is a good idea to step into a fun house and see our reflections in the distorted mirrors.) For me, however, this was really a revelation: the attitude that has been adopted in Japan to confront the problem of woman's place in society and the roles that she has to play; an attitude that crystallizes into a Women's Love Movement as opposed to Women's Lib.

You were able to learn about it due to the presidential visit to the Far East, when the pages of Mexican newspapers and magazines were full of facts about different aspects of life in that region. I learned about it thanks to the visit to Israel made by Mrs. Kasagi, journalist, teacher, lecturer, expert in the rehabilitation of the deaf and mute, and, in her spare time, passionate leader of Women's Love.

Mrs. Kasagi made the following revelation: a woman who is gracious, kind, and on the surface submissive is able to conquer a man and, without his realizing it, impose upon him her own points of view. Remember, you catch more flies with honey than you do with vinegar, and that an angry, hysterical woman will only generate antagonism from members of the opposite sex and pity or merciless laughter from members of her own sex.

I yield the floor to Mrs. Kasagi, who confirms the fact that raising the banner of love and rejecting the militancy of demanding and violent women simply reflect her own philosophy of life. This does not mean that she does not work, and very actively, for the emancipation of the Japanese woman, but, rather, her methods are different, more in keeping with the oriental feminine image in which woman embodies the values of delicateness and charm.

Why reject this image and adopt another that would be extremely foreign to them, like the one contemporary Western culture proposes? On the contrary, Mrs. Kasagi's activity is directed toward salvaging a series of practices that were on the verge of being lost immediately after the Japanese defeat at the end of World War II.

Traditionally, in the Japanese family, the mother handed down to her daughter the elements required in order to be considered a real woman. That is, in the bows due her elders and those superior to her (which was practically everybody), she taught her how to bend in a correct and gracious manner; she showed her how to wear her kimono properly and how to arrange flowers. Instructing her in how to conduct herself at the table (and other more private pieces of furniture) and how to perform the refined tea ceremony were also included.

What happened at the end of the Second World War? Women went out to work and earn money, and now they had no time to practice what they had learned and even less to teach their daughters how to conduct themselves like ladies. Naturally, the daughters were not capable of passing on to their own daughters a wealth of knowledge that is no longer part of their heritage.

Mrs. Kasagi embarked upon retrieving such important material, and in Tokyo she has opened up something that could be considered the equivalent of what we call a "charm school." There, this diamond in the rough, that is, an adolescent girl, is polished until she becomes an item of luxury that displays the wealth and fine taste of its owner and constitutes a secure investment that never ceases to yield dividends.

The training that is acquired at Mrs. Kasagi's institution of learning is so complete that a woman educated there can be intelligent without showing it in the slightest way; she can be ambitious without scaring men away; she can hold important positions, private as well as public, without awakening the competitive spirit of her opponents, but, better yet, she can appeal to their chivalrous spirit to help and protect her.

As you already know, the Japanese man (like some of your countrymen) is very touchy in these matters. He demands complete submission, and whenever he is opposed he knows how to inflict punishment with an iron hand. Do you not remember, for example, that ex–Prime Minister Sato's wife confided to a journalist something about her husband's habit of beating her? This item of information did not provoke any governmental crisis or deterioration of the government's image. It is better this way than the opposite.

We must, then, recognize the given facts and act accordingly. Mrs. Kasagi can serve as an example to her pupils. She has obtained permission to act and even travel on her own, as her stay in Israel proves. One has to attribute such daring not to her methods, as she herself admits, but to the fact that her husband is very progressive and broadminded.

So broad that he would wait for her during an absence of five days when she accepted the invitation of an airline company to visit a country in the Middle East. And as for her son, who is now twenty years old, he can choose from among his mother's pupils the one who obtains the best grades.

Tel Aviv, July 20, 1972

Translated by Laura Carp Solomon
El uso de la palabra (1974)

Herlinda Leaves

Until now, I've had two long servanthoods, and I use that word with the full consideration of its ambivalence. Because both of them served me to exactly the degree to which I consented to become a creature dependent upon their care, oriented to their efficiency, obedient to their routines, flexible to their whims, resigned to their limitations. Which of the two was the most subject, servant or mistress? That remains to be seen.

Each one of the protagonists—a complementary adversary—will claim for herself the largest dosage of suffering. I can only affirm that when I have lived in circumstances in which this relationship, which has always seemed to me to be a fatal one, did not exist, I was able to breathe more than easily, just as I liked, without remorse, regrets, or irritation, without that bother of having precise rules established, without that feeling of being at the mercy of another's good intentions, and that the margins—of tolerance or abuse—can be set up as one goes along. How much can I ask for? How far should I give in? According to what rituals? Intuition showed me the way. But reflection paralyzed my acts until the time came when external circumstances enabled us to untie the knot that was mutually choking us and enabled us to say (with regret for the past, fear for the future, and neglect for the present) good-bye!

The first person of the two whom I referred to at the beginning of this essay was María Escandón. Her mother gave her to my mother when we were both children in order for her to become my "carrier," or *cargadora*.

That institution—I don't know if it is still practiced in Chiapas where they tell me so many things have changed—was in all its splendor then. It consisted of the fact that the master's child had, in addition to toys that were few and simple ones, a child of his or her own age as a companion. That child was at times a playmate with initiative and inventiveness, who participated actively in games. But sometimes the child was a mere object on which the other child exercised frustration: a child's unending energy, boredom, anger, possessive jealousy.

I don't think I was exceptionally capricious, arbitrary, or cruel. But no one had taught me to respect anyone else except my peers, and of course my elders. So I let myself be carried along by custom. The day when it was revealed to me in a blinding way that the thing that I made use of was a person, I made an immediate decision: to ask pardon of the person whom I had offended. And I made another vow for the rest of my life: not to take advantage of my position of privilege to humiliate another person.

What happened then? Was a relationship of respect established between a grateful María and a scrupulous Rosario? No. Between a startled María and a defenseless Rosario there was no possible contact. Furthermore, we had grown up and I was going to school or the teacher came to the house to teach me. María was more useful helping with the cleaning and housework and gradually getting used to the sacred territory of the kitchen.

Although near one another, we led parallel lives, and I can only remember her during my mother's final illness when María was a much more devoted and sacrificing nurse than I was. Because she loved my mother with a deeper more daughterly affection, she consented to fulfill my mother's last wishes: to take care of me.

She did it in such a way that I never even needed to order anything: everything was always ready. The bath at just the right moment, clothes laid out properly for each occasion, the meals on time and according to the rules. What did I do in exchange? Accept her discipline with comments that were only praises. Not to cross my boundaries, which were the study, the bedroom, and the parlor. Not to ask questions or make inquiries of any kind. To hand myself over with total confidence and passivity. To which María corresponded by not abandoning me even when the doctor who diagnosed my tuberculosis said it was contagious. Not even when I decided to go to work for the Indigenous Institute in Chiapas. Not even when I got married. But both of us knew that after that she was relieved of her duty to me, because I was then—as they say in my part of Mexico— "under a man's hand."

So then María went to work for Gertrudis Duby, who never got over the surprise (and she told me so reproachfully) that after all those years of living with me I had never even taught her to read well or to write. There I was off playing Quetzalcoatl, the great white civilizing god, while right next to me someone was walking around ignorant. I was ashamed. I made a promise that the next time (if there was to be a next time) it would be different. My policy in regard to Herlinda Bolaños was totally different. But I would not venture to say that it was more appropriate.

During our stay in the United States, and especially when we arrived in Israel, I took care of her while she took care of my son. On the trips and outings I made sure she had fun and that she learned something. She had

already finished primary school and had done well; she had natural initiative and courage to face new situations. But centuries of tradition,
prejudice, dogmas that we assumed every single day in judgment weighed
on all of that like a tombstone. I used my arguments to discredit everything that Herlinda patiently brought up from her memory and loyalty to
ancestral duties.

In Israel she acquired full awareness of her importance. And that, I
must confess, was not thanks to me but to the company of a group of Latin
Americans who worked in Tel Aviv. To the degree that her awareness developed, so did her demands. Less work, better salary, paid vacations,
health insurance, retirement pension.

I agreed—in principle—but in practice I tried to convert her not into
my adversary in the class struggle but into my accomplice. I authorized
her to command the others and we would both comment—as mistresses
always do—about the ineptitude of their subordinates.

Suddenly, she realized something: she had been working her entire life
and she had some savings. What better way to spend them than on a trip?
I organized a tour for her through Italy, France, and Spain with final destination Mexico, where she planned to retire and live off her income.

Mission completed, we could say. And what about me and Gabriel and
everything else? It's summer and like the locust I sing Solveig's song that
says that the land is full of roads.

Tel Aviv, August 24, 1973

Translated by Maureen Ahern
El uso de la palabra (1974)

THEATER

. . . It's not good enough to imitate the
models proposed for us that are answers to
circumstances other than our own. It isn't
even enough to discover who we are. We have
to invent ourselves.   —Rosario Castellanos
The Eternal Feminine, Act III

The Eternal Feminine

Translated by Diane E. Marting and Betty Tyree Osiek
  from *El eterno femenino*

Notes by Diane E. Marting except where noted

CHARACTERS

Whoever appears. But ten actors will be sufficient—seven women and three men—if and only if they are versatile and understand that this is a text, not of characters but of situations. This means that the protagonists should define themselves by their actions (which at times will be singular), by their words (which will be few), and, fundamentally, by their costumes and surroundings.

The solution to the problem falls upon the set designer. He or she should not try, at any time, to be realistic, but rather to capture the essence, the definitive characteristic of a person, of a style, of an epoch. Exaggeration is advisable, in the same way in which caricaturists use it, who with a few lines make the models who inspired their figures recognizable to the public.

As should be clear from the beginning, the text is a farce, which in certain moments becomes sentimental, intellectual, or grotesque. The equilibrium of those moments, the maintenance of a general tone, and, above all, the rhythm of the plot's development should be achieved by the director.

And I would appreciate the entire cast and crew not forgetting Cortázar's saying, which might well have served me as an epigraph, that laughter has always dug more tunnels than tears.[1]

ACT I

OPENING

A beauty salon in a middle-class suburb of Mexico City. The Martian appearance of the customers seated under the dryers should be emphasized. The Hairdresser is about to finish putting rollers, a hair net, and ear protectors on a customer. The Owner watches, with an eagle eye, the proper functioning of her business. Entering by the door is the Salesman, an old acquaintance in those parts, with whom the Owner exchanges the customary greetings. The Owner takes him to a spot where they can discuss and write up the order in comfort. The Salesman takes his ace in the hole from his briefcase: a new catalog.

SALESMAN. This time, Señora, it's something sensational, unheard-of, unusual: a new product.

The Hairdresser, who has led her customer to the hair drier, approaches, listening with curiosity. The Owner obviously perceives this as a lack of respect. But she does not dare to protest, neither against the Hairdresser's presence nor against her interruptions, which always seem insolent to her, because she fears losing her employees. For the moment, these are the consequences, felt to the quick, of the beginning stages in the process of development in a Third World country.

HAIRDRESSER (*surprised and pleased*). Another?

OWNER (*reproachfully*). But we haven't finished paying the installments on the last new product you brought us. It was just two months ago.

SALESMAN. Progress moves fast, Señora, and no one can stop it. As far as the previous equipment goes (if that is what is bothering you), the company will accept it as a down payment on the new one. Besides, as you already know, you are my favorite customer. The rest you can pay as you wish, when you wish.

HAIRDRESSER. And if she really doesn't want to pay?

SALESMAN. There's no problem. The deposit paid at the beginning covers us against all risks.

HAIRDRESSER. Careful, aren't you?

SALESMAN. In Latin American countries, where cripples walk tightropes, people frequently change their minds, residence, name, temperature, and even government. A house of business is obliged to take precautions.

HAIRDRESSER. Sounds like the White House.

OWNER (*to the Hairdresser, harshly*). Don't butt in!

SALESMAN (*undaunted, continuing his sales pitch*). The managers of our company have kept in mind the peculiarities of our clientele while designing their credit system in order to be protected from any contingency.

HAIRDRESSER. Who is protected?

SALESMAN. The company . . . I mean, the clientele. (*Turning to the Owner, and referring to the Hairdresser*) What a charming girl! Where did she learn to ask questions?

HAIRDRESSER. In a different place from where they taught you to answer them. That's why we never agree.

SALESMAN (*with an ingratiating smile to the Owner*). Señora, would it be any trouble to offer me a cup of coffee? I would be delighted if the young lady would prepare it with her delicate impish hands.

HAIRDRESSER. Wouldn't you like me to make some tea that takes a long time to brew? (*Without expecting an answer, she goes away.*)

SALESMAN (*to the Owner*). I wanted to speak to you privately because the product is still in an experimental stage and it's a secret. Look at your customers, with their heads stuck under the driers. How long do they stay like that?

OWNER (*in a neutral tone, in order not to commit herself*). It depends on her hair.

SALESMAN. The average, according to statistics, is one hour. One hour! Doesn't that seem monstrous? One hour in which there can be no chatting, no listening to the radio, no watching television, because, with the noise, you can't hear a single word. She can't even read since her hands are being manicured. Nothing. And then the heat. One hour! How many times a week do your customers come?

OWNER. The sloppy ones, once; the run-of-the-mill, twice. The pampered ones, daily.

SALESMAN. On the average, that makes a minimum of fifty-two hours a year. Fifty-two hours of hell!

OWNER. One must suffer to be worthy. Don't you think? No pain, no gain.

SALESMAN. It already costs them money and it already costs them time. Isn't that sufficient?

OWNER. No sweat, no sweets.

SALESMAN. Please excuse me, but that isn't the philosophy of the firm I represent. Our motto is: "Enjoy it if you can and don't pay . . . (*Mephistophelian*) if you can help it."

OWNER. Yes? That's what my dead husband used to say and, as you can see, he passed on without leaving me a cent. If it hadn't been for that . . . Do you think I went to work for fun? If there's any justice, God must have him sizzling in the teeming pits of hell.

SALESMAN. Don't worry, Señora. With our firm there aren't any problems of eternal salvation. In this deal, you won't have any debts to be paid in heaven. Everything will be paid before your trip.

HAIRDRESSER (*with a tray and several cups*). I made coffee for all three of us.

SALESMAN (*resigning himself to a witness he can't get rid of*). Thank you. One must think of the clientele, of the well-being of those who have a right to it. The hair drier will no longer be an instrument of torture!

HAIRDRESSER. Bravo! Are they going to change the hairstyles? Are they going to make them simpler, quicker, cheaper?

OWNER. Do you want to take the very bread out of our mouths? You're crazy!

SALESMAN. Good insight, Señora. It isn't a question of harming the interests of private enterprise by simplifying, by diminishing, or by creating an overabundance of the products it offers. In this particular case, the question is: while the hair is drying—the length of time will not change—how will the customer be entertained? Our experts did a survey: what does a woman do when she is reduced to total inertia for an hour?

HAIRDRESSER. Gets bored.

OWNER. Sleeps.

SALESMAN. We expected those two answers and I must confess that we were not too worried about them. But then it was discovered that boredom or sleeping were only transitory, and that there could be other consequences . . . well . . . then it was necessary to invent something to ward off the danger.

HAIRDRESSER. What danger?

SALESMAN. That women, without realizing it, might begin to think. The proverb says it: think the worst and you'll be right. Thinking, itself, is bad. It must be avoided.

OWNER. How?

SALESMAN. With this gadget that I'm going to show you. (*He unwraps a package and displays a tiny electronic device.*)

OWNER (*disappointed*). That flea?

HAIRDRESSER. What's it for?

SALESMAN. It's for hanging where the drier's electric current is generated. Apart from giving off vibrations that deaden the unpleasant sensations of the drier—the noise, the heat, the isolation, etc.—it fulfills a positive function. I should say: extremely positive. It induces dreams.

OWNER. Dreams?

SALESMAN. Marvelous dreams! During the whole time the customer is subject to the action of this device, she dreams.

HAIRDRESSER. And what does she dream?

SALESMAN. Whatever you want. Look here, operating this button gives one absolute control over the . . . topics. There's a complete catalog of possibilities: she dreams that she is the prettiest woman in the world; that all men are falling in love with her; that all women envy her; that her husband gets a raise in salary; that there's no price increase in the basic cost of living; that she finds an efficient and inexpensive maid; that she gets pregnant this month; that she doesn't get pregnant this month; that her children get an A average in school; that her daughters need bras; that her mother-in-law dies; that she becomes a widow and collects on a huge life insurance policy . . . In short, there are dreams for all situations and all tastes.

HAIRDRESSER. But those are the most ordinary dreams!

SALESMAN. Well . . . if you have a special clientele, we'll provide you with special devices. Naturally, they're more expensive.

OWNER. That's what I thought. They must cost an arm and a leg.

SALESMAN. No, no. If it's the cheap model, like the one you need, there's no problem. And keep in mind how much you can raise the value of your work. You know as well as I do that you're not the one who pays: it's the customer. At the same time, you're doing a good deed. People are capable of giving you everything as long as they are kept from thinking. Yes, thinking: the great risk of leisure. Do you realize the danger we risk if . . . ?

OWNER (*horrified*). Don't even think about it.

HAIRDRESSER (*looking contemplatively at the device*). The solution to the problem is here.

SALESMAN. Exactly. There's no longer any need to worry.

HAIRDRESSER. It's like some kind of drug, like LSD.

OWNER. How dare you make those comparisons? Drugs are a filthy habit for degenerates. This is a respectable device.

SALESMAN. Shall we write the order?

OWNER. No. Leave it for me to look over. I don't want to jump into anything.

SALESMAN. Try it! You won't be sorry.

HAIRDRESSER. Why don't we try it first on Lupita? It would be like a gift. (*To the Salesman*) It's a very special occasion: she's coming today to have her hair done for her wedding.

SALESMAN. We have exactly what's needed in this case. Where do you want me to put it?

HAIRDRESSER (*leading him to a hair drier*). Here.

OWNER. Watch how it's done. Maybe you'll learn something.

SALESMAN. It's quite easy. (*He works at putting it on, observed very closely by the Hairdresser.*) Ready. Shall I leave it set to a particular dream?

HAIRDRESSER. Yes. Where it says: What does the future hold for me?

OWNER (*still apprehensive*). Won't that be very risky?

SALESMAN. Please, Señora. Don't insult me. Who do you think planned that dream? An ordinary person? No way. A genius? Not at all. Ordinary people are very limited; geniuses are crazy. We turned to something better than the two of them put together: a machine, a computer, an electronic brain, something that never makes a mistake. The dream will be pleasant.

And now (*transfigured by his gestures into a Master of Ceremonies of Salón México*),[2] Ladies and Gentlemen, we have the pleasure of dedicating our play *What Does the Future Hold for Me?* especially to our dear friend, Lupita, and to her companions. Take it away, Lupita . . .

Dance Music

*   *   *

THE HONEYMOON

Lupita is sitting on a sofa, with a bridal veil covering her face and dressed in the most conventional and pompous bridal gown imaginable—after all, it is only once in a lifetime. On the train of the dress there is a bloodstain, which would not be clearly visible if she had not carefully arranged the folds so that the spot would be in full view. While she is occupied with this task with a virtuous precision, Juan, her husband, walks up and down like a caged animal. Other than the flesh-colored bathing trunks—which should produce, as much as possible, an impression of nakedness—he is wearing only a top hat, celluloid collar, cravat, starched cuffs fastened with flashy cuff links, high socks, and patent leather shoes. He gestures as if he were counting on his fingers and finally decides to consult a kind of enormous lawbook lying open on a lectern. With a goose-quill pen he places checkmarks beside the things that have been accomplished.

JUAN. Let's see: Paragraph IV, section C, on Conjugal Duties. Carried out. Section F. Mission accomplished. Section H . . . The letter "h" is silent in Spanish, which means . . . I'm not very sure . . . but neither am I very unsure. In case of doubt, dot-dot-dot. Now that's done. Section N . . . (*triumphantly*) Ah, ha, ha!

He leaves the book and charges with the impetus of a bull to the place where Lupita is sitting; she has taken advantage of her husband's distraction, has raised her veil, and is licking her lips with obvious signs of pleasure. Juan scrutinizes her disapprovingly, takes her by the shoulders, shakes her violently, and orders:

JUAN. Look me in the eye!

Lupita obeys without blinking and Juan backs away horrified.

JUAN. Shameless hussy! How dare you to look at me like that! Lower your veil, *ipso facto*, brazen woman! Now then. Look me in the eye and tell me: Has this been the first time?

LUPITA (*in one of the obvious asides of the ancient theater*). What a mania men have for asking the same question! (*To Juan, with an innocent voice*) I don't know what you're talking about.

JUAN (*taken by surprise; evidently this was not the answer he expected; he improvises*). I asked if it was the first time you were married.

LUPITA. Oh, well, certainly. Naturally.

JUAN (*solemn, with his hand on his heart*). And have you remained pure until marriage?

LUPITA (*pointing proudly to the bloodstain*). Don't you see?

JUAN. I see, but I'm not much of an expert. It looks like catsup.

LUPITA. Catsup? It's plasma. Of the best quality. I bought a quarter of a liter at the Blood Bank.

JUAN. Very good answer. (*He goes to the book and makes a check while Lupita continues talking.*)

LUPITA. I would have liked to buy something pretty with that money: a dress, some stockings . . . but my friends advised me against it; first things first, they said, and . . . well, it was necessary.

JUAN. Your friends were right. (*He leaves the book and returns to Lupita's side.*) And now the sixty-four thousand dollar question: Did you like it?

LUPITA (*indignant*). Like it? Me? A decent girl? Who do you take me for?

JUAN (*hopefully*). You didn't like it?

LUPITA (*firmly*). It seemed repugnant, disgusting.

JUAN (*beside himself*). Thanks, Lupita. I knew you weren't going to fail me in the moment of truth. Thank you, thank you.

LUPITA. I'll never let you come near me again.

JUAN. Not even if I force you?

LUPITA. Would you be capable of that?

JUAN. Naturally. What would stop me? I have the strength and I have the right. Besides, you vowed to obey me before the altar.

LUPITA. I made the vow out of ignorance, in my innocence. And now you're taking advantage of my situation. Cad!

JUAN. You're going to see what's in store for you! Do you think you've already drained the cup of pain to the dregs? Ha, ha, ha! Allow me to smile. What happened today was only a small sample.

LUPITA. But it was terribly painful. You hurt me. Look! (*She points dramatically to the stain.*)

JUAN (*petulantly*). Well, that's nothing. And the moment will come when you won't complain that it's too difficult but rather too often.

LUPITA (*on her knees*). Have pity!

JUAN (*like an executioner*). I won't have pity on you even if you beg me

on your knees. (*Lupita crawls snakelike on the floor and makes all the useless gestures that signal the approach of an inevitable catastrophe.*) Do you think that a Mexican Macho is going to allow himself to be moved by some crocodile tears? No, I'll just keep right on until . . .
Darkness.

THE ANNUNCIATION

Lupita is dressed in some very tight-fitting toreador pants. She is very pretty and jubilantly happy. With a dust cloth she is swirling "verónicas" and other figures of the bullfight while an invisible multitude shouts "¡Olé!"[3] *Lupita makes a bow to the public and begins to imitate an announcer's voice at the microphone, alternately playing the roles of the bull and of the bullfighter.*

VOICE. It's the *alternativa*, the night of becoming a full-fledged bullfighter, and, after an unforgettable performance, the *matador* struck the death blow. With only one thrust, he conquered the bull, which had so nobly played the game. The multitude fluttered their white handkerchiefs, claiming for the *matador* both ears and tail, which were conceded to him after he had made various turns around the bullring.

The voice fades. Lupita bows to the applauding audience; she pretends to toss the trophies to the crowd, and then returns to where she was: her home.

LUPITA. That noble bull, which showed true greatness and skill against the cape, with wide-spread horns, is I, your humble servant, Lupita. It isn't that I like to show off, but when I compare myself with others . . . with Mariquita of number seven, for example, who returned alive to the corral. Or, for example, Carmen, who after several inept jabs to the bone, had to be finished off by the young men of her quadrille.[4] I'm certain that what they did didn't last. Good blood, good breeding. They were bred for punishment. What was needed was my Juan's bullfighting spirit.

The background music changes from the "paso doble" (appropriate for a bullfight) to the "bolero" (romantic). The lights fade.

LUPITA. It's true that the atmosphere helps: moonlit nights, shellfish, the cliff divers at Acapulco. (*The music ends. Bright lights.*) Although the huge hotel bill can't help but make one nervous. And from nerves to being frightened, there's only one step . . . which, thank God, my Juan did not take. But he had to hear, why deny it, the reminder given by the bullfight's judge, and, sometimes, he has had to suspend the programmed fight because of the bad weather.[5] But here, in his own home, his laurels have become green again. Twirls, *verónicas*, passes on his knees, movements like the famous Manolo . . .

wife's fruitless struggle to keep it "presentable." The housewife, Lupita, has just lost another round in the unevenly matched battle and is recuperating while seated in the most comfortable easy chair. Her appearance matches that of the furniture. Rollers in her hair, her face covered with rejuvenating cream, a robe that has seen better days. To give herself the illusion that she is resting, she begins to read a woman's magazine and to eat chocolates which are not going to contribute to improving her appearance. In the next room is heard the noise of two children—a boy and a little female, as they say—who are fighting. Tousled and dirty, they appear alternately and fleetingly.

LUPITA II. Mama! Juanito pinched me!

LUPITA (*without pausing in her reading or interrupting the satisfaction of her gluttony*). You scratch him, so that you'll be even.

(*Immediately a scream is heard and Juanito appears.*)

JUANITO. Mama! Lupita scratched me!

LUPITA. Pinch her. Can't you think of anything at all? (*Juanito leaves and obeys the order. The corresponding scream ensues.*) If they didn't take after someone I know, I wouldn't have believed that my kids were a pair of blockheads. You have to tell them everything. To eat, not to hang out the window because they are going to fall, to take a bath, to . . . As if I didn't have more important things to do than to look after them. (*Reading aloud from the magazine*) "The education of your children is a very delicate matter which cannot be left in the hands of just anyone." (*Without a transition Lupita continues her monologue, interrupted here and there by the chocolates.*) God deliver me from the nursemaid who raises them badly or from the kindergarten that returns them to you cold-hearted. The one who must sacrifice herself is the mother. The mother who accepts complete responsibility. For the children. And also for the house. Thank God, mine is a little gem. (*As though illuminated by a lightning flash, ghosts of her women friends appear who sniff the air and who pass their fingers over the surfaces and find everything filthy. They make gestures of disgust and disappear.*) Not a speck of dust. And, as for myself, I have never been careless with my appearance. What better way to keep a husband than a woman who is always smartly dressed, always slender, nice looking? That's why my poor Juan is more in love with me every day. Every week, as infallible as the Pope, he gives me a bouquet of flowers. When it's not a bouquet of flowers, it's a piece of jewelry. They say that gifts derive their value from the virtues of the giver. (*The door-bell rings. It is a messenger who deposits a tiny package in the hand of the housewife. Lupita signs the re-*

ceipt and does not give a tip. She closes the door in the messenger's face and looks for the card. She reads.) "For my Little Kitten from her Big Kitty Cat." How funny! Juan never before called me his little kitten. Oh, men are so capricious! (*She unwraps the package and takes out a bikini, unbelievable because of its size. She contemplates it in a stupefied way.*) Well, there's been a mistake here, because as for fitting me (*holding up the bikini against her clothes*), not even in my dreams. I'll speak to Juan's secretary who's in charge of sending me gifts. (*Lupita goes to the telephone, dials a number.*) Hello? Yes, Señorita. Señora Pérez here. Yes, to speak to you about a package I just received. No, no, no, no. No, no, no, no. The bikini seems to be a very good idea. But the size . . . It's too large for me. Enormous. Could you arrange for an exchange in the store? I know that with clothing it's very difficult, but when it's a matter of such an obvious error . . . What's the matter with you? Where did you get the idea that you, too, could call me Little Kitten? I am Señora Pérez to you. The legitimate wife, understand? Would you do me the favor of explaining what you said to me? Hello? Hello? (*She hangs up, furious.*) I was cut off.

Darkness. On the curtain at the back of the stage a silent film is projected illustrating the ballad[6] *that is going to be sung next.*

In the year of seventy-three
I remember very well,
in a building called Aristos
when the disaster us befell.

Kukita, the secretary,
was writing with good will;
when Juan's little wifey
appeared on the window sill.

With the cry, "Death to all
who wear size thirty-two!"
into the chest of Kukita
the pistol bullets flew.

The policeman quickly came
and tried to take away her arms.
No way, she said, first I must kill
that Juan in all his charms.

For a traitor and a playboy,
now his life is done,

he played cards with two decks,
and with neither of them won.

The little swallow flies along,
the lift goes up and down,
the story spreads to every ear,
about the basest rake in town,

who quickly found his fate;
with his life he had to pay
for all the shameful actions
of those who helped him stray.

Let this be a warning,
for our story now is done,
he is a threat to many
who already has killed one.

Darkness. When the lights go up on the scene, a newsboy appears.

NEWSBOY. Extra! Extra! "I killed him for love, declares the self-made widow . . ." Extra! Extra! (*The pedestrians buy the newspaper; they eagerly read the headlines and comment excitedly among themselves.*)

"The fatal triangle . . ." "Secretary or mistress?" "My children will cry for their dead father, but they will not curse an unfaithful husband."

Darkness. A light centers on a television screen. The face of the announcer fills it completely.

ANNOUNCER. Ladies and Gentlemen: tonight we suspend our weather report to allow the presentation of a news item, hot off the wire. As your reporter, I am always anxious to serve you, at whatever cost. I have obtained an exclusive interview, and, until now, the only interview, with the sensational Lupita, the self-made widow who climbed in the window, the one who killed for love, the one who faced the horns of her dilemma: secretary or mistress? But, why continue? Who doesn't know the story? Ladies and Gentlemen . . . here with you . . . the one and only Lupita . . . !

The camera focuses on a glamorous, sophisticated, and triumphant Lupita.

ANNOUNCER. Lupita, we don't need to ask you how you are because your looks tell all. You look great! Really great!

LUPITA (*arranging her skirt provocatively*). I don't understand your allusions, sir, so therefore you can continue making them. As far as I am concerned . . .

ANNOUNCER. Tell us, Lupita, in terms of news, do you have any plans for the future?

LUPITA. Well, as soon as the court case is finished, with my innocence established by the judge, I have to fulfill a promise: to enter the Basilica of Our Lady of Tepeyac on my knees for the protection that she has given me and because she saved me from the great danger I faced.

ANNOUNCER (*to the public*). That proves, once again, that Lupita embodies the archetype of the Mexican woman: long-suffering, self-sacrificing, devout. (*To Lupita*) And afterward?

LUPITA (*unenthusiastically*). I have to decide among several offers. Film producers want me to play the leading role in my own drama.

ANNOUNCER. That's practically launching you into stardom.

LUPITA. But the scripts are . . . how should I say it? Until now none of them has appeared convincing.

ANNOUNCER. What's your version of what happened?

LUPITA (*properly nostalgic*). My husband, Juan, and I were so happy . . . We used to have lunch at Mom's house on Sundays. We would go to the movies once a week and to Acapulco for the Christmas vacations. He had paid the down payment on our little house in the subdivision . . .

ANNOUNCER. Please don't say the name; we don't provide free advertising.

LUPITA. Well, in a subdivision that is very popular and that gives such easy terms . . .

ANNOUNCER (*reproachfully*). Lupita . . .

LUPITA. And suddenly . . . (*expectant pause*) suddenly the owner of the subdivision declared bankruptcy.

ANNOUNCER. And why didn't you kill him?

LUPITA. Why should I kill him? That was men's business. Besides, I wasn't in love with him.

ANNOUNCER. Nor were you in love with the secretary.

LUPITA (*confidentially*). Do you want me to tell you the truth, the complete truth? I killed her because she was so ugly.

ANNOUNCER (*remembering*). Well, in reality, she was not so bad looking.

LUPITA. No? (*She takes some photos out of her purse and shows them to the announcer.*) Don't tell me that she could compete with me!

ANNOUNCER (*examining the photos carefully and yielding to the evidence*). Well, in reality she does not look so very seductive, so to speak. But it must be kept in mind that these photos were taken in the morgue, after the autopsy.

LUPITA. And that seems to you a sufficient excuse? Tell me how you die and I'll tell you who you are. She never had the least idea of how to fix herself up. The results are quite obvious.

ANNOUNCER. And, nevertheless, this woman—whom you so rightfully scorn—took your husband away from you. How do you explain such an aberration?

LUPITA. It's useless for me to be conceited about being pretty, because we all know very well that beauty is somewhat fleeting and that it lacks importance. When a woman is horrible, she's always called virtuous.

ANNOUNCER. Then she was a virtuous woman.

LUPITA. Virtuous? An adulteress? Are you mad? Why don't they cancel this immoral program? Doesn't censorship exist for things that compromise public morals?

ANNOUNCER. We understand that your nerves are a little on edge, but the question still stands. What can explain your husband's conduct?

LUPITA. It's obvious. His secretary was lacking in virtues, both physical and moral. Well, then, she gave him a love potion.

ANNOUNCER. Which one?

LUPITA. I could give you the recipe, but not without first warning you that the patent has already been applied for.

ANNOUNCER. Dear audience, Lupita is going to reveal to us one of her secrets; go ahead, Lupita.

LUPITA. You start to boil old typewriter ribbons and mix them with three-fourths of a family-size bottle of . . .

ANNOUNCER. Please, without mentioning names.

LUPITA. But it's an indispensable ingredient.

ANNOUNCER. Let's leave it to the imagination of our listeners.

LUPITA. Can we say, at least, that the drink has cola in it?

ANNOUNCER. Darn! She finally got her way.

LUPITA. You add five drops of it each day to his eleven o'clock coffee and that's that. There's no boss who can resist it. Juan wasn't able to be the exception. In reality, the poor guy was no good for confirming anything.

ANNOUNCER. Do you have any witnesses?

LUPITA. That he wasn't even good for confirming the rule?

ANNOUNCER. No, that he drank the love potion.

LUPITA. Oh, that, too: all the office employees. And the doorman of the building, who's an authority on black magic. And it's not that I have racial prejudices, but I struggled with all my strength against that sorcery: I had attacks of hysteria, I brought my mother to live with us so that she could serve as witness and judge of what was happening, I paid a private detective to watch my husband's wrongdoing. I warned him three times as required. And do you believe it? All that for nothing. I had nothing left but to do what I did. What would you have done in my place? (*The question is directed to the invisible audience. Darkness.*)

TWILIGHT

The light goes up in Lupita's living room, now modernized. That means that the furniture, after so many years, no longer appears old; it has become antique. There are two focal points in this room: the parrot cage and the television screen on which Lupita's questioning face is seen. Lupita herself gets up from a chair: she is in house slippers, gray-headed, fat, and slovenly, but now much older and with the indelible mark of her life as a housewife. She turns off the set reluctantly and turns on the light. While the image disappears one continues to hear the question, "What would you have done in my place?"

LUPITA. What I would have done in her place . . . What I do always: make a soufflé.

LUPITA II. Oh, Mama, how old-fashioned you are! Nowadays everyone does yoga.

PARROT. Oh, my child, how old-fashioned you are! Nowadays everyone does judo.

LUPITA. In any case, there isn't the slightest need to kill one's husband. I mean, to shoot him. It's so easy to do it with a small kitchen knife.

LUPITA II. Quite easy. But who would write about you in the newspaper, interview you on TV, and give you a film contract?

LUPITA. Virtue, my child, does not praise itself.

PARROT. It only gives benefit dinners.

LUPITA. Besides, what a way she had of showing herself off with such a tiny miniskirt. Who's going to believe that she's a decent woman?

LUPITA II. Isn't it extremely boring?

The two of them prepare the table for their afternoon snack.

LUPITA. Decency extremely boring? I never thought of that. Yes, I believe it is; but it has its compensations.

LUPITA II. In heaven, I suppose.

LUPITA. And here, also, don't you think?

LUPITA II. Like what?

LUPITA. They call you "Señora" and no one ever looks at you pityingly, mockingly, or distrustfully, as they do at old maids.

LUPITA II. Who sees you? You are always shut inside.

LUPITA. Well, the groceryman, the man from the dry cleaners, the milkman and the mailman . . .

LUPITA II. What a distinguished audience.

LUPITA (*making a visible effort to raise the category*). The lawyer, the family doctor, the visible people, I guess.

PARROT. They are visible. Thus, they see.

LUPITA II. And how do they see you?

LUPITA. As if you were a saint.

PARROT (*singing*). "Let them gossip . . . it doesn't bother me that they gossip . . ."

LUPITA II. But a glance, a word, from those whom you don't even really know . . . That's really paying very dearly.

LUPITA (*meaningfully*). There are other, more intimate things, which are priceless.

LUPITA II (*with morbid curiosity*). Yes? What are they?

PARROT. Three days of Holy Week spent in Veracruz, now and then a lousy movie theater, and, if there's a real celebration, a bunch of charcoal-broiled tacos.

LUPITA (*to the Parrot*). What did you say, vulgar boy? Charcoal-broiled tacos? That's what you would like. An afternoon snack at Sanborn's.[7]

LUPITA II (*with a decided air*). Mama, definitely, I'll never get married.

LUPITA (*insisting*). An afternoon snack in Sanborn's. With the children and Mama and the cousin from Aguascalientes.

LUPITA II. I'll never get married.

LUPITA. And does it seem such a little thing to go for a day in the country? And to row on the lake in Chapultepec Park[8] on Sundays?

LUPITA II. That's what I have done since I was born. I want things to change; oh, that something, anything, might change.

LUPITA (*dogmatically*). Always, when anything changes, it's for the worse.

LUPITA II. How do you know that?

LUPITA. Haven't I bickered with maids all my life? They got worse and worse until there weren't any more. Now we have to do the work ourselves.

PARROT. "An important company advertises for a presentable young girl, good salary, future possibilities."

LUPITA. Perhaps you'll marry the supervisor. Or the supervisor's son. If the super is an old sot.

LUPITA II. Supervisor, son, sot. So many *s*'s! Perhaps I'll go sightseeing around the world on one of those tours where you "travel now and pay later."

LUPITA. Sightseeing begins with an *s*.

LUPITA II. Nothing is perfect, but something is something.

LUPITA. Nothing. What is there in the world but people who don't know you, who don't know if you are wearing a new dress for the first time, or if you're long-suffering or frivolous . . . ?

PARROT. And they say that the world is a handkerchief. What would they say of the universe, which is infinite?

LUPITA II. And if I were to go to college?

LUPITA. Are you mad? That den of Communists?

LUPITA II. What is so bad about being a Communist?

LUPITA. Communists go to Hell!

LUPITA II. And if there is no Hell?

LUPITA. Do you dare to doubt it after all that happens in this life?

PARROT. Between Hell and a housewife's life, the difference is only a matter of degree. But the degree can be above zero. It all depends. The optimist sees the glass half-full, the pessimist sees it half-empty.

LUPITA. Nevertheless, I'm not going to let you go.

LUPITA II. To Hell? But, I'm already there!

LUPITA. To the university. Over my dead body!

PARROT. Don't give her any ideas.

LUPITA II. Can one know the reason why?

LUPITA. Because you aren't going to be different from what I was. As I'm not different from my mother. Nor my mother different from my grandmother.

PARROT. This Lupita is a fanatic for stability. Persons, times, fashions. If she were in charge, there wouldn't have been any history. "O Zeno, cruel Zeno, Zeno of Elea."[9]

LUPITA. And if you don't obey me willingly, I'll tell your brother to watch you so that you don't go out.

LUPITA II. And if I go out anyway?

LUPITA. I'll ask your father to intervene. And they will both support me so that you behave as you should.

LUPITA II. I am a person . . .

LUPITA. Not any more or any better than I was.

LUPITA II. I have a right to . . .

LUPITA. Nor more intelligent.

LUPITA II. I want to live my own life.

LUPITA. Nor freer.

LUPITA II. I want to be happy!

LUPITA. Nor happier.

PARROT (*sighing*). Nothing quite compares to maternal love!
Darkness.

APOTHEOSIS

*The lights come on once more in the same living room; several years have
passed, with the changes that this implies and the deterioration showing.
Seated in a rocking chair and listening peacefully to the radio, while she
caresses the cat sleeping on her lap, we see Lupita converted, finally, into a
typical white-haired old lady. She only needs to speak in order to be Sara
García.*[10] *The clock on the wall chimes a few times and Lupita jumps up.
She throws the cat to the floor, turns off the radio, and exclaims:*

LUPITA. Heavens! It's time for my tonic.[11]

*She takes off the white wig and the robe behind a folding screen and re-
appears in the costume of a "China Poblana."*[12] *She takes out a Mexican
cowboy's wide-brimmed hat and starts to dance the "jarabe tapatío" of
Guadalajara. While she dances, she sings.*

LUPITA. I'm dancing on your grave, Juanito. You can't escape in order
to make my life difficult. (*Mimicking the action of what she is saying*) "Has
the consommé boiled enough? It needs salt! Seasoning! Seasoning! Oh,
when will your cooking compare with that of my sainted mother, may she
rest with God in His Glory." But now, Juanito, now you're near her,
hanging onto her apron strings, as always, although I don't think that you
could be with Him in His Glory, instead you must be in the teeming pits
of Hell, which is what you deserve. And as for me, ha, ha, ha! A free
woman. With your life insurance and your pension, I am living regally.
Take a little turn now and then through the house. You aren't going to
recognize it. I arranged it as it pleased me, and only me. As if you had
never existed or had any opinions. And the bed is mine, completely mine,
and at night I turn and roll over from left to right and from right to left and
I don't bump into . . . what I bumped into when you were here. And I
sleep completely relaxed; without worrying whether the lord and master
will or won't come home; or if you crashed at some corner because of
driving while drunk. And no one leaves me already dressed to go to the
movies and upset because there was a business meeting. And no one forgets my birthday, or my wedding anniversary, or makes excuses for not
attending the graduation party of my children. And, concerning the children, I fulfilled my duty of seeing them placed in life. The girl turned out
to be somewhat wild, but she couldn't get away with it around me, and

now Juanito and Lupita are both well established; each is respectably situated. Oh, finally, I got them out of my hair! They come to see me now and then so that I can take care of the grandchildren. I take care of them, naturally; I pet them and spoil them so that when they return to their parents they're unbearable. That way we're even.

Lupita continues dancing, giving cheers and carousing, until someone knocks on the door. With a swiftness inappropriate to her age she goes behind the folding screen and again disguises herself as a white-haired old lady. She sits down in an easy chair and holds the cat again, which goes to sleep immediately. When the scene is set, she answers with a quavering voice.

LUPITA. Come in.

The door opens and a horde of camera men, mariachi band players, masters of ceremony, etc. enter. They play the birthday song, "Las Mañanitas."

Chorus. Oh hear the birthday song
which great King David sang,
now for the sweet old ladies
it is sung here by the gang.

MASTER OF CEREMONIES (*microphone ready*). Ladies and Gentlemen, dear audience: on this day consecrated to the celebration of the most sublime love, of the most unselfish mission, on this Mother's Day we have the privilege of entering into the bosom of a home in which the Mexican people's dearest essence is preserved. A home in which our idiosyncrasies are quite visible. A home which is, at the same time, emblem and mirror of all Mexican homes. The home of Señora. . . . (*To Lupita*) Señora, would you like to introduce yourself to our refined audience?

LUPITA (*demurely*). With great pleasure. I am Guadalupe S., widow of Sr. Pérez, at your service and in the service of God.[13]

MASTER OF CEREMONIES. A very good answer. Perfectly answered! Lupita, for having so aptly answered our first question, you have won a prize granted to you by the Paris Perfumery, whose products smell . . . and smell good, to our audience.

LUPITA. I thank you very much . . . (*She chokes.*)

MASTER OF CEREMONIES. . . . the Paris Perfumery, whose products smell . . . and smell good . . .

LUPITA. . . . and smell good.

MASTER OF CEREMONIES. Hurrah! What a memory! She has all her faculties, unchanged. It's astonishing at her age.

LUPITA. . . . for this undeserved gift.

MASTER OF CEREMONIES. Undeserved? The one who loved us before knowing us deserves everything. Because of that, "Canex, the company that *can* because it has a complete selection of cans," gives you these cans of soup, of sauce, of marmalade . . . Señora, know that you, too, *can*; open a can. Canex provides you with everything that your kitchen needs. Can, no. Canex, yes.

LUPITA (*who is beginning to be surrounded by the objects accumulating around her, confused by what is happening*). How pretty! But, really, I don't know . . . It's too much. Since I am alone . . .

MASTER OF CEREMONIES. Alone? Solitude does not exist for someone who, like you, has paid her debt to nature and to society by becoming a mother. Solitude doesn't exist for those who have sacrificed themselves for others. Your children, Señora, are with you in spirit.

LUPITA. Were my children the ones who sent you here?

MASTER OF CEREMONIES. No, Señora. This event has been organized by the BGT chain of stores. B: buy. G: good. T: things. You turned out to be the winner of the BGT contest. Buy good things.

LUPITA. I won the contest for the best Mexican mother?

MASTER OF CEREMONIES. No, Lupita. That would have been impossible. All, absolutely all, and every single one of Mexico's mothers are the best.

LUPITA. But whom are they better than?

MASTER OF CEREMONIES. Better than those who aren't mothers, or who, while mothers, are not Mexicans. It's very simple.

LUPITA. I won the contest for the most popular mother, then.

MASTER OF CEREMONIES. The most popular mother, Señora, is the one immortalized in the golden verses of the bard, Guillermo Aguirre y Fierro, whose "Bohemian's Toast" is going to be recited by the magician of the microphone, Pedrito Mora. Pedrito . . . to the microphone, and give it all you've got!

PEDRITO. Thank you very much, Ladies and Gentlemen, esteemed audience, Lupita, I have the honor of reciting for you all . . . for you . . . the moving verses . . .

LUPITA (*deeply moved*). How beautifully he speaks! It seems like music!

PEDRITO. Around a table in the tavern, . . . et cetera.

While Pedrito shouts himself hoarse, Lupita wants to dispel her doubts.

LUPITA (*to the Master of Ceremonies*). Then, who chose me?

MASTER OF CEREMONIES. You weren't selected, it was a raffle. You had it bestowed upon because you were holding the number . . .

PEDRITO. . . . I drink a toast to woman, but not because of that . . .

LUPITA (*disillusioned*). A raffle?

MASTER OF CEREMONIES. Yes, luck, grandmother, luck!

While Pedrito screams himself hoarse and the Master of Ceremonies explains and Lupita resists, they unload upon her blenders, washing machines, stoves, pastries, forming a pyramid that buries her. On top of the peak is a cake with one candle. Lupita, feeling that she is suffocating, cries out from the bottom of the abyss.

LUPITA. Help me! Help! Get me out of here! I'm suffocating! I'm suffocating . . . Help me . . . Help . . .

Darkness. When the lights come up again, we are once more in the beauty salon. The Owner and the Hairdresser run to disconnect Lupita's drier and help her to get out from under it. Stumbling, held up by her saviors, she exclaims.

LUPITA. What a horrible nightmare! I never would have believed it . . . Horrible . . . nightmare . . . horrible . . .

CURTAIN

ACT II

The action continues without a break from the previous act. It is the same beauty salon, the same customers, the Owner and the Hairdresser. All try to calm Lupita, who is drinking a spiked cup of tea because of her fright. Taking advantage of the women's commotion, the Owner speaks to the Hairdresser.

OWNER. Go on, hurry it up. Take that junk off the drier that good-for-nothing salesman tried to con us with.

The Hairdresser pretends to obey, but, after assuring herself that the Owner is distracted, she doesn't remove the device but rather changes the setting to produce other dreams.

LUPITA (*who has gone from agitation to fatalism*). This had to happen to me today of all days.

OWNER (*benevolently*). It's natural. You have the "opening-night jitters," as actors say.

LUPITA (*putting down her cup of tea*). No jokes, okay? Or when I return from my honeymoon, I won't tell you anything.

CUSTOMER I. There's nothing new under the sun, dear. And much less under the Acapulco sun.

CUSTOMER II. You've been around, haven't you?

CUSTOMER I (*as one who throws down a winning ace*). Divorced three times.

LUPITA (*at the height of astonishment*). Married three times!

CUSTOMER II. The classic case of the optimist and the pessimist. The optimist sees the glass half-full and the pessimist sees it half-empty.

LUPITA. Three times! I'm getting married for the first time today and I can't even get my hairdo finished. (*The Hairdresser leads her again to the drier and helps her to get comfortable.*) This time I'm certainly not going to go to sleep. I've had enough bad dreams.

After this emphatic promise, Lupita is seen struggling against the sleepiness that invades her. Little by little she lets herself be conquered by a force superior to her own, surrendering to a state that must be pleasant if one judges by the expression on her face and the relaxation of her body. The lights and images of the beauty salon disappear slowly and, suddenly, we see Lupita at a fair with its games, its hawkers, and its freak shows. Lupita strolls along, eating a popsicle. She stops before a brightly colored tent and gaudy advertisements drawn by an ingenuous painter. At the entrance the Hawker announces his wares.

HAWKER. Ladies and Gentlemen, distinguished audience, come on in, come on in to see the most extraordinary phenomenon in the world: the woman who was turned into a serpent because she disobeyed! Señora, show this example to your daughter to teach her to be docile. Young woman, come in and look at yourself in this full-length mirror. Distinguished public, this is a show for the whole family, a performance recommended by both the ecclesiastic and the civil authorities. A spectacle combining entertainment with the teaching of sacred moral principles. Enjoy yourself and be patriotic, helping to preserve the sacrosanct traditions that form our idiosyncrasies. For a peso, mark it well, for only a peso, you get all this: healthy enjoyment and protection from exotic ideas! How many tickets? How many? Who said, "Me"?

People, who flee on principle from anything didactic, begin to disperse and Lupita alone remains; she buys her ticket and enters the inside of the tent. In it there is a representation of what is commonly understood to be Paradise: a pleasant garden, with babbling brooks, an apple tree, and a woman covered with a scaly leotard who naps until a light awakens her. Momentarily blinded, she lifts her head and scrutinizes what should be her audience. When she discovers that there is no one but Lupita, she gives a huge yawn.

EVE. One can't say that this is a success.

LUPITA (*embarrassed*). If you don't think it's worth the trouble of bothering yourself for me and want to cancel the show . . .

EVE. Oh, no. I have too much professional conscience to do that. Why do you think we don't have an audience?

LUPITA. There's a lot of competition.

EVE. That must be it. Because my story hasn't stopped being interesting. On the contrary. With all this about Women's Lib, I'm like chewing gum: in everyone's mouth. Some praise me, others damn me, but no one forgets me. As far as I'm concerned, I've never been in better shape than today. It's the opportune moment for . . . but my manager is irresponsible: he signs contracts with the first passerby and then completely neglects the publicity. Under such circumstances, it's a miracle that you're here. A real miracle. (*There is a pause, which Lupita does not know how to end.*) For centuries I have dreamed of someone to tell the true story of the loss of Paradise to, not that version for the mentally retarded that has usurped the truth. Perhaps you . . . Are you curious?

LUPITA. If I weren't, I wouldn't be here.

EVE. Humm. That answer reeks of a famous phrase. But anyhow, one can't expect very much. Let's begin.

Eve takes off her scale-covered leotard and she has beneath it another, which is flesh colored. She sits down, with an air of total boredom, beneath the apple tree. Adam, also in a leotard suggesting his nakedness, appears. With the air of a country schoolteacher, he warns Eve.

ADAM. . . . and don't you forget it: your name is Eve. Repeat that. Eve.

EVE. Why?

ADAM (*confused and, naturally, angry*). What do you mean, why? A decent woman doesn't ask those questions. She obeys and that ends it.

EVE. I don't see the reason for it.

ADAM (*who does not see it either but trying to conceal it*). You love to oppose everything, to make yourself interesting. Why don't you follow everyone else's example? Look. (*Acting out what he says*) You are called a tree. T-r-e-e. And, you, an ant. A-n-t. Without a *u*, because with one it's your father's sister.

EVE. I don't hear anyone answering at all.

ADAM. That's precisely what I want you to learn. Not to talk back.

EVE. How do you expect a tree or an ant to reply if they're mute? That's not even funny! Why don't you talk with a parrot? Because he can answer you back, right?

ADAM (*with his feelings hurt, but generous*). How mistaken you are, dear, how mistaken! I don't talk to things or to animals. That would be to lower myself. I don't even talk to you.

EVE. That would be to raise yourself.

ADAM. Don't be insolent.

EVE. It's not a matter of being insolent, but logical. Then who are you talking to?

ADAM. I'm not talking *to* anyone. I'm speaking *for*. I speak with Posterity.

EVE. You mean that you're speaking for our great-grandchildren.

ADAM. Please, woman, don't be prosaic. I place the problem on a spiritual plane and you reduce it to its most vulgar biological elements.

EVE. Without those elements, without my collaboration, I mean, who would be your audience?

ADAM. Eternity, God.

EVE. Jehovah?

ADAM. He can create beings from nothingness. He formed me from clay and you . . .

EVE. Yes, I already know, don't repeat it to me. He made me from one of your ribs.

ADAM. Don't you see? You're not indispensable. And it's good that you remember it, once and for all. Your condition is absolutely contingent.

EVE. The same as yours.

ADAM. Oh, no! I'm essential. Without me, God couldn't be known, worshipped, or obeyed.

EVE. Don't deny to me that this God you speak of (and whom I've never seen) is vain; he needs a mirror. Are you sure he isn't a Goddess?

ADAM. Don't be irreverent! God—because he is made in my image and likeness—wished to crown creation with a consciousness. *My* consciousness.

EVE. It sounds very pretty . . . but, what did He ask you for in exchange?

ADAM. To catalog whatever exists, to put it in order, to take care of it, and to make all His creatures subject to His law. Beginning with you. Therefore, repeat what I've taught you. What's your name?

EVE. What did you call me?

ADAM. Eve.

EVE. All right. That's the pseudonym under which I'll go down in history. But my true name, the one *I* call myself, that I won't tell anyone. And much less to you.

ADAM. Obstinate! I'm not going to continue wasting my time with you. (*Looking over his agenda*) Today, I must devote myself to the Lepidopteras.

He goes away, with his clipboard in his hand, pointing with his pencil, and writing down names. Eve stays in her place. She yawns, stretches, is about to die of boredom.

SERPENT (*who has been hiding behind the tree and who shows himself now as an asexual figure with reminiscences of a reptile; he sings*).

Boredom is a peacock
which dies in the light
of the afternoon . . .

EVE. What's that?

SERPENT. It's Posterity singing.

EVE. Don't be gauche. Tell me, where have you come from?

SERPENT. If I were to tell you, you wouldn't believe me: from the same place you came from.

EVE (*scornfully*). Are you another walking rib?

SERPENT. Go on, go on, don't tell me you believe in those fairy tales. And, by the way, where's Adam?

EVE. Wandering around over there. You already know what he spends his time doing: naming everything.

SERPENT. Do you mean he's a poet? I must remind you that that's an activity that's very poorly remunerated.

EVE. For all that we need . . .

SERPENT (*observing her*). How horrible! You don't have anything to wear!

EVE (*with a gesture of modesty*). How shameful! And before a stranger!

SERPENT. I'm not a stranger. I know your real name.

EVE (*without worrying about verifying it, wanting to confide in him*). How did you find out?

SERPENT. You would be amazed if I told you everything that I know. I've been in various paradises before winding up in this one, and I assure you that I've never seen a more disappointing place.

EVE. And if the others were so pretty and this one so horrible, why did you come here? Why do you stay? Why don't you return?

SERPENT (*mysterious and sad*). I'm a political exile.

EVE. What does that mean?

SERPENT. That I disagreed with the regime. You know tyranny doesn't tolerate criticism.

EVE. Did they throw you out?

SERPENT. I requested asylum. I thought that things would be different. And, actually, the place is agreeable . . . I mean, to spend a short vacation.

EVE. A vacation here! Here no one works.

SERPENT. Is that possible? Now I understand the . . . let's say, the scarcity of your wardrobe.

EVE. Tell me, what do women wear . . . out there?

SERPENT. This season, grape leaves. Of different colors, in different combinations. It's the latest fashion.

EVE (*seductively*). Would it be possible to get one for me?

SERPENT. Well . . . that costs money. And I fear, because of what you have told me about Adam's activities, that he doesn't earn much.

EVE. I don't want to depend on him, either. I want to be self-supporting. He already rubs in that stuff about his rib too much.

SERPENT. And do you know how money is earned?

EVE. I don't even know, actually, what money is.

SERPENT. It's compensation for work.

EVE. And what's work?

SERPENT. It's the best cure for boredom. See that field there in front of you?

EVE. Uh-huh.

SERPENT. How does it look to you?

EVE. So-so.

SERPENT. It's going to waste, truly to waste. It's a perfect field for sowing vineyards.

EVE (*catching his idea immediately*). Lots of grape leaves. For all the seasons of the year, for every hour of the day, for solemn occasions, and for daily use . . .

SERPENT. Don't go so fast. The first thing that would have to be done is to obtain a growing permit.

EVE. A permit? From whom?

SERPENT. The owner.

EVE. The owner is egotistical and stingy. Did you know that He has forbidden us to eat the fruit of that tree?

SERPENT. Why?

EVE. Oh, he doesn't condescend to give any reasons why. Simply and basically, just *because*. It makes my blood boil.

SERPENT. Then why don't you eat one?

EVE (*vacillating*). As a matter of fact, I'm not much in the mood.

SERPENT. As a matter of fact, you're afraid.

EVE. I wouldn't want to gain weight.

SERPENT. Fruit isn't fattening; that has been scientifically proven. Besides, if you work, you have to be well nourished.

EVE. Is it hard to work the land?

SERPENT. When one isn't accustomed to it . . . (*He cuts an apple and offers it to Eve.*) Have some.

EVE (*taking the apple*). You don't look like a farm worker.

SERPENT. What do I look like?

EVE. I don't know. Perhaps like . . . an intellectual.

SERPENT. I would have liked it better if you had said that I looked intelligent.Because an intelligent person thinks up ways to do what he or she wishes and to pay the least possible for it.

EVE (*concentrating, as if to figure out something*). And if I eat that apple . . .

SERPENT. You will have shown one thing: that you're free. Now then, liberty is worth a lot. But it costs much more.

EVE. It doesn't matter to me! I don't obey arbitrary orders, nor do I believe in fairy tales, nor . . .

A *lightning flash, momentary darkness. When the lights go on again the serpent is no longer there, only an accusing Adam.*

ADAM. What have you done?

EVE. I've discovered that the field needs a crop. Grape vines would grow well.

ADAM. What are you talking about?

EVE. That it's shameful that we two walk around as naked as beggars.

ADAM. We don't need clothing: this is the Land of Eternal Spring.

EVE. Tourist propaganda. No spring is eternal. And I'm not interested in waiting until autumn to gather fallen leaves. I want to prepare my wardrobe now. So let's get to work.

ADAM (*incredulous*). You mean to say that you're thinking of working?

EVE. What's so bad about that?

ADAM. You get tired. And you sweat.

EVE. I won't get tired because *I* am well nourished. Try this apple.

ADAM. How dare you? It's the fruit that Jehovah has forbidden us to eat.

EVE. Why?

ADAM. Just because.

EVE. And you don't dare ask Him His reasons?

ADAM (*who is losing face*). Do I dare; as they say, "am I game" . . . why not? But it would show a lack of respect. And Jehovah is so respectable: he has a great white beard.

EVE (*disillusioned*). He's old? Now, I understand it all. He has forbidden us to touch that fruit out of envy. He wants us, in the flower of youth as we are, to be as weak and impotent as He is. Do you know what that apple has? (*Adam shakes his head negatively.*) Vitamins. We must eat a balanced diet if we want our children to be healthy.

ADAM. Children?

EVE. Of course. One has to think of them. I would like to leave them a little farm as an inheritance, with dairy cows and chickens and . . .

ADAM (*who has been nibbling distractedly on the apple, chokes*). Who's put those ideas into your head?

EVE. Ideas are not put into heads: they come out of heads. How was the apple? Tasty?

ADAM (*looking horrified at the core*). My God!

EVE. Don't call Him. What do you want Him for?

ADAM. To ask Him not to punish us.

EVE. What greater punishment do you want than this lazy life without possibilities for progress or change, without anything?

ADAM (*nostalgic*). But we were so happy . . . We didn't need anything.

EVE. We didn't desire anything, which is different. And we weren't happy. We were selfish and cowardly. Being human is not a gift one receives; one must fight for it.

ADAM (*on his knees*). Lord, I am not worthy. Lord, have mercy on us.

CAVERNOUS AND DISTANT VOICE. You will bear your children in pain!

EVE. I will pay the price of fulfillment. I swear that I will not rest until pain is conquered.

VOICE. You will die! You will be lost!

EVE. Death will be the proof that we have lived.

ADAM (*trying to stop her*). Eve, I beg you, turn back.

EVE (*continuing to advance*). It's not possible. History has just begun.

Darkness. Lupita begins to scream hysterically. "Blasphemy! Slander! Where is the hawker who sold me the ticket? I want my money back! Swindler! Bandit! Heavens, I'm running around in circles. This is a labyrinth. Hawker! Hawker!" When the lights come on again we find Lupita, with an air of being lost, in front of a wax museum, where Malinche, Sor Juana, Josefa Ortiz de Domínguez, Empress Carlota, Rosario de la Peña, and Adelita are found, represented in the most conventional manner possible, in a series of niches.[14] *Brought to life by the hullabaloo, they come out of their niches.*

SOR JUANA (*putting her hands to her head*). My heavens! Can't one live in peace even in a museum? Even here, must the sound of the community's voices follow me, a noise that, like the gadfly, has tormented me all my life?

ADELITA. Noise of the community? Squeamishness of a nun! I would have liked to see you right in the middle of the Revolution: cannon blasts, trains exploding in the air, cavalry charges. And all for what? So you can walk around (*pointing to her nun's habit*) disguised as a scarecrow, as if the Constitution didn't exist.[15]

JOSEFA (*energetically*). Show respect for her habits; they're sacred.

CARLOTA. It isn't a question of respect; it's a complete lack of manners, as is usual in this country. (*To Adelita*) How dare you speak to someone who hasn't even been introduced to you?

ROSARIO (*trying to mediate*). Perhaps you knew each other from before.

ADELITA. Me! Know her? Not even her name.

SOR JUANA (*ironic*). Such is the posterity for whom I wrote!

JOSEFA (*calling on her sentiments of charity, and referring to Adelita*). The poor thing doesn't even know how to read. She is a total illiterate. I, on the contrary, have had the privilege of being your reader. (*To Sor Juana*) And I admire you so much!

SOR JUANA (*without paying attention to the praise, looking at Adelita and at Malinche*). But such ignorance must be remedied in some way. (*Suddenly inspired*) Why don't we play school?

Everyone reacts unfavorably, each in her own way. Rising above the chorus of negative exclamations, the voice of Lupita imposes itself.

LUPITA. I believe I'm the only one here who has the right to give an opinion because I paid for my ticket. And I want them to give me what they promised me: a show, not a class.

CARLOTA (*dreamily*). To act! The dream of my life.

SOR JUANA (*to Lupita*). But you also have to take part. Each one of us will choose an outstanding moment in her life. And you will have to identify us.

JOSEFA. That won't be hard to do. We Mexican women who have gone down in history are so few!

SOR JUANA. It is going to be difficult. Because they have made us submit against our will to a stereotyped, official version of history. And now we are going to present ourselves as what we were. Or, at least, as what we think we really were.

CARLOTA. Is the order of priority to be according to protocol? Because, in that case, I'm first.

SOR JUANA. Let's try to proceed in chronological order. (*To Malinche, who has not opened her mouth and has limited herself merely to observing*) Madam, the stage is yours.

Darkness. When the lights go on, one sees an improvised campaign tent. Inside, Cortés cannot manage to get comfortable because of his armor, which is irritatingly in the way. It is obvious that the coastal heat oppresses him. Malinche fans him with a rustic palm leaf.

MALINCHE. I told you so: we can't stay here.

CORTÉS. Nor go up there, much less return to Cuba. Oh, what I wouldn't give to have in my hands for a minute, only one minute, that sailor who started smoking in the hold of the ship and then fell asleep!

MALINCHE. You should be more tolerant. Tobacco is a vice your soldiers have just discovered. It's our way of repaying the gift of syphilis that you brought to us.

CORTÉS. But what a catastrophe it produced! Not one trace remained of any of the ships.

MALINCHE. No trace of that smoker, either. That man could have been an inconvenient witness. Why don't you take advantage of the circumstances to have the rumor spread that you, you yourself, burned the ships.

CORTÉS. I? What for?

MALINCHE. In order to cut off the return to Cuba. There are many cowards and one or two traitors in your army who would like to return. Now they can't do it and they have no other remedy than to face up to the facts.

CORTÉS. Which can't be more unfavorable: a hellish climate, a formidable empire . . . Help me to take off my breastplate.

MALINCHE (*firmly*). No.

CORTÉS. How dare you to say "no" to me? You are my slave, my property, my object.

MALINCHE. I am your tool, I agree. But at least learn to use me for your benefit.

CORTÉS. Which, according to you, consists of melting myself inside my armor.

MALINCHE. If you take it off, the Indians will see what I have seen and do not tell: that you are a man like any other. Perhaps weaker than some others. In your armor you seem like a god.

CORTÉS (*flattered*). Give me a mirror. (*He looks at himself and agrees*) True. And this role of a god fits me to a T.

MALINCHE (*smiling indulgently at Cortés' vanity*). A god whose return the Indians have awaited from the beginning. Waited for him, to submit to him, in order to return to him what belonged to him: absolute power. Because all the prophecies announce his return and also his victory.

CORTÉS. Do you believe in that farce?

MALINCHE. What I believe doesn't matter. I'm not a slave of Moctezuma because I escaped from the power of the Mayan lord who's paying tribute to him. Now I belong to you.

CORTÉS. You like the role of goddess consort, don't you?

MALINCHE. I would like Moctezuma to drink a cup of his own bitter chocolate. He's a cruel master.

CORTÉS. More than me?

MALINCHE. You're brutal because you're in a hurry. He thinks he's the owner of eternity.

CORTÉS. It won't be easy to set him straight.

MALINCHE. But it's possible. Many hate him. That empire, which you see raised before you like a great wall, is full of cracks. Through any one of them, you'll be able to infiltrate with your army.

CORTÉS (*trying to embrace her*). Oh, women, women! Why has Divine Providence given them the superfluous gift of speech?

MALINCHE (*struggling to get out of his grasp*). In my particular case, so that I might serve you as an interpreter and transmit to you the message of the emissaries of Tlaxcala, who request an audience with you.

CORTÉS (*lewdly*). Malintzin!

MALINCHE (*denying herself to Cortés for the present, promising for later*). You're in a hurry, remember. The situation of your men is desperate and the Tlaxcalans are your only hope. Receive them. They'll show you the safe road to Tenochtitlán.

CORTÉS. The city of gold!

MALINCHE. The center of power. Captain, go up to the highlands and tear from Moctezuma the high-backed throne and the rod of authority. You'll be king.

CORTÉS (*who has never heard of Shakespeare and, even less, of the witches of Macbeth*). Riches, glory, power. I'll leave an empire to my children!

While Cortés rambles on, Malinche polishes his armor, combs his hair, etc. When his appearance seems satisfactory, she goes to the door of the tent and calls to those who wait outside.

MALINCHE. The Tlaxcalan emissaries may enter.

Darkness. Once again the wax museum. Carlota's expression is scornful; Adelita's, fascinated; Josefa's, respectful; Sor Juana's, ironic. Only two faces express the most complete frustration: Rosario's and Lupita's. The former is restrained by her good manners and by the fact that she is a wax figure. But Lupita is impelled by the cost of her ticket. She protests.

LUPITA. And the romance?

MALINCHE. What romance?

LUPITA. You were in love with Cortés, with the white, bearded man who came from across the ocean.

MALINCHE. In love? What does that mean?

SOR JUANA (*didactic*). Probably, the lady is referring to love, a genuinely Western product, an invention of Provençal troubadours and of the Castilian ladies in twelfth-century European castles. Probably Cortés, in spite of his stay in Salamanca, never knew it or practiced it.

MALINCHE. That's why he didn't import it to America. And as for us . . .

SOR JUANA. We know already. Love has nothing to do with the indigenous cultures.

CARLOTA. Nor with convent life.

SOR JUANA. It's for that reason that I give the floor to one who has experience, my colleague, Rosario de la Peña, alias Rosario, friend of Acuña.[16]

JOSEFA. Colleague?

SOR JUANA. Because they called me the Tenth Muse and she was the muse of the Pleiades, of intellectuals.

ROSARIO. Oh, yes. Through my salon passed some of the most notable men of the time. Although I must admit that the epoch was quite mediocre. I preserved in my album the signatures of all of them. They admired me; they rendered me homage; they called me the inspiration for their works.

SOR JUANA. But you owed most of your celebrity to Manuel Acuña. He committed suicide because of you, isn't that so?

ROSARIO. So says the legend. But, like all legends, it's a lie. What I'm going to tell you is the truth.

Darkness. An extremely poor attic apartment appears. It belongs to a young romantic of nineteenth-century Mexico who would like to appear as a young romantic of nineteenth-century Paris. Manuel Acuña has all the noble signs of malnutrition, insomnia, and, perhaps, some addiction. Feverish, with dark circles under his eyes, he writes a few lines and then, standing up, he recites.

MANUEL. And now, I need—to tell you that I love you—to tell you I adore you—within my deepest heart . . . etc.[17]

The door opens silently and on the threshold Rosario appears, upset by the emotions that overpower her and by the many stairsteps she has had to climb. A thick veil covers her face, as is usual for nineteenth-century heroines who make clandestine visits to young gentlemen, alone. For some moments she listens rapturously to his recitation until, not being able to restrain herself any longer, she runs—with wide-open arms—toward the poet.

ROSARIO. Manuel!

Manuel looks at her as though she were Banquo's ghost and rejects her coldly.

MANUEL. Young lady, restrain your impetuosity and remember that your presence, at this hour, under these circumstances, in the house of a single man, can cause your dishonor.

ROSARIO (*vehemently*). That doesn't bother me in the least, Manuel. I scorn the judgment of a petty and hypocritical society that doesn't understand or admire you. (*She raises her veil.*) I know very well what I was defying by daring to come here. But, nevertheless, I didn't hesitate. The first sacrifice that I make on the altar of Eros is my reputation.

MANUEL (*his perturbation makes him show that he is offended*). What is it that you dare to propose to me?

ROSARIO. Marriage.

MANUEL (*horrified*). Marriage? Don't make me laugh. After the step that you just took—and that wouldn't be taken, for any reason, by a decent young woman . . .

ROSARIO. Well, since you want to know, I'll tell you. I'm not a decent young woman. (*As if reciting*) I'm a woman in love.

MANUEL (*with real curiosity*). With whom?

ROSARIO. What do you mean, with whom? With you.

MANUEL (*now his perturbation makes him appear Machiavellian*). Yes? And how can I be sure that you haven't told the same thing to all those men who form your retinue of admirers? To Manuel M. Flores and to José Martí, to cite no more than the best known among them.[18]

ROSARIO. Why would I have told it to them?

MANUEL. Because you told it to me. He who makes one basket makes a hundred, according to the proverb.

ROSARIO. But you're the man I love.

MANUEL (*not falling into such a clumsy trap*). If you loved me, you wouldn't put me in front of this precipice.

ROSARIO. What precipice? I don't understand.

MANUEL. You were my ideal love, ergo, impossible.

ROSARIO. I was?

MANUEL. Naturally. With the step you've just taken, you've destroyed everything. My dearest illusions: those of living in a fantasy world in which you would always be in love with me and I would always be satisfied. (*He stands still as though paralyzed for an instant and then runs to write what he recites in a loud voice.*) "And between us, my mother, like a God."

ROSARIO (*retreating*). Now I begin to understand: between us, your mother like a God. Like the sword between Tristan and Isolde.

MANUEL. Who ought to have been our models.

The door to the attic apartment opens and a laundress enters with a basket of clothes.

LAUNDRESS. A good and pleasant afternoon to you, Manolo. (*Upon noting the presence of Rosario, she is embarrassed.*) Señor Manuel, why didn't you let me know that you were to have visitors? I would've prepared something she would like. Tea or coffee. (*Identifying the woman with the veil, with ingenuous and sincere admiration*) You're Rosario, the famous Rosario!

ROSARIO (*between annoyed and flattered*). I, on the other hand, have not had the pleasure of meeting you.

LAUNDRESS. I'm Petra, the laundress, at your service and serving God. I'm the one who keeps house for the young master.

MANUEL (*to the Laundress, covering his face with his hands*). Shut up, for God's sake!

ROSARIO (*who has not failed to capture the reality of the situation, to Manuel*). Why should she be silent? The mouths of the innocent always speak the truth.

LAUNDRESS (*showing her advanced pregnancy*). How could I be innocent, Señorita? Manolo says that I'm the one who keeps house for the child and keeps a child for the house.

ROSARIO (*applauding*). Hurrah! Hurrah! She knows how to make puns. Manuel, you must bring her to my house, it's absolutely indispensable.

MANUEL (*overwhelmed*). Would you please stop torturing me?

ROSARIO (*reprovingly, to Manuel*). You're ashamed of her, but you don't fail to take advantage of her generosity, her ignorance, or her humble station. It's clear that you haven't placed your mother as a protecting figure between this woman and yourself. (*Manuel tries to speak, but Rosario Olympically ignores him; to the Laundress*) Señora, the friends of my friends are also friends of mine. I would like to beg you from this day forward to consider yourself invited to my literary gatherings.

LAUNDRESS. Oh, Señorita! What in the devil will I do there? I'm so uncultured. And Manolo has told me that all of you are very intelligent.

ROSARIO (*with a triumphant glance at Manuel and letting her veil fall*). I admire, above all, moral virtues. And for that reason I would like to be your friend.

Both walk away talking to each other while Manuel, in the center of the stage, recites the last stanzas of the "Nocturne." While he recites, he gradu-

ally becomes conscious of the fact that he has made himself completely ri-diculous. As he recites the final verses, he takes hold of a revolver. He fires just as the Laundress returns, who puts her hands to her head in a gesture of complete desperation.

LAUNDRESS. My God! He has spattered blood all over the clean clothes! Now I have to wash them over again.

Darkness. Return to the wax museum.

SOR JUANA (*laughs quietly*). Forgive me, but I can't help it. I thought until now that I had been the only one, although my case was never as extreme as yours. In my case there never was a suicide. Men, who fled from me as though from the plague, never did go that far. And I, to say the truth, was not ugly. I knew, also, how to please. But I must have had a Medusa's head paralyzing with horror all those who looked at it. Only on one occasion was I on the point of ending my isolation. But, of course, everything came to nothing, a comedy of intrigues.

LUPITA (*urging her*). Tell the story.

SOR JUANA. All right. You all know about my penchant for disguises . . .

Darkness. The light goes on in the drawing room of a colonial house. Juana Inés, fifteen years old, writes with a goose-quill pen on parchment. Far away is heard the melody of a "viola d'amore." Distractedly, Juana Inés nibbles now and then on a piece of cheese. She stops, reads to herself while she chews, and, after swallowing a bite, rises to her feet and recites, counting the syllables to see if they are correct.

JUANA. . . . The soul, then separated
      from out the body's rule,
      immersed in daily chores
      —for good or bad the day was spent—
      albeit the soul, not far removed,
      in semblance, separate and alone.[19]

Separate and alone . . . separate and alone . . . What follows, good heav-ens, what follows? (*Crumpling the parchment*) Nothing. My thought is gone, flown away. Everything was so different when I began, so easy. I put one word down, and after it, pursuing it, chasing it, catching its prey, came all the others that followed it. "But you speak in verse," my visitors told me, amazed. Now, on the contrary, each concept hides from me like an armadillo in its shell. And I have to smoke the word out so that instead of suffocating, it shows itself. And when it appears, it's as lean, as tasteless, as withered as a nut. That was before. But, before, of course, I was inno-cent and grace rained on me from the heavens. Now, on the contrary, banished in frivolity, a glutton for everything: for cheese, which causes the most rapier wit to become dull, for the gossip of the court, for the praise of the educated and the admiration of imbeciles, avid for universal applause. (*Changing her tone and contemplating herself fixedly in a mirror*) Juana Inés, I declare you to be guilty of vanity, of laziness, and of ignorance. And I decree that a head so empty of information ought not be covered with adornments and trifles. Let the sentence be fulfilled. (*As if her double, and with the slowness of ritual gestures, Juana Inés takes from her desk a pair of scissors and cuts off, with sure strokes, the mass of hair which was her pride and joy. Her appearance has changed completely. With a gesture, she compares her shorn head and her clothing, and she says to the mirror*) No, it is not logical. (*She goes behind a folding screen to change her clothes. While she changes her courtesan's dress to a page's habit, she sings softly.*)

> . . . I only know that I came here
>   so that if I be woman,
>   no one can truly say . . .

When she has finished the process, she looks at herself again: she has the equivocal appearance of an adolescent boy, which pleases her. She hears steps and automatically puts out the light. Scarcely a second afterward, Celia enters.

CELIA (*feeling her way, trying to touch a body that escapes from her. Juana and Celia advance and retreat in regular and harmonious movements as in a dance*).

> Stay, shadow of my elusive love,
> image of the charms that I adore,
> fair illusion for whom I gladly die,
> sweet fiction for whom I sadly live.[20]

JUANA (*apart*). She is reciting.
(*To Celia*) Señora, do consider

> the owner has consecrated
> this house to the Muses—
> to them it's dedicated.

CELIA. Unknown to me that Edict
> from the Crown of sovereign Spain.
> Or does presumptuous Juana
> usurp that kingly claim?

JUANA. If trumpets sound her daring,
    they do not praise her fame.
    By being modest, good, and wise
    she gained honor for her name.
CELIA. Quiet, knave, who did not come
    to court these ghosts inside,
    but to pay a debt of honor
    to me, made pregnant, at your side.
JUANA. Señora, please restrain your tongue.
CELIA. Would that I'd held my virgin door
    under lock and key from you
    my prowling nighttime suitor.
JUANA. Señora, did I promise give,
    of name and marriage vows?
CELIA.   And ornaments so gay,
    to replace with precious gems
    the priceless one you stole away.
JUANA. Now open-eyed you would collect
    what you so freely gave away;
    and does it not surprise you
    that to this room I find my way?
CELIA. I gather that you understand
    how sacred are its walls;
    you're hidden not by one alone
    but by nine sisters' shawls.
JUANA. I own but to the tenth.
CELIA.   The tenth?
    Juana, . . . is she the one you name?
    But, no, I have no jealous heart.
    For that, one single bastard[21]
    is not a daunting rival.
JUANA. Fool! Be silent!
CELIA. With a dowry of four sheepskins,
    while beneath her petticoat
    are naught but syllogisms.
    Find a more momentous foe!
JUANA. Her beauty is apparent.
CELIA. True, when one is young,
    but it only lasts one morning.

JUANA. And do you have a magic pact?
    Does time let you go free?
CELIA. I am a female of my race,
    and like the fertile land
    I sprout again with every child,
    eternal life within my hand.
JUANA. And her?
CELIA. She's like a withered nut.
JUANA. And is she truly sterile?
CELIA. She births ideas every day,
    puns and shadowy webs of grace;
    they are the pages of her books,
    which autumn's coming does erase.
    But worst of all, she has no dowry!
JUANA. But aren't you green with envy?
CELIA.   Of Juana?
    And the myths around her name?
    The Phoenix rare of Mexico?
    No, the Vicereine shaped her fame,
    but the Graces have undone her.
    To rouse my jealous ardor
    find more compelling merit.
    Be she equal or above me,
    but through abounding human charm,
    perchance she may defeat me,
    by my own weapons foiled.
    You err. It is unwise
    to mingle oil and water,
    the cooing dove and abstruse owl,
    and apples mixed with pears offend.
JUANA. And can you tell between them?
CELIA. My heart is not deceived.
JUANA. What says your heart today?
CELIA.   That you love me,
    and I love you.
JUANA.   For my high rank?
CELIA. For your figure and your face,
    which like a sovereign star
    does all the other orbs efface.

JUANA. For the fortune that I have?
CELIA.   My fortune is
        to have you in my bed
        and sacrifice to Love,
        until the light of dawn
        comes down from above
        to end or to extend the battle.
JUANA. And would you change me for another?
CELIA. Is gold exchanged for silver?
        Do stars reverse their course?
        Do arrows return to their quivers?
JUANA. And if I am not I?
                    I would die!
        My heart is not deceived!

After a dramatic pause, Juana strikes a light.
JUANA (*shining the light directly on her own face*).

Do you know me? The one
for whom you'd gladly sigh,
for whom you'd gladly die,
for whom you'd lose your soul.

CELIA. Juana!
There is, in the pronunciation of this single name, an uneasiness that does not crystallize into rejection, but rather into a kind of bewilderment. Celia opens her arms, as she did at the beginning, in darkness, and Juana doubts a moment between flight and surrender. Finally, she reacts vehemently.

JUANA. No, no longer call that name,
        nor talk of deeds and tales,
        that for my shadow claim
        the ranting tongues of slander.
        Here perishes for evermore
        the woman in me. Here ends
        all this time of strife
        twixt powers and the soul.
        The trunk forever hewn
        of my descent. In a shroud
        enclose my earthly body:
        let my imprisoned soul go free[22]

Good-bye, good-bye, my youthful days,
good-bye, sweet music, brilliant scene
of numbers and of quiet talks.
Good-bye to what I never was,
and to what I was too much.

CELIA. To where will you retreat?

JUANA. To where the noble intellect
is solitude in flames.

The two contemplate each other for a moment, both paralyzed by con-trary forces: one that attracts them—which must be suggested very deli-cately—and one that separates them. Darkness. When the lights go on again, they light up the wax museum. The spectators of the previous scene seem confused and do not know which way to react. Carlota fans herself, majestically, and finally decrees.

CARLOTA. We are not amused. We are not amused at all.

JUANA (*taking things lightly*). But what you have seen in only an enter-tainment. It's, perhaps, just one version.

ROSARIO. Finally, I choose to stay with the classic version; I mean, the romantic one—the impossible love, the convent.

LUPITA (*to Rosario*). You, with your experience, dare to believe in im-possible love?

JUANA. In principle, all love is impossible: an obsessive idea that seizes control over solitary spirits. The rest do not fall in love; they form a union.

ROSARIO (*to Sor Juana*). But in your time there was still that graceful exit: taking the veil. In mine there were only two soups to choose from. And I didn't pick the one with noodles. An old maid, and that ended it.

JOSEFA. That's what's called dumbbell soup.

SOR JUANA. But I didn't enter the convent as a vocation or from dis-appointment, but because of common sense. I don't know why they per-sist in inventing so many other motives, when I wrote very clearly in a letter the reason why I was entering the cloister. More than because I was attracted to that form of life, I was impelled by the "total repugnance which marriage inspired in me."

LUPITA. Repugnance? How can that be? I don't understand.

JOSEFA. You will understand soon. You're on the verge of understand-ing. I remember, for example . . .

Darkness, in order to change the scene to the living room of a Creole[23] family in Guanajuato. A Canon is playing a game of cards with the Mag-istrate. At the end of the room, his wife, Josefa, much younger than her husband, restless, sated by a life that has no outlet, embroiders. She looks insistently at a wall clock, which, according to her sense of impatience, does not move.

JOSEFA. Isn't it time for chocolate?

MAGISTRATE. Oh, my child! When will you learn to calculate time? We have just barely finished eating. Isn't that true, Reverend?

CANON. Certainly, Your Honor. Although I understand that your wife at her age . . .

MAGISTRATE (*extremely surprised*). Since when do decent married ladies have an age? Those frivolities are left for loose women.

Nevertheless, the Magistrate feels some doubt, since he turns to inspect Josefa as though he were seeing her for the first time. While doing so his critical judgment is suspended, because the expression on the Magistrate's face is inscrutable.

CANON. Young women like serenades, excursions, and dances.

MAGISTRATE. When they are frivolous or when they have no one to watch out for their honor. But Josefa is a respectable married woman. Therefore she is beyond those diversions, which you, Reverend, know about thanks to the confessional. As our Holy Mother Church teaches us, they endanger the soul's salvation.

CANON. And even the body's health. A health which, nevertheless, I find here to be undermined. (*He rises and approaches the embroiderer; he acts out what he says*) Her hands are icy, while her cheeks burn with feverish heat. Do you feel well, Señora?

MAGISTRATE (*without deigning to pay attention to the person mentioned*). Why shouldn't she feel well? She is the legitimate wife of a high dignitary of the crown of Spain; she lives in a palace; she has numerous servants at her command; she'll inherit the family jewels and all the dresses, hats, shoes, and cosmetics, which no longer fit in her closets.

CANON. Perhaps something is still missing.

MAGISTRATE. She lacks what a woman needs to be complete, a·son. A son whom she ought to have in order to continue the line, to pass on the family name. But perhaps she doesn't understand that obligation. (*Without looking at her*) Did you hear, Josefa? The Reverend ordered you to have a son.

CANON (*rectifying*). Far be it from me to have the audacity to order her. Perhaps I would dare to suggest.

JOSEFA (*flushing from wounded modesty and anger*). If it were up to me . . . but I assure you that it isn't in my hands, Reverend.

MAGISTRATE. It's well known that in these cases there's no better advice than to put yourselves at the mercy of Our Lady of Perpetual Help. Why don't you make a vow to go to visit her at her sanctuary?

CANON. Right now perhaps it isn't prudent, Your Honor. One hears rumors of discontent everywhere. There are ambushes on the roads; there's hunger in the countryside.

MAGISTRATE (*laughing softly*). When has it ever been otherwise?

Josefa has stopped her work and follows the conversation with a rapt interest that the others do not notice.

CANON. It's as though the whole land were sprinkled with fuel, ready for a fire that anyone could set. I listen to so many things in the confessional that I think we've reached the end of time and I see the coming arrival of the Antichrist!

MAGISTRATE. The people are given to making a great fuss; one mustn't pay much attention to them. Bread and circus, counseled the Romans, and their Empire fell. Bread and blows, I say. And that's that.

JOSEFA (*unable to contain herself*). And if it's not enough?

MAGISTRATE. The army not enough? Spanish fury not enough to drown in blood . . . what? Something that doesn't even have a form, to which no one can give a name.

JOSEFA (*stubbornly*). And if it's not enough?

MAGISTRATE. Then it must be something supernatural, which our Holy Mother, the Catholic Church, will have to concern itself with; God promised that the devil would not prevail against the Church.

CANON. And if I were to tell you, Your Honor, that it's in the very bosom of the Church where the uprising is being born? That it's from the pulpits that the multitude is being stirred up?

MAGISTRATE. But they're mad! That's to bite the hand that feeds them, if you will forgive the proverb.

CANON. Those priests—I must continue calling them that since they haven't yet been judged or excommunicated—have read books that speak about equality among all men.

MAGISTRATE. Since when has the Inquisition permitted those books to enter and circulate freely in the kingdom of New Spain?

CANON. From the very moment New Spain was founded, Your Honor. The Inquisitors are susceptible to certain gratifications that I don't want to specify.

MAGISTRATE. Men to the last! For that reason, the most certain deterrent, I've always maintained, is to keep the people in ignorance. If you were as careful with your flock as I am with mine, we wouldn't have these headaches. (*To give an example*) Josefa, do you know how to read?

JOSEFA. No, Husband.

MAGISTRATE. Do any of your maids, your female relatives, or your friends know how to read?

JOSEFA. None of them, sir.

MAGISTRATE (*to the Canon, triumphantly*). See? It's very easy. Thus there can be no way for them to find out about anything, or for them to disseminate it.

CANON. And you, Your Honor, do you know how to read?

MAGISTRATE. Only well enough to fulfill my obligations. But I swear to you, except for that, I never read at all.

CANON. And your friends? Those who frequent this house? Captain Allende? Jiménez? The priest, Miguel Hidalgo, does he know how to read?

MAGISTRATE. I don't know for sure, but the poor man is a saint.

CANON. If I were to make an inspection of Father Hidalgo's library— because he has one, and very well stocked—I bet that we would find very interesting things, although not surprising ones.

JOSEFA. Oh!

CANON (*solicitous*). What's the matter, Señora?

MAGISTRATE. Nothing. She must have pricked her finger with the needle. As always.

JOSEFA. I'm so silly . . .

MAGISTRATE. It's your duty, and you fulfill it very conscientiously. In that sense, I have nothing to complain about.

CANON (*returning to the theme*). And if we did make that inspection anyway?

MAGISTRATE. It isn't worth the trouble of wounding feelings. And dear Father Miguel is, begging my wife's pardon, who appreciates him so much, a real simpleton.

CANON. Madam, we are boring you with our conversation.

JOSEFA. Oh, no, not at all. Who am I to get bored in the presence of such learned people?

MAGISTRATE (*condescending*). A very good answer, Josefa. Because if you had said that the conversation interested you, you would have appeared presumptuous. One becomes interested when one understands. And if you had said that you were not paying attention to the conversation, you would've seemed impolite. But in this way, you put yourself in the appropriate place—woman's place—and you put us in our proper place. You may continue embroidering, Josefa.

CANON. If it wouldn't be too much trouble, I would ask the Señora to give me a glass of water.

MAGISTRATE. Water? Josefa, tell the servants to bring us a glass of sherry and cookies.

Josefa stands up and, against her will, goes to ring the bell, but the Canon interrupts.

CANON. I would appreciate it very much if you, personally, would bring me that glass of water with your own hands. Do you understand? With your own hands. You must forgive an old man's eccentric wishes.

JOSEFA. I'll do it right now. (*Leaves.*)

CANON. Forgive me for what seems to be a lack of respect or an extravagance. But it's urgent that I speak to you alone.

MAGISTRATE. We have been alone all afternoon.

CANON. And Señora?

MAGISTRATE. Señora, like all the ladies, doesn't count. You know quite well that she's my wife.

CANON. That's precisely the point. There's a conspiracy.

The Canon just finishes saying this last syllable when Josefa enters hurriedly.

JOSEFA. Your glass of water, Reverend.

MAGISTRATE. A conspiracy against whom?

CANON. The water is delicious, Señora. I have no doubt that it is so by virtue of your kind hands that brought it to me. Would you do me the favor of bringing me one more glass?

JOSEFA (*maliciously*). Won't it give you dropsy?

MAGISTRATE. I insist, a conspiracy against whom?

CANON (*waiting until Josefa has left again*). Against the Crown.

MAGISTRATE. Why do you mutter in that way? How do these people, who have never been in Spain, know what the Crown really is? I myself, who came from there, don't clearly remember. The Crown of Spain! It's something so . . . remote that I can't understand how they can conspire against it.

CANON (*finally letting it out*). Ask your wife.

JOSEFA (*entering hurriedly*). Your glass of water, Reverend.

CANON (*trapped*). I was referring precisely to you.

JOSEFA. Can I serve you in any way, Reverend?

MAGISTRATE. He wants me to ask you . . . (*To the Canon*) What did you want me to ask her?

JOSEFA (*pretending innocence*). Some cooking recipe, perhaps?

CANON. I'm afraid, Señora—and I say it at the risk of seeming impolite—that cooking isn't your strong point. Or, in any case, that you prefer highly seasoned dishes.

JOSEFA. Salt and pepper, nothing else.

CANON. Nothing else? Among your ingredients isn't there some gunpowder?

MAGISTRATE. But who would think of such a thing? Go on! That's unmitigated foolishness. Gunpowder isn't a spice.

JOSEFA. Perhaps the Canon thinks that I can use it when I make powdered-sugar cookies.

CANON. Did you say powder-coated or powder-loaded?

This game of wits is too much for the Magistrate, who has fallen asleep and is now snoring placidly. The two interlocutors speak softly in order not to awaken him.

CANON. A word to the wise is sufficient, Señora. The only thing left for me is to advise you to separate yourself, as soon as possible, from those who are about to fall into the hands of the law.

JOSEFA. My husband is the law here, and I fell into his hands a long time ago. Look at him snoring like an innocent child! If you have the same luck that I've had, you won't be able to wake him up.

CANON. I'll try at this point to do the impossible. And, if it's really impossible, I'll have to resort to other methods.

JOSEFA. That was what I did.

CANON. But you aren't the mistress—God pardon me for that word!—of any of the conspirators in this dirty business.

JOSEFA (*very tranquil*). Mistress, no. Their accomplice.

CANON (*unable to keep from shouting*). God have mercy on us!

MAGISTRATE (*waking up*). Huh? Huh? What's going on?

JOSEFA. The time for dark chocolate and clear explanations has finally arrived. The Canon has a secret to tell you.

MAGISTRATE. A secret?

CANON. Señora, you're driving me to do something rash!

JOSEFA. I'm going to check that everything's ready. (*She leaves.*)

CANON (*trying to inspire the magistrate to action*). Stop her before it's too late!

MAGISTRATE. Have you gone crazy?

CANON. Hurry! She's going to get away from us. Close the doors, the windows, the exits.

Confused sound from the outside. Two servants drag Josefa in.

MAGISTRATE (*furious at the Canon*). Will you do me the favor of telling me what this is all about?

JOSEFA. And do me the favor of letting me loose. I don't intend to flee.

CANON. It so happens that your wife is a spy of the insurgents and, if she hadn't been stopped, she would've revealed to them that their conspiracy had been discovered.

MAGISTRATE (*making an effort to put his ideas in order, ideas that are few in number and not easily organized*). My wife? A conspiracy in which MY WIFE is involved?

JOSEFA (*suddenly fierce*). Yes, your little Josefa, the one you wouldn't give five cents for.

MAGISTRATE (*stunned*). Josefa . . . My little Josefa . . . Why have you done this to me?

JOSEFA (*stonily*). Because I was bored.

Darkness. Return once again to the wax museum.

CARLOTA (*who finally feels that she is in her medium*). Boredom . . . Don't I know it? Boredom is one of the great movers of history. And women's capacity to be bored is much greater than men's; it's not easy for me to explain. A game of chess, a fishing pole, is enough for them; men consider themselves satisfied. Sometimes even less is sufficient. Let me mention, for example, the case of Max. He could spend hours and hours watching the ocean.

SOR JUANA. Living in Ocean View, what else could he do? To make you forgive me for that bad joke, I'm going to propose a hypothesis: perhaps he was thinking.

CARLOTA. About what? He didn't have any prospects. His venerable mother enjoyed the luxury of having such numerous offspring that the probability of his inheriting a European throne was minimal.

JOSEFA. Unless Max had been a genius of intrigue or of crime.

CARLOTA. Poor Max! He's immortalized in history thanks to my hysteria. Oh, how well I remember the great scenes I organized regularly in our retreat! Thanks to them, our life together wasn't completely a desert.

LUPITA. And at just the right moment, the Mexican reactionaries' emissaries supplied you with an illusion: coming to reign over Mexico.

CARLOTA (*poetically, and deeply moved*). Mexico! How exotic and mysterious it seemed from far away! How unpronounceable! And the mission Divine Providence had entrusted to us was finally made manifest in all its splendor: to redeem, reconcile, unite, and civilize the Mexican people.

MALINCHE. Exactly the same thing that Hernán Cortés' propagandizers said. Never, until now, did I realize that the failure of his undertaking had been so complete.

Darkness. The terrace of Chapultepec Castle. Maximiliano enters and Carlota runs toward him, receiving him with more respect than warmth.

CARLOTA. I have followed you with my eyes, down the entire length of that big avenue that we had built, from the time you left the palace until you reached the castle.

MAXIMILIANO (*ironically*). Were you afraid I'd get lost?

CARLOTA. I was afraid that they would assassinate you.

MAX. Why? The natives aren't savages. And if they were, Rousseau has shown that savages are essentially good.

CARLOTA. That's not the point. The Mexicans have been half-corrupted by civilization. That's what makes them dangerous.

MAX. Civilization: the gift from the House of Austria. Is that why I'm obligated to undo wrongs? Besides, who are the Mexicans? The Creole elite? The *mestizos*? The native masses?

CARLOTA. In charge of the Indians is their equal: Benito Juárez.

MAX (*rancorously*). And you, who pushed me into this, you, tell me, what are you in charge of?

CARLOTA. Of playing the role of empress before a people who have adopted Spanish etiquette but have converted it into a mixture of rigidity and of laxity that as a result is impossible to understand, to predict, or to control. Sensitive as well as cruel, they give themselves over to you with an effusiveness only equaled by the scorn with which they leave you.

MAX. The hand that rocks the cradle is the hand that moves the world. But I don't see the cradle, Carlota. Where is it?

CARLOTA (*tense with suppressed anger*). Max, let's not start again.

MAX. I'm not starting anything; I'm continuing because of inertia. And what I would like is to finish once and for all, to know what to rely upon. Will what I build in this country without memory collapse at the moment of my death? Won't I even have an heir to my dreams, to my work, to my blood?

CARLOTA. Don't change the subject. First one has to have a throne. Afterward, only afterward, does one think of a successor.

MAX. Don't you feel the need for a child?

CARLOTA. Until I have prepared a good place in the world, no. A child, like you or I, who doesn't fit into any social class, who's at the mercy of any adventurer, on the hunt for any throne, no, a thousand times, no.

MAX. Very well. Then I refuse to continue acting out a farce whose only end can be catastrophe.

CARLOTA. Is the situation that serious?

MAX. The French consider finished what they call "their military ramble through Mexico," and now they're returning, covered with glory and a few other trophies, to their homeland.

CARLOTA. That had to happen sooner or later. As long as there's a foreign army supporting you with their bayonets you can't really govern. You knew that the troops' presence here was temporary. They were giving you time to organize your followers.

MAX. What followers?

CARLOTA. The nobles, if one can call by that name the *pulque*-drinking aristocrats and the other landowners.[24]

MAX. I would say *the* landowner, the Church.

CARLOTA. So much the better: The Church and the monarchy always go together.

MAX. When the monarchy is strong. When it's tottering, like ours, they call me—oh, praising me, of course!—a free-thinker. That label permits the faithful to follow their own logical thread, which brings them even to believe in my secret association with the Masons.

CARLOTA. We must take drastic measures. Beginning tomorrow morning, we will go to Mass daily and take communion, very solemnly, in the Cathedral.

MAX. They'll accuse us of being sacrilegious.

CARLOTA (*walking up and down, concentrating on her thoughts*). Nor is there a bourgeoisie to turn to; there's no middle ground between the two extremes. Between the well-off and those who die hungry, there's only hatred, lack of trust, and violence.

MAX. But now that hatred, that lack of trust, that violence has a name: Maximiliano. I'm the blight of the crops, the slaughter of the animals, the children's stomachs swollen with worms. Oh, Juárez has known quite well how to take advantage of all the adverse circumstances—which they won't be freed from when they're freed from me—he just attributes them to me.

CARLOTA. Well, then, the French are still indispensable.

MAX. There's another alternative.

CARLOTA (*anxious*). What?

MAX. Return with them.

CARLOTA (*furious*). Are you mad? We would be the laughing-stock of Europe.

MAX. What are we here?

CARLOTA. The usurpers. They abhor us, but they don't mock us.

MAX. Not yet.

CARLOTA (*determined*). Never. Do you hear, Max? Never!

MAX. What new fantasy have you thought of?

CARLOTA. I'll get ahead of the returning French fugitives . . . I'll go to Napoleon's court; I'll explain to him what's occurring here. I'll convince him that his troops' retreat is still premature, that we just need time . . . time.

MAX. Napoleon believes that we've had more than enough.

CARLOTA. But scarcely yesterday . . . was it yesterday? Sometimes I confuse dates, times. Sometimes—because everything here happens with a slowness that makes all changes imperceptible, everything returns to the beginning, like a circle that closes and like a serpent that bites its own tail—sometimes I have the impression that the clocks in the castle have stopped.

MAX. The clocks in Versailles, on the contrary, work perfectly. No, Carlota. Your argument lacks force.

CARLOTA. Napoleon has to understand. I'll make him understand.

MAX. Is it worth the trouble to work so hard for a foreign country that rejects us, that would like to remove us as though we were a malignant tumor killing it?

CARLOTA. I'm not talking about the country. It doesn't matter to me. I'm speaking of us: they educated us to reign and we don't know how to do anything else.

MAX. A king without a crown . . . without descendants . . .

CARLOTA. A queen with willpower. I swear to you, Maximilian, I'm going to triumph or die in the struggle.

Darkness. Return to the wax museum.

CARLOTA (*with satisfaction*). It was a sensational death: all the newspapers described it. There were pilgrimages made from all over the world to contemplate the body of the sacrificed empress. Among the many homages, I must confess that I forgot Max completely. Tell me, who was his heir?

ADELITA. Don't pretend you're crazy. You know very well that we shot him on Bell Hill.

CARLOTA (*disappointed*). Execution by firing squad in a place with that name can't be tragic.

JOSEFA. It wasn't tragic, but it was worthy.

CARLOTA. How absurd! We kings and queens are trained from infancy to die *comme il faut*.[25]

SOR JUANA. Given the circumstances, it was a logical outcome.

ADELITA. Who would think to ask for pears from an elm tree? It's well known (*for Carlota*) that whoever doesn't know God goes around kneeling everywhere. Instead of playing crybaby to the powerful, you should've talked to the people—then you would've heard a song of a different tune.

CARLOTA (*admitting for the first time that Adelita exists*). Forgive me, Señora, but I believe we have not been introduced.

ADELITA. Señorita, although it may be difficult for you to say the word.

LUPITA (*extremely surprised*). Señorita?

ADELITA. An honorable unmarried woman. Even the colonel respected Adelita.

SOR JUANA. The poor thing! Her, too. Wouldn't it be interesting and even revealing to survey how many women in Mexico have hit the jackpot through disrespect. I mean . . .

Darkness. A revolutionary ballad is heard. The lights go on inside a military tent. Two Colonels, absolutely identical—or at least undistinguishable because their uniforms are alike—are seated in front of a table where there is a bottle of tequila and two glasses. Nothing else.

COLONEL I. Wal, General . . .

COLONEL II (*modestly*). Only Colonel, Colonel.

COLONEL I. Don't be insubordinate, good buddy. You have just this moment been promoted to General. For merit in action.

COLONEL II. Thank you very much, Colonel.

COLONEL I. Why do you call me "Colonel"? Aren't you going to promote me? You leave me out and I'll fill you full of lead.

COLONEL II (*sweating and saluting him with military discipline*). As you command, General.

COLONEL I. Tit for tat: That's how you play the game. Now that we are equal and neither one feels superior to the other, why don't we make a toast?

They fill their glasses and are on the point of making a toast when Adelita enters and strikes the table with her hand, making the bottle of tequila wobble; both officers jump to its rescue at the same time.

ADELITA. Just a moment, Gentlemen. May I ask what you are doing?

GENERAL I (*timidly*). Wal, you see now . . . here we're just getting ready to celebrate.

ADELITA. To celebrate what?

GENERAL I. Wal, look. It all began when the General here . . .

ADELITA. General? (*To the one referred to*) Don't let them make you swallow that lie. Colonel it is, and be grateful. Besides, you're our prisoner of war.

GENERAL I (*guiltily*). Wal, there's no reason for you to know, my dear

Adelita, nor even less for me to tell you, but the whole truth is that I pardoned him.

ADELITA (*without exploding yet*). In exchange for what?

GENERAL II. Look, Miss, when you grabbed me with your own hands on the field of battle . . .

ADELITA. . . . because you yourself came to me personally and surrendered to me. What did you want me to do?

GENERAL II. Wal, I had already prayed to our Lady of Tepeyac, and she surely guided me to you. And who could've been better? You with your heart of a mother . . .

ADELITA. I? Mother? Mother?

GENERAL II. Wal, I drew myself up and I said to myself: Go ahead! And here you see me, pardoned. And even promoted.

General I makes frantic signs to him to shut up, but the other does not pay any attention.

ADELITA (*standing with legs akimbo*). And who promoted you, if you're at liberty to say?

GENERAL II. Wal, here, the General did.

ADELITA. Uh, wal, this is already becoming an epidemic. And you (*to General I*), since when are you a General?

GENERAL I. From this very moment. That was what we were going to celebrate.

ADELITA. So, eagles everywhere, right? (*To General II*) And who promoted you?

GENERAL II. Who else could it be, Señorita? Wal, the General here did.

ADELITA. As they say, while giving and giving, the bird flies away.

GENERAL II. So we were going to celebrate it here, and now that you've come into range, why don't you join us?

ADELITA. Because you (*pointing to General I*) have no power over him (*pointing to General II*), unless it's to shoot him.

GENERAL II. Look at that. So pretty and so untamed! Why would he shoot me?

ADELITA. Because you're the enemy.

GENERAL II. That depends on how you look at it. Because back there on my side, they said that you're the enemy. With so much confusion, who can understand?

GENERAL I (*who has been drinking and who begins to show it*). Wait a minute . . . Wait a minute . . . Enemies are those on the other side of the line. Even the line itself is called the enemy line.

GENERAL II. Here, confidentially, *compadre,* have you ever seen that line?

GENERAL I. Never in this world.

GENERAL II. Neither have I. Because when I went over to see it, I was already, if you will forgive me saying so, in the lady's arms.

A song is heard outside:

because she has two rifles for arms,
because she has two bullets for eyes . . .

ADELITA. I fulfilled my duty and handed him over to my superior so that he could fulfill his duty of trying him.

GENERAL I. And what else did I do? The only bad thing is that by talking one understands people and, once we had talked, we decided to sign a peace treaty.

GENERAL II. That was what we were celebrating when you came in as though you were halfway irritated, and . . .

ADELITA. And I spoiled the party. Because this matter has to be explained more fully to me. Where are the papers?

GENERAL I. Papers? what in the devil do you mean? The important thing is a man's word.

GENERAL II. A man's word to a man.

ADELITA. And what is that famous word? What does it say?

GENERAL I. Wal, that everything was OK, right? That a cup was broken, and everyone could go home.

ADELITA. Very pretty. And the thousands of dead men? What about them?

GENERAL II. Why do you worry so about those things? The buzzards have already eaten them.

ADELITA. But why in the devil did they die?

GENERAL I. Because it was their turn. That's all.

GENERAL II. And it wasn't our turn because of pure luck. But we all took the same risks. We all joined the Revolution.

A voice outside, singing:

a whirlwind came and swept us away . . .

GENERAL I. Joined? They forced us! They put a rifle in my hand and told me: "If you don't shoot, we'll shoot you or they will."

ADELITA. And everyone, like madmen, bam, bam, bam. Playing at war games. You, why didn't you grab a rifle and use it to kill the one who gave it to you?

GENERAL I. That's exactly what I did do. And then with two rifles, they named me chief. And then I started to make a career of it.

ADELITA. But what were you after?

GENERAL I. What do you mean, what was I after? The others were running after me! The only thing that I was trying to do was to escape.

GENERAL II. And, sometimes, just by a hair . . . Gosh, General! This Revolufio is serious business.

ADELITA. It's a terrible disaster.

GENERAL I. That's life, brother! But now is the time to settle down. And my old lady and my small fries are there in the village. I have to take care of them.

ADELITA. Of course, and the other guy must have his virtuous little girlfriend, and, us, let the devil take us.

GENERAL I. Adelita, you know that I've never done you wrong.

ADELITA. I'm not talking about myself, but about all the others who have been with you. What have we solved, really, for sure?

GENERAL I. Forget it, and let each one live with his or her conscience. Mine is as clear as can be.

GENERAL II. And as I already said, "Enough." And when I say enough, that means enough.

ADELITA. And now you're talking about returning. Where to?

GENERAL I. The hacienda, where I was a day laborer and they furnished me with a house.

ADELITA. We burnt that hacienda and we hung none other than the overseer because the owners were somewhere around Uruapan.

GENERAL II. I have a secure job in the mines.

ADELITA. What mines, child of God? The ones that didn't flood we blew to pieces with dynamite. Like the trains. So, even if there had been somewhere to return to, there wouldn't be any way to get there. Because, in case you don't know it, Mexico is deserts, mountains, and swamp.

GENERAL I (*reaching rapidly for his gun*). No one's going to insult my country to my face.

ADELITA (*without showing any emotion*). Put that toy away, General; keep it for when you can really use it. Because a general has no other place to go than the battlefield.

GENERAL I. But who do I fight? This guy (*pointing to General II*) is my brother, my true buddy.

ADELITA. That's even better. Now the two of you join forces and give it to them, just like in the Christmas parties, when they break the *piñata*.

GENERAL II. But who is the *piñata*?

ADELITA. Wal, don't you see it? Big and fat, swaying high above us all, full of sweets, of fruits, of gifts to be given, to divide among everyone. The *piñata* is the rich.

GENERAL I. But we keep hitting out—blindfolded—against the other poor people like us.

ADELITA. That happens because we are ignorant. But if we were to make a plan . . . (*She goes to the table. She removes the bottle and the glasses and looks at the cleared surface.*) There ought to be some paper here.

Darkness. Return to the wax museum.

ADELITA. There was paper, many papers. For the modest price of ten million casualties we were able to convert Mexico into an immense archive.

SOR JUANA. But the history books say that the Revolution was a success.

ADELITA (*pointing to Lupita*). If it had triumphed, would this girl be here? Would there still be girls like her, with parents like hers, with sweethearts like hers, with a life like hers?

LUPITA (*beside herself*). Well, then I compare myself with you, with any one of you, I think that I was very lucky and that I hit the jackpot and that . . .

The lights flicker and then there is total darkness. The shadows let us guess that we have returned to the beauty salon.

OWNER. That was all we needed. A blackout.

LUPITA. And my hair is still damp and they can't fix it, and today I'm getting married, and . . . My God, what am I going to do? My God, what am I going to do?

CURTAIN

ACT III

When the curtains open, we are once again in the beauty salon, still in darkness because of the short circuit. Lupita's choked sobs and the Owner's, the Hairdresser's, and the other customers' conventional conciliatory remarks are heard. Someone lights a match; the Hairdresser finds, finally, a candle, which she places strategically in such a way that Lupita's furious yanking out of her rollers can be seen. Her hair, still damp, falls down, mussed and ugly. With such hair as raw material, nothing can be done and no one endeavors to hide such an evident fact. Lupita looks at herself and starts to cry like a baby.

LUPITA. That's the limit! That's the limit! Nothing like this has ever happened to me in all the days of my life. First, the nightmare, or rather the nightmares, because there were lots. And then to top off ruining everything, the fuses blew.

OWNER (*very sensitive about her establishment's prestige*). You will admit that nothing like this has ever happened to you before. I can testify that nothing like this has ever happened to you in *my* salon. Nor to me either.

HAIRDRESSER (*putting her foot in her mouth*). Could it be because of the gadget on the dryer?

OWNER (*looking daggers at her*). Of course not. The whole block is blacked out.

CUSTOMER I. What gadget?

OWNER (*trying to beat about the bush*). As you know, I always try to be up-to-date about new inventions and to offer my clients fully guaranteed products of the highest quality. The drier, the driers rather, are the most modern ones made in the United States. For that reason they can't be defective. We reject that possibility. But I wonder . . . (*She raises Lupita's chin and examines her face scrupulously, as if she wished to find some identifying sign.*) Could this whole series of mishaps be some kind of warning?

LUPITA (*trembling under the owner's inquisitive glance*). Warning of what?

OWNER. That your fiancé isn't right for you.

LUPITA (*as a conclusive argument*). But I don't have another one. And it was even hard to find him, to make him fall in love, to convince him to marry me. . . . All that just for you to tell me now that he won't work out.

HAIRDRESSER. You have to submit him to the test of fire: if he sees you with that stringy hair and he still insists on marrying you . . .

LUPITA. And if he doesn't insist?

CUSTOMER II. Marriage isn't eternal life. If you were to ask my advice, I'd tell you that . . .

HAIRDRESSER (*jumping for joy*). But why didn't we think of it? The solution is so very easy. (*To Lupita*) Why don't you wear a wig? Actually we have just received a lovely selection. And you can try them all on and choose the one you find is best.

LUPITA (*who, while the hairdresser goes to look for the recently discovered treasure, appears bewildered and not very convinced*). This getting married in a wig gives me a strange feeling. . . . It's as if I weren't a virgin.

CUSTOMER III. Being a virgin or not isn't important at all any more. I know an infallible method my grandmother gave me . . .

She begins to whisper in the bride's ear, while the Hairdresser begins bringing out the wigs—each one on its respective plastic head—so that they may be studied in all their splendor and appreciated in all their differences and in each of their details. Lupita looks at them without deciding. One must keep in mind that neither her humor nor the poor light helps her. Finally, she points to one at random.

LUPITA. This one.

HAIRDRESSER (*puts it on her while she praises it*). It's a very fine model, very elegant. It's called "The Life of a Single Woman."

The Hairdresser brings the light close to her so that the face of Lupita is well reflected in the mirror. What we are going to see is projected on a screen formed by the curtain at the back of the stage. The film shows a sad-looking and severe hairdo, a face without makeup and with puckered lips. In short, that severe, vaguely accusatory, and guilty expression of old maids. Simultaneously, a voice begins to recite a poem. While the text proceeds, the images follow one after the other. There is no exact correspondence between word and images, nor is the latter an illustration of the former. It should not be understood in that way, but as in "Hiroshima, Mon Amour,"[26] the film complements the written text: it does not duplicate it.

Text. THE LIFE OF A SINGLE WOMAN[27]

Being alone makes one ashamed. All day long
a terrible blush burns on her cheek.
(But the other cheek is eclipsed.)

The single woman strains at her ashy toil,
labor with neither merit nor fruit;
and at the hour when relatives gather
around the fire, when stories are told,
the scream is heard
of a woman's cry in a boundless desert
where every crest and every trunk
crumbled by forest fires, each twisted
branch, is a judge
or a witness without mercy.

At night the single woman
lies down on her bed of pain.

The anguished drops of sweat fall on humid sheets,
and the emptiness is peopled
with invented men and dialogues.

And the single woman waits, waits, waits.

She cannot be born in her child, in her flesh,
and she cannot die
in her body, remote and unexplored,
a planet the astronomer deems to exist
but which he has never seen.

Facing an opaque crystal, the single woman
—extinguished star—paints onto her lips
the blood she does not have.

Smiling at the solitary sunrise.

THE LIFE OF A SINGLE WOMAN

Images.

1. *A huge blackboard. Lupita, with her back turned, in a black suit, writes in a beautiful, clear, Palmer handwriting, the present tense conjugation of the verb "to love."*

I love	*We love*
You love	*You love*
He loves	*They love*

When she finishes she turns around to face a completely empty classroom.

2. *A secretary's office. Lupita types rapidly and precisely on a typewriter, copying from notes in shorthand. When she has finished she takes the paper out of the typewriter and tries to read it. Her eyes, that is, the lens of the movie camera, focus on a completely blank sheet of paper.*

3. *The interior of a hospital room. Lupita, a nurse, pushes one of those rolling tables for transporting medical instruments. Lupita stops next to a bed and begins to examine the instruments that will be used to treat the sick person. The delicacy of her movements is exquisite. But on the bed lies only a statue, beyond any kind of human help. Lupita puts the instruments back in their place and goes to sit down in a chair next to the window.*

4. *Lupita's face behind the pane of another window, opaque due to the dawn mist. With her hand Lupita cleans a part of the glass so that she can*

look outside. In the street, anonymous bicyclists, street sweepers, school buses still without children, and a pregnant woman with a shopping basket on her arm pass by. The view becomes misty again until it disappears completely, caused now not by the outside humidity but rather because of the onlooker's tears.

Darkness. Return to the beauty salon. Lupita hurries to take off the wig.

LUPITA. No, not this one. It looks horrible on me.

OWNER. But here in Mexico, it's used a lot.

LUPITA (*as though threatened*). It doesn't matter to me if it's been used a lot or not. The fact is that I'm not going to wear it.

HAIRDRESSER (*solicitous*). Perhaps this'll look better on you. It has a lovely name . . . although a bit daring. It's called "The Soiled Flower." [28]

CUSTOMER I. Oh, that one never goes out of style.

Darkness. A street. A lamp post. Lupita, all painted-up and in a prostitute's outfit, leans against the light post in a highly conventional posture of waiting. She smokes. She walks, swinging affectedly her hips and shoulders, like the fighters who shadowbox before encountering their real adversary. She returns to her place. Suddenly Cinturita[29] appears, also in his respective (pimp's) costume. Far away is heard, with perfect clarity, a poet-musician, coughing out one of his great creations.

Sell your love dearly, adventuress.
Give your past the wages of sorrow;
and he who your honeyed mouth would kiss
should pay with diamonds for your sin-n-n.

CINTURITA (*approaches, deviously, his prey*). Good evening, Señorita. Could you do me the favor of telling me the time?

LUPITA (*inexperienced*). Excuse me, young man, but I don't have a watch.

CINTURITA. You haven't been able to buy a watch or did they steal it from you already? Lady, Lady, no matter how much one hurries, one always runs the risk of arriving too late.

LUPITA. Too late for what?

CINTURITA. To protect you. How can you be so foolish? Walking around at this hour of the night, and in this neighborhood . . . Anyone could make a mistake and take you for something that you aren't.

LUPITA. But I *am*. I have my Health Department license and everything.

CINTURITA. I mean . . . make the mistake of thinking that you're a student, a secretary, the daughter of a good family. Not everyone has the expert eye that I have.

LUPITA. And supposing they make a mistake, so what?

CINTURITA. So what? They can rob you of your watch . . . or of whatever you have on you. Women, as you know from experience, should never walk around alone, but, on the contrary, always under a man's protective arm. And you, why would you run under the horses' hooves when right here you have your very own fancy man?

Cinturita tries to embrace the novice without noticing that another prostitute has been observing the scene and is gradually and threateningly approaching the two of them.

PROSTITUTE (*to Cinturita*). Whose very own fancy man?

CINTURITA (*rudely*). Get out of here, you old slut. Don't you see that I'm hustling trade?

PROSTITUTE (*without letting herself be impressed by the technical term*). The only thing that I see is that some hustling hussy has come to stand under *my* lamppost and has started making a play for *my* man.

LUPITA (*cocky*). The street belongs to everyone.

PROSTITUTE. You're wrong, little girl. The street belongs to whoever works it, as someone said. So wing it out of here, right now, and shed your lice somewhere else.

LUPITA (*defiant*). What? So you can say that stupid dame went away? No way. I'm staying here. We'll see who can make me go.

PROSTITUTE. Well, don't keep me waiting. Come on, put 'em up.

Both roll up their sleeves, spit on their hands, and get ready to fight like hornets. Lupita, from the beginning, adopts a defensive attitude. The other, violent, is forcibly held back by Cinturita.

PROSTITUTE. Let me go, you louse. Don't you see how angry I am? (*Truculently*) I can taste the blood in my mouth! My hands are going to bury you.

LUPITA. Oh, who's scared? Come on you, just try it.

CINTURITA (*with an authoritarian voice that paralyzes the two of them*). Just a minute! Who gives the orders around here?

PROSTITUTE (*letting her hands fall in a resigned way*). No need to ask that. Everyone knows you do.

CINTURITA. Then, why are you going off half-cocked if you've got nowhere to go?

LUPITA (*to Cinturita*). You're the witness. She started it all. I was here, easy and quietlike, without bothering anyone, because there wasn't any reason to, when this woman jumped on me like a half-sister to a stick of dynamite.

PROSTITUTE. This woman has a name, in case you didn't know.

LUPITA. But I'd better not say it because you'll say I'm trying to provoke you.

PROSTITUTE. Oh, yes, so innocent. If I jump, it's because I'm stepped on. (*To Cinturita, as if he were the one who has to decide*) You're a witness: that woman was trying to swindle me out of my rights.

LUPITA. And what do I know about your rights? Maybe that lamppost has a sign saying that it's the private property of the whoringest bitch of the whores in this neck of the woods?

The prostitute again becomes infuriated and Cinturita again restrains her.

PROSTITUTE (*surrendering*). Bah! (*To Cinturita*) You explain it to her, because I don't know if she's dumb or if she's just pretending to be.

CINTURITA (*to Lupita*). You know how this business works?

LUPITA. Well, not completely, since I'm new at this.

PROSTITUTE. Har, har, har. (*Singing*) "Kind sir, I cannot—give you my love—for I am a virgin—among the flowers." Go on. Go on. Tell me another one.

CINTURITA (*to the Prostitute*). Shut up. (*To Lupita*) Well, if you don't know, all the more reason to teach you. Pay attention: the streets are divided into districts. In each district there's a group of women working. Each group's radius of action (*he takes out a map, which is projected on the screen at the back of the stage, identical to those used to chart war plans*) is completely determined. The units are movable, of course; they can advance, retreat, head for one flank or the other, according to tactical necessities. But what they can't ever do, under any circumstances, is to invade another's district.

LUPITA (*open-mouthed*). It's really complicated! And who watches that things happen by the book?

CINTURITA. In this district, I do. From the moment when we are open for business—and we're more punctual than a bullfight and more trustworthy than the lottery—I walk around patrolling, making sure that there won't be any difficulties or misunderstandings like between you two a while ago. And I have an eagle eye. You saw it: you hadn't even finished leaning up against the lamppost . . .

PROSTITUTE. Against my lamppost.

CINTURITA. . . . when I approached you. And just in case, in order not to insult you, I asked you a very decent question. By the way, it's not good for you to be walking around without a watch.

LUPITA. Why?

PROSTITUTE (*laughing loudly*). They brought this one down from the hills with the drums beating. She doesn't know anything. Why? Har, har.

CINTURITA (*patiently*). Because we set and we collect the price depending on the time.

LUPITA. We set and we collect? Sounds like a lot of people to me. Who is "we"?

CINTURITA. You and I.

PROSTITUTE. And me, too. Or am I some policeman's daughter for you to treat me like a nobody, just like that?

CINTURITA. You two aren't the only ones. (*To the Prostitute*) Don't you get any ideas or give any to your partner here.

PROSTITUTE. No, we already know that nobody but you calls the tune and whoever doesn't want to step to it can go to . . . and stay there.

LUPITA. So the man is very popular.

CINTURITA. What happens is that everybody has their own personality. Besides I am always on guard, but I never get rough. If I do a good job, why shouldn't I earn a good salary?

LUPITA. Just for watching?

CINTURITA. And also for protecting. If I hadn't been here when she attacked you, you'd be making your peace with Saint Peter right now.

LUPITA (*aggressively*). She's not so hot at the ol' one-two! And don't think that I'm one-armed either!

CINTURITA (*professionally*). It's easy to see that you're not. You lack nothing, as they say, nothing.

LUPITA. I don't look too bad for a native product, do I?

CINTURITA. For just that reason you have to be careful and not go around exposing yourself to slaps in the face by getting into a tight corner.

LUPITA. In that case, I already owe you a favor.

CINTURITA. Let's just say it's a free sample. If you like the product, buy it.

LUPITA. And if not?

CINTURITA. You have to go to another territory . . . organized exactly like this one. And what would the advantage be? The competition is the same, the guardsman in charge has the same functions and requires the same pay. We take care of the thinking. For you, the act of going from one district to another . . .

LUPITA. . . . like butterflies from flower to flower . . .

CINTURITA. Doesn't look good at all. Not at all. You get a bad reputation; they think you're an undisciplined worker . . .

PROSTITUTE. . . . unruly . . .

CINTURITA. . . . and we act accordingly. If you don't understand with good treatment, we tighten the screws. And if you don't understand with bad treatment (*he makes the sign of cutting a throat*), kaput!

PROSTITUTE. Go on, stop reading me the riot act.

LUPITA. So, as one could say, with my first step in this territory, I made my choice. Here I am and here I'm staying.

PROSTITUTE. Not *here*. *I'm* the one who works here.

CINTURITA (*to Lupita*). We'll look for a place for you now. Don't worry. But remember this, whatever the place is like we designate for you, you have to know the basic rules of the game. Here's a manual for you. (*Cinturita hands a little book over to her.*) Read it, study it, learn it by heart, because it's going to be very useful for you.

LUPITA (*flipping through it*). And if there's something that I don't understand?

CINTURITA. Consult me. Or you discuss it with some of your colleagues. (*Looking at his watch*) There's no more time to lose. I have to continue my rounds. (*To the Prostitute*) I leave her in your charge. Watch that she doesn't put her foot in it.

PROSTITUTE (*rancorous*). If I were any good as a nursemaid, I'd be in a palace. And not here, day and night. (*Cinturita disappears without paying any attention; the Prostitute resigns herself and holds out her hand to Lupita.*) Buddies, okay? From here to eternity, with a stop at the hospital on the way.

LUPITA. As you say. As far as I'm concerned, no hard feelings.

PROSTITUTE. Put it there. Listen, how did you wind up doing this?

LUPITA (*unworried*). Just for fun. Ever since I was a little girl, I have always liked to paint the town red, and once I no longer had my father's respect, I struck while the iron was hot and I said to myself, now you're leaving.

PROSTITUTE (*looking at her suspiciously and, upon convincing herself of her sincerity, looking all around to make sure no one has been listening*). Shhh, shut up! Never say that.

LUPITA. Why not?

PROSTITUTE. Because you discourage the clientele. The john, hammer this into your head, is an enemy. And what he likes to think is that he's screwing you over. You're wretched, so unhappy that you don't even notice if he's virile or not. You're so miserable that, even if he's a miserable bastard, you're the one who's pitiful, not him. And who's going to believe in your disgrace if you didn't fall against your will?

LUPITA. Okay. Who pushed me into it?

PROSTITUTE. That's the least important part: your boyfriend who stood you up, all decked out and flustered. Your father, who died and left you an orphan, with a swarm of younger brothers and sisters to support. And poverty. The incurably ill relative who has to be kept in the hospital. Your little sister who boards at a school run by nuns and who knows nothing of your life—the evil life you lead in order to protect her purity. Lower yourself. Don't be afraid. The more you show your misery, your impure life, the more they'll pay you.

LUPITA. Or the more they'll hit me.

PROSTITUTE. That, too. But that's a very expensive fancy.

LUPITA. What I fail to understand is how the johns can be such suckers to think that somebody winds up here because there's no other way. What about other jobs?

PROSTITUTE. You tried them all and they didn't turn out well for you. Bosses paid your salary late, badly, or never. Bosses grabbed you behind doors. Sons of good families only wanted to screw you. On the other hand, here, here . . . Here, my girl, you collect in advance. Because then if they come out with the story that they forgot their billfold in their other pants . . . or that this was the first time, which is like crossing yourself—it brings you good luck . . .

LUPITA. And isn't it true?

PROSTITUTE. Certainly not, dummy. Or afterward they get you to swallow some lie like "they're trying you out" to see if they'll redeem you and marry you . . . and that they're going to buy you diamonds . . . and that . . .

While the two women talk, they are moving away. The light from the lamp goes out and we return to the beauty salon, where a disgusted Lupita takes off the wig.

LUPITA. But how vulgar! How . . . what's the word?

OWNER. But it fit as though made especially for you.

HAIRDRESSER. How many wouldn't even dream of being able to wear it!

LUPITA. But not me. All those piled-up curls, made like a beehive . . .

OWNER. You're not going to deny that the curls are lovely?

LUPITA. But you can't distinguish one from the other. I'd like a simpler wig, not that pelt of some Blackamoor.

HAIRDRESSER. Now, I understand what you want. Something very simple. A single curl, but well done, to make your fine features stand out.

LUPITA. My God! Is this blackout never going to end?

OWNER. What does it matter now if it ends or not. There's no way that we'd have time to do your hair. You'll have to brave it with a wig.

LUPITA. What bad luck! All these misfortunes on the very day of my wedding.

OWNER. It's a day like any other.

LUPITA. No, it's not a day like any other, not in the least. It's a special, a unique day.

OWNER. That depends. But don't go around blabbing about it, because we aren't to blame. My salon is listed in tourist guidebooks, recommended for foreigners who pay in dollars, and is recognized as first class. If the lights go out, it's the government's fault. We were so well off before the electric company was nationalized. But everyone knows it: whenever the government expropriates or buys something, it's because it doesn't work any more.

LUPITA (*following her own train of thought*). Could it be a kind of warning, an omen?

OWNER. Not at all. Business, purely business. Things arranged between the front men, on the one hand, and Mexican traitors, on the other. (*A little uncomfortable because of the seriousness of such words, she hurries to add*) That's what my brother-in-law says.

LUPITA (*in horror*). Because, maybe it's God's will that I stay single.

CUSTOMER 1. Between dressing saints or undressing drunks, neither one nor the other is the way to go.

OWNER. . . . and my brother-in-law is an authority on political matters. Ever since they fired him from his job as customs inspector because of office politics.

LUPITA. It can't be! It can't be! (*To the Hairdresser*) Miss, hurry up.

HAIRDRESSER. Here it is. (*She shows her the wig.*) How does that look?

LUPITA (*doubtful*). Well, it's pretty . . . but let's see how it looks on me.

OWNER. It's a very traditional, discreet model. It's called "The Usurper."

Darkness. A bedroom is suggested, dark also, in which the voice of Lupita is heard issuing from a tape recorder.

LUPITA. Miss Lonely Hearts: will you dare to publish this letter in your column? Because it isn't asking for advice, it's a declaration of principles: love, yes, love, is the only thing for which life is worth living.

Many women know it intuitively, with the sixth sense that nature gave them. But they prefer to obey the conventions of a hypocritical, plainly hypocritical society, caring only for appearances. There are others who, coming very close to love, haven't known how to recognize it because selfishness and fear blind them. Others, poor things, never saw their lives illuminated by that ray of sunlight; creatures who withered, like the blighted rosebush, without ever flowering. The first have my scorn; the last have my compassion. Because I, Miss Lonely Hearts, have been one of those chosen by Cupid, the god of Love. I knew love and, as our immortal musician-poet says . . . "It's very beautiful!"

He and I met because destiny would have it so. He thought he was already in the sunset of life. "The snows of time had whitened his temples." I was in the fullness of my springtime and I was his secretary. I guessed that behind those stern features, behind that executive's desk, lay a secret heartache. His wife didn't understand him. He who had sacrificed his youth and his happiness to repay, like a gentleman, a debt of honor. She, his wife, wore, with a shamelessness without limits, a white dress made of guipure lace, which her inconstancy had already blemished, a corsage of artificial orange blossoms, which her passion had already stained red. He accepted that mockery of virtue's sacred emblems in order not to humiliate her, she who had sinned. He did it, in short, in order not to ruin the ceremony. And the wedding ring was the first link in the chain restricting his freedom, he who had always flown, light as a bird.

When he and I met, he had already renounced any hope in living. He was vegetating. But love, our love, imparted a new impetus to his soul, new dreams to his future, new directions to his horizon. He opened various branch offices of his business, and the man who had forgotten how to smile, smiled again when he learned that I returned—with interest—his feelings.

Pigmylike humanity! How many obstacles they tried to place between us. My parents disowned me, my friends turned their backs on me or asked me for my secret, my superiors made lewd proposals to me.

But I always held my head very high before them all. Sinner? No. In love. And it was love that led me . . .

Still in darkness another voice is heard, irritated and real, which says:

MAID: The cow is in the corn again. (*She trips against something.*) Oh!

The tape recorder falls. The maid turns on the light. We see the details of the bedroom now. Lupita is stretched out on her stomach on a double bed, snoring. The maid approaches and, without hesitation, shakes her to wake her up.

MAID. Señora!

LUPITA (*turning over furiously*). Leave me in peace! Can't you see that I'm sleeping? Don't I even have the right to do that?

MAID. Sleeping with the tape recorder playing.

LUPITA. I need to hear someone's voice. I'm afraid to sleep alone. Always, ever since I was a little girl. And you go up to your top room without even thinking of me.

MAID (*trying to put some order in the chaos*). Everybody has her place, Señora. What would your gentleman say if he were to arrive suddenly and find me down here?

LUPITA (*bitterly*). He never arrives suddenly. Only on the regular days.

MAID. Today is one of his regular days.

LUPITA (*recuperating, immediately, her lucidity*). Today? What day is today? Wednesday?

MAID. Wednesday.

LUPITA. And what time is it? Why didn't you wake me up earlier? He's going to come and find me like this, looking a fright, no hairdo, in my robe and house slippers . . .

MAID. Just exactly like his wife.

LUPITA. Fix my bath, go on. Hurry up! Put bath salts in the water. I want my whole body to smell good, like a flower.

The maid hides a mocking smile and disappears. The sound of the water filling the tub is heard. Lupita inspects herself in the mirror.

LUPITA. My manicure is still good; it'll do. But as for my hair . . . (*Shouting to the Maid*) What do you think I should put on?

MAID. Whatever is the most difficult to take off.

LUPITA (*laughing*). Why?

MAID. So that he can dream that he's subjecting you to his will, that he's forcing you.

LUPITA. Where did you learn so many tricks?

MAID. I have worked for other women, in other love nests. You yourself read my letters of recommendation.

LUPITA. Yes. And your mistresses seemed to like you very much. Why did they leave you or why did you leave them?

MAID. They didn't leave me and I didn't leave them. The work ended.

LUPITA (*petrified*). What?

MAID. The love nests were closed down.

LUPITA. But that can't be. Did the man stop coming?

MAID. Little by little, not suddenly. First the visits were farther and farther apart.

LUPITA. And shorter. He had to work, he had family obligations . . .

MAID. And I, what do I know? No one explained anything to me. I only saw that he would come in and leave again as fast as lightning. Sometimes he didn't even have time to go up to see the lady and he would leave the expense money with me.

LUPITA. And the women?

MAID. It gave the ladies quite a turn, as is to be expected.

LUPITA. And didn't they do anything?

MAID. What?

LUPITA. Talk to him on the telephone . . .

MAID (*realistic*). How would they dare? They were absolutely forbidden.

LUPITA. And the next time, when they were with their lover, didn't they complain?

MAID. Well, that depends. If the lady was in a hurry for it to end (perhaps she had already found another gentleman) . . .

LUPITA. What do you mean, another? But if he's the only one?

MAID. The only one. While it lasts. I'm going to see if the bathtub is full. (*She leaves.*)

LUPITA (*anguished*). That can't happen to me. Ours is true love. I've given up everything for him. I've consented to live in isolation, like a leper, in order not to disgrace his name. I've never asked him to take me out, nor to show me off in public. Each time that I've gotten pregnant, I've managed to get an abortion. Without even saying anything to him, so that he wouldn't feel guilty or disgusted. Without asking him for money for the procedure, but squirreling it out of what he gives me. And whenever he comes, he finds me dressed up and happy. Whenever he comes . . . (*To the Maid*) Do you remember how it was at first? He came every day. . . .

MAID. Oh, yes, what a mess! I had a heap of work: three meals, the dirty sheets . . .

LUPITA. You never protested.

MAID. It wasn't worth the while to complain. I knew that it wasn't going to last. Like all of them. The bed's brief spark.

LUPITA. Then he began to come every other day.

MAID. I can tell you, Señora. Each and every one of them are the same.

LUPITA. And now he only grants me Wednesdays. Because on Saturday he has to take his wife to dinner and to the theater.

MAID. Don't envy her, Señora; for her, poor woman, everything goes just about like it goes with you. Or worse. Cooking, washing, dusting, fighting with the children the whole week long. That even I wouldn't do.

LUPITA. And Sundays he has to go to mass and to eat dinner with the family.

MAID. He has to fulfill his obligations.

LUPITA. And Monday is the weekly executives' meeting; Tuesday, dinner at his club.

MAID. And Wednesdays are your turn. As it should be.

LUPITA. Not at all as it should be. Why not Thursdays and Fridays? Let's see you explain that to me. Why not?

MAID. Perhaps they are changeable holidays (so the date changes).

LUPITA. But why didn't I think of it? He has a new secretary, did you know that? But, truly, I swear by my mother who died of the sorrow of seeing me dishonored, that if he's cheating on me, I'll kill him. I'll kill him. I'll kill him.

Telephone. The two women look at the telephone, which keeps on ringing. Finally, the maid picks up the receiver.

MAID. Hello. Yes. Yes. Here she is right now. (*Covering the receiver with her hand and giving the telephone to Lupita*) It's him.

LUPITA (*she takes the telephone with a kind of reverence and fear and makes signs to the maid to leave*). Yes, my darling, yes, it's me. (*A long silence during which Lupita's face goes from an expression of painful surprise to disillusionment and the effort to hide her anger.*) Yes, of course. They arrived suddenly. No, no. How can I be angry? Sad, yes, because I love you. But it makes me happy to know that you're happy. No, no, don't worry. You know that I never get bored. There's always something to do in the house. Until . . . until when, then? Until next Wednesday? It's like a century for me. But, no, don't be upset. When we see each other again, it'll be like a honeymoon. (*Tense silence.*) Forgive me. I know you don't like me to say things like that . . . but . . . (*She continues looking at the telephone, from which is heard distinctly the "click" that cuts off communication.*)

The maid enters, on tiptoe, as though it were a wake.

LUPITA (*showing the receiver as proof of her innocence; with tears in her voice*). Did you see that? That louse left me with the words in my mouth.

MAID. His wife must have been prowling nearby.

LUPITA (*who still cannot believe it*). He cut me off! He hung up on me!

MAID. Don't take it that way. His heart is going to bleed, as they say in my part of the country.

LUPITA. The wife. She can never call herself anything else. On the other hand, I'm the lover. And the lover is loved.

MAID. The word itself says so.

LUPITA (*dejected*). Do you know what? I guess I don't feel like a bath any more.

MAID. That's wasteful; God will punish you for it. The water smells glorious!

LUPITA. You use it.

MAID (*incredulous and happy*). Really, Señora? Truly?

LUPITA. Certainly. It'll benefit you more than it will me. You have a boyfriend, don't you?

MAID. We don't say it like that, but it comes down to the same thing. Oh, and how nice! Because he was already asking me about it. And your bubble bath, he was saying to me. Be calm, I answered him. Soon it'll be time. And just what I told him is happening. The time has come.

LUPITA (*vulgar*). Well, make it snappy, it's hot stuff. You were with me in the stormy weather and now you'll enjoy the sunshine. Oh, before getting into the bathtub, bring me a bottle of cognac and a glass.

MAID. That's not good, Señora.

LUPITA. Why not? I'm going to toast to pleasure, love, and life, like a bohemian.

MAID. It isn't good to get used to cognac, Señora. Because afterward there isn't going to be any. Why not begin right now with tequila?

LUPITA. And, in addition, I'll be patriotic, consuming what the country produces. Bring anything, but quickly.

When the maid goes to carry out the order, Lupita closes the curtains, turns off the light, and connects the tape recorder again.

VOICE. Miss Lonely Hearts, will you dare to publish this letter in your column?

Silence. The light comes back on to illuminate the beauty salon.

LUPITA (*taking off the wig*). Ah, no, definitely no.

OWNER. It suits you so well, you look so romantic, so sad . . .

LUPITA. But, no, it's not what I want. Something more original, less common.

HAIRDRESSER. How does this one look to you? It's new. They've just been put on the market. We haven't sold a single one yet.

LUPITA (*taking the wig and reading the label*). "Woman of Action." Hmmm. The name isn't very attractive.

OWNER. But try it on. You can't lose anything by trying it on.

LUPITA. Except time . . .

Darkness. Then, under a spotlight, Lupita is dressed as a reporter, active, energetic, enterprising, and audacious. Among her job equipment are papers and a tape recorder. She reads her instructions aloud.

LUPITA. Interview . . . (*she skips the names*). Emphasize the person's human side. Point out her exemplary private life. Don't mention her religious beliefs, even if she's Catholic, or discuss her political ideology, even if she belongs to the PRI.[30] Any text will be subject, before publication, to revision and correction by the newspaper's Editor-in-Chief. The company doesn't pay for anything but approved and published articles. Okay, okay. I understand already. (*Opening an envelope*) What's this? Oh, the invitation to the annual banquet celebrating freedom of the press. The cost is enough to make you drop dead. Well, I'd better conform. No other way.

Darkness. Another spotlight. Lupita faces the Celebrity she is interviewing. Both are seated. Lupita prepares the tape recorder for use. The Celebrity is reclining against the back of the chair and she gropes without looking for her husband's hand. He is also her bodyguard, her manager, her chief of public relations, her oracle, her administrator, etc.

LUPITA (*ready*). Would you give me your name, please?

CELEBRITY (*offended*). Well . . . that's very curious. I thought that you already knew it.

LUPITA. Why should I have known it?

CELEBRITY. Well . . . because I'm famous.

LUPITA. And who made you famous?

HUSBAND (*conciliatory, to the Celebrity*). Don't argue with the fourth estate, dear. My wife is Lucrecia Galindo.

LUPITA (*occupied in watching the functioning of her tape recorder and in noting on her pad the most revealing details of the surroundings, she does not glance at either of her interlocutors; thus, she does not see the Celebrity's expression when she throws out her second question*). And what do you do?

LUCRECIA. That really is the limit!

HUSBAND (*rubbing her back, like one rubs a cat, to calm her down; to Lupita*). She is a piano virtuoso and she's just won an international competition in Moscow.

LUPITA. No, that can't be.

LUCRECIA. Why not? I have the certificate right here . . . (*She tries to get up to show it, but her husband stops her.*)

HUSBAND (*to Lupita*). Do you doubt our truthfulness?

LUPITA. It doesn't matter to me if it's true or not. What can't be in the article is Moscow. Do you understand?

It is obvious that the Celebrity does not understand anything, but that her husband is more objective and more intelligent.

HUSBAND. Well, what difference does it make if it's one place or another? Moscow or Washington makes no difference to the readers.

LUCRECIA (*stubborn*). But the certificate . . .

LUPITA. And what was the prize? Money?

HUSBAND. It's a scholarship to study in the conservatory of . . . By God, I was on the point of committing an indiscretion and revealing something that ought to be a secret. It's not worthwhile to enter into details.

LUPITA. Does the Scala of Milan seem all right? It's neutral.

HUSBAND. As you wish.

LUPITA. You are married, naturally?

LUCRECIA. By both the religious and civil ceremony.

HUSBAND. By all three ceremonies. (*With a vague hope that Lupita will know to what he is referring*) You know that joke, don't you?

LUPITA. Ha, ha. And you, sir, have you ever opposed your wife's career?

HUSBAND (*magnanimous*). On the contrary. I try to support her in every way I can. Isn't that true, Dear?

LUCRECIA. If it weren't for him . . . He gives me counsel; he guides me; he directs me; he manages me. Not even the bank account is in my name!

LUPITA. How romantic!

HUSBAND. And in those moments when an artist loses hope and courage, my wife always finds in me a stimulus to continue struggling.

LUPITA. Do you have children?

LUCRECIA. No.

LUPITA. Would it be a disadvantage for your wife's career? Have you avoided it?

HUSBAND. By no means. God has not seen fit to bless our union.

LUCRECIA (*to her husband*). But you promised me that upon ending this tour, we could . . .

HUSBAND (*squeezing her shoulder fiercely so that she will be silent*). The young lady is discreet, like all reporters, but we don't have to discuss, in her presence, our intimate relations.

LUPITA (*matter-of-fact*). Any anecdotes?

LUCRECIA (*consulting her supreme authority, her husband*). Shall I tell her how I met you?

Darkness. Another spotlight illuminates Lupita, with her tape recorder and her shorthand pad, before a desk. Behind it is a female public official.

LUPITA. As I understand, you're the first woman in the history of Mexico to fill the office of State Governor. How do you feel about this triumph?

PUBLIC OFFICIAL. I consider it my Party's triumph. Its democratic methods, its dynamism, its capacity to interpret the thoughts of the people and to satisfy their needs . . .

LUPITA. Just a minute! I don't want speeches. I want you to talk to me about yourself. Why did you declare yourself a candidate?

PUBLIC OFFICIAL. Out of loyalty to the Party.

LUPITA. Didn't you aspire to this post?

PUBLIC OFFICIAL. My only desire has been, always, to serve my country. In whatever trench they assign me. No post is insignificant when one has the will to help. And the higher one reaches, one acquires greater responsibilities, not greater privileges.

LUPITA (*undaunted by this rhetorical display*). Whatever made you decide to throw your hat in the ring?

PUBLIC OFFICIAL. I won a speech contest in my prep school. They invited me to speak in the Youth Court. In those days the presidential candidacy of the honorable Doctor . . . was about to begin.

LUPITA. Let's not go back to prehistoric times. Do you think that being a woman has been an obstacle in your career?

PUBLIC OFFICIAL. Why would it have to be? The Constitution guarantees equality before the law to all Mexicans, without sexual, religious, racial, or age discrimination . . .

LUPITA (*cutting her off*). Are you married?

PUBLIC OFFICIAL (*rigid*). No, I am single.

LUPITA. Do you believe that success has made you less feminine?

PUBLIC OFFICIAL. Not in the least. Each time the Party gives me some freedom, I run to spend time in the kitchen. I make some chilies in nut sauce that make you lick your fingers. If you wish, I'll give you the recipe.

LUPITA. No, thank you. What's your favorite color?

PUBLIC OFFICIAL. How can I choose from among green, white, and red, the colors of our flag? The three are lovely. All three.

LUPITA. What is your political platform?

PUBLIC OFFICIAL. It's my Party's platform: to protect the farmer and the worker, to stimulate the development of industry, to clean up public administration . . .

LUPITA. Etcetera. In your particular case, add nurseries, rural social centers, and all that. Good. To finish up, any anecdotes?

PUBLIC OFFICIAL (*as though caught off guard*). Of course . . . well, you see . . . (*After a moment of doubt, she decides to ask*) What is an anecdote?

Darkness. A spotlight shows a dusty old sofa. Cats. Lupita, her tape recorder, and her pad. A woman more than middle-aged, a little bit senile.

LUPITA. Señora . . .

ASTRONOMER. Señorita . . . although it's a bit more bother to say.

LUPITA. In any case, it was certainly up to you to bother or not.

ASTRONOMER (*putting her hand behind her ear*). What did you say?

LUPITA (*shouting*). I asked if it's true that you have discovered a new star?

ASTRONOMER. Oh, yes, certainly. I named it Amparo, in memory of my sweet mother, may she rest in peace.

LUPITA. And how did it happen?

ASTRONOMER. Well, the poor woman had been suffering from rheumatism for a long time. And she never complained . . .

LUPITA. I mean, the discovery of the star.

ASTRONOMER. Oh, well, it was pure chance. I was like a tortilla in the frying pan, as they say, because these blessed cats wouldn't let me sleep with their caterwauling. So I jumped up and I said to myself: let's take a glance through the telescope. And I did. And what did I discover but Amparo, very obvious, very tranquil, as though waiting for someone to discover her. What do you think of that?

LUPITA. And how did you happen to have a telescope?

ASTRONOMER. I inherited it from my daddy, may he rest in peace. He taught me how to distinguish between the constellations, to name them all. Since back then there wasn't any television, we didn't have much to entertain ourselves with.

LUPITA. And did you like astronomy?

ASTRONOMER. Well, do I like it? Why should I lie to you? No. But my dear daddy was so good and so determined that I didn't have the heart to go against his wishes. He was so good . . . Do you know what the first gift he gave me was? I was still a baby. He gave me an abacus, so I could learn to count. And then after that: multiplication tables, logarithms . . . Since he had to stay in bed because of his infirmities, we amused ourselves a lot of the time with numbers.

LUPITA. And when he died . . .

ASTRONOMER. The government decreed that this house was the property of the nation, who knows why. Something like a museum. And no matter whether we liked it or not, we had to reconcile ourselves to it, my mommy and I.

LUPITA. And do you have any more family?

ASTRONOMER. No. I was an only child. For that reason my daddy wanted me to receive the best education, by the best teachers available then. Although you wouldn't believe it: just as you see me, I know how to play the piano, to embroider, to paint in water colors. I never learned how to do that blessed leathercraft, though.

LUPITA. Don't worry. It's no longer in fashion.

ASTRONOMER. Just like everything else. Look how much commotion there is over my Amparo now. Tomorrow, nobody will remember. The ways of the world are so changeable.

LUPITA. But while the run of luck lasts, one must take advantage of it, right?

ASTRONOMER (*hopefully*). Do you think that, with this hubbub over the discovery of Amparo, they'll approve a budget for repairs to the roof of the house? There are so many leaks that during the rainy season I don't know where to go.

LUPITA (*mechanically*). Let's hope so. Any anecdotes?

ASTRONOMER. Oh, so many. Look, this little pussy cat who looks so serious and proper, well, you aren't going to believe it but one night . . .

The voice, the light, and the persons vanish slowly, and we return again to the beauty salon.

OWNER (*seeing the signs of Lupita's opinion about the wig*). No?

LUPITA. No. (*She tries to excuse herself, but that does not stop her from returning the wig.*) It suits me like two pistols would suit Christ.

HAIRDRESSER. Let's not argue any more. Here you have our latest model.

OWNER. And it is, truly, the last.

HAIRDRESSER. It's called "At the Edge of the Storm."

Darkness. The light is going to illuminate now one of those mixtures of parlor and classroom, so frequent among the ladies of the Mexican bourgeoisie who have just discovered that culture is an adornment and who dedicate to culture, if not their most arduous efforts, at least their best hours. On this occasion, the group is very select, which means very small. They chatter with great gusto during the interval between classes.

LADY I (*doubtful*). I don't know if I should stay or go. I have a date at the Golf Club.

LADY II. How do you pronounce *Club*? Like in English, French, or Spanish?

LADY III. Aw, you, it's not important, even if the word were *chocolate*.

Lupita enters, dressed soberly and elegantly. It is obvious that she has an academic degree but that it has made her more conscious of her femininity, more careful of her appearance. For example: she is near-sighted. It is not a misfortune; it is an opportunity to use spectacles designed in a way to make her appear mysterious, not intelligent; attractive, not capable. She moves with great sureness and efficiency, but, in each sure and efficient movement, she lets it be understood that she is ready to abdicate her independence at the first convenient opportunity. And to abdicate means to follow the example of her mother or her mother-in-law.

LUPITA (*sits down before the teacher's table, places her briefcase and her papers in a convenient manner, and, when she has finished, rings the little bell to impose silence*). Señoras, remember that, from this moment on, there'll be a fine levied against anyone who talks about her husband, children, or recipes.

LADY I. Can one talk about maids?

LUPITA (*with a sense of humor that her students appreciate and laugh about each time she shows it*). About maids, yes, because that is a serious subject.

There is a pause during which some students get ready to take notes in their notebooks and others start their tape recorders. This permits them not to pay attention; but they give the excuse that, later, they will listen to the recordings in their husbands' company. In this manner, the ones who have gained high administrative posts or who are rich and have influence can play their role with self-confidence in any social gathering, since they are knowledgeable about the themes that are discussed and can give their opinion, on divine and human subjects, without excessive risk that they will put their foot in their mouth. Or, to know, with certainty, when it is necessary to refrain from giving an opinion.

LUPITA (*doctoral*). Señoras, on this occasion we are going to put off the theme that until now we have been developing, that is, "The Function of the Pedestal in the Colonial Architecture of New Spain," to touch on another subject that, although it isn't as important, is more urgent. First, I want to ask you a question: are you aware of what's happening, with the authorities' knowledge and forbearance? Did you know that our most revered traditions, our dearest symbols, are being mocked in a theater in the capital?

LADY II (*to her neighbor*). Who are they ridiculing?

LUPITA. They're ridiculing one who is a pillar of our society, one who transmits the values that are sustaining us for future generations; they are ridiculing the Mexican woman.

LADY II. What woman?

LUPITA. I should say, "woman in the abstract." But the attack is specific and is directed against mothers' selflessness, against wives' virtue, against brides' chastity, that is, against our proverbial attributes, the attributes that form the base of our most solid institutions: family, church, and country.

LADY IV. It can't be important if it hasn't been prohibited by the censor.

LUPITA: Because, since we are a democratic country, we respect freedom of expression. But *that* isn't freedom, it's licentiousness.

Excited voices, curious now, with their interest aroused.

LADY I. Where is it?

LADY II. I couldn't hear well, but I think in the theater.

LADY III (*to Lupita*). What is the name of the work?

LUPITA. It's called *The Eternal Feminine*. Let's not pay any attention to the title's lack of originality; it's merely a commonplace, plagiarized literally from Goethe. Let's not consider it from the critical point of view, because we'd have to condemn the arbitrariness of its progression, the unrealistic situations, the utter inconsistency of its characters. Those are technical problems of the dramatic structure, which do not concern us, neither do the hodgepodge of genres or the abuse of untheatrical tactics, nor, above all, the language, which, when it isn't vulgar, tries to be ingenuous or lyrical and doesn't reach the level of anything but pretentiousness. There's something else that we won't take into account either, at this moment: the manner in which she treats our history. The author, obviously, doesn't know it. Because she's ignorant of it, she's incapable of interpreting it, and, as if such a thing were acceptable, she invents it. And her invention always tends to degrade us and to make us look ridiculous. But she's just spitting into the wind.

LADY III. What's the author's name?

LUPITA. Oh, you've put your finger on it. The person responsible for this monstrosity isn't, as logic decrees, an author, a man. No. It's . . . let me put it this way so as not to sin against Christian charity . . . it's a woman. If this term can be applied to someone lacking decorum and scruples and who rejects the mission which nature has given her, to be the dove for the nest. But neither does she transform herself into a lion for combat. Her cowardice comes out into the open when she takes advantage of being out of the country and, on thinking herself to be beyond good and evil, out of the reach of the critics, safe from reprisals of decent people, she casts her stone.[31] And she doesn't even take the trouble of hiding the hand she threw it with.

CHORUS OF LADIES (*rhythmically*). Names! Names!

LUPITA. Her name . . . it's not that I want to hide, I'm just sure that it won't mean anything to you. The author of the poor mulligan stew is Rosario Castellanos.

LADY I. But that can't be! *Paths of Emotion* is a lovely work and very edifying.

LADY II. Well, now you can see that she's pulled a switch on us. It's like my husband says: this world is full of turncoats.

LUPITA (*severely*). Señoras, do me the favor of not confusing a writer worthy of all our respect, a lady—as was Rosario Sansores until the last seconds of her life—with a . . . well. Let's not try to classify her at all, because, after all, what we're talking about is really unmentionable. But I want to appeal to the pious sentiments of each of you. That . . . "woman" deserves our scorn. But let's not give her the gift of our pity, keeping in mind that she is a pitiful, resentful woman, envious and bitter.

LADY I (*as though about to give a diagnosis*). Is she single?

LADY II. If she's single, it's probably because she likes it. Manuel Acuña committed suicide because of her.

LUPITA (*with a murderous look*). Permit me to make a correction. The Rosario whom you have just mentioned is Rosario de la Peña and she lived in the nineteenth century. A person as delicate as she would never have descended so low as to cause this scandal.

LADY I (*shock of recognition*). Oh, yes, now I know. She's the one they call Rosario of Amozoc.

LUPITA (*patient*). No, not her either. Rosario of Amozoc—or more correctly, *the Rosario of Amozoc*—is a kind of legend that isn't pertinent. Rosario Castellanos is the author of a book that isn't at all bad if you take into account that it's about Indians. I'm referring to her novel, *Chilam Balam*.[32]

All write down this fact industriously. Thus is history made.

LUPITA (*pedagogically*). In those pages the author, although limited and mediocre, seems, at least, tender, simple, sweet. But in the new light of her present actions, we can confirm that she was nothing more than a hypocrite. Ever since she wrote *Chilam Balam*, my analysis will permit our discovery of the serpent hidden in the grass. And what venom, ladies, what venom!

LADY I (*like a refrain*). Is she single?

LUPITA (*as if her foot were being stepped on*). What does it matter if she's married or single? Marriage and the shroud, the proverb says, come down from heaven. The proverb, as with all sayings, expresses popular wisdom; in this case, it tells us that finding a compatible partner, is, in the majority of cases, a matter of pure luck. Now, then, you aren't ignorant of the fact that luck and merit rarely accompany each other.

LADY I. But is she single?

LUPITA (*resigning herself to coming clean*). No, Rosario Castellanos doesn't even have the excuse of being single. It's worse: divorced, which, by my way of thinking, doesn't justify her in any way but does explain her cynicism, her shamelessness, and her aggressiveness. Her marital failure, for which, no doubt, she's the only one to blame, encourages her to slap the cheek of a society to which she is no longer worthy of belonging.

LADY II (*bored*). Let's ignore her.

LADY I. Let's make her realize that it bothers us no more than a fart bothered the Patriot. (*Embarrassed by the vulgarity of the proverb*) Forgive me.

LUPITA. No. I fear that responding by keeping quiet is a subtlety that Señora Castellanos won't grasp. She'll presume that she's left us with no arguments to refute her.

LADY III. We can't refute her if we don't see the play.

LADY II (*to Lady I*). I'm glad you said that. Because I'm beginning to want to see it . . .

LADY I. Me, too. But keep still. Later we'll decide if we can go to see it together. Right now, we have to see what we're going to do.

LUPITA. I think that, if the attack has been cunning, the counterattack shouldn't be direct. It will have to be demonstrated, with facts, that the Mexican woman isn't that caricature—or that self-portrait—that Señora Castellanos presents. No. The Mexican woman is an aware and responsible human being, who acts according to deeply rooted moral, scientific, philosophical, and religious principles. I said that women *act*, and I want to underline it, because now it's a matter of going into action.

LADY I. Let's organize a bingo night! For charity, naturally.

LUPITA (*with deceptive sweetness*). What for? To buy the Castellanos woman a husband with the funds we collect?

LADY II. Oh, yes, indeed, and what would she rather have? A lemon lollipop?

LADY III. I propose that we use the money to compensate her ex-husband for the time that he had to put up with her.

LADY II. Or it could be the reward for his skill in having gotten rid of her.

LUPITA. Señoras, let's not continue to be blinded by what the poet has called domestic stars.

LADY III. What if we started a political party?

LUPITA. What would its ideological platform be?

LADY III. To fight to be given the right to vote.

LUPITA. We Mexican women have had the right to vote since January 18, 1946.

LADY III (*startled*). How come we never . . .

LUPITA (*in the tone of "Elementary, my dear Watson"*). That proves the pointlessness of the idea.

LADY IV. With or without the vote, we Mexican women continue being oppressed.

LADY I. By girdles and by bras—terribly oppressed.

LADY II. Which is already an improvement. Our grandmothers wouldn't allow themselves to go out without a corset.

LADY III. Oppressed by Italian-style shoes.

LADY I. We are slaves of beauty salons, of rollers and pin curls, of hair dye, rejuvenating mud masks, and low calorie diets, and . . .

LADY III. Let's fight for a society without makeup!

LUPITA. And what man would we please in that way?

LADY IV. Is it always a matter of pleasing men?

LUPITA. There's no other alternative, if we consider our mission in the world is to perpetuate the species.

LADY IV. If science continues in the way that it's going, soon the species is going to reproduce in laboratories.

LUPITA. And if it doesn't continue?

LADY IV. At any rate, we already have artificial insemination available, right now.

LADY I. Oh, how revolting!

LADY IV. What I'm trying to show is that, if we limit ourselves to motherhood as our sole function, we won't be indispensable for very long. We'll be converted into useless mouths that will be allowed to die of hunger in times of want; we'll be treated as an object of either experimentation or luxury, a superfluous object that will be thrown away when it's time to clean things out.

LUPITA. What an apocalyptic picture that is!

LADY IV. But not impossible. Not even improbable. Nor even remote.

LADY I. We'll always be men's companions.

LADY IV. We've never been companions. Servants, yes. In time of peace. And after the victory, the warrior's repose. But now we aren't even that. We've been successfully replaced by drugs: from the sophisticated LSD to the common ordinary marijuana.

LADY II. I agree that we aren't companions. When we do well, we're competitors. When we do badly, we're appendages.

LADY I. I'd say it the other way around.

LADY IV. No matter the order of the factors, you still get the same product. And the product stinks. Like death.

LUPITA (*from whom they have taken her role*). What would you suggest? Organize a kingdom of Amazons?

LADY IV. I'm not so utopian. In a culture like ours, the most adaptable structure would be a beehive: the queen bee, worker bees, and drones, who aren't eliminated as long as they are useful.

LADY I (*very anguished*). Oh, no, I love my husband and my children. I love my house. Don't change anything, anything. Ever.

LADY II (*letting her subconscious speak*). I want my daddy to take me by the hand to the park. I don't want him to ever let men come close to me. I want him to die in my arms, like it should be.

LADY I. That isn't how it should be; the New Testament says that you should leave your father and mother to follow your husband.

LADY IV. The Bible is a very beautiful book that one should read, that one should enjoy, but that one doesn't have to take literally. According to Engels in his treatise *The Origin of the Family, Private Property, and the State*, woman's condition is nothing more than a superstructure of the economic system and of the way in which wealth is distributed.

LUPITA (*wanting to regain leadership*). And Bachofen proves the historical existence of the matriarchy.

LADY IV. And what else but a matriarchy is the Mexican family? Machismo is the mask which Tonantzin hides behind in order to act with impunity.[33] Bad faith, in the Sartrean sense of the word, is what makes our backbones so flexible. But one shouldn't trust us. When we bow down, it is not to submit but to stretch the cord that'll let the arrow fly.

LUPITA (*to Lady IV*). Have you seen *The Eternal Feminine*?

LADY IV. I don't need to go to the theater to assimilate ideas—like some of my friends—or to think. I think on my own.

LUPITA. And you think the worst.

LADY IV. Then, as the proverb says, I get it right.[34] That's why when you said that the time to act had arrived I agreed. Now we have to agree on exactly how.

LADY II. I belong to the Christian Family Movement.

LADY IV. What do they say about the pill?

LADY IV. That it's a problem of conscience.

LADY IV. Of whose conscience? Your confessor's? Your husband's? Of your social class? Or simply of *your own* conscience?

LADY II. Oh, stop bothering me.

LADY IV. And don't forget that the government is now beginning to intervene. Family planning is a political matter, not a private one.

LADY II (*to Lady IV*). And what do *you* propose? That we form lesbian groups like in the United States? That we publish pornographic magazines with male nudes?

LADY I. Please, how scandalous!

LADY III. I am old-fashioned. For me Lysistrata's example is still valid.[35]

LADY I. What does Lysistrata say?

LADY III. In a few words, those two (*pointing to her breasts*) pull more weight than two carts.

LADY II. I fear that with unisex fashions, poor Lysistrata couldn't handle even one.

LADY I (*irritated*). So what then?

LUPITA. Let's summarize. There are various options. First, defend traditions, modernizing them, of course, in order to up-date them.

LADY I. Yes, yes, great, great, hurrah, hurrah!

LUPITA. Second, break with the past as our blonde cousins have done, our good neighbors.

LADY III. Yankees, go home!

LUPITA. But they aren't the only ones: the Scandinavians and the English too . . .

LADY III. And how are they doing?

LADY I. Dreadfully. They work inside and outside the home and, furthermore, when they die, they're going to hell.

LADY IV (*to Lupita*). Isn't there a third way for those of us who belong to the Third World?

LUPITA. Industrialization?

LADY I. Get thee behind me, Satan. I don't set any store by motherhood, matrimony, and all that paraphernalia. Let our principles perish, but save the servants!

LADY IV. The third way has to reach to the heart of the problem. It's not enough to adapt to a society that changes superficially, while its roots remain the same. It's not good enough to imitate the models proposed for us that are answers to circumstances other than our own. It isn't even enough to discover who we are. We have to invent ourselves.

What has been kept under control until then breaks out: an attack of collective hysteria. Some women go down on their knees and ask public forgiveness for their sins. Some call out, crying, for their mothers. Other women throw their bras in the waste can. Others cry out for children, for husbands, for men, for sex, for liberty, for economic independence. Others sing: "We don't want a tenth of May, we want liberation." [36] *On the whole, it's pandemonium that Lupita, in spite of her bell-ringing, cannot bring to order.*

LUPITA (*shouting*). Señoras, please be quiet. Señoras, you're behaving like ill-bred nobodies. Señoras! (*No one pays any attention to her.*) Enough! Enough!

Infuriated, Lupita takes off the wig, throws it to the floor, and stamps on it. Momentary darkness. When the lights come back on, we are once again in the beauty salon, but Lupita continues throwing her tantrum in spite of the fact that other customers, the Hairdresser, and the Owner try to prevent her from doing it. Finally, the latter is successful in retrieving the wig— now a revolting mess, of course.

OWNER. You're certainly going to pay for this one. Just look what you've done to it! And you probably still want us to let you try on others. Well, you're mistaken. The fat's in the fire, and I don't tolerate insolence in an exclusive salon meant for decent ladies. Get out of here before I forget who I am and give you what you deserve! Get out of here!

LUPITA (*incoherent*). But my hair isn't done.

OWNER. And what does that matter to me?

LUPITA. I was going to be married . . .

OWNER. Too bad for you. If you don't like anything that I've offered to you, well, fix your own hair just as you darn well please.

LUPITA (*seeing that the battle is lost, becomes defiant*). And do you think that I can't?

OWNER. That doesn't matter to me. Pay me what you owe me and we're through. The rest is *your* problem.

LUPITA (*upset, looking at the audience as though searching for help*). My problem? Ha!

CURTAIN

BALLADS

Translation of the corridos *in rhymed verse by Betty Tyree Osiek*

I

My song I now begin,
a very well-known hit;
the subject found therein
is the eternal feminine,
about which wise men write,
in books, on parchment thin.

The Bible of God's reign
says that it was an error;
he made man's body and his brain,
the mud he used, half-spoiled;
and without skill he did attain
a man as good as good could be.

One day, asleep within the sack,
in Eden's grassy park so green,
God took a rib, without a crack,
and placed it in a woman's skin;
since now he had the knack,
she came out first, not second rank.

Adam and Eve, naked in space,
were going from here to there
to all gave names, with subtle grace,
their job within the garden:
"You are a bull for fighting;
a horse, now you must race."

While Adam named them all,
poor Eve got bored, the pretty maid,
and went to lean against a tree,
where a serpent calmly laid;
he told her, "Try an apple
of the very finest grade.

"If you eat it you will know
how far from bad to good,
what you ought to like,
and what you never should,
and how they will deceive you,
if they think they ever could."

Not slow, nor lazy either,
Eve bit close to the core,
and at that moment in her head
the light it did restore;
with her new view of Paradise,
she understood much more.

With a little bit of work,
improvements can be known;
to cook a little meal,
to build a little home,
and take the sign right down
that makes the apples not our own.

But Adam was so lazy,
and did not desire to aid,
because he also feared so much,
and Jehovah made him so afraid,
because of threats to punish him,
by exit from their lovely glade.

Adam would never listen well;
no need to talk or to explain.
He was not born to govern,
but obey, as though he had a chain.
He will not bite the apple,
unless I bake a pie again.

I'll tell you how to make it,
the snake told Eve, as bait,
and uncovered other secrets,
her trust to captivate,
to encounter other friendships,
to help his power accelerate.

At last, as you are bound to know,
God learned of his mistake;
an angel with a huge bright sword
threw them out with many a quake;
now Adam and Eve were naked;
damnation followed in their wake.

And, since then, suffering humans
work, for a life of ease is past;
fill the world with people,
and, if it ends, renew it fast
and keep your books quite well
of acts today and in the past.

Adam walked along in tears
and looked back on his way
to view a paradise now lost,
with no return, to his dismay;
and Eve, she thought of history
that had just begun that day.

Dear friends, I beg your pardon,
with my good-bye, you're free.
The serpent snakes his way around
in this poem, as you can see,
where the ballad tells the many acts
of the eternal feminine she.

II

My song I now begin,
a very well-known hit;
the subject found herein
is the eternal feminine,
about which wise men write,
in books, on parchment thin.

They say Eve ruined humanity,
both the fat ones and the lean,
by gnawing on an apple
placed by God in quarantine;

because she was from her first breath
disobedient and just plain mean.

Thus she bears her children
in sadness, with pain ever near;
so don't ever let her enter
the church, except in her bier;
nor as teacher in a class,
nor in the shop should she appear.

She ought to be enclosed inside,
for, if her eyes the fields traverse,
to rack and ruin go the crops,
and fruits are made much worse;
and hunger is their only food;
in cities and towns fall a curse.

If she decides to see the beach,
a storm its rains converge,
and sea monsters come to greet
their ally most perverse,
since just like her they move along
in a dark and shadowy universe.

She speaks out from the shadows,
mysteries and prophecies she asserts;
she works within the darkness,
to all spells and charms alert,
and she knows no other light
than that her body does disperse.

When they burn her in the squares,
as an example and a threat,
when shriven by the flames,
she goes to Heaven like a jet,
where God accepts her there,
his reign to establish and abet.

On the loving lap of woman,
the Redeemer she did guide,

on that maternal softness,
the humble pastor sat in pride,
and before Him the kings bowed low,
and the sun reveres His might.

With the cherubims around her,
the angels sing and smile;
and the archangels rise above her,
to the highest throne they fly,
where the Holy Virgin Mother
ends the devil's power so vile.

With deep pity viewing others,
the Only One without sin,
she looks at them, for they were left,
lost, shut out, to their chagrin;
they fill the earth so broad,
with the evil and lies they revel in.

They are snakes in their disguises,
and for paradise they do pine,
to return there to destroy it,
to prove again their power malign
and their unyielding strength of will,
the eternal feminine to enshrine.

Fly, fly, little pigeon;
salute them as you soar;
bored Eve and maligned Malinche,
Sor Juana and Xtabay[37] of yore,
and also the sweet Guadalupan,[38]
in Tepeyac once more.

Now, I must say good-bye,
and not forget a soul that's here,
and not leave out a single woman,
for ballads are a hard career;
what one deserves, my ladies,
is not received, I fear.

Notes

I would like to recognize the indirect contribution of M. E. Levine to this translation and to thank her for her help. Several years ago, Levine and I translated this play in a very rough form, which has influenced my contribution to the present translation. Osiek had translated the whole drama separately, and, when she discovered that I was already negotiating with a publisher, we agreed to join forces rather than to publish two different translations of the same work. Later, Maureen Ahern generously assisted in the editing. Consequently, this translation is the work of Osiek and myself and she and I are responsible for any faults that may be found in it.—D.E.M.

1. Julio Cortázar (1914–1983), contemporary Argentinean short story writer and novelist of international stature. Many volumes of his works exist in English translation, including *Blow-up and Other Stories, End of the Game and Other Stories, Hopscotch,* and *A Manual for Manuel.*

2. A place where discussions occur. It may be a radio station, a television talk show, or a room in a cultural institution.

3. This scene employs a great deal of technical bullfighting terminology, which has no exact English equivalent. The following descriptions are very general but may prove useful:

alternativa—ritual ceremony of confirmation as a *matador.*

banderilleros—assistants on foot who work with the cape and drive their *banderillas* (darts with streamers attached) into the bull.

cuadrilla—troupe consisting of two or three *banderilleros* and two or three *picadores* per *matador.*

manoletinas—extremely dangerous movements named for their first practitioner, Manolete (Manuel Rodríguez, 1917–1947, b. Spain), which consist of holding the *muleta* (smaller than the cape) behind the bullfighter's back and only at the last moment moving the cloth to the side. To be properly executed, the bullfighter cannot move his or her feet.

pase de rodillas—very dangerous movements where the bullfighter is on his knees and thus practically immobile during the bull's charge.

revoleras—dangerous movements of turning in a full circle in front of the bull, thus exposing the bullfighter's back during the bull's charge.

verónica—a fairly common, relatively simple pass with the cape.

4. When the *matador*'s helpers have to finish off the bull, it is a humiliation for the *matador.*

5. The judge of the bullfight, *el juez de la plaza,* monitors the ethics of the contest as well as gives out the rewards (like the bull's ears and tail). Heavy fines and even jail sentences have been given, for instance, if a *torero* touches the bull with the *estoque* (the sword for the kill) at any moment other than the kill (see *Encyclopedia Britannica,* 1982).

6. Literally, *el corrido*, a traditional Mexican verse form of eight-syllable lines that is usually sung.

7. Sanborn's is a chain of restaurants. One of the best-known branches is in the famous building La Casa dc los Azulejos in Mexico City.

8. A huge park in Mexico City containing a historic castle, children's rides, several important museums, and large open areas.

9. Zeno of Elea (448?–430? B.C.), early Greek philosopher of the Eleatic School, follower of Parmenides, known for his arguments (paradoxes) against motion and multiplicity, including the famous paradox of Achilles and the Tortoise.

10. Sara García was a character actress on Mexican Radio and television.

11. The Spanish word *jarabe*, translated here as "tonic," is an untranslatable pun meaning both a syrup (tonic) and a specific type of Mexican folk dance.

12. *China* originally meant the female of any animal in the Andean language, Quechua. The China Poblana is a *china* from Puebla (Mexico) who is a *mestiza* woman, representing beauty, wearing traditional costumes, who performs traditional dances, like the *jarabe tapatío* mentioned here, which is typical of Jalisco, Mexico.

13. In the Spanish name system, upon marriage a woman keeps her maiden name and adds her husband's name, separated by *de* (of), e.g., Juana López marries Juan Rodríguez and becomes Juana López [or Juana L.] de Rodríguez. If widowed, she may choose to reflect the fact by adding the word "widow" (*viuda*, abbreviated *vda.*) before *de*, e.g., Juana López vda. de Rodríguez.

14. For the rest of Act II, Castellanos playfully retells the life stories of women from Mexican history. Hence, it is important to know the traditional legendary version of their stories, which she expects her audience to know.

La Malinche (sixteenth century). Daughter of a powerful Indian leader, she was sold as a slave at an early age by her mother. Eventually, she was sold as a slave to the Spanish, where she quickly and easily learned Castilian. Baptized as "Marina" (her Indian name was "Malintzin," pronounced "Malinche"), she later became the personal interpreter, advisor, and lover of Hernán Cortés himself. Because she helped the Spanish cause, Octavio Paz (in *The Labyrinth of Solitude*) and many other Mexicans see Malinche as representing the supreme traitor. To be "Malinche" or "Malinchista" in present-day Mexico is to place foreign over national interests, or favor foreign things or ideas.

Sor Juana Inés de la Cruz (1651–1691). Juana Ramírez was an illegitimate daughter who was born into humble circumstances, but, because of her surprising intellect and beauty, she was the favorite of the Vicereine, the Marquesa de Mancera. Juana's beauty, talent, and intelligence made her popular at Court and enabled her to enter a convent, where she could pursue her scientific studies and her literary career in relative peace. Many hypotheses have been advanced to explain why she entered the convent, the most popular being that her lover died or spurned her. Although Juana wrote much love poetry, both before and after entering the convent, the only autobiographical statement that she left us was in *Letter in Reply to Sor Philotea*, where she wrote that she entered to avoid marriage, implying that she preferred her independence to living with a husband. See Castellanos' essay on Sor Juana in this anthology.

Josefa Ortiz de Domínguez (d. 1829). Nicknamed "La Corregidora," "the [female] Magistrate," Josefa was active in the revolution of 1810 against Spain, despite being jailed in various convents by her husband, the actual Magistrate of Querétaro, Mexico, to prevent her from engaging in such activities. There is a statue of her in Mexico City.

The Empress Carlota (1840–1927). Daughter of Leopold I, King of Belgium, Carlota married the Archduke Maximiliano, who became emperor of Mexico in 1864. During her tenure as empress, the conservatives of the upper and middle classes imitated European, especially French, customs and dress. In 1867 Carlota went to Europe to ask Napoleon III for help in maintaining their rule, but her husband was killed by the revolutionaries while she was gone. Symptoms of madness had appeared before Carlota left Mexico and it is unclear whether the news of her husband's execution precipitated or merely aggravated her mental illness.

Rosario de la Peña (b. 1847). A very beautiful and talented woman whose literary salon was frequented by major poets during Mexico's romantic period in the nineteenth century. According to Francisco Castillo Nájera (in *Manuel Acuña* [Mexico City: Imprenta Universitaria, 1950], 48–67), whose testimony appears condescending and biased, Rosario encouraged Manuel Acuña until she discovered his involvement with his laundress. There is speculation that Acuña's laundress had a child by him. Because one of Acuña's last poems before his suicide, "Nocturno," was dedicated to Rosario, her rejection of him (for infidelity) is often seen as the cause of his death.

Adelita (twentieth century). A familiar character in *corridos*, or popular ballads, of the revolution of 1910 and after, Adelita was one of the *soldaderas*, who, since Mexico did not provision its soldiers during this period, followed the armies and fed, clothed, nursed, and sometimes loved the soldiers. A few *soldaderas*, including Adelita, actually took part in the fighting; the songs about her, however, "focus more on love than on women's ability on the battlefield. . . . [the famous ballad] 'Adelita' drew its inspiration from a Durangan woman who had involved herself at an early age in the Maderista movement" (Shirley Ann Soto, *The Mexican Woman: A Study of Her Participation in the Revolution, 1910–1940* [Palo Alto, Calif.: R and E Research Associates, 1979], 27). According to Armando de María y Campos (*La revolución mexicana a través de los corridos populares*, vol. 1 [Mexico City: Biblioteca del Instituto Nacional de Estudios Históricos de la Revolución Mexicana, 1962], 43), the original Adelita, Adela Maldonado, was killed in 1934 by a rival lover.

15. The Mexican Constitution of 1917 was a product of the Revolution. In it the "Church was debarred from public education. Civil marriage was established. Members of the clergy lost the right to vote and to hold public office" (Germán Arciniegas, *Latin America: A Cultural History*, trans. Joan Maclean [New York: Knopf, 1967], 494). Members of the clergy also lost the right to wear their religious habits in public.

16. Manuel Acuña (1849–1873), popular Mexican romantic poet who died a tragic death. His love poetry stressed the spiritual over the physical.

17. These lines are from Acuña's poem "Nocturno," dedicated to Rosario and one of the last poems he was to write.

18. Manuel M. Flores (1850–1885), author of erotic, sensual, and romantic love poetry. According to Castillo Nájera (49), the story that Rosario and this Manuel were lovers is untrue. Additionally, he writes that she first met Flores in 1874, months after the death of Acuña. There was some speculation that they would marry but Flores contracted a serious illness at an early age.

Jose Martí (Cuba, 1835–1895). One of the most important poets of Latin America, Martí participated in De la Peña's literary salon in 1875 (i.e., two years after Acuña's suicide) during a stay in Mexico. Also, in 1875, he addressed several tender letters to her.

19. The Spanish original can be found in Alfonso Méndez Plancarte, ed., *Obras completas de Sor Juana Inés de la Cruz*, vol. 1, *El Sueño* (Mexico City: Fondo de Cultura Económica, 1951), 340.—Betty Tyree Osiek

20. Ibid., vol. 2, 287; This is the first stanza of sonnet 164.

21. Historians have only recently discovered that Sor Juana was illegitimate.

22. These lines have multiple meanings but often in Sor Juana's poetry she uses "prison" and its derivatives to refer to the incarnation of the soul, trapped inside the body during life.—Betty Tyree Osiek

23. Persons born of Spanish parents in the New World, in contrast to Spanish born in Spain, who held many privileges over other settlers.

24. *Pulque*, a local alcoholic beverage made from the century plant, having an unpleasant odor but an acceptable taste.

25. As is necessary, i.e., appropriately.

26. *Hiroshima, Mon Amour*, film script by Marguerite Duras, film by Alain Resnais. An unusual story of an erotic involvement between a French actress traumatized by the German occupation of France and a Japanese man who lost his family in the atomic blast. She is on location in Hiroshima making a film about peace.

27. Included in Rosario Castellanos, *Poesía no eres tú*, 175.—Betty Tyree Osiek

28. *Flor de fango*, a novel by Vargas Vila.—Luz María Umpierre

29. Cinturita, a nickname meaning "small-waisted."

30. The Mexican government party, Partido Revolucionario Institucional, has remained in power since the period just after the Revolution (1910–1917).

31. Castellanos completed this play while serving as the Mexican ambassador to Israel.

32. The ignorance of the character, Lupita, is obvious in her error of giving the credit to Castellanos for the Mayan indigenous work of several books, transcribed after the conquest, entitled *Chilam Balam* (see *El libro de los libros de Chilam Balam* [Mexico City: Fondo de Cultura Económica, 1948]). One of Castellano's novels has a title very similar in sound: *Balún Canán.*—Betty Tyree Osiek

33. Tonantzin, the virgin mother goddess of the Aztec gods, including the war god, Huitzilopochtli. Also known as Coatlicue, she nursed both the gods as well as the Mexican people, whom she created. In modern times her identity has merged with that of the Virgin of Guadalupe, beautiful and benevolent mother deity who lovingly defends her Mexican children (see William Madsen, *The Virgin's Children: Life in an Aztec Village Today* [Austin: University of Texas Press, 1960], 4, 28–29).

34. *Piensas mal y acertarás* roughly means "Think the worst and it will come to pass."

35. *Lysistrata*, a comedy by Aristophanes where the women refuse all sexual favors until the men agree to end the war.

36. May 10 has been celebrated as Mother's Day since 1922, when it was initiated as a holiday by journalist Rafael Alducin, founder of *Excélsior.*—Betty Tyree Osiek

37. Xtabay, pre-Columbian goddess of love and music.

38. Guadalupan, the Virgen de Guadalupe, patroness of Mexico.

Notes on the Editor and the Translators

Maureen Ahern is professor of Spanish at Arizona State University where she teaches Latin American literature and literary translation and theory. A former Institute of International Education and Fulbright fellowship recipient, Ahern studied at the National University of Mexico and the University of San Marcos in Lima, Peru, where she received her doctoral degree. She is co-editor with Mary S. Vásquez of the first volume of critical studies on Rosario Castellanos, *Homenaje a Rosario Castellanos*, which includes her critical bibliography of Castellanos' writing and has published a selection of Castellanos' poems in translation in *Looking at the Mona Lisa*. Her critical studies and translations of contemporary Mexican and Peruvian poets have been published in journals and anthologies in this country and in England, Mexico, Peru, and Spain, including *Peru: The New Poetry* and the poetry of Antonio Cisneros, *At Night the Cats*, with David Tipton and William Rowe.

Diane Marting is assistant professor at the University of Nebraska-Lincoln where she teaches Spanish American literature and Spanish language. She received her doctoral degree in comparative literature from Rutgers University and spent a year in Brazil on a Fulbright fellowship studying sexuality and feminism in the works of Brazilian women writers. She has edited *Women Writers of Spanish America: An Annotated Bio-Bibliographical Guide* and *Spanish American Women Writers: A Bio-Bibliographical Source Book*, a collection of essays by various authors.

Betty Tyree Osiek is professor emerita at Southern Illinois University where she taught Spanish and Latin American literature from 1966 to 1986. Her major publications are *José Asunción Silva: Estudio estilístico de su poesía* and *José Asunción Silva*. Since 1981 she has organized several panels on the work of Rosario Castellanos at regional and national conferences and is presently working on a book on the life and works of Rosario Castellanos.

Ruth Peacock translated the novella "The Widower Román" as an assignment for Raúl Ortiz y Ortiz' seminar in literary texts at the National University of Mexico. She presented it as part of her thesis for the Master of Arts degree in Spanish language and Latin American literature at the National University of Mexico prior to its publication in the *Texas Quarterly*. She lives in Guadalajara, Mexico.

Lesley Salas is a free-lance translator and writer who graduated from San Francisco State University. She has lived and studied in Mexico and presently works in Austin, Texas.

Laura Carp Solomon is a Master of Arts degree candidate in English at Arizona State University with a concentration in linguistics. She resides in Carlsbad, California, where she teaches a bilingual first grade and is completing her thesis on the translation of Castellanos' novel *Oficio de tinieblas*. Her translations of the Mexican author's prose began as a project in Ahern's seminar in literary translation.

Index

Acuña, Manuel, 307, 352, 365n.14, 366n.16
Adam, 358–360
Addressee: feminine, 27
Adelita, 53, 303, 365n.14
Agosín, Marjorie, 43
Agustini, Delmira, 255, 258
Álbum de familia, 36
Al pie de la letra, 6, 227, 257
Ambiguity: and translation, xvii–xviii, 11
América, Revista Antológica, 2
Angel in the House, the: as metaphor, xviii, 42; as Victorian ideal, 45, 239, 244n.1
Apuntes para una declaración de fe, 226
Archetypes: female, xiv
Arguedas, José María, 32
Armendáriz, Emma Teresa, 54–57
Artes Hispánicas, 3
"Attempt at Self-Criticism, An," 33, 51, 226–228
Autobiography: of Sor Juana Inés de la Cruz, 39; of women, 16, 59n.19

Bakhtin, Mikhail, xiii
Balún-Canán, 31, 227
Beauvoir, Simone de, xiv, 264; as mentor, 4, 40–41; on myth, 236; on woman as Other, 62n.41
Bécquer, Gustavo Adolfo, 26, 109
Berryman, John, 26
Biography: as dramatic strategy, 55–56; and servanthood, 50
Blood: as feminine sign, 20–21, 60–66n.28; as symbol, 14, 60–61n.28
Bolaños, Herlinda, 50, 268–269
Boston Globe, 39
"Brief Chronicle," 14, 20–21, 95
Burke, Carolyn, 53

Calderón de la Barca, Fanny (Marchioness), xviii, 45–47, 245–248, 248n.1
Canon: literary, 30; poetic, 9
Carballido, Emilio, 2, 31
Carballo, Emmanuel, 6, 30
Cardenal, Ernesto, 2
Cárdenas, Lázaro, 2, 36, 232–235, 235n.1
Cargadora, 267–268
Carlota, Empress, 365n.14; as female character, 53, 303
"Cartas a Elías Nandino," 32
Cartas marcadas (García Flores), 6
Casas, Fray Bartolomé de las, 231
Castellanos, César, 1
Castellanos Figueroa, Rosario: autobiographical references of, 100–101, 226–228, 232–235, 254–258; 267–269; biography of, 1–5; as object of dramatic satire, 55–56, 351–353; on solitude, 35
"Castration or Decapitation?" (Cixous), 51–52
Castro, Dolores, 2, 3
Chamula Indians, 1; oppression and

rebellion of, 31–32, 230–231; in Yalentay, 219–221

Chiapas: Comitán, 1, 35; cultural oppression in, 31–36; cultural programs, 3; as cultural region, 1, 57n.2; discrimination in, 229–231; as metaphor, 36; as poetic motif, 3, 6; San Cristóbal de las Casas, 220, 230–231; women in, 35–36, 219–221, 232–235

Chilam Balam, 352, 367n.32

China Poblana, 293, 364n.12

Ciudad Real, 32–33, 228

Cixous, Hélène, xvi, 40; on language, 51–52; on silence, 43; on writing the body, 1, 20, 61n.28

Comitán, 1, 35

Confrontaciones: Los narradores ante el público, 3

"Consciousness," 8, 14, 90–91

Contexts: and biography of Castellanos, 1–5; feminist, 37

Los convidados de agosto, 33–35, 228

"Cooking Lesson," xvii, 36–38, 207–215

Corridos, 358–363, 364n.6

Cortázar, Julio: on laughter, 273, 363n.1

Cortés, Hernán, 6, 225n.1, 305–307

Cruz, Sor Juana Inés de la, xiv, 362, 364–365n.14; as archetype, 42–43; autobiography of, 39; in *The Eternal Feminine*, 53, 55, 303; in Mexican letters, 222–225; and silence, 43

Daly, Mary, 43, 58n.11

Darío, Rubén, 253n.2, 254

Daughters: in Castellanos' prose, 33–35; in Chamula culture, 219–221. *See also* Female characters; Women

Death: in Castellanos' family, 2–3; as literary theme, 5, 7–8, 62n.36; of

Rosario Castellanos, 5

"Death without End," 5

Debunking: as dramatic strategy, 53, 55–56

Descartes, René, xviii, 22

De la vigilia estéril, 226, 257

Dependency: of women, 50, 261–262

Dialogue: as discursive strategy, 46–47; feminist, 45–47

Díaz Cuscat, Pedro, 230

Díaz del Castillo, Bernal, 6, 58n.10

Díaz-Diocaretz, Myriam: and feminist discourse and negativity, 62n.35; and speech acts and feminist discourse, 58n.14; and subtexts and intertexts, 24–25, 27, 29, 61n.31, 73; and translation, xvi, xviii–ix, 1, 10–11

Díaz Puijla, Catalina, 32

Dickinson, Emily, xvii, 61n.30

"Difference of View, The" (Jacobus), 30

Discourse: and domesticity, 52–53; feminist, 58n.14; feminization of, 36–38, 46–47; formats, 25; gender identity and markers, 10–13; modes of representation, 33, 46–47; and negativity, 68n.35; subversive, 17–18

"Discrimination in the United States and Chiapas," 22, 36, 57n.2, 229–231

Domesticity: as discursive strategy, 52–53; as poetic discourse, 14–17; as sign, 52–53; and subversive discourse, 16–17; and textuality, 14–17, 38

Duby, Gertrudis, 268–269

"Eagle, The," 33, 120–128

Eco, Umberto, 30

Écriture féminine, xv, 51

Eliot, George, 26

Escandón, María, 2, 267–268

Essays: analysis, 39–53; bibliography, 39
Estaciones, 31
El Estudiante, 5
Eternal Feminine, The, 271–367; and biography, 50–56; bullfighting terminology in, 280–281, 363–364n.3; dramatic strategies, 53–57; satirization of, 351, 355; staging of, 54–55; translation of, 56–57, 63n.51
Eve, 358–362
El Excélsior, 39

Felsteiner, John, 16
Female body, 239–241; and writing, 1, 21, 51, 60–61n.28. *See also* Blood; Pregnancy
Female characters, xviii, 28; as archetypes in Mexican culture, 44–45; as daughters and friends, 33–35; in *The Eternal Feminine,* 55–56; in European literatures: Amelia, Ana de Ozores, Anna Karenina, Dorotea, Hedda Gabler, Melibea, 243, Iphigenia, 240, Marchioness de Marteuil, 243, Celestina, la Pintada, 244. *See also* Angel in the House; Cruz, Sor Juana Inés de la; Malinche
Female experience: literary reconstruction of, 6, 28–30, 38. *See also* Motherhood; Pregnancy; Women
Female images, 16–17, 42–43, 236–244
Female literary tradition, 28–30, 111, 236–244
Female sexuality, 19–21, 60n.26, 60–61n.28, 62n.43, 112–115
Female stereotypes, xv, 44–45; satire of, 53–56
Feminist communication, 37, 58n.14. *See also* Language; Women
Feminist drama, 54–57

Feminist ideology, 40–41, 54–55
Feminist scholarship, xvi
Figueroa, Adriana, 1
"Fleeting Friendships," 33–34, 145–154
Flores, Manuel M., 308, 366n.18
Forster, Merlin H., 43
French feminist writers, xv, 21, 40, 51, 63n.47

García Flores, Margarita, 6, 9
García Márquez, Gabriel, 252
Gender: feminine identity markers, 10–13; and otherness, 9, 41; of poetic speakers, 11–12, 22. *See also* Feminist communication; Language; Rhetoric
Generation of 1950, the: members of, 2; role of, in Mexican literature, 31–32
Goodman, Ellen, 39
González, Otto Raúl, 2
Gorostiza, José, 5
Greene, Gayle, xvi, 38, 45
Guardia, Miguel, 2
Gubar, Susan, 7, 20, 24, 58n.12, 60n.28
Guerra, Ricardo, 4
Guerra Castellanos, Gabriel, 4
Guillén, Jorge, 6, 255

"Herlinda Leaves," 49–50, 52, 267–269
Hernández, Efrén, 2
Hernández, Luisa Josefina, 2
Hidalgo, Miguel, 318
"Hiroshima, Mon Amour," 331, 366n.26
"Home Economics," 15, 39, 103–104
Humm, Maggie, xvi; on Virginia Woolf, 41–42, 44–45
Humor: ironic, xvii, 38; as poetic theme, 6, 257–258; translation of, xvi–xvii, 56–57

Ibarbourou, Juana de, 255, 258
Ideology: cultural, xiii–xiv, 40; feminist, 40–41, 54–55; and translation, 29–30
"If Not Poetry, Then What?," 51, 255–258
Illescas, Carlos, 2
Images of women, 16–17, 42–43, 236–244
"Incident at Yalentay," 35, 219–221
Indigenist Institute, 3–4, 32, 220
Indigenist writing, 31–33
"Inscribing Femininity" (Jones), 40, 43
Intertextuality: definition of, 24–25; discursive strategies of, 26–27, 61n.31; feminist, 26–27, 44; and subversion, 27
Irigaray, Luce, 23, 40, 51. See also French feminist writers
Israel, 4–5, 268–269

Jacobus, Mary, 1, 30
Japanese women, 264–266
Jelinek, Estelle C., 16
Jones, Ann Rosalind, xvi, 43
"Joyful Mysteries," 227
Juárez, Benito, 322, 323
"Judith," 6
"El juego de las encantadas" (Mendoza), 43
Juhasz, Suzanne, 16
Juicios sumarios, 39–42

Kahn, Coppélia, xxiv, 38, 45
Kamenzain, Tamara, 43
"Kinsey Report," 19–20, 112–115
Kramarae, Cheris, 59–60n.21, 60n.24
Kristeva, Julia, 51

"Lamentación de Dido," 6, 257
Language: and alienation, 7; and culture, 51–52; and female speakers,

23, 60n.24; humorous, 54; and identity, 11–18, 51–52; and liberation, xxi, 252–253; Mexican speech patterns, 56–57; as oppression, 21–24, 50–52, 230–231, 250–253; and race, 250; and sexuality, 19. See also Discourse; Translation
"Language as an Instrument of Domination," xxi, 22, 50–52, 250–253
Latin American women poets, 10, 59n.18, 255, 258
"Laugh of the Medusa, The" (Cixous), xvi; on silence, 43; on writing and the female body, 1, 20–21, 51, 61n.28
"Learning about Things," xvii–xviii, 17–18, 105–107
Lerner, Gerda, 45
Letter in Reply to Sor Philotea (Sor Juana Inés de la Cruz), 39, 225n.1, 365n.14
"Liberation of Love, The," xviii, 47–48, 264–266
Life in Mexico: The Letters of Fanny Calderón de la Barca (Calderón), 45–47, 321–332
"Life of a Single Woman, The," 331–332
Lívida luz, 227
"Looking at the Mona Lisa," 27–28, 116
Looking at the Mona Lisa, xviii, 58n.8
Lopéz Mirnau, Rafael, 54–57
Lotman, Jurij, 10
"La lucidez como forma de vida" (García Flores), 7, 9
Lysistrata, 355–356, 367n.35

McDonald, Regina Harrison, 50–51
Machismo, 355; and female sexuality, 19–20
Magaña, Sergio, 2
"Malinche," xviii, 6–7, 96–97, 97n

Malinche, xv, 63 n. 44, 303, 362, 364 n. 14; as archetype, 42–43, 62 n. 41; and Cortés, 6, 58 n. 10, 225 n. 1, 307; as myth, 7, 53; as sign, 7, 42–43; as symbol of sexuality, 7, 222–223

"Man of Destiny, A," 35–36, 52, 232–235

Marriage: critique of, 37–38. See also "Cooking Lesson"

Martí, José, 308, 366 n. 8

El mar y sus pescaditos, 39

Massacre in Mexico (Poniatowska), 13, 59 n. 16

Materia memorable, 8–9

Maximiliano, Emperor, 323, 365 n. 14

"Meditación en el umbral," 29

"Meditation on the Brink," xvii–xviii, 9–10, 28–30, 111

Mejía Sánchez, Ernesto, 2

"Memorandum on Tlatelolco," xviii, 13–14, 98–99

Méndez Plancarte, Father Alfonso, 224, 225 n. 2

Mendoza, Maria Luisa, 43

Mentors: feminine, 40–42

Messages: subversive, 17. See also Signs

"Metamorphosis of the Sorceress," xviii, 28, 93

Metaphor: Angel in the House, xviii, 42, 44, 239; blood, 14, 20; domestic, 15–17; female body, 51; feminine, 21, 37–38, 43; pregnancy, 21, 61 n. 29; in prose, 227

Mexican women: in Chiapas, 33–35; and culture, 349; a dialogue of, 45–47; as dramatic characters, 53–57, 350–353, 364–365 n. 14; legal rights of, 262–263; and maternity, 48–49, 241–242, 261–263, 354–355; in Mexican history, 304, 364–365 n. 14; in nineteenth

century, 45–47, 245–249; and self-sacrifice, 47, 261–263; speech patterns of, xvii–xviii, 56–57

Middlemarch (Eliot), 26

Miller, Beth, 40

Mistral, Gabriela, 6, 257, 258

"Moment of Truth, The," 52

"Monologue of a Foreign Woman," 7, 84–86

Monsiváis, Carlos, 39

Monterroso, Augusto, 2

Motherhood: and dependency, 48–49, 241–242; and self-sacrifice, 261–263, 354–355

Mujer que sabe latín, 39–40, 44–47

Muller, Ingrid, 47–48

Myths: destruction of, 53–57; about marriage, 37–38, 207–215; reversal of feminine, 6–7, 9–10, 20, 58 n. 11; about women, 42–43, 208, 236–244

Nandino, Elías, 31

Napoleon III, 324

National Indigenist Institute, 3–4, 32, 220

National University of Mexico, 2, 4

"Nazareth," 7, 118

Negation: through language, 22–23, 30, 62 n. 35; See also El ninguneo; "Nobodying"

Negative signs, 28–30

New York Times, 39

Nicholson, Irene, 3

Nigro, Kirsten F., 53, 56

Nine Guardians, The, 31, 227

"Nineteenth-Century Mexican Woman, The," 45–47, 245–249. See also Calderón de la Barca, Fanny

El ninguneo, xvii, 22–23, 117 n

"Nobodying," 21–23, 117

Oficio de tinieblas, 32, 228
Olsen, Tillie, 43, 58n.12
"Once Again Sor Juana," 40, 42–43, 222–225
On Feminine Culture, 3, 40
On Lies, Secrets, and Silences (Rich), 43, 58n.12
Oppression: cultural, in Chiapas, 31–36, 229–231; linguistic, 21–24, 50–52, 230–231; Simone Weil and paradigms of, 33
O'Quinn, Kathleen, 53
Ortega, Julio, 43
Ortiz, Raúl, 4, 54
Ortiz de Domínguez, Josefa, 303, 315–321, 365n.14
Other, the: concepts of, 8, 26; as text, xv; woman as, 62n.41. *See also* Otherness
Otherness, xiii; and creativity, 9, 26; and death, 8; expanding concepts of, 7–11; and gender, 9. *See also* Other

Pacheco, José Emilio, xiii, 39
Parler femme, 51
"La participación de la mujer mexicana en la educación formal," 18
"Passage," 12–13, 89
Patmore, Coventry, 244n.1
Peña, Rosario de la, 303, 307, 352, 365n.14
"A pesar de proponérselo," 52
Petul, 35, 219–221. *See also* Teatro Petul
Pfandl, Ludwig, 43, 224, 225n
Pineda, Vicente, 230–231
Poemas: 1953–1955, 6
Poesía no eres tú, xvii, 5, 9, 254–258
Poetic language: evolution of, 5–10, 254–258; as political protest, 60n.27. *See also* Latin American women poets

Polyphony: and translation, xviii
Poniatowska, Elena: on Castellanos' biography, 1–2, 4–5, 57n.3; on Castellanos' writing, 15, 31, 35, 41, 55; and Tlatelolco, 13, 59n.16
"Postscript," 18, 108
"Power and Danger: Works of a Common Woman" (Rich), 23–24
Pregnancy: Cixous on, 21; metaphor of, 21, 102
President, The (Asturias): and language, 251, 253n
Problems of Dostoevsky's Poetics (Bakhtin), xiii
"Professions for Women" (Woolf), 244
Prose: development of Castellanos', 227–228
Prostitution, 335–338
Punning: poetic, 25–27; as sociolinguistic sign, 22–23

Quetzalcoatl, 50, 268

Reading: act of, 10, 58n.13; concomitant, 35–36; criterion, xviii; *The Eternal Feminine*, 55; and gender identity, 10–11; and translation, xvi–xix, 1
Reader: as accomplice, 258; active, xvi; female, 37; expectations, 58n.13; and ideology, xix; of other feminist writers, 40–42; participation in text, 47–48; prior 11; and translation, xvi–xix
"Re: Mutilations," 15, 110
Representation. *See* Discourse
El rescate del mundo, 6, 257
Rhetoric: male, xviii, 48; poetic, 6
Rich, Adrienne, 26; on language as oppressor, 23–24; on "re-vision," 46; on silence, 58n.12
"Rito de iniciación, 4, 228
Rivero, Eliana S., 10

Room of One's Own, A (Woolf), 41
Rosario Castellanos: Una conciencia femenista en México (Miller), 40
"Rosario Castellanos: ¡Vida, nada te debo!" (Poniatowska), 1, 4–5, 15, 31, 35, 41, 55, 57 n. 3
"Routine," 8, 14, 87

Sabines, Jaime, 2
"Salome," 6
San Cristóbal de las Casas, 220, 230–231
Satire: of male rhetoric, xviii, 48; of Mexican history and myth, 53–54; of Rosario Castellanos, 351–353
Second Sex, The (Beauvoir), 41, 62 n. 41
"Self-Portrait," 15, 100–101
"Self-Sacrifice Is a Mad Virtue," 48–49, 259–263
Servanthood, 49–50, 267–269
Sexuality. *See* Female sexuality
Signs: appropriation of, 24–30; displacement of values, 38; intertextual, 44–45; of patriarchal authority, 17–18; perversion of, 33; positive and negative transformation of, 28–29; social, 22–23; subversive, 17–19; systems, 24–25; as transcultural acts, xiii
Silence: in Castellanos' poetry, 5–10; in female experience and culture, 6–7, 40, 42–43, 47, 58 n. 12; as meaning, 7; and myth, 6–7; and otherness, 7–10; and Sor Juana Inés de la Cruz, 259; in women's language, 59–60 n. 21, 60 n. 24
"Silence Near an Ancient Stone," 11–12, 81
"Silences in Literature—1962" (Olsen), 43, 58 n. 12
Silencio e imaginación (Agosín), 43
"Simone de Beauvoir o la lucidez," 41
Sobre cultura femenina, 3, 40

Solitude: in Castellanos' childhood, 2, 31; in Castellanos' poetry, 4; and women in Chiapas, 34–35
Speakers: and addressees, 10–24, 58 n. 14; gender identity of, 10–13; generic, 13–15; feminine, 12–17, 60 n. 24
"Speaking of Gabriel," 21, 102
Speculum of the Other Woman (Irigaray), 23
Speech acts, 17, 59 n. 20; and negation, 23
"Splendor of Being," 227
Stereotypes. *See* Female stereotypes
Stevenson, Anne, 30
Storni, Alfonsina, 255, 258
Subtexts: definition of, 24–25, 61 n. 31; visual, 27–28

Tablero de damas, 53–54, 63 n. 50, 227
Taranovsky, Kiril, 24, 61 n. 31
Teatro Petul, 3, 53. *See also* Petul
Telenovelas, xvii, 49
Testimonial voices, 13–14
El texto silencioso (Kamenzain), 43
Theory of Semiotics, A (Eco), 30
Third World: and women's issues, 27–28, 116
Three Guineas (Woolf), 41
"Three Knots in the Net," 36, 129–143
Tlatelolco, 13–14, 59 n. 16
"To a Tiny Mayan Badger," 6, 82
Tonantzin, 355, 367 n. 33
Tone: and translation, xvii–xviii
Translating Poetic Discourse: Questions on Feminist Strategies in Adrienne Rich (Díaz-Diocaretz). *See* Díaz-Diocaretz, Myriam
Translation: criterion, xv–xviii; of cultural and lexical equivalences, xvii, 23; of *The Eternal Feminine*, 56–

57, 63–64n.51; of feminist ideology, 29–30; of gender, 11–13; as mediation, 1; of Mexican culture, xix; of Mexican speech patterns, 56–57; and otherness, xv–xix; of poetry, xv–xix, 11–13, 29–30; policy, xviii; and reading, xvi, xix, 1, 11; of satire, xviii; and semiotics, xvi–xviii; theory, xvi; of tone, xvii–xviii; of *umbral* 29–30, 40; and writing 1; of "You," 11, 59n.15

Translator, the: notes of, and meaning, xvii, 23; as prior reader, 11

Trayectoria del polvo, 5–6, 226, 256

Tzotzil, 31. *See also* Chamula Indians

Umbral: translation of, 29–30, 40

El uso de la palabra, 39, 52

Varo, Remedios, xviii, 28, 93

Vásquez, Mary S., 54, 57n.3

"Virginia Woolf o la literatura como ejercicio de la libertad," 41

Virgin of Guadalupe, 225n.1, 362, 367n.38; as archetype, xiv, 42–43; as symbol, 222–223

Vives, Luis, 243

Voice. *See* Speakers; Testimonial voices

Voss, Norine, 16, 19, 59n.19

Weil, Simone: influence of, 4, 40–42, 258n.1; on love, 255; paradigms of oppression, 33

"When We Dead Awaken" (Rich), 46

"Widower Román, The," 31, 33–34, 155–206

Wittig, Monique, 51, 53. *See also* French feminist writers

"Woman and Her Image," 42, 44–45, 236–244

Women: autobiographies of, 16, 59n.19; and biography, 50; in Chiapas, 33–36, 219–221, 232–235; as daughters and friends, 34–36, 219–221; and dependency, 48–49, 50, 261–262; as Enigma, 62n.41; free, 41; Japanese, 264–266; and language, xvii, 11–13, 22–24; lives of, in Mexico, 45–47, 245–249, 256–263; in Mexican letters, 34–35, 56–57; and myth, 44–45, 236–244; as objects of exchange, 34–35; as Other, 62n.41; relationships of, to each other, 34–35, 267–269; roles of, 41; and self–sacrifice, 48–50, 256–263; as signs, 28–30, 57, 62n.38; as signs of conflict and solitude, xiv, 31–36; and silence, 42–43; speakers, 14–17, 60n.24; as symbol, 62n.41; and writing, 51, 61n.28. *See also* Mexican women

Women's Liberation Movement, 4, 50, 264

Woolf, Virginia: and the Angel in the House, 239, 244n.1; influence of, xiv, xviii, 4, 40–42; rhetorical features, 41. *See also* Mentors

Xtabay, 362, 367n.37

"You": translation of, 11, 59n.15

"You Are Not Poetry," 9, 25–26, 109

You Are Not Poetry, 254–258

"You Are the Text" (Berryman), 26

For authorization to translate the poetry, prose, and play by Rosario Castellanos we are grateful to her heir, Gabriel Guerra Castellanos and the following Mexican publishers: Fondo de Cultura Económica, Editorial Joaquín Mortiz, Universidad Veracruzana, Ediciones Era, *El Excélsior*, Ediciones SEP Setentas, and Revista "Universidad de México."

For permission to publish the translations of the poems, short fiction, essays, and play by Rosario Castellanos we are grateful to the translators Maureen Ahern, Diane Marting, Betty Tyree Osiek, Lesley Salas, Laura Carp Solomon, and Ruth Peacock.

For permission to reprint poems and short fiction that were first published in English translation in magazines and anthologies in the United States and Great Britain we are grateful to the following:

Ambit for "Self Portrait," which first appeared in 82 (1980).

Brooklyn College Press for "To a Tiny Mayan Badger," "Presence," "Speaking of Gabriel," "Nobodying," and "Cooking Lesson" from *Contemporary Women Authors of Latin America: New Translations*, ed. by Doris Meyer and Margarite Fernandez Olmos. Copyright © 1983 by Brooklyn University Press. Reprinted with permission of the publisher.

Caliban, which first published "Meditation on the Brink," "Memorandum on Tlatelolco," and "Nazareth" in 2, no. 2 (1978) and "Home Economics" in 3, no. 1 (1979).

Calyx: A Journal of Art and Literature by Women, which first printed the translation of "Kinsey Report" in its International Issue, 5, nos. 2 & 3 (1981).

Colorado State Review for "Malinche," which was published for the first time in New Series, 7, no. 1 (1979).

Denver Quarterly for "Metamorphosis of the Sorceress" and "Speaking of Gabriel," which first appeared in 15, no. 1 (1980).

Latin American Literary Review/Press for "Monologue of a Foreign Woman," "Learning about Things," "Postscript," "You Are Not Poetry," "Re: Mutilations," and "Looking at the Mona Lisa," which first appeared in earlier versions in 8, no. 15 (1979). Earlier versions of "Silence Near an Ancient Stone," "Malinche," and "Home Economics" were reprinted in *Woman Who Has Sprouted Wings*, ed. by Mary Crow. Copyright © 1983 by Latin American Literary Review Press.

Longman Inc. for permission to reprint "Woman and Her Image," which first appeared in *International Literature by Women*, ed. by Marian Arkin and Barbara Sholler. Copyright © 1988 by Longman Inc.

New Letters, which first published "Routine" in 46, no. 1 (1979).

Perivale Press and Nora Jácquez for "Speaking of Gabriel," "Learning about Things," and "Meditation on the Brink." First versions of these translations were published in their *Looking at the Sun: A Bilingual Anthology of Latin American Women Poets*, ed. by Nora Jácquez Wieser. Copyright © on critical essays and English translations by Nora Jácquez Wieser, 1979; Perivale Press, 1979, 1982.

Rivelin/Ecuatorial for "Brief Chronicle" and "Self-Portrait," which originally appeared with twenty-three other poems by Rosario Castellanos in *Looking at the Mona Lisa*, trans. by Maureen Ahern; copyright © by Maureen Ahern, 1981.

Spectacular Diseases for "The Other," which originally appeared in the Latin American Issue, 7 (1984).

Texas Quarterly and Raúl Ortiz for "The Widower Román," which was first published in 16, no. 2 (1973).

Thirteenth Moon for "Silence Near an Ancient Stone," "Consciousness," and "Home Economics," which were first published in earlier versions in 4, no. 2 (1979).

Translation for "Chess," "Nazareth," and "Passage," which were originally published in 6 (1978–1979).